BLACK APOSTLES

Afro-American Clergy Confront
the Twentieth Century

BLACK APOSTLES

Afro-American Clergy Confront
the Twentieth Century

Edited by
RANDALL K. BURKETT
and
RICHARD NEWMAN

G.K.HALL&CO.

70 LINCOLN STREET, BOSTON, MASS.

Library of Congress Cataloging in Publication Data
Main entry under title:

Black apostles.

Includes index.
CONTENTS: Shepperson, G. Introduction.—Pierson, R. M. Alexander
Bedward and the Jamaica Native Baptist Free Church.—Henriksen, T. H.
African intellectual influences on Black Americans, the role of Edward W.
Blyden.—Burnham, K. E. Father Divine and the peace mission move-
ment. [etc.]
1. Afro-American clergy—Biography—Addresses, essays, lectures.
I. Burkett, Randall K. II. Newman, Richard.
BR563.N4B56   200′92′2 [B]   78–6697
ISBN 0–8161–8137–3

This publication is printed on permanent/durable acid-free paper
MANUFACTURED IN THE UNITED STATES OF AMERICA

To the Memory of
James H. Robinson
and
Gladstone St. Clair Nurse

Contents

Preface

This volume brings together in one place a collection of biographical studies of individuals who helped shape the directions of black religion in the United States in the first half of the twentieth century.

The book is primarily an effort to encourage and facilitate research in Afro-American religious history. We found the number of articles from which we could draw for this collection to be surprisingly small, an indication of the significant amount of basic work which remains to be done in this field. In spite of the considerable importance, for example, of sects and cults in the post World War I period, there is little scholarly material on Daddy Grace, Elijah Poole, Elder Lightfoot Solomon Michaux or Prophet F. S. Cherry.

We have sought to include essays on individuals from as wide a denominational spectrum as possible. There are representatives of the African Methodist Episcopal, African Methodist Episcopal Zion, African Orthodox, Baptist, Black Jewish and Pentecostal Churches, as well as of the predominantly white Congregational, Presbyterian and Protestant Episcopal Churches. We have also sought to include representatives of the ideological spectrum: conservatives, radicals, moderates, integrationists, separatists, fundamentalists and social gospellers.

We are especially pleased to be able to include four previously unpublished articles. Samuel K. Roberts' essay on George E. Haynes, Kenneth Burnham's study of Father Divine and David W. Wills' analysis of the early life of Reverdy C. Ransom are all based on recent research done for doctoral dissertations. Herbert M. Smith's essay on Harold M. Kingsley is a chapter from his important but unpublished M.A. thesis written at the University of Chicago in 1935.

It is no longer quite so necessary to point out the significance of the black church and the black clergy for an adequate understanding of black history. The paucity of material is clear evidence, however, that the most important institution in the black community and the most important leadership group among black people have been seriously neglected over the years. Only recently has scholarship begun to discover this gap, to realize the extent of the loss, and to place new emphasis on the investigation and appreciation of Afro-American religion.

Randall K. Burkett
Richard Newman

Introduction

In 1951 an Afro-American author, William H. Piper, published a book entitled *Say Amen, Brother! Old-Time Negro Preaching: A Study in American Frustration.* The fifteen articles in *Black Apostles: Afro-American Clergy Confront the Twentieth Century* does not lack evidence of the survival of the heritage of the old-time black preacher well into the new century; but their main emphasis is on a more sophisticated approach to religion amongst Afro-Americans and their Caribbean cousins. What this book, however, does have in common with *Say Amen, Brother!* is the spirit of its subtitle: a study in American frustration.

The twentieth century, of course, with its mixture of hopes and horrors, of rising and declining expectations, has been a time of frustration for all, whatever their racial or ethnic origins, who have had the privilege and predicament of living in it. But, in the gap between theory and practice in democracy in the New World, the twentieth century has surely been a time of acute frustration for the descendants of the slaves in the United States, particularly as the promise of the Civil War remained so long unfulfilled.

The spokesmen for these Afro-American frustrations, in their multiplicity of forms, have often been, as in other countries, persons of predominantly secular status and calling. But, as *Black Apostles* demonstrates, the religious vocation has frequently been the means through which Afro-Americans in the century of the common man have attempted to overcome their dilemmas and distresses.

This religious vocation has usually assumed a Christian character; and the articles in this book bear witness to this. But they also provide some indication of other religious callings, traditional and original, in which both Islam and Father Divine co-exist. Ranging across black North America and the West Indies, with their volatile mixtures of religious orthodoxy and unorthodoxy, *Black Apostles* suggests the intricate interaction of all of these forms from the islands of the Caribbean to mainland America. A picture emerges in this book of considerable religious complexity amongst black folk in the New World.

The compass of this collection of studies, however, is necessarily limited; and it cannot be expected to reveal the many complications and religious ramifications of Afro-American pulpit personalities and their disciples in their responses to the challenges of the twentieth century. Indeed, it could be claimed that this book performs a useful service to students of black history by stimulating them, through the very omissions and differing degrees of emphasis which a selective survey cannot avoid, to recognise these elements in it and, in this way, to make their own contributions to this complex field of study.

For example, some will notice that women play little part in *Black Apostles*. There is, it seems, no Sojourner Truth in the twentieth century. And the black apostles singled out for special mention are those whose careers are relatively well documented—although ,one longs for greater documentation for some of them, especially that fascinating figure, William J. Seymour, black father of modern pentecostalism. Other black apostles, humbler figures, remain only in the folk memory. It is to be hoped that one effect of this book will be the encouragement of the discovery and description of these humbler figures, the less articulate and the inarticulate amongst the many kinds of black clergy in their confrontation with the stresses and strains of the modern spirit.

Who, for example, were the three blacks who accompanied the Trappist monk, Father Vincent de Paul, when he went to minister to "the wants of the poor, neglected inhabitants" in the cold interior of isolated Nova Scotia in 1815?[1] At this early date, they could have been, as many blacks in Nova Scotia were at this time, refugees from the United States.

Mention of such anonymous black Catholics in North America indicates another aspect of the black apostolate which, no doubt for reasons of space, this book is obliged to skim over: Roman Catholicism and the Afro-American in the twentieth century.[2] And yet it was an Afro-American Catholic, Countee Cullen, who expressed so well in his poem of 1929, *The Black Christ*, the anguish which many black men and women have felt about the contradictions of the twentieth century:

> O World grown indolent and crass,
> I stand upon your bleak morass
> Of incredulity and cry
> Your lack of faith is but a lie.
> If you but brushed the scales apart
> That cloud your eyes and clinch your heart
> There is no telling what grace might
> Be levelled to your clearer sight.[3]

"Anguish" (*Angst*) and "alienation" have become such trendy words in the world after the Second World War, under the stimulus of popularized existentialism and neo-Marxism, that one hesitates to use them for fear they may have lost any real force they once had. But how can they be avoided when one is speaking of people of a religious temperament in North America and the Caribbean countries: people who have had more than their fair share of anguish and alienation meted out to them in the twentieth century? It could be that, in exploring these qualities amongst them, the true and unhackneyed meaning of these emotive terms could come to light again.

Black Apostles provides good material for such an exploration. It presents us with a gallery of portraits of talented and vocal black men in confrontation with the anguish and alienation of the new age represented by Gobineau, Darwin, Marx and Freud. Some seek the way of escape, into the past or into the future, often through the search for Africa abroad and, in spirit, at home. As Jamaican-born Claude McKay on the eve of the Harlem Renaissance cried out in an invocation of the spirit of his ancestors:

> Thou who from out the dark and dust didst raise
> The Ethiop standard in the curtained days,
> Before the white God said: Let there be light!
> Bring ancient music to my modern heart. . . .[4]

Others grapple with an Afro-American version of the Social Gospel, with its focus less on the past or the future and more on the present, in their search for an equitable distribution of the fruits of the earth and the rights of man. The savage marks of the First and Second World Wars and of the Depression of the 1930's are plainly apparent in this book; and it seems that they spurred on many Afro-Americans to seek in their religious activities not so much for the means of escaping from or of changing the hard realities of existence but for consolation and the courage to endure.

To some who approach this book, the use of the word "apostle" in its title may seem misleading or fanciful. But is this really so? In the original Greek, "apostle" has the meaning of "one who is sent out," of "a messenger." In this manner, it was taken up in the Christian New Testament and has since gained the broader significance of "a principal proponent or champion of a cause or a new system." Some of the figures in this book fit into the strictly Christian use of "apostle"; for others, the broader meaning is relevant. All of them, I feel, have in them, explicitly or implicitly, something of the spirit of the two black men who are mentioned in *The Acts of the Apostles* in the New Testament, the symbolism and significance of whom has been cherished by many generations of black preachers: "Simeon that was called Niger," one of the "prophets and teachers" in the early Church at Antioch (XIII, 1); and, in particular, that "man of Ethiopia," the servant of a black queen, who, from his reading in the fifty-third chapter of *The Book of the Prophet Isaiah* in the Old Testament, was brought to baptism by the Apostle Philip (VIII, 27–39).

This episode was made the subject of one of the noblest sermons that was preached before an Afro-American audience by Edward Blyden, the great black messenger of both Christianity and Islam whose life and works spanned America, the West Indies and Africa and who rightly occupies a prominent place in this anthology of black apostles. A passage from Blyden's sermon on *Acts*, VIII, 27–39, which I like to think that readers with contrasting views on the Afro-American past, present and future, will interpret in different ways, provides, I believe, a fitting conclusion to this introduction. This book should not fail to interest and to challenge the assumptions and attitudes of all who are concerned with the plight of human beings, white as well as black, in the stormy twenty centuries since Philip's "man from Ethiopia," having received the Apostles' good news of liberation, "went on his way rejoicing." To end, then, with Edward Blyden to his congregation of Afro-Americans:

> Tell me, now, ye descendants of Africa, tell me whether there is anything in the ancient history of your African ancestors, in their relation to other races, of which you need to be ashamed. Tell me, if there is anything in the modern history of your people, in their dealings with foreign races, whether at home or in exile, of which you need to be ashamed? Is there anything, when you compare yourself with others, to disturb your equanimity, except the universal oppression of which you have been the victims? And what are suffering and sorrow but necessary elements in the progress of humanity? Your suffering has contributed to the welfare of others. It is a part of the constitution of the universe, that out of death should come life. All the advancement made to a better future, by individuals or races, has been made through paths marked by suffering. This great law is written not only in the Bible, but upon all history. "Without shedding blood there is no remission."[5]

George Shepperson

University of Edinburgh
February 1978

Notes

1. Rev. Luke Schrepfer, O.S.A., *Pioneer Monks in Nova Scotia* (St. Augustine's Monastery, N.S., 1947), pp. 98–104.

2. For a useful background bibliography see Maria Genoino Caravaglios, *The American Catholic Church and the Negro Problem in the XVIII–XIX centuries* (Rome, 1974), pp. 355–68, to which should be added Albert S. Foley, S.J., *Bishop Healy: Beloved Outcast* (Dublin, 1956).

3. Countee Cullen, *The Black Christ and other Poems* (London and New York, 1929), pp. 63–64.

4. "Invocation," originally published in *Seven Arts*, volume 2, October, 1917, p. 741; quoted in Wayne Cooper, ed., *The Passion of Claude McKay. Selected Poetry and Prose, 1912–1948* (New York, 1973), p. 117.

5. Edward W. Blyden, *Christianity, Islam and the Negro Race* (first published, London, 1887; Edinburgh edition, 1967), p. 162.

Acknowledgments

The editors express their appreciation to the individual and institutional holders of copyright who have granted permission for their essays to be included in this book:

George Shepperson, "Introduction."

Roscoe M. Pierson, "Alexander Bedward and the Jamaica Native Baptist Free Church," *Lexington Theological Quarterly*, 4, 3 (July 1969).

Thomas Henriksen, "African Intellectual Influences on Black Americans: The Role of Edward W. Blyden," *Phylon*, 36, 3 (March 1975). Atlanta University.

Kenneth E. Burnham, "Father Divine and the Peace Mission Movement."

Kenneth J. King, "Some Notes on Arnold J. Ford and New World Black Attitudes to Ethiopia," *Journal of Ethiopian Studies*, 10, 1.

Louis B. Weeks III, "Racism, World War I and the Christian Life: Francis J. Grimke in the Nation's Capital," *Journal of Presbyterian History*, 51, 4 (Winter 1973).

Raymond Gavins, "Gordon Blaine Hancock: A Black Profile from the New South," *The Journal of Negro History*, 59, 3 (July 1974). The Association for the Study of Afro-American Life and History, Inc.

Samuel K. Roberts, "George Edmund Haynes: Advocate for Interracial Cooperation."

J. Carleton Hayden, "James Theodore Holly (1829–1911) First Afro-American Episcopal Bishop: His Legacy to Us Today," *The Journal of Religious Thought*, 53, 1 (Spring-Summer 1976).

Herbert M. Smith, "Harold M. Kingsley: Preaching to the White Collar Class."

Gavin White, "Patriarch McGuire and the Episcopal Church," *Historical Magazine of the Protestant Episcopal Church*, 38, 2 (June 1969). Published by the Church Historical Society.

David Wills, "Reverdy C. Ransom: The Making of an A.M.E. Bishop."

James S. Tinney, "William J. Seymour: Father of Modern-Day Pentecostalism," *Journal of the Interdenominational Theological Center*, 4, 1 (Fall 1977).

Edwin S. Redkey, "Bishop Turner's African Dream," *Journal of American History*, 54, 2 (September 1967). Organization of American Historians.

George M. Miller, "The Social Mission of Bishop Alexander Walters," *The A.M.E. Zion Quarterly Review*, 88, 2 (Summer 1976).

Philip S. Foner, "Reverend George Washington Woodbey: Early Twentieth Century California Black Socialist," *The Journal of Negro History*, 61, 2 (April 1976). The Association for the Study of Afro-American Life and History, Inc.

Alexander Bedward and the Jamaica Native Baptist Free Church

Roscoe M. Pierson

Where Duke Street comes to an end at the water's edge in Kingston Harbor, the Royal Mail Dock continues out into the bay. The western side of this dock is bounded by a concrete wall upon which the following inscription has been carefully, though crudely, printed in black paint:

> During 1920 Jamaica knew two prophets
> One called Bedward attempted to fly. He was
> tried and placed in asylum. The other
> rank by far the most important prof. He was
> Marcus Garvey who founded the Universal
> Negro Improvement Association in the U.S.A.
> Proclaimed Black nationalism and preached Africa
> for Africans at far land abroad. One God,
> one aim, one destiny.[1]

Though this inscription is more concerned with Marcus Garvey than with the prophet who "attempted to fly," and was probably printed by the same sort of person who has written "Birth control plan to kill Black people" on countless exterior walls in Kingston, the first named prophet is the immediate concern of this paper.

In intellectual circles in Kingston, as well as in other major cities, Black nationalism is in vogue. Numerous articles and books have been, and are being, written on nearly every phase of the Negro's history. Accordingly, less than one week after the above transcription was made there appeared an article on Alexander Bedward in Jamaica's fine newspaper, the *Sunday Gleaner*.[2] From some cursory research that had been done while preparing a bibliography of West Indian church history, this writer recognized some discrepancies in this newspaper account and the information previously discovered in general reading. His interest thus tantalized he made the effort to learn as much about Bedward and his followers as was possible in the time available to him. Nearly every item in the files of the Institute of Jamaica was copied on an electrostatic copier; numerous interviews were attempted, and several field trips to important sites were enjoyable interludes amid his other studies. The results are incorporated in the remainder of the paper.

The Background

Harrison E. Shakespeare Woods, an American Negro, arrived in Jamaica in the nineteenth century, probably after the War Between the States, and settled in Spanish Town. By about 1876 Woods had moved to St. David's and made his home in a cave, probably not far from the present-day community of Dallas Castle, in St. Andrew, no more than three or four miles from the present campus of the United Theological College of the West Indies. There are numerous caves on Dallas Mountain, and from time to time Shakespeare, for this was his common appellation, came forth preaching and prophesying. In June, 1879, he prophesied that Dallas Castle would be destroyed by a flood. When a cloud-burst destroyed the Wesleyan Chapel and several other buildings five months later, on October 11, 1879, his fame as a prophet spread.

The Hope River flows in the valley that lies between Dallas Mountain and Long Mountain, to the west, and the village of August Town lies mainly on the west bank of that river. It was here, or near here, that the young Alexander Bedward lived when, in December 1888, Shakespeare came prophesying the destruction of August Town:

> Thus saith the Lord, behold the sins of August Town have come up before me, and I will destroy the place as I did Dallas Castle except the people repent and obey me. I will sink the valley and make the two hills meet.[3]

In April of 1889 Shakespeare called a meeting of all the three churches in August Town—Anglican, Baptist, and Methodist—and informed them that if they would follow him they would be blessed, but if they did not they would face his predicted destruction. Accordingly, on April 19, 1889, numerous people, mostly from the Baptist and Methodist churches, assembled on Papine Pasture for a momentous meeting. After a breakfast at 3:00 p.m. Woods withdrew to a private dwelling and selected twelve men and twelve women to be Elders of this gathering. He then named Robert Ruderford,[4] a Baptist, and Joseph Waters, a Wesleyan, to be the chief leaders. Apparently he directed the followers to return to their original churches, but to observe a monthly fast; predicting that "fruits would so abound in August Town, that, from various parts of the world, people would come to enjoy them."[5]

After prophesying further that "A fountain would be opened in

August Town, but that the man to rule it was not yet ready," Shakespeare moved back to Spanish Town in 1889, leaving the two appointed chief Elders in command.

Alexander Bedward

Although there is no accurate record of the date of Bedward's birth, it is likely that he was born in 1859. All accounts agree that he was born in the parish of St. Andrew, probably on the Mona Estate, near Matilda's Corner, no more than three or four miles from August Town. In his family he was the only son, though there were two daughters.[6] He seems to have had little or no formal education and when he reached young manhood he became a worker on the Mona Estate. His obituary states that he was a cooper by trade.[7] In these early years he is reputed to have been (1) troubled by some mysterious disease,[8] (2) immoral and lascivious,[9] (3) a partner in an unpleasant marriage,[10] (4) a practitioner of necromancy,[11] and (5) a very religious member of the Providence Wesleyan Church at Matilda's Corner.[12]

From this superficially contradictory background there emerges one solid fact: he left Jamaica for Colon, then Colombia, now Panama, in 1883, when he was about 23 or 24 years of age. Whether this was for reasons of health, as Brooks categorically states, or because of the unpleasantness of his family life, as possibly can be inferred from Brooks' *History,* is not certain. He did, nonetheless, leave his wife and children,[13] quite possibly to seek employment on the Panama Canal, which was being built at that time by the French corporation.

He worked in Colon for two years, until August 1885, when he decided to return to Jamaica; according to all accounts he was successful, at an unspecified job, and "is said to have made a lot of money."[14] Bedward arrived in Kingston on a Monday, but by the next Saturday disease, burdens, and oppressions, physical and spiritual, had so beset him that he once again embarked for Colon, vowing never to return to Jamaica. Upon his return to Panama, he got his job back, but his health did not improve. On the sixth night after his return to Colon he had two dreams which changed the course of his life.

In the first dream, a man appeared before him and commanded him to go back to Jamaica. "If you stay here, you will die and lose your soul, but if you go back to Jamaica you will save your soul and be the means of saving many others." When Bedward complained that he had no money for another passage, he was told by the apparition to see several men who would provide the means for his passage.

Later in the night Bedward had another dream in which he found himself on the Constant Spring Road in Kingston. He tried to enter into a gate, but the gatekeeper informed him that he could not do so, for he was lost. Frightened by this he dreamed that he turned back crying at the top of his voice, "I am lost, I am lost." Soon he met a man on the road who said to him "Come here, I do send you to August Town. . . . Go to August Town, submit yourself to Mr. Ruderford for instruction, with fastings on Mondays, Wednesdays, and Fridays. Then be baptised: for I have a special work for you to do.[15]

Late the next day, Bedward had a vision of a man in white apparel who asked him if he had done as he was ordered in the previous dream. When he replied that he had not, the man commenced to beat him with a whip. Some companions of Bedward were astonished that their friend was speaking to someone they could not see, and that he appeared to be in agony. Immediately Bedward went to those who had been announced to him, they supplied him with the money needed to return to Jamaica, and he arrived in Kingston on August 10, 1885.

According to Brooks, Bedward at once sought out Mr. Ruderford and commenced his preparations for baptism. These preparations lasted for several months, for Bedward's baptism by Ruderford finally took place on the second Sunday in January, 1886.

Bedward returned to his work on the Mona Estate, and presumably to his family. Whether he lived at Matilda's Corner and again attended the Wesleyan Church, or whether he now lived nearer to August Town cannot be determined. Possibly his relationship with Ruderford, and his Baptist baptism is sufficient evidence to conclude that Bedward easily changed denominational affiliation. He must have been active in religious work, for when Shakespeare called the meeting on August 19, 1889 at Papine Pasture, Bedward was present and was one of the twelve men chosen to be Elders.

This is puzzling, since the only available evidence of any value is Brooks' *History*, and Brooks is an ardent disciple of Bedward. It is possible that Brooks is writing his narrative to connect the two local charismatic leaders, when there was little or no connection. In his description of the appointment of the twelve Elders, Bedward is not mentioned in the natural narrative (pages 6–8). As he is describing events at least four years later, Brooks offers Shakespeare's prophecy, that there was among the Elders one who would succeed him, as part of Bedward's credentials as a prophet:

> When he stood among the twenty-four elders on the 19th of April 1889 and heard Shakespeare's prophetic remark. [sic] "One of you shall succeed me &c." he had not the slightest idea that it was he. But later towards the fulness of time when he was assured that he was the chosen successor, he shirked, refused and begged to be excused, chiefly on the ground of his lack of education, and impediment of speech. But when, like Moses fully convinced that it was the Divine Will, he acquiesced, only trusting in his God.[16]

Furthermore, in the pages discussing the normal development of Bedward's life, more or less in chronological order, there is no mention of Shakespeare's influence on Bedward, not even the election to eldership under Shakespeare. In this narrative, Brooks proceeds from his baptism in January 1886 to October 10, 1891, when he reports that Bedward "was specially called by God for sanctification. And this dates the commencement of his public ministry."[17].

Bedward's Public Ministry

On December 22, 1891, Bedward with approximately two hundred followers gathered on the bank of the Hope River, near August Town, and Bedward proclaimed the healing qualities of the river's water. Earlier, Shakespeare appears to have alluded to the special qualities of this water,[18] but it was Alexander Bedward who gave it strong national importance. From the large group that had gathered by the river, only seven would drink the water as medicine. These seven were, according to the accounts, immediately cured and the fame of Bedward and his healing stream began to gather momentum.

Two hundred people do not gather by a river bank without some preparatory activities. What Bedward did to arouse the interest of his followers is not to be found in the printed accounts. He must have done some public preaching to call forth his first adherents, possibly as an active worker in the local Baptist Church. On Christmas day, 1891, the Gospel Worker of the Baptist group, V. Dawson, became his co-worker, or as Brooks notes "as Moses and Aaron in the congregation of Israel, so stand these two, Bedward and Dawson in Bedwardism."[19].

Some charismatic leaders are imposing in appearance, but it has been difficult to obtain a coherent and reliable description of Bedward. One newspaper reporter who interviewed him before the earthquake of 1907 reminisces in an article written more than fifty years later, "I recall him as a black man taller and burlier than the average, his round face wearing a rather mild expression. His moustache and short side whiskers were just beginning to turn grey."[20] Another reporter, however, describes him as a stout little peasant.[21] Brooks, who idolizes his leader, does not comment on Bedward's physical appearance, nor mention that this influenced his leadership.

The mystique that enabled Bedward to become a charismatic leader may be complex—the prophetic descendant of Shakespeare, his assured manner, his message of assurance and healing, the latent Black nationalism that was developing—but he steadily developed a large following. Even though the discipline of fasting was arduous, and his followers were urged to fast from midnight to about 1:00 p.m. each Monday, Wednesday, and Friday when a communion-type service using bread and the water of the Hope River was held, the number of disciples grew.

The most famous services were the healing services at a pool of the Hope River to which the sick and infirm from all over the island were invited. Large numbers of people came to be baptized by Bedward or to bathe in or drink from the river. Many miraculous cures were attested to, and the pilgrims carried jugs of water to every part of Jamaica, for themselves and for friends or relatives too ill to make the trip to August Town.

In 1893 Bedward "was Divinely instructed to build an house for the Service of God."[22] And in June, 1894, the corner stone for a large stone edifice was laid at Union Camp, August Town, by the Rev. S. S. Carr, the Baptist minister in August Town. This became, and still is, the headquarters of the Jamaica Native Baptist Free Church.

The British authorities were not unaware of the large groups that were gathering in August Town, nor of the racial overtones to some of Bedward's preaching. Bedward was fond of passages in the Bible as "Ethiopia shall stretch out her hands to God" (Ps. 38:31),[23] and he made a personal identification with Paul Bogle, the Baptist leader of the uprising at Morant Bay in 1865.[24] Roberts quotes Bedward as proclaiming: "There is a white wall and a black wall, and the white wall has been closing around the black wall; but now the black wall has become bigger than the white wall. Let them remember the Morant War."

On January 21, 1895, the government, thoroughly aroused by the preaching of Bedward, sent a company of about forty-five men to his home in Union Camp, and arrested him after dark. He was taken to Spanish Town and there spent four months in jail before being brought to trial on the charge of sedition. The writer has not seen the official records of that trial and does not know what actually took place. According to Brooks he was uncondemned, yet not acquitted";[25] later newspaper accounts are in agreement that he was judged insane.[26] There is no doubt that he was remanded to the Lunatic Asylum where he spent a month before his lawyer, Philip Stern, was able to get him released.

Bedward came out of this episode a martyr to his followers, and his fame was spread rather than tarnished by his trial and imprisonment. The crowds who gathered in August Town continued to grow and the number of Bedwardite groups enlarged until there was no area in Jamaica without his followers.[27] A number of his disciples had gone with the banana industry to Port Limon, Costa Rica, and a missionary was chosen to labor among them.[28]

The healing water of the Hope River was the corner-stone of the ritual of Bedwardism. The Lord revealed this to Bedward in a vision, of which he reports: "An' de Lard takes me by de han' and leads me to a place in the 'Ope River an' says to me, 'Bedward, my prophet, dip up dis water, pour it into big Spanish jars, bless it an' whosoever shall drink of it shall be heal in both body and soul.'"[29]

Several popular songs derived from the healing service. One of the more popular ones was written out by a student at the United Theological College of the West Indies, at Mona, and was given to me. It is transcribed here exactly as it was received:

> One day we go down to August Town, but we never go up to Mona;
> We were invited to that place by a young man called Bar-Jona.
> And when we go down in August Town, and look in a da healing stream
> We see breda Bedward dipping de people, deep down in a de healing stream.

> *Chorus*
> Dip dem Bedward, dip dem
> Dip dem in de healing stream
> Dip dem fe cure de bad feeling
> Dip dem Bedward dip dem
> Dip dem in de healing stream
> Dip dem sweet but not too deep
> Dip dem fe cure bad feeling

> Dome come from the east wid long belly fe de feast
> Fe go dip in a de healing stream,
> Some come from the west just a perfect mess (pess?)
> Fe dip in a da healing stream.

> *Chorus*
> Some come from de north
> Fe come ketch quattie bath
> And dip in a de healing stream
> Some come from the south
> Wid dem big yabba mouth
> Fe dip in a de healing stream

> *Chorus*

Another aspect of Bedward's preaching received wide attention. From a pulpit nearly fifteen feet high,[30] he proclaimed that the powers afforded to those who had faith were boundless; even to the extent of walking on water and flying like birds. Though Bedward himself never attempted to fly, some of his followers did. They climbed up into the trees at Union Camp and crashed into the ground when they attempted to soar from their perches. Unabashed, Bedward is reported to have said that it merely reflected the limitations of their faith.[31] No one is reported to have been killed in attempting to fly, though there are numerous records of broken limbs, for those of little faith.

The civil authorities did not take lightly these demonstrations of enthusiasm, especially when they may have once again taken on overtones of Black racialism;[32] and especially so after December, 1920, when Bedward proclaimed that he was Jesus Christ and that, like Elijah, he would ascend into Heaven in a flaming chariot on December 31. Bedward had a replica of this chariot made and would sit on its white cushions in a white robe and turban promising that three days after his ascension he would return for those who faithfully followed him to take them with him into Glory. He would then raindown fire upon those who were not among the elect and destroy the whole world.[33] Many of his followers sold all their possessions in preparation for their earthly departure.[34] When the stated time arrived and Bedward was not taken to Heaven, he postponed the ascension until the following April. His followers were not dispirited by his failure, rather they seem to have been even more certain that the delay was granted for them to be prepared to go with their leader.

Feelings and emotions were at such a pitch in April that the government felt it must act to prevent a march by Bedward and his followers from August Town to Kingston. Sir Leslie Brobyn, the Governor, directed Resident Magistrate S. C. Burke to intercept the march and break it up.[35]

Mass' Sam Burke took a contingent of sixty police and, with little difficulty, arrested Bedward and marched his entire company to the police station at Half Way Tree. Bedward was charged with assaulting a consable, but refused to plead. Burke then "remanded him into custody for medical examination."[36]

The legal proceedings of this arrest would make an interesting article, suffice it to say that this time the court declared Bedward insane and committed him to the Asylum, now Bellevue Hospital, on Windward Road, Kingston, where he remained until his death, Saturday, November 8, 1930.

In spite of damage from the earthquake of 1907, and the ravages of hurricane Charlie in 1951, which did more damage, the walls of Bedward's church still stand in the compound at 67 August Town Road. There is yet a following of faithful who live near the church and carry on much of the ritual of their deceased leader. Squabbles over leadership[37] have split the ranks of the membership, and they have become wary of strangers, especially from the University and from the press. In 1967 and 1968, this writer tried several times to gain admittance to Union Camp, but could not. At the entrance to the compound, persons refused to acknowledge even that they knew where Bedford's church was located, or that they had ever heard of Alexander Bedward. Perhaps a person of darker pigmentation who took time to gain their confidence might assuage the hostility of the Bedwardites of today. In 1963 there were between two and three hundred people still living in the compound; how many there are today I could not find out.[38]

Bedward's reputation today does not depend upon the vitality of his existing followers. He has passed into folk-lore. Plays, by Carmen Manley and Louis Marriott, this last on television in 1960, have been written of him. Short stories in pamphlet and newspaper have been published; and he would be the fit protagonist for a local novel. His revivalistic influence has penetrated Jamaican revivalism which has been admirably studied by the noted sociologist George Eaton Simpson.[39] His present standing is legendary, otherwise the anonymous epigrapher would never have written the inscription on the wall of Royal Mail Dock.

Notes

1. This inscription was first seen by the author in December 1966, and was photographed and transcribed on November 4, 1968. The writing has weathered somewhat and is not immediately legible; perhaps it has been there for at least five years.

2. A.E.T. Henry, a regular columnist, wrote "Dip dem Missa Bedward, dip dem . . ." for the *Sunday Gleaner*, Nov. 10, 1968, p. 8, a humorous article on the experiences of the Bedwardities who attempted to fly.

3. A. A. Brooks, *History of Bedwardism; or, Jamaica Native Baptist Free Church, Union Camp, Augustown, St. Andrew, Ja., B.W.I.* (2d ed. rev. and enl.; Kingston, Gleaner Co., 1917), p. 6. Brooks' *History* is the best source of this information known to the writer; there is no copy of the first edition in any of the major libraries in Jamaica, England, or the United States. Other sources of information on H.E.S. Woods seem to be dependent upon Brooks, but some offer slightly differing details, e.g., William E. Hemming, "Bedward's Remnants Mourning Still," in *Jamaica Times*, August 6, 1949; W. Adolphe Roberts, "Bedward the Revivalist," in *The Sunday Gleaner*, January 31, 1960; and pseudonymous article, "Tattered Flock Awaits Return of Dead Leader," in *The Star*, June 24, 1963, p. 6.

4. This name is given variously as Ruderford and Raderford; I have chosen the first form in Brooks, *History*, p. 7.

5. Brooks, *History*, p. 7.

6. Brooks, *History*, p. 13.

7. *Jamaica Mail*, November 11, 1930.

8. Brooks, *History*, p. 9; *Jamaica Mail*, November 11, 1930.

9. Brooks, *History*, p. 9.

10. Brooks, *History*, p. 9.

11. *Jamaica Mail, idem.*

12. *Jamaica Mail, idem.*

13. Brooks, *History*, p. 10, writes concerning his second visit to Colon that he left "wife, children, and all. . . ." If he left children at the start of this trip, he must have left them in 1883 also.

14. *Jamaica Mail, idem*; Brooks, *History*, pp. 9–11.

15. Brooks, *History*, p. 11.

16. Brooks, *History*, p. 14.

17. Brooks, *History*, p. 12.

18. Brooks, *History*, p. 6. Shakespeare placed his Bible on a jar of water from the river before he ordained his twenty-four Elders.

19. Brooks, *History*, p. 12.

20. W. Adolphe Roberts, *Sunday Gleaner*, January 31, 1960.

21. Randolph Williams, "The Prophet of August Town; Bedward—Reformer and Blasphemer," *Jamaica Standard*. This is a clipping from the files of the Institute of Jamaica; the date has been mutilated so that it cannot be determined.

22. Brooks, *History*, p. 20.

23. Brooks, *History*, p. 17.

24. Roberts, *Sunday Gleaner*.

25. Brooks, *History*, p. 15.

26. Roberts, *Sunday Gleaner*; his obituary in the *Jamaica Mail* hints that Bedward's wife requested the lunacy hearing.

27. Roberts, *Sunday Gleaner*; Williams, *Jamaica Standard*.

28. Roberts, *Sunday Gleaner*.

29. Williams, *Jamaica Standard*. The use of dialect is correct, but Williams is a hostile witness. W. A. Roberts says he spoke "dialect with a broad, guttural accent."

30. Wilbert E. Hemming, "Bedward's Remnants Mourning Still," *Jamaica Times*, August 6, 1949.

31. All the references quoted above refer at length to these episodes. Cf., e.g., the article cited above, n. 2.

32. In an article in *The Star*, June 24, 1963, a pseudonymous writer, The Saint, interviewed a still-living disciple of Bedward who spoke of " 'the sceptre, the sword, the Lion of the Crown,' which he said were stolen from the 'Black Man' by the British and kept in England; those things returning to Ethiopia to the Blackman. If Bedward did not come those things could not be returned to the Blackman." [*sic*, entire quotation] There is a community of Ras Tafarians now living in August Town, not far from Union Camp. The writer tried to establish a relation between the two groups, to no avail.

33. George Eaton Simpson, *Jamaican Revivalist Cults*, p. 337; this is a long book-length article published as the entire issue of *Social and Economic Studies*, Vol. 5, no. 4, December, 1956 (Mona, University College of the West Indies, 1956).

34. Williams, *Jamaica Standard*, describes this wave of enthusiasm very well.

35. All the official documents relating to this arrest have been collected and mimeographed as Jamaica Historical Society *Bulletin*, Vol. 2, no. 15, n.d.

36. Jamaica Historical Society *Bulletin*, p. 248.

37. See articles in the *Star*, March 6, 1965, "Press lies about us claim Bedwardites"; and previously quoted article from the *Star*, June 24, 1963, for treatment of dissension.

38. *Star*, March 6, 1965.

39. See note 33.

African Intellectual Influences on Black Americans: The Role of Edward W. Blyden[*]

Thomas H. Henriksen

The origins of black American cultural ethnocentrism are historically diverse and geographically distant. One significant source of presentday black pride is derived from the late nineteenth-century influence of Edward W. Blyden and fellow West African intellectuals. Yet this fact has not been acknowledged by many scholars of Afro-American thought.[1] African civilizations have been credited with making substantive contributions to human progress, but the impact of African thinkers on black American thought is scarcely recognized. Indeed, there is a paucity of studies that illuminate the fascinating transfer of ideas between Africans and black Americans.[2]

Instead, the link between the New World and Africa is most often confined to expressions of African survivals in the physical and institutional behavior of black Americans. The retention of motor habits, speech patterns, cooperative labor groups and kinship systems are claimed as some of the transferred Africanisms. Much of the research underpinning this view was provided by Melville J. Herskovits' book, *The Myth of the Negro Past*.[3] Whatever the merits of his study, Herskovits' scope precludes an examination of the exchange of ideas between the two continents.

Not surprisingly, most scholars of black American history of the late nineteenth century—a period of renewed and intensified communication with Africans—fail to record the commerce of ideas between Africans and black Americans.[4] Prevailing scholarship, in fact, traces one important impetus of African cultural nationalism with its attendant political overtones to black Americans, while omitting any mention of a partial African

[*]Thanks are due to the Penrose Fund of the American Philosophical Society and the State University of New York/Research Foundation for their financial support of the research for this study.

genesis of black thought in the New World. Although African students returned home inflamed by the racial themes of Marcus Garvey, W. E. B. DuBois and the Harlem Renaissance,[5] they really carried back a measure of African ideas that had been disseminated among black Americans in the previous century.

For black Americans and Africans alike, the late nineteenth century was a time of despair and hostility. European powers partitioned Africa at such a rapid rate that the race for colonies has been dubbed the "scramble for Africa." In the United States, particularly the South, the black Americans' political influence was effectively curtailed by the use of violence, fraud, and complicated registration and voting procedures following the collapse of the Reconstruction governments in 1877. The notion of racial superiority was used to justify the unchecked rule of white over black. Obviously, the rulers benefited from the fabricated and hollow myth of the inherent social and technological backwardness of the Negro race stemming from biological deficiencies and evidenced in its lack of cultural and historic achievements.

Against the racial prejudice of the Victorian age a handful of black spokesmen strove to refute the dominant orthodoxy. Disenchanted by Western values or rebuffed by Europeans in their attempt to assimilate Western culture, some West African intellectuals began to assert their Africanness.[6] This ideological counterattack has had intensifying reverberations to the present not only in Africa but also in the United States. Many black Americans had long possessed a sentimental attachment to and interest in Africa, and so the ideas of West Africans struck an especially responsive chord. The anti-Western reaction in West Africa was demonstrated by a return to traditional dress and ceremonies, by separatist churches and small political groups; but it was most forcefully articulated in the racial philosophy of Edward Wilmot Blyden.

Born of free and pious parents in 1832 on the Danish West Indian Island of St. Thomas, Blyden at a young age manifested high scholastic aptitude which was nurtured by the tutoring of his mother, a school teacher. Under the guidance of a friendly American missionary, young Blyden's religious and secular education was furthered, as were his aspirations to become a clergyman.

In 1850 Blyden failed to gain admission to three different theological colleges in the United States because of his race. He rightly concluded that the United States in the 1850's was no place for a black man. His friends urged him to emigrate to Africa. Fortunately, he became associated with prominent members of the American Colonization Society which repatriated people of African descent back across the Atlantic to Liberia.

Independent since 1847, Liberia both symbolized the hopes of the black world then held in bondage and beckoned to young blacks of

Blyden's caliber to assist in the building of an exemplary black nation. Although a poor West African state, it fired the imagination and race pride of this West Indian-born African, who later believed that the well-being and progress of Africans everywhere was bound up with the success of Liberia.[7] Without questioning the narrow motives of the Society, he sailed to Liberia on December 21, 1850.

Once in Monrovia, the capital of Liberia, Blyden made rapid progress in his many endeavors. His accomplishments were numerous: he became an ordained Presbyterian minister at the age of twenty-six, held the presidency of Liberia College, served two appointments as Ambassador to the Court of St. James and one as Secretary of State, and briefly edited the *Liberia Herald* and the *Negro*—a newspaper in Freetown, Sierra Leone. His fame, however, does not rest with the holding of prestigious offices but rather with his spirited championing of the Negro race.[8]

Spurred by a desire to vindicate his race from the simplistic and unjust conceptions held by whites and absorbed by some blacks, Blyden wrote prolifically and lectured widely.[9] He railed against the pyramidal ordering of races with Anglo-Saxons mechanically placed at the apex and Negroes instinctively assigned to the base.[10] For his task, he gathered information from historical, sociological, anthropological, and even biblical sources. Like all wise men, Blyden was never satisfied with his knowledge and sought to increase his "efficiency to promote and accelerate the Negro's progress."[11] He increased his research skills by teaching himself Hebrew and Arabic so as to read the original sources upon which Europeans based some of their prejudice and to study North African civilizations. Some of his accounts romanticized African life, but his view frequently reflected a truer image of Africa than that of Western observers who noted only savagery and paganism.

Blyden emphasized four main themes in the defense of the Negro race: it possessed past achievements worthy of pride; its African traditions and culture must be preserved; its progress was thwarted by adherence to Christianity and enhanced by the pursuit of Islam; and it had intrinsic qualities which he termed the "African Personality." By resolutely propounding his vibrant philosophy, Blyden proved to be a spiritual father of the reassertion of black pride that is so characteristic of the mid-twentieth century.

He was among the first of his race to write at length about the important role Africans played in the early history of man.[12] Realizing the significance of history to racial pride, Blyden wrote extensively that African contributions to Egypt and beyond to the ancient Mediterranean world shared in the development of human civilization. Along with praise for Ethiopia and other African kingdoms, he lauded the unacknowledged labors by Africans in the commerce and agriculture of the New World.[13]

The Negro Society for Historical Research founded by black Americans in 1911 recognized his achievements by placing his name among the original list of honorary presidents.[14] W. E. B. DuBois, the brilliant Afro-American race protagonist of the twentieth century, paid tribute to the pioneering work of the Liberian scholar. In his book, *The Negro*, which in itself is a persuasive assault on the prevalent notion that Africans lacked historical accomplishments, DuBois in 1915 extolled Blyden as "the prophet of the renaissance of the Negro race."[15] While editor of *The Crisis*, the publication of the National Association for the Advancement of Colored People, DuBois devoted at least two separate articles to Blyden.[16]

Just as Blyden was adamant about Africa's place in world history, so was he convinced that Islam exercised a salutary effect on African people. During the 1870's he undertook a serious examination of Islam in Africa by frequent visits to Muslim towns and cities as well as by archival research. Over the years he published the results of his inquiries in a series of essays that were printed in 1887 in the book, *Christianity, Islam and the Negro*.[17] Whereas Christianity conditioned "the Negro . . . that to be a great man, he must be like the white man,"[18] Islam, according to Blyden, discouraged racial discrimination, allowing Africans to achieve positions of distinction while retaining their Africanness. He also gave high praise to Muslim society for fostering scholarship, for developing urban civilization, and for creating an egalitarian spirit which "bound tribes together in one strong religious fraternity."[19]

Blyden's enthusiastic endorsement was a corrective to the low regard in which most Europeans held Islam, although contemporary scholarship has been less unqualified in its praise. He pin-pointed, more importantly, a central contradiction of the Christian world that confronted black people: they were expected to emulate the values of them who held them in contempt.[20] In this he anticipated the dilemma of contemporary black Americans, some of whom have attempted to avoid its implications by espousing Islam or rejecting Christianity.

Blyden's most profound impact remains with his conception of the African Personality and its future role in mankind's progress. His concept of race acknowledged racial differentiation. But he refused to accept the European assumption of the inferiority of the Negro race or the European scale of achievement that relegated blacks to the bottom. Like his West African predecessor, Africanus Horton,[21] Blyden berated the racial anthropologists of the mid-nineteenth century for measuring the attainments of superb examples of Europeans against the most unfortunate specimens of another race.[22]

For Blyden races were simply different, not better or worse; "each race was equal, but distinct."[23] Shaped by the environment, each race evolved its own traits and accomplishments, making impossible and unfair the ranking of peoples on a scale prejudicially derived by one race. It was God's grand design that unique qualities of each racial group complement others in order to succor all mankind.[24] A later generation of Afro-American leaders of such diverse thought as DuBois, John E. Bruce, and W. H. Councill held similar judgments of innate racial differences and the special genius of the Negro race.[25]

What were the common qualities that the Negro race possessed? Indeed, what special role was it to play in human development? Blyden zealously advanced three elements of traditional African society that could substantially benefit world civilizations: the communality of African life; the African conception of wealth and ownership; and the fundamental spirituality of its life.

Geography and poverty of resources, Blyden concluded, dictated mutual help and cooperation among villagers. Only a community that worked together closely could survive and grow. The extended family with the interdependence and considerate care of its members—young, old and sick—was the foundation of the community and a microcosm of it. On the rare occasion that the family failed, the community assumed its place. The economic considerations that impeded sharing and proved so divisive in Western society were generally missing in much of African life.

What enabled individuals and African society as a whole to develop without the materialism and selfishness that characterized Western life? To Blyden's mind the answer lay in the African's view of land and wealth. Many African societies regarded land, water, and trees as belonging to everyone in the community, like sunlight and air. Without the grasping acquisitiveness that caused starvation and suffering in Europe, he held much of sub-Saharan Africa escaped the bitter class conflict that destroyed communal spirit. From Africa, Blyden preached, the Western world of competition and self-seeking could learn the principles of cooperation and sharing. In his most ambitious book, *African Life and Customs,* and in many articles and lectures he vigorously advocated preservation of the institutions and customs that nurtured the wholesome aspects of traditional life against the intrusion of European value.

Above all, Blyden believed that the African psyche possessed a certain spirituality that others would do well to emulate. This spiritualness was a result of the African's close communion with nature. Africans made no clear-cut distinction between religious and secular life; rather the two were inextricably interwoven in the seamless fabric of daily experience—planting and harvesting, political and religious ceremonies, birth and death. Africa's tolerance toward Christianity and Islam and its pronounced traditional religious sense prompted Blyden to conclude that "Africa may yet prove to be the spiritual conservatory of the world."[26]

Blyden perceived his mission as not only to challenge the negative assumptions about the Negro race but also to instill a sense of pride in black people in Africa and diaspora: "As a race you are independent and distinct, and have a mission to perform."[27] His ideas anticipated as well as helped spark the black cultural renaissance of the twentieth century.[28] In so doing, Blyden was a principal precursor of much of the awakened African consciousness in America.

His ideas are present today in the United States partly because he assisted in spreading them here. He traveled to the United States twelve times between 1872 and 1890. Some of his visits were sponsored by conservative white backers of the American Colonialization Society which promoted the emigration of black Americans to Africa. Although not in favor of "wholesale emigration," Blyden advocated the settlement of skilled emigrants or those with investment capital.[29] He traveled widely with Bishop Henry M. Turner, the foremost black American proponent of emigration to Africa in the nineteenth century, lecturing to groups and writing in local newspapers about African society and history as well as settlement in Liberia. Believing that black Americans lacked sufficient race confidence and adopted white values too readily, Blyden struggled tirelessly to change the Western image of Africa. His listeners and readers learned that he was fiercely proud of his ancestry and African institutions.[30]

He worked diligently on behalf of South Carolina's Senator Matthew C. Butler's bill calling for federal assistance to black emigrants to Africa. His name and message spread throughout the nation, albeit the passage of the bill failed in 1890. One renowned historian of Back-to-Africa plans wrote that Blyden and Turner created an " 'African fever,' a burning desire on the part of some blacks to leave the United States."[31] The twentieth century emigration movements of Chief Alfred C. Sam from the Gold Coast (Ghana) and Marcus Garvey from Jamaica drew heavily on the earlier campaigns of Blyden and Turner. Even though the great majority of black Americans rejected African emigration, the attention and interest of some were drawn to Africa. Books by Blyden and other Africans sold briskly in such black communities as Harlem.[32]

Interest in Africa was further stimulated, whether for emigration, missionary work, or simple curiosity, by two important conventions that met in the 1890's. The Chicago World's Fair in 1893 provided an excellent opportunity to learn about Africa at the Liberian exhibit as did the week-long World's Congress on Africa held in conjunction with the fair. Sponsored by the American Missionary Association, the Congress was probably the first scholarly conference on Africa.[33] Momolu Massaquoi, admirer and friend of Blyden, spoke and Samuel Johnson, eminent African historian of the Yoruba people in Nigeria, sent a paper.[34]

Two years later the Stewart Missionary Foundation for Africa convened a conference in Atlanta on "Africa and the American Negro" in December, 1895. The Reverend W. J. Stewart of the Gammon Theological Seminary hoped his foundation and the conference would popularize interest in Africa and encourage black Americans to seek missionary work there. Blyden was unable to attend but sent a paper. Speakers included Bishop Turner, Alexander Crummell, and John H. Smyth.[35] These three black Americans had come under the influence of Blyden's ideas, and aided in conveying them to the United States.

Bishop Turner maintained correspondence with Blyden, even visiting the Liberian scholar in Monrovia. On a card inviting Blyden to the festivities of his thirtieth wedding anniversary, Turner penned: "If not the greatest, certainly one of the greatest Negroes that tread the globe."[36] More significantly, Turner lectured and wrote on topics dear to the heart of Blyden. He subscribed to Blyden's beliefs that God had planned a great destiny for black people, that Islam uplifted Africans in their search for education, and that Africa represented the proper home for the Negro race.[37]

Alexander Crummell, an Anglican divine, served twenty years in Liberia where he was Blyden's colleague on the faculty of Liberia College. Returning to the United States in the early 1870's, he became the rector of a successful Episcopal church in Washington and a leading black intellectual of the period. In spite of a high regard for Anglo-Saxon civilization, the former missionary to Liberia, like Blyden, ruled out assimilation of European culture. Couching his arguments in Blydenesque terms, Crummell called for a separate and unique identity for the Negro race because "races have their own individuality."[38]

Another black American who participated in the conference on Africa and Negro Americans and embraced Blyden's brand of racial ideology was John H. Smyth. Stationed in Liberia from 1878 to 1885 as the United States minister, Smyth became the "dear friend of E. W. Blyden."[39] Blyden as president of Liberia College awarded an honorary Doctor of Laws to Smyth in 1881. Amplifying Blyden's racial sentiments, he declared in an American address in 1887: "Race allegiance is compatible with the highest patriotism.... We are bound ... to make ourselves—not on the pattern of any other race, but actuated by our peculiar genius in literature, religion, commerce, and social intercourse—a great people."[40] Turner, Crummell and Smyth led long activist careers in behalf of black Americans. Their efforts were sure to have been influential on the development of Afro-American thought.

Not all the important black conferences of the age were called on the American continent. The first attempt to convene a Pan-African conference started with the agitation in 1897 by a group of knowledgeable and moderately prosperous Africans in England who were alarmed by the brutality of British conquests in what is now Rhodesia and Botswana and by the continuation of the slave trade along the East African coast. For these and fraternal reasons, they formed "The African Association."[41] Henry Sylvester-Williams, a West Indian barrister who performed legal duties for Africans, actually organized the conference which met July

23–25, 1900, in London. DuBois attended the conference along with eleven other black Americans.[42] Although the Pan-African conference movement lay dormant until 1919 when DuBois revived it, the idea was promoted in the formative days by Africans. Much of the organizational side grew from the pan-Negro sentiments expressed by Africans as well as by black Americans.[43]

If Blyden was the most prominent African spokesman, he was not the only active one. John Payne Jackson, editor of the Nigerian *Lagos Weekly Record*, provided instructive and influential columns to his contemporaries for almost a quarter century after 1890. The tone and content of Payne's editorials and the regularity with which he printed Blyden's letters and articles attest to the influence of the Liberian scholar on him. Like Blyden, he encouraged the return to African names and the sympathetic treatmen of African history and traditions.[44] His thoughts on racial exclusiveness and distinctiveness closely approximated the Liberian's ideas, as did his belief in the rejuvenative powers of traditional life: "go back to the simplicity of your fathers—go back to health and life and continuity."[45]

Black Americans attentive to things African often subscribed to the *Lagos Weekly Record* and other West African papers. One of the most faithful readers of the Lagos paper was the Afro-American journalist, John Edward Bruce, who with Arthur Schomburg founded the Negro Society for Historical Research in 1911.[46] For his frequent articles Bruce used information from African newspapers and correspondence from African leaders, including Mojola Agbebi and J. E. Casely Hayford.[47]

Of all Blyden's followers, Casely Hayford was perhaps his most fervent disciple. The Liberian vindicator made a life-long impact on him in Sierra Leone where Casely Hayford was a student in the early 1870's.[48] Casely Hayford, a lawyer, became in his own right a race champion of some renown. As well as being the foremost architect of the National Congress of British West Africa—an important forerunner to widespread African nationalism—he persistently charged European missionaries with a "de-Africanizing influence."[49] Drawing considerable inspiration from Blyden, the Gold Coast (Ghana) barrister ardently defended African culture. In *Ethiopia Unbound,* he paid exulted, if not worshipful, tribute to Blyden and his racial philosophy.[50] Interestingly enough, it was Bruce who served as the American agent for *Ethiopia Unbound* and thus contributed to spreading Blyden's influence in another way.

Still another African intellectual and Blyden adherent with heady ideas for black Americans was Mojola Agbebi. Dr. Agbebi, a Baptist-trained minister, established with Blyden's encouragement probably the first independent African church in West Africa.[51] Humble in origin and largely self-educated, Agbebi rose to prominence in Lagos by founding Hope Institute, an agricultural and technical school, and by eloquently describing Africa's social systems and culture. Blyden, who was too ill to travel, had reason to be proud of and heartened by his close friend of twenty years at the sixth session of the Universal Race Congress. The Congress was significant because its international forum lent prestige to race egalitarians. Convened in London in 1911, it was attended by Africans and black Americans, among them DuBois who delivered a paper. During the proceedings Agbebi also read a paper, "The West African Problem," which showed his firm agreement with Blyden's racial beliefs.[52]

Before this Blyden had warmly congratulated Agbebi for his inaugural address at the first anniversary of the "African Church" in Lagos in December 21, 1902;[53] he referred to Agbebi's sermon as "the earnest utterance of a genuine African."[54] The Nigerian commended African traditional institutions, endorsed Islam and acclaimed Africans' unique attributes.[55] Bruce wrote Agbebi requesting consent to print the sermon after reading excerpts of it in the *Sierra Leone Weekly News*. In the letter, he displayed a jubilant sense of racial pride that has a contemporary ring: "I am black all over, and am as proud of my black skin, and that of my forebears, as the blackest man in Africa."[56] Other black Americans recognized Agbebi's contribution to delineating a distinct African Personality.

Under Bruce's leadership an Afro-American organization, the Men's Sunday Club of Yonkers, New York, observed October 1, 1911 as "Agbebi Day." One hundred and seven distinguished West Africans applauded the observance of the Yonkers group. The Africans stated in a signed scroll to the club that they admired its "resolution to immortalize in him (Agbebi) an African Personality."[57] Further participation in black American history by Agbebi's family was evidenced when a kinsman of Mojola, Akinbami Agbebi, worked actively although unsuccessfully, managing Garvey's Black Star steamship line.

Marcus Garvey, the charismatic Jamaican who organized one of the first genuine black American mass movements in the half-decade following World War I, encountered African nationalist ideas from 1912 to 1914 in London, just as had Chief Alfred C. Sam. While in London—Blyden's former ambassadorial post—Garvey met frequently with Africans and West Indians and developed a keen interest in Africa. In all likelihood, he discovered Blyden's racial ideology either through his voracious reading at the British Museum or through Africans such as the Egyptian nationalist of Sudanese descent, Duse Mohammed Ali. As editor of the *African Times and Orient Review*, an anti-imperialist paper printed in London, Duse Mohammed argued for Egyptian home rule and condemned Anglo-Saxon color prejudice.[58] From him, Garvey learned of the slogan "Africa for the Africans"[59]—a phrase long popularized by Blyden.[60] When Garvey established the Universal Negro Improvement Association, Duse Mohammed was employed by the movement's paper, *Negro World*, and became one of its ideologues.[61]

The conferences on Africa, emigration plans, lectures, West African newspapers and voluminous correspondence between African thinkers and their black American associates all provided valuable opportunities for Afro-Americans to learn not only an African version of African life and history but also experience a sense of racial worth. Doubtless, African intellectuals contributed to a maturity of racial consciousness—a new sense among black people that they had something of value in common.

Blyden and his spokesmen made a far-reaching impact on the black intellectual response to white views of the Negro race. Their sentiments have been expressed in countless ways in art, literature, politics and even in the unarticulated feelings of racial dignity. DuBois, the preeminent black American leader of this century, put forth a racial manifesto in 1897 that strikingly paralleled Blyden's thought and language: "Their (Afro-Americans) destiny is not absorption by the white American... not a servile imitation of Anglo-Saxon culture, but a stalwart originality which shall unswervingly follow Negro ideas.... Negro people, as a race, have a contribution to make to civilization and humanity, which no other race can make."[62]

DuBois's familiarity with the ideas of Blyden is greater than is often realized.[63] George Shepperson, the British historian, noted that DuBois "knew Blyden and his writings well,"[64] but this writer has been unable to substantiate the assertion that DuBois even met Blyden. It is entirely possible that DuBois may have heard Blyden speak or encountered him at a gathering of black Americans. He certainly read Blyden's work and credited their contribution to African history and to enhancing racial pride. Less directly, DuBois also came under the influence of the Liberian scholar. During his early career, DuBois was closely associated with at least one of Blyden's most active adherents in the United States. DuBois knew William S. Scarborough, a classics teacher, whom he replaced in 1894–96 at Wilberforce University, a black American school in Ohio.[65] Scarborough unreservedly endorsed the Liberian's emigration plans and efforts to intensify black pride. For Scarborough's scholastic attainments Blyden conferred on him an honorary degree a decade and a half before the Greek and Latin teacher met DuBois.[66]

Black American interest in and identification with Africa soared in the twentieth century. It was Africans who had helped nurture and quicken this African awareness. The increased development of racial identity and ethnocentric culture in the 1920's was a variation on earlier themes which have persisted into our own time.[67]

That black Americans played a contributory role in the growth of African nationalism is a story well popularized.[68] But that Africans shared at an earlier date in the evolution of black American racial thought is largely ignored. The careers of Kwame Nkrumah and Nnamdi Azikiwe, who studied in the United States before the Second World War, are cited as examples of formative black American influences on future African political leaders. Yet Azikiwe and Nkrumah had been politically conscious before their American student days, or even before learning of significant black American leaders.[69]

Admittedly, black Americans forged unique attitudes that influenced young Africans, but this should not detract from African contributions to black consciousness in the United States. The ideological current that flowed from the United States to Africa had been at first generated in part by African intellectuals.

Notes

1. For example, August Meier, *Negro Thought in America, 1880–1915* (Ann Arbor, 1963); Sterling Stuckey, *The Ideological Origins of Black Nationalism* (Boston, 1972); and Earl E. Thorpe, *The Mind of the Negro: An Intellectual History of Afro-Americans* (Baton Rouge, Louisiana, 1961).

2. For one of the best accounts, see George Shepperson, "Notes on Negro American Influences on the Emergence of African Nationalism," *Journal of African History,* I (February, 1960), 299–312.

3. Melville J. Herskovits, *The Myth of the Negro Past* (New York, 1941). For others of the same view, see Lorenzo D. Turner, *Africanisms in the Gullah Dialect* (Chicago, 1949) and Romeo B. Garrett, "African Survivals in American Culture," *Journal of Negro History,* LX (April, 1966), 239–45.

4. Benjamin Quarles, *The Negro in the Making of America* (rev. ed., New York, 1969); Kenneth G. Goode and Winthrop D. Gordan, *From Africa to the United States and Then: A Concise Afro-American History* (Glenview, Illinois, 1969).

5. Colin Legum, *Pan-Africanism: A Short Political Guide* (rev. ed., New York, 1965), p. 14; E. U. Essien-Udom, "The Relationship of Afro-Americans to African Nationalism," *Freedomways,* II (Fall, 1962), 104.

6. Robert W. July, *The Origins of Modern African Thought* (New York, 1967), pp. 208–10.

7. Blyden like many immigrants, famous or not, assumed the outlook of his adopted land. He regarded himself as an African not only culturally and ethnically but also in citizenship.

8. Hollis R. Lynch, *Edward Wilmot Blyden: Pan-Negro Patriot, 1832–1912* (New York, 1967), pp. 3–5.

9. Blyden's numerous writings were published in newspapers, pamphlets, periodicals, and books. His best-known books are: *Christianity, Islam and the Negro Race* (1887, reprinted by Edinburgh University Press, 1967); *African Life and Customs* (1908, republished by International Publishing Service, 1970); *Vindication of the Negro Race* (Monrovia, 1857); *The Significance of Liberia* (Monrovia, 1906).

10. For a synopsis on how Europeans viewed Africans in the late nineteenth century, see Ronald Robinson, John Gallagher and Alice Denny, *Africa and the Victorians: The Official Mind of Imperialism* (London, 1965), pp. 2–3.

11. Blyden to William E. Gladstone, September 7, 1860, *British Museum*

Add. Mss. 44394/102. Gladstone at the time was British Chancellor of the Exchequer and later became Prime Minister.

12. Lynch, *op. cit.*, pp. 54–55.

13. Edward W. Blyden, "The Negro in Ancient History," *Methodist Quarterly Review*, LI (January, 1869), 71–93.

14. Other Africans associated with the Society at the time of its founding as members or in honorary roles were Lewanika of Barotseland, Casely Hayford, and Duse Mohammed Ali.

15. W. E. B. DuBois, *The Negro* (New York, 1915), p. vii. This work has been reprinted by Oxford University Press, 1970.

16. *The Crisis*, III (January, 1912), 103; *The Crisis,* III (March, 1912), 187.

17. Among the most significant are "Mohammedanism and the Negro Race," *Fraser's Magazine*, New Series, XII (November, 1875), 598–615; "Mohammedanism in West Africa," *Methodist Quarterly Review*, LIII (January, 1871).

18. Edward W. Blyden, "Christianity and the Negro Race," *Fraser's Magazine*, XIII (May, 1876), 556–57.

19. Edward W. Blyden, "Mohammedanism in West Africa," *op. cit.*, p. 70.

20. Lynch, *op. cit.*, p. 72.

21. J. A. B. Horton, *West African Countries and Peoples* (London, W. J. Johnson, 1868), pp. 39–43, 52–55.

22. July, *op. cit.*, p. 215.

23. Edward W. Blyden, "Africa and the African," *Fraser's Magazine*, XVIII (August, 1878), 191.

24. Edward W. Blyden, *African Life and Customs* (London, 1908), pp. 11–12.

25. Meier, *op. cit.*, p. 267.

26. Edward W. Blyden, *Christianity, Islam and the Negro Race* (3rd ed., Edinburgh, 1967), p. 125.

27. *Chicago Inter-Ocean*, November 5, 1889.

28. Robert W. July, "Nineteenth-Century Negritude: Edward W. Blyden," *Journal of African History*, V (January, 1964), 73–86.

29. *Washington Post*, October 14, 1895.

30. Edwin S. Redkey, *Black Exodus: Black Nationalist and Back-to-Africa Movements, 1890–1910* (New Haven, 1969), pp. 54–58.

31. *Ibid.*, p. 71.

32. Richard B. Moore, "Africa Conscious Harlem," *Freedomways*, III (Summer, 1963), 316–17. Moore lists a number of books written by Africans that were sold in Harlem. Among the more important were: Samuel Johnson, *History of the Yoruba People*; Duse Mohammed, *In the Land of the Pharaohs*; Casely Hayford, *Ethiopia Unbound, Gold Coast Native Institutions*; Sol T. Plaatje, *Native Life in South Africa*; and John Mensah Sarbah, *Fanti Customary Laws.*

33. Frederick Perry Noble, *The Redemption of Africa* (Chicago, 1899), p. 491.

34. Momolu Massaquoi was born in Sierra Leone and later served in the Liberian government as assistant to the Secretary of Interior. Although missionary trained, Samuel Johnson spent years compiling a massive history of the Yoruba people in Nigeria.

35. John W. E. Bowen, ed., *Africa and the American Negro* (Atlanta: Gammon Theological Seminary, 1896), pp. 1–3.

36. Blyden to William Coppinger, September 20, 1886, quoted in Edith Holden, *Blyden of Liberia: An Account of the Life and Labours of Edward Wilmot Blyden, LL.D. as Recorded in Letters and in Print* (New York, 1966), p. 569. Coppinger was secretary of the American Colonialization Society.

37. Edwin S. Redkey, "Bishop Turner's African Dream," *Journal of American History*, LIV (September, 1967), 278, 285–88.

38. Alexander Crummell, *The Future of Africa* (New York, 1862), p. 87.

39. James A. Padgett, "Ministers to Liberia and Their Diplomacy," *Journal of Negro History*, XXII (January, 1937), 60.

40. Washington *Bee*, June 25, 1887. In his address at the conference, Smyth mentioned J. A. B. Horton's name as one who attempted to correct European opinions of Africans. See Bowen, *op. cit.*, p. 78.

41. George Padmore, *Pan-Africanism or Communism?* (London, 1956), p. 117.

42. Alexander Walters, *My Life and Work* (New York, 1917), pp. 253–55.

43. Clarence G. Contee, "The Emergence of DuBois as an African Nationalist," *Journal of Negro History*, LIV (January, 1969), 50.

44. July, *The Origins of Modern African Thought, op. cit.*, pp. 355–56.

45. *Lagos Weekly Record*, October 19, 1912.

46. Bruce also subscribed to the *Sierra Leone Weekly News*, the *Gold Coast Aborigines*, and the *African Times*. See John E. Bruce Papers, Schomburg Collection, New York Public Library. Arthur Schomburg's personal library was bought by the Carnegie Foundation in the 1920's. It formed the small nucleus of the present collection.

47. Bruce also wrote in African Papers. For his correspondence, see John E. Bruce Papers.

48. Lynch, *op. cit.*, pp. 240–42.

49. Joseph C. Casely Hayford, *Gold Coast Native Institutions* (London, 1903), p. 105.

50. *Ethiopia Unbound* (London, 1911), pp. 162–64.

51. *Sierra Leone Weekly News*, August 29, 1896.

52. G. Spiller, ed., *Papers on Interracial Problems: First Universal Race Congress* (London, 1911), pp. 343–47.

53. Mojola Agbebi, *Inaugural Sermon Delivered at the Celebration of the First Anniversary of the "African Church,"* (Edgar R. Horworth, Printer, Yonkers, New York, n.d.), Schomburg Collection.

54. Blyden to Agbebi, March 17, 1903, attached to *Inaugural Sermon Delivered at the Celebration of the First Anniversary of the "African Church,"* p. 17. Blyden also wrote in the same letter: "Bishop Montgomery, of South Africa, at the last meeting of the Church Congress, in England, said that 'Africa is struggling for a separate personality'; and your discourse is one of the striking evidences of this."

55. Agbebi, *op. cit.*, pp. 7–8, 10–14.

56. *Ibid.*, p. 27.

57. Agbebi to Bruce, August 27, 1907, John E. Bruce Papers.

58. E. David Cronon, *Black Moses: The Story of Marcus Garvey and the Universal Negro Improvement Association* (Madison, 1955), p. 15.

59. Moore, *op. cit.*, p. 322.

60. George Shepperson and Thomas Price, *Independent African: John Chilembwe and the Origins, Setting and Significance of Nyasaland Native Rising of 1915* (Edinburgh, 1958), p. 504.

61. Duse Mohammed eventually parted ways with Garvey because of jealousy over Garvey's success and skepticism of his linking African nationalism to black American redemption. Cronon, *op. cit.*, p. 43.

62. W. E. B. DuBois, "The Conservation of Races," originally published in the American Negro Academy, *Occasional Papers*, no. 2 (Washington, D. C., 1897). Among other places it has been reprinted in Howard Brotz, *Negro Social and Political Thought, 1850–1920* (New York, 1966), pp. 483–92.

63. DuBois may not have acknowledged Blyden's influence because of the Liberian vindicator's well-known dislike of mulattoes. So great was Blyden's hatred of mulattoes that it may have stopped him from attending the 1900 Pan-African conference in London.

64. George Shepperson, "Pan-Africanism and 'Pan-Africanism': Some Historical Notes," *Phylon*, XXII (Fall, 1962), 350.

65. Francis P. Weisenburger, "William Sanders Scarborough: Early Life and Years at Wilberforce," *Ohio History*, LXXI (October, 1962), 203–26.

66. Lynch, *op. cit.*, p. 154.

67. Nathan Irvin Huggins, *Harlem Renaissance* (New York, 1971), pp. 4–7.

68. Legum, *op. cit.*, pp. 13–15; Shepperson, "Notes on Negro American Influences on the Emergence of African Nationalism," *op. cit.*, p. 312; Martin Kilson and Adelaide Hill, eds., *Apropos of Africa: Afro-American Leaders and the Romance of Africa* (Garden City, 1971), p. 346.

69. K. A. B. Jones-Quartey, *A Life of Azikiwe* (Baltimore, 1965), pp. 56–57; Kwame Nkrumah, *Ghana: The Autobiography of Kwame Nkrumah* (New York, 1957), pp. xii, 16.

Father Divine
and the Peace Mission Movement

Kenneth E. Burnham

The Peace Mission Movement is the name by which several thousand people in several countries designate themsleves. Whatever their past religious convictions, race or nationality they hold that Major Jealous Divine, also known as Father Divine, an American citizen of dark complexion, was and is to be God incarnate in a human body. They believe that even though God has not animated the body of Major Jealous Divine since September 10, 1965, he will return in another body, and that meanwhile God is still present everywhere in the world and is to be addressed as Father Divine.

I. *Origin and Growth*

Major Jealous Divine first came to the notice of the wider public in connection with a dramatic court case on Long Island, New York, in the Spring of 1932. Interracial religious services at his home in Sayville were raided by the police on the evening of Sunday, November 15, 1931. Eighty attenders were arrested, fifteen of them of the American racial majority and the rest minority group members. They were charged with "disturbing the peace" and fifty-five pleaded guilty and paid a five dollar fine; twenty-five and Father Divine pleaded not guilty. Major Jealous Divine was found guilty on May 25, 1932. Despite a judge's recommendation of leniency, Judge Lewis J. Smith sentenced him to the maximum penalty under the law: one year in the county jail and a five hundred dollar fine. The Bill of Particulars stated:

> Defendant claimed to be the Messiah returned to earth; conducted so-called religious services, at which services colored and white people did congregate in large numbers, and did then and there encourage, aid and assist those present in shouting and sing-

ing in loud tones of voice, annoying neighbors in the vicinity of the defendant's place.

And did then and there permit and encourage large numbers of people on foot and in auto to gather around the place; and did encourage said singing, shouting, exhorting and stamping to continue past midnight, keeping them awake at all hours of the night and morning.[1]

Followers of both races defined the trial as based on racial antagonism because of the integrated nature of Father Divine's fellow-worshippers. Despite testimony that the sounds from the Divine home could not be heard outside it, neighbors claimed it was the noise and crowds of people in a residential area which perturbed them. Followers felt that the remarks of the Judge were irrelevant and prejudicial. He had claimed:

His name is not Devine ... he is not an ordained minister ... he is not married to the woman he calls his wife ... he has another woman as his wife ... and has children living ... he takes his follower's wages and has used them for his own purposes ... he has failed to cooperate.[2]

Major Divine's followers held that all of these were either of no significance in the charges against him, or were simply not true. There has never been any evidence that he was not married to Penninah, or that he had another wife or any children. They saw the raid, the arrest, and the sentencing all as a pattern of persecution of a minority, those who believed that God made all people of one blood.

The case received national publicity as a matter of civil rights and religious persecution. Lawyers from Harlem, who were not followers, served in the defense. Followers of all complexions testified that Father Divine was God and that his finances were a spiritual matter. The Judge questioned the sanity of those who frequented the house on Macon Street, but he could find no one who had been committed to a mental hospital from that address.

Then came a turning point in Father Divine's career ... it was an incident that has become the prototype of many others since. Judge Smith, an apparently healthy man, died suddenly of heart disease just three days after he pronounced sentence. This was immediately interpreted by the followers as an act of retribution brought about by Father's wrath.

Ever since this day, June 7, 1932, the newspaper of the movement, the *New Day*, has publicized incidents of death and suffering which are predicted to happen or have occurred to those who oppose Father Divine or his principles. The *New Day* is replete with such threats. I quote a few to illustrate their nature.

Major Divine says: "If I do not have free access to any part of this country and especially where they oppose me, ambulances and doctors and the Red Cross will go to see them."[3]

In a telephone conversation with a reporter in connection with the refusal of the Yonkers, New York, officials to grant a license for a parade, Father says:

> You see, when prejudice tries to bar the peaceful access and the peaceful assemblage of any peaceful people, naturally the cosmic forces of nature go forth destructively and act as they would desire to act towards those to whom they are prejudiced (but) my home will not be disturbed, even as it was not disturbed the other week. All the telephone communication was cut off in that community and also in New Rochelle, and my home was in perfect contact with the outside world. So that . . . those who are malicious to that degree, or prejudiced they might know, if they try to bar Me, I will bar them through the cosmic forces of nature or in some other way they may not think.[4]

In a letter to the president of an international airline Major Divine states that certain air accidents were due to disregarding his message and to the practice of discrimination and that other calamities are also due to the same facts. The Second World War could have been avoided "had they taken cognizance of My message." The "very ground itself is cursed" when "men seek to segregate themselves and place restrictions on deeds and papers." "Where prejudice, division, bigotry and strife exist, disaster also exists or follows. The Texas City fire, the floods in the Middle West and the many airplane crashes, train wrecks, and automobile wrecks attest the fact."[5]

Many followers were convinced of Father Divine's control of cosmic forces by the death of Judge Smith and agreed with their leader's explanation of the causes of disasters. Father Divine was more powerful than the government. If someone in government or industry or the community practices discrimination against Father Divine, persons of his complexion, or his followers or those who accept his principles, retribution may occur, and Father Divine will have confirmed his powers.

The anticlimax to the judge's death was reversal of the conviction by the Appellate Division of the Supreme Court in Brooklyn. A new trial was called for because "prejudice was excited in the jurors by the comments, rulings and questions by the court." The case was never retried. And its significance was never forgotten by the followers. Only God could punish the judge and overcome the law. Father Divine was free again although he had spent 33 days in jail. Nor was he driven from Macon Street in Sayville. To this day followers live in the house and others make pilgrimages to it from all over the world.

From this time on there was little doubt among the followers of the divinity of their leader. They proclaimed it at meetings, at parades, at the various legal proceedings which involved the movement, and in the weekly newspaper. Although accused of being evasive in court, Major

Jealous Divine had no hesitance in declaring himself God before his followers and visitors, nor in having this printed for all to read.

One of the devices that has given a sense of unity and continuous participation in the activities of God, Father Divine, to the followers has been the weekly publication of the movement's "newspapers" in which all the public utterances of Father Divine are printed. To the followers these utterances are God's commands for their lives and nothing is too great or too trivial for the Father to control. As Wilson observes:

> Sectarians often display a high regard for charismatic authority whether this be offered as an incarnation of God in man, as a special anointing by God as a prophet, or merely as a marked natural ability, special wisdom, knowledge, lucidity or unction. The leader is responsible, at least initially and in part, for the precepts and examples which his votaries accept, and for the primary articulation of values to which they subscribe: his self-interpretation conditions their behavior and beliefs.[6]

I shall return now to describe the origins of the "family" which had endured arrest with Father Divine in 1932. There is disagreement about the origins of Father Divine. The popular books[7] about him held that he was born in Savannah, Georgia, in 1878 or 1880. Court records in Mineola, Long Island, claim that he was born in Providence, Rhode Island, in 1880. The movement holds that he was first married June 6, 1882, and refuses to discuss his birth.

One of Father Divine's answers as to his origin is the following:

> I have spoken of My first record as having moved out upon the face of the waters when I was intangible, invisible and without form, and spoke into outer expression first the most greatest or biggest tangibilization of creation which was the material earth, when I said "Let dry land appear!"[8]

There is reason to believe that Major Jealous Divine did preach for a number of years in various parts of the South, and that he preached against discrimination. He often described the hardships he endured by the phrase that he had been "lynched" 32 times.

At any rate it is a fact that by 1914 he had been for some time in New York City. He was living in an apartment in Brooklyn which he shared with his wife Penninah and a group of followers. The followers worked in the community, but shared common meals with Major Divine and his wife. Perhaps they pooled some or all of their incomes to meet expenses. They worshipped together at meals and hence this was the origin of the communal living and the "communion" meal which all true followers of Father Divine still practice.

Major Divine seemed to take pride in the statement that he had no formal education, nor ordination by any religious group. He identified with the segment of the population which had been enslaved and still suffered great indignities. He held that much of the legal action taken against him was because of his attack upon the unconstitutional practice of racial discrimination. He explained his manner of speech and his appearance as God's way of reaching the people who needed to hear God and were not being reached by the ordinary preachers.

In 1919 Mr. and Mrs. Divine, with the earnings of Penninah, bought a single home in a residential area of Sayville, Long Island. Sayville, a small village, surrounded by summer estates, furnished domestic jobs for followers and a pleasant place to live. He claimed that no one knew who he was when he came to Sayville, but there were soon followers living in the home, and he acted as both a spiritual adviser and an employment agent for them. Apparently his reputation was spread by word of mouth and through the years between 1919 and 1932, a steadily mounting tide of individuals, finally busloads, began to come to worship with him, some to tarry at the home for various lengths of time. There are many testimonies in the *New Day* as to the services rendered to those who were looking for physical, material, and spiritual salvation and who felt that they found it at the worship services that went on during the "communion" meal at Sayville.

Attempts were made to impugn the sexual purity of the leader and his followers, but none of them succeeded.

In the late fall of 1931 and the winter of 1932 Father Divine was in such demand at meetings in Harlem that he was traveling back and forth almost daily, a trip of about 120 miles. Charles Calloway, a retired railroad worker, leased several apartments on 135th Street, which he offered to Father Divine as a headquarters for himself and his immediate family and guests. For about eight months after March 1932 this property was often referred to as the Peace Mission, a term that was spreading among the followers. Later in 1932, Lena Brinson, who also often invited Father Divine to her home, leased a building at 20 West 115th Street. This was used for meeting rooms, restaurants and dormitories. Meals were ten to fifteen cents and sleeping quarters were two dollars a week. Mrs. Brinson urged Father Divine to be her guest and to speak at some of her meetings. By November 1933 she had placed at the disposal of Father Divine an office and apartment on the top floor of the building. Charles Calloway and his wife closed their home and moved in with Mrs. Brinson to cooperate with her in maintaining the 115th Street home.

Thus was the pattern of "communal living" established which persists among the American followers to this day.

In the glare of publicity attending the trial and subsequent events, 20 West 115th Street became generally known as Father Divine's Peace

Mission Headquarters and the suffering and the curious came there from all over the world.

In the depth of the depression there was always free or inexpensive food, a place to sleep, and work to do. For soon other followers started dormitories, restaurants, sewing rooms, and other small businesses which furnished employment for many.

During the next ten years Father Divine traveled up and down the Eastern Seaboard from Connecticut to Washington and as far west as Detroit. Followers in many places he visited established homes in which to welcome the Father. Although there were mass meetings in the largest halls that followers could find to hire, the communal meal became the highlight of Father Divine's visit. The ritualized serving of this meal is the most impressive worship service of the Movement. It not only furnished sustenance for the body but was felt to prove the power of Father Divine, for who else but God could furnish such an abundance of food in the depression. Participants were allowed to donate for this meal.

In the late thirties city followers were encouraged to return to the land by Father Divine and they began to buy farm properties and hotels in Ulster County, New York. Even during World War Two rationing, the farms helped to furnish food in abundance for the communion tables.

Californians visited New York and took back the ideals of Father Divine to found small groups in several California cities. Canadians carried the message back to their homes. In the 1930's Walter Clemow Lanyon, an English writer of metaphysical and inspirational books, visited and returned to preach the message in England and on the continent. This resulted in "families" in England (most of whom have since migrated to the United States), Germany and Switzerland. The faith reached Australia and today the several active groups there regularly send visitors to the followers in the United States and several individuals have migrated here.

II.   *Theology and Ideology*

Father Divine is God Incarnate.

"It is through our recognition of Father Divine and who He is that has brought us together. We have come to Father from many nations throughout the world and many classes of people. Father has something that is satisfying for all people. Being God incarnate ... he would automatically have that satisfying portion for all people."[9]

Father Divine is the father of one family—
all mankind.

"We live together as one family and recognizing God as our father, we are all brothers and sisters in reality. This does away with the consciousness of races and nationalities and this is the way it was in the beginning. Out of one blood God created all nations for to dwell upon the face of the earth, and this is what it is to be in the end."

Father Divine exemplifies the life of Christ
here on earth.

"Father has stressed the necessity of living the life of Christ that Christianity preaches and which all people who profess Christianity should live. We are founded on the Sermon on the Mount and Father has made the precepts of the Bible a living reality to us. Christianity is a Principle, the Life that Jesus lived and it must be lived by everyone in order to get the desirable results. And it is here and now, not in some imaginary heaven after we die."

Death, disease and sickness are abolished if one
lives by the mind of Jesus.

"Father has taught us that, as Jesus said, 'If a man keep My sayings he shall never see death!'—that it is the mortal versions of the carnal mind that man functions under, that produces sickness and disease and death, but if he lets this Mind be in him that was also in Christ Jesus, then that Mind will give him victory over sickness, disease and death."

Science and religion are one and will bring the
Kingdom of Heaven into existence on this earth.

"Father upholds science because it is God's revelation or God's inspiration to man for the good of His children and the bringing of the Kingdom of Heaven on the earth plane to us. Father said years ago that he was working cancellation on the imaginary Heaven, and we can see through the advances science has made that the religious world is beginning to realize it must change its concepts to cope with the modern world."

On the relationship between the sexes.

"We don't have any relationship with the opposite sex except on business. One must direct their mind and attention on the Fundamental in order to get the victory over the carnal nature. That is why the virtuous life is a necessity. We make a self-denial of the pleasures of the world but yet we find our pleasure and happiness in Father and in the Peace Mission. We find a happiness and joy that far surpasses in our estimation what one finds in mortal pleasures."

Attitude toward proselyting.

"We do not believe in proselyting, as many churches do. People have been attracted to Father from many nations and they have carried the message back to those nations."

The apocalyptic role of Father Divine.

"We know that Father's coming is the bringing of the Heaven to the earth plane, as spoken of in Revelation; the first Heaven and the first earth were passed away and he (John) saw a new Heaven and a new earth."

Father Divine's wider influence.

"Of course Father is by no means confined to the Peace Mission. All those who think righteously are following Father, but they may not be conscious of it. Father would not by any means allow us to confine Him."

The exemplary role of the Followers.

"We as individuals feel that if we lift up a standard within ourselves, like Jesus said, 'And I if I be lifted up from the earth I will draw all men unto Me'—it means so much more to put your energy into living this Life than to just talk it and not live it. I feel this is where Christianity has failed to some degree—they have not really practiced true Christianity."

*Father Divine's apparent death was for the
redemption of mankind.*

"Father is the lamb that was slain before the foundation of the world, as a sacrifice—a complete sacrifice—for the redemption of mankind. As Father often said, 'If anyone should be sick, I should be the one, if anyone should appear old, I should be the one, because it is written "He took upon Himself our infirmities and bore our diseases and by His stripes we are healed!"' Father said we should not even stump our foot nor should we have a blowout in the tires of our cars if we are conscious of God's presence and live the Life of Christ; everything should work harmoniously and systematically and we should not even age."

*The goal of man is to be one with his maker
and creator.*

"We must be free from conventionality and free from tradition in order to get the inspiration from God to go on and bring the Christ to fruition: this is the goal of man and eventually he will be one with his maker and creator."

The omnipresence of God, Father Divine.

Father did not personally go to any other country "because he said it was nothing he did as a person (in fact he refused to do things from a personal point of view to try to help or bless anyone), but as people would call on Father's name and think sympathetically and harmoniously on Father, their prayers would be answered. It is not necessary for God to go anywhere because He fills all space and is absent from none, and this is what Father wants us to grasp; that wheresoever we are, God is there, and that we can call on Him and get the answer to our prayer; but at the same time, though, that God is personified in a bodily form."

Why God came in the bodily form of Father Divine.

"And the beauty of Father Divine coming in the bodily form to the underprivileged and to the downtrodden is that there would be no child of His that would feel that he could not have his salvation. If God had come as the majority of the people would expect God to come ... there would be so many that would feel they would not have a chance."

Importance of recognizing the personification
of God in Father Divine.

"Father says, if you recognize God in body, God will recognize your body and take care of the needs of your body, but if you only recognize God in the Spirit, you might be saved spiritually but your physical body will not be."

Even though he has apparently left his body,
Father Divine will return in a bodily form.

"He will return in a bodily form: Father, to me is God, and therefore he is the victory over every situation and every circumstance, and as I see it, what Father did, he willed it that way."

Influence of Father on the founding of
American democracy.

"Father was really with the Founding Fathers, they took the principles of Christianity and made laws, that was their inspiration for a perfect form of government. This nation was conceived in liberty and dedicated to the proposition that all men are created equal. The freedom to worship God according to the dictates of your own conscience allows the Christ within each individual to be developed."

The American form of government
is the perfect form.

"Father came to America that he might be called an American and he has advocated the Constitution of the United States and the Declaration of Independence, the American form of government as the perfect form of government—that is, if it is lived."

Father Divine's social, political and
economic message.

During the early years of the movement a number of political parties sought the support of Father Divine and some followers who were interested in many panaceas called a convention to draw up a platform representing Father Divine's social program. In January, 1936, such a convention was held in New York City. Father Divine endorsed the Righteous Government Platform which has since been reprinted in the *New Day* periodically.

The following are the provisions of the "Platform."

1. The United States government is to ban every form of discrimination or segregation because of race, creed or color.
2. The adoption of one world language. (Mother Divine is now advocating that English be this language.)
3. The repeal of all laws and ordinances for compulsory insurance, employers liability, or any other form of compulsory insurance.
4. The establishment of a minimum wage scale.
5. Payment of fees to employment agencies by employers rather than employees.
6. Government control of idle plants and machinery where owners cannot operate them at full capacity. They are to be run on a co-operative, non-profit basis by government experts with the wage scale to be at least a living wage and increased as conditions permit. Plants would be returned to owners if they could run them at full capacity.
7. Useful government work projects such as tunnels and roads for all who wish to work.
8. The doing away of relief rolls.
9. "Immediate abandonment of all state and national crop control, destruction of foodstuffs and other products, and the establishment of an efficient and equitable distribution system."
10. Abolition of all tariff schedules and obstacles to free trade among the nations.
11. Legislation limiting the amount of profit to be made on any article or product, but leaving the individual free to sell for as little as he chooses.
12. Government to print its own money and make it illegal to hoard it.
13. Government to redeem all its bonded debts and to lend the money to cooperative, non-profit enterprises; to abolish all interest and make it a criminal offense to take usury or interest, or to receive dividends that exceed three and one half percent, or money without labor performed or practical service rendered.
14. Government ownership and operation of the financial system.
15. "Legislation making it a criminal offence to spend money except

for necessities of life, while an individual owes a just debt to any other individual or organization. The followers of Father Divine will not owe one another nor buy on the installment plan."

16. "Immediate destruction of all counterfeit money by those who have acquired it, rather than attempting to pass it on, and a change in the currency to eliminate all counterfeits in circulation. The followers of Father Divine destroy all counterfeit money they find in circulation at their own expense."

17. "Immediate destruction by both nations and individuals of all firearms and instruments of war within their borders saving those that are used for law enforcement. The true followers of Father Divine will refuse to fight their fellowmen for any cause whatsoever." (When the Second World War was declared many followers were conscientious objectors. As the war continued Father encouraged his followers to buy war bonds. At the end of the war he claimed he had inspired the invention of the atom bomb and warned the Russian Communists he would authorize its use against them. Followers now serve in the armed forces unless their consciences will not allow them to; the by-laws of the churches define such behavior as being up to the individual conscience.)

18. "Legislation making it a crime for any newspaper, magazine, or other publication to use segregated or slang words referring to race, creed or color of any individual or group, or write abusively concerning any."

19. Abolition of capital punishment in all states and countries.

20. "Legislation in every state and country requiring children or adults to submit to vaccination, or treatment by physicians imposing equally binding obligations upon the medical authorities taking charge of the patient physically guaranteeing a complete cure and the life of the individual or be liable for damages in the event of death."

21. Legislation to abolish lynching and outlaw members of lynch mobs in all states and countries.

22. "Legislation requiring immediate return to owners of all stolen goods or their equivalent, not only by individuals but by nations; this to include all territories taken by force from other nations."

23. "Legislation making it a crime for any employer to discharge an employee, when even circumstantial evdience can be introduced to show that it was on account of race, creed or color.

24. "Legislation establishing a maximum fee for all labor union memberships, requiring them to accept all qualified applicants and to give them equal privileges regardless of race, creed, color or classification. Any labor union which limits the hours and days of work per week, must guarantee at least that much work per

week to its members, and if it calls a strike, pay its members while they are out of work, the full amount they are demanding from the employers; otherwise all obligations for dues must cease."

25. "Immediate repeal of all laws ... requiring individuals to designate themselves as being of a race, creed or color in signing any kind of papers; this to apply especially to immigration, citizenship, passport or legal papers."

26. "Legislation making it unlawful for employers of skilled or unskilled, technical or professional help, to have different wage scales or salaries for what they term different races, creeds or colors; or to discriminate in any way in the hiring of help."

27. Support of the public schools, integrated and open to all.

Personal Morality.

The movement has adopted an "International Modest Code" which calls for: No smoking. No drinking. No obscenity. No vulgarity. No profanity. No undue mixing of the sexes. No receiving of gifts, presents, tips or bribes.

III.   *Subsistence and Economic Basis*

As far back as there is any record (1914) members of the movement have worked outside as well as in the group to earn a living. Some have started their own businesses; grocery stores, barber shops, cleaning and tailoring shops, shoe repair stores, trucking services, restaurants, and others have been civil service employees, public school teachers, factory workers, nurses and domestics.

Mother Divine described the position of the movement in 1966:

> Father has said that any able-bodied person should seek a position and qualify themselves to become upright and independent citizens, and pay cash for everything and buy nothing on the installment plan or on credit. And you see the results of following this. As individuals began to live this way, they changed for the better and they were able to pay back the bills and to owe no one, and by being honest they were able to obtain responsible positions and to better their standard of living. And Father through feeding the hungry and allowing them to be able to live and be housed and sheltered at such a low cost ... they were able to take care of their responsibilities and to raise and educate their children, if they had any, and then eventually they were able to save money ... with which they bought properties ... and become to be a blessing to other people.

As we have noted, by 1914 followers of Father Divine were living as one household and perhaps sharing in the expenses. And by the 1930's followers were opening inexpensive restaurants and sleeping accommodations which served the public at rates which could only be achieved by the use of volunteer labor and self-sacrifice. These followers either worked outside the movement at paying positions in order to do their volunteer work or lived on a subsistence basis within the movement. Some were retired school teachers and railroad or civil service workers on pensions.

Through the years various groups of dedicated followers, by voluntary investment, bought as co-partners many properties in which they live, worship and carry on business. The maintenance of these many buildings furnishes labor for some followers. Several of them are large centrally located hotels which are open to the public, but which are also home to many of the owners as well. Such hotels served an almost unmet need for minority group members who were seeking lodgings in a strange city. Only people of dark complexion in this country realize the difficulty there has been to find hotel lodgings without painful experiences of discrimination.

In Philadelphia, where Father moved his headquarters in 1942, there are about 24 properties. These include two large hotels, the Divine Lorraine on North Broad Street, near center city, with 300 rooms, and the Divine Tracy, adjoining the University of Pennsylvania campus, with 200 rooms. Besides garages and stores there are at least 20 other properties which furnish living quarters for members. Even the five buildings which are used for worship purposes also include residential areas, and two of them contain public restaurants and other shops run by followers.

In New York City there are three "church" buildings which are also homes, as well as at least five other residential properties. Located in the suburbs, Tarrytown, New York, is a 70-acre estate which is home to a number of followers. Sayville still is home to the owners, as well as a shrine for the movement. Several groups live in rural Ulster County, New York.

In Jersey City, New Jersey, the Hotel Fairmount serves the public and its owner-devotees with one hundred and seventy rooms and an excellent restaurant. Jersey City also supports a church and other activities.

Followers identify buildings as part of Father Divine's Peace Mission Movement in Los Angeles; Washington, D.C.; Chicago; the Republic of Panama; Vancouver; Vienna, Austria; Goeppingen, West Germany; Rheinck, Switzerland; Campbellville, British Guiana; and Victoria and Sydney, Australia.

The Movement, as such, owns no property; nor do Father and Mother Divine. Each piece of property is owned by a group of individuals who have invested their money in it as co-partners. Dozens may own a hotel, several own the newspaper, a single one may own a shoe repair store. Also, a single follower might have an interest in more than one hotel or business.

Another form of ownership is by incorporated churches which have branches in the countries named above. These are the Circle Mission Church, Home and Training School, Incorporated, of New York; the Unity Mission Church, Home and Training School of New York; The Nazareth Mission Church, Home and Training School of New York; Peace Center Church and Home Incorporated of New Jersey and the Palace Mission Church and Home Incorporated of New Jersey. The churches are supported by the secret donations of their members, they take no public collections at worship services and will not accept donations from non-members. Father Divine is considered the pastor or minister of each church and there is no paid minister. Father Divine received no salary, but was a guest in the property of the followers who provided for all his needs. He appeared whenever and wherever the spirit led him, often at several different churches or communion tables in one day with no pre-arranged or announced schedule. Mother Divine practices the same flexibility of movement. Each church maintains one apartment for Father Divine and a separate one for Mother Divine. Although legally married, in keeping with the separation of the sexes taught by Father Divine, they always occupied different living quarters.

In 1953 the Palace Mission Church of New York bought for $75,000 cash a 73-acre estate called Woodmount with a 32-room French Gothic mansion in the fashionable Mainline suburbs of Philadelphia. It was to be the home of Father and Mother Divine and a mecca for followers from all over the world. During the years many thousands of dollars have been poured into improvements in landscaping, a swimming pool, tennis courts, living quarters for staff and visitors and rehabilitation of the mansion. During 1965 and 1966 a $300,000 marble shrine was built on the grounds to house the body of Father Divine. Followers continue to come to the estate and the shrine. Mother Divine leads followers daily in worship services over communion banquets in the chapel of the mansion as well as around the shrine.

IV. *Social Patterns*

The true follower has severed his connection with his original family and considers himself a child of God, Father Divine. He sings sincerely (to the tune of "Tiptoe Through the Tulips").

> Now we have a Father
> Now we have a Mother
> Real dear and true Holy Parents
> Father gives us wisdom
> And He leads us onward
> Into Eternal Life,
> That's why we are—
> So glad we don't have to
> Die to travel

At the light-rate speed
To reach God
So far up in the sky!
We know that Father is here.
He's wiped our tears away.

In 1946 Father Divine was married to a blond Canadian follower, Edna Rose Ritchings, who had migrated to Philadelphia. He explained that she was the reincarnation of his first wife who had become dissatisfied with her former body because she was so much larger than Father Divine. So he finally let her "pass" after years during which she had asked for that privilege. The new marriage was looked upon as a symbol of the interracial, international and supernatural nature of Father Divine's power and mission. The followers expressed themselves in song about it as follows:

I believe in the Sacred, Holy
Spiritual Marriage of Father Divine,
Who is our Father, Mother God,
To His Spotless Virgin Bride, Mother Divine,
Who before the world was, was predestined to be
And now is the Symbol of the Church
Without spot or wrinkle!
I believe that the Marriage of Father Divine
To Mother Divine was predestined to be,
That it is the marriage of the Lamb and the Bride
And that it symbolizes the Marriage
Of Christ to the Church
The union of God and man
And the fusion of Heaven and Earth.

The true follower accepts his status as a brother or sister of everyone else in the movement. No prior marriage is any longer valid (although before being accepted to live in the family one must meet any legal obligations to spouse or children), and the once married member will no longer live with his mate but in a room or dormitory segregated by sex. Hotels have separate floors for men and women. The sexes are separated at the communion table and at worship services. Mother is always accompanied by a chaperone.

Children who are brought into the movement are cared for by surrogate parents, not their own, and are taught that Father and Mother Divine are their only true parents. They often live at Woodmount or on one of the farms in Ulster County. They are sent to public school, but spend their leisure time at home with the followers. When they are old enough they share in the "housework" and are expected to help support themselves eventually by whatever work they can do in the larger community. Several have graduated from college and at least one has a Ph.D. in physical chemistry. Needless to say, no children are born in the movement. Father Divine taught that there were already too many bad parents and too many poor children in the world and urged that there be no more. The intimacy and quality of life in the homes is such that there can be no sexual promiscuity; those who do not accept the strict sexual and moral code soon leave the "family of God."

There are no clothing taboos except that women must wear clothes that do not emphasize their sex: slacks and miniskirts are forbidden. Cosmetics are not noted. Men dress as do those in the larger community, except for a taboo on shorts.

There are no food taboos. The great variety at meals allows each to pursue his own tastes. Only liquor is forbidden.

The process of socialization into the "family" is continuous, for, once one has moved into the property of a group of followers, one is never free from the voice of Father Divine or of one of his followers. When wire and tape recordings became available, buildings were supplied with amplifiers, and recordings of Father's addresses were played periodically. When a worship service or a communion is in process it, too, is amplified throughout the building.

Worship services are part of each meal, eaten at long tables which may accommodate from 50 to 100 followers. Unity is symbolized and developed by each item of food and each plate passing through the hands of Father and Mother Divine (or over their seats if they are not physically present) and then through the hands of everyone at the table. This is done in rhythm and with songs, tapes of Father Divine's messages, and testimonies of healing and good fortune ascribed to the influence of Father Divine.

There are also evening worship services at which anyone may read to the assembly Father Divine's words from the *New Day*, sing one of the hundreds of songs created within the movement, testify to healings, relate conquests over temptation, dance in the aisles, or speak in tongues.

The services are led by followers if Father or Mother are not present. There are no ordained ministers, followers take turns as they are inspired so that almost anyone may lead the worship at any given moment.

Each morning there are Bible study groups in which Father Divine's interpretation of the Bible is learned. This is to be found in the *New Day*, in the thousands of extemporaneous messages which have been printed since the 1930's.

All recreation is arranged within the family. There are carefully chosen movies shown in the church hall, television programs, religious plays written and acted by followers all of the same sex, and various forms of interpretive dancing emphasizing some message of Father Divine and once again maintaining separation of the sexes.

Much time and effort goes into preparation of the decorations, choral activities and food for the annual celebration of Father's marriage and now his "sacrifice." Open house is held at Woodmount for several days each year and most of the followers who are not visiting from afar are busy as guides and hosts, or in skits, plays and banquet (communion) preparations and service.

Each church owns a number of large automobiles in which members of one church travel to visit services and communions at the other churches. Visits to Woodmount, periods of volunteer work there, and worship at the new shrine or communion table are privileges sought by all including those in foreign countries.

Literally the time not devoted to labor to earn a living and to carry on the public restaurants and living accommodations is spent on activities having to do with the worship of Father Divine. Little time is devoted to anything else.

V. *Polity*

The Peace Mission Movement is certainly a textbook example of charismatic leadership and organization. It was the qualities ascribed to Major Jealous Divine which first brought him followers, and the present followers are no less convinced of his supernatural powers. He had no position of power in the larger community. He was not legitimated by any religious organization, nor by formal education, nor political power. But he was convinced that he had a mission and he demanded obedience and demonstrated his powers to those who had faith in that power. In this respect he is the prototype of Weber's charismatic leader.

> The charismatic leader is a man who demands obedience on the basis of the mission he feels called upon to perform. His claim is valid if those he seeks to lead recognize his mission; and he remains their master as long as he proves himself and his mission in their eyes. . . . The leader is called by a higher power and cannot refuse, and the followers are duty-bound to obey the leader who possesses the charismatic qualification. This relationship of ruler and rules is typically unstable, because the leader may lose his charisma—he may feel that his god has forsaken him or that his power has left him. For the charismatic leader derives his authority solely from the demonstration of his powers and from the disciples' faith in that power whatever that power is conceived to be.[10]

Individual followers may have lost their faith and hence Father Divine was no longer their leader, but for those who have remained loyal, even after the apparent death of his body, he remains a charismatic leader, and the center around which the polity of the movement still is organized. The followers of Father Divine, by their own testimony, give him complete obedience for one or several of the following situations, all of which they feel are proof of his mission to bring spiritual and material salvation to anyone who will follow his commands.

1. The reformation from the commission of crime or indulgence in sex was due to Father Divine.
2. The cure of alcoholism or drug addiction was due to Father Divine.
3. The physical healings to which many followers testify were due to him.
4. The employment opportunities that came their way during and since the Depression were created by Father Divine.
5. The complete integration and mutual respect among the various races were due to belief in him.
6. The progress toward legal enforcement of non-discrimination is due to him.
7. The control of the Nazis and the Communists in and after World War II was because Father willed it.
8. The success of the followers in accumulating property was due to him.

The following song expresses the followers' attitude toward Father Divine.

> Father has taught us the mystery
> Of happiness and health,
> He has given us the abundance
> Of prosperity and wealth,
> He said, "Take all you want
> But don't forget the Best,
> For if you do you will lose all the rest!"
> We love you, Father, we will never forget!
> We love you, Father, we know you are the Best!
>
> Father, we appreciate the abundance
> That You give,
> We love the Holy Life
> You have taught us to live,
> But most of all we love
> Your beautiful Body, dear,
> And love you for bringing
> Our precious Mother here!
> We love you, Father, we will never forget!
> We love you, Father, we know you are the Best!

As individuals in the 1930's voluntarily invited Father Divine to use their properties so the pattern continues to this day. Mother Divine now is welcomed in every Church and Home of the Movement and is always addressed as though Father was with her in person. There has been no modification in the rigid morality of the movement and Father's words are printed and reprinted in the weekly *New Day*. His precepts are still followed in the conduct of daily life. The question raised is always, "What would Father have us do?"

Leadership of the various groups for many years was chosen by Father Divine. Anyone he favored with his presence was designated as a kind of leader for the local group—but never was she or he the paramount leader—always Father's opinion was asked and followed. Anyone who did not receive his blessing found himself out of favor with the other followers.

Very early he began to designate women as his secretaries, and allow them to share his office, to travel with him, to record his words, and to sit near him at the Communion Table. The *New Day* verbatim reports of his words were from their notes until recording on wire and tape was adopted. The number of secretaries varied. To be a secretary was a reward given to those who Father selected for whatever reason he might have. Through the years as property and responsibilities accumulated one secretary came to head up housekeeping, another coordinated transportation, another what might be called public relations, still another food services, and so on through a variety of activities. These are very capable women who have had these responsibilities for many years. They devote their full time to this and were in constant touch with Father Divine and now with Mother Divine.

A number of followers incorporated to publish the newspaper, compose it, sell advertising and to distribute it. The bulk of its contents are statements of Father Divine ranging back to 1930. Letters and their answers to Mother and Father Divine are also printed as well as remarks of visiting non-followers and testimonies of followers. News which illustrates the progress of Father Divine's statements on government and the overthrow of discrimination is featured.

The incorporated churches each have an annual open meeting at which officers are elected, including President, Secretary, Treasurer and a Board of Trustees. But these officers must all be approved by Father Divine and now by Mother Divine before they are put up for election. The panel is approved by a show of hands and at the several meetings I have attended I am not aware of anyone failing to receive a unanimous vote. A Treasurer's report is given at the meetings, but no specific figures are quoted; rather an enumeration of the physical improvements made by the church is given and the fact that they were all paid for in cash. Financial affairs are confidential. It is doubtful that anyone other than the Treasurer of each church, perhaps Father or Mother Divine and the very able Philadelphia (non-follower) lawyer, knows the actual contributions of each member.

The spokesmen of the movement follow Father Divine's lead in refusing to discuss the actual membership of the several churches in terms of numbers or names. Only the names of the officers are published in the *New Day* and no membership lists are available.

Father and Mother Divine and various members of the Peace Mission feel that they have been of service, through healing, inspiring, feeding and housing to many millions of people. During the period from 1932 to 1942 when Major Divine was preaching up and down the Eastern Seaboard from Connecticut to Washington he did speak to many thousands of people. The parades which the followers staged in Harlem and Brooklyn during this period received much publicity; as did the inexpensive excursions by steamboat from New York City to the properties in Ulster County. The major news media found Father Divine and his followers an interesting source of news. And Father said "even the knocks were boosts."

But it was the person who would voluntarily accept the will of Father Divine as his will, and who would subject his behavior to continuous scrutiny by other followers, who became the resident of the properties publicly identified as affiliated with Father Divine. In order to live the carefully ordered life of the follower in community with other followers he must be able to share in the expression of the kind of relationship to Father Divine found in this song, which is only one of many containing similar sentiments.

> You are the beating of my heart,
> You're the twinkling of my eye,
> You're the joy when I'm living,
> You're the sunshine of my smile,
> You're the rainbow when it rains,
> You're the music when I sing,
> You're the love in my love songs,
> Darling, You're my everything!
>
> You're the beauty of the winter,
> You're the tenderness of spring,
> You're the romance of summer,
> Darling, You're my everything!
> You're the keeper of my heart,
> You're the little birds that sing,
> You're the true blue of heaven,
> Darling, You're my everything!
>
> I have found a loving sweetheart,
> I have found a loving friend,
> I have found a darling Father,
> I have found the dearest one.
> I have found a diamond clear,
> I have found a friend so dear,
> I have found Father Divine.

In the earliest days of the movement persons of all ages were attracted and spent some time as members of various groups; many have stayed loyal for forty or more years. The core of secretaries appear to be beyond middle age as are the visitors who come from abroad. Both the secretaries and the foreign visitors seem to be long time followers, all having been influenced by Father from fifteen to forty years ago.

Since the largest number of adherents are located in Philadelphia, New York and New Jersey, generalizations about age, sex and minority group status must be made from them. Although indeterminate numbers of people must have been touched by Father Divine and served by the followers who have lived communally with him, only a few thousand appear to have committed themselves wholly to the community segregated by sex which surrounded Father Divine. One measure of the size of this group is the circulation of the *New Day*, which all true believers secure every week. It has been about 9,000 for the last ten years.

Often one of the groups of followers has been a haven for someone who apparently lives with it until he can face the "world" again. There must be many thousands of persons who have sought and found help in the movement and then returned to the larger community. There must have been many who found the life too difficult; any of the several demands made upon them might lead to defection—the denial of sexuality, the continuous labor, the moral demands, the subordination to the will of Father Divine, the lack of any private life, the separation from the former family.

Essentially the polity of the movement is still based on charisma; i.e., the voluntary obedience to the standards and way of life established by Major Jealous Divine and perpetuated by his wife and the secretaries who were closest to him, and now to her. This obedience is still based on the conviction that the good fortune in health, material security, and moral purity which the believer feels to be his lot is due to the ever presence of Father Divine. Anyone who can no longer accept this conviction would find his life too difficult and leave the group.

On the whole the population is aging, with more than half over fifty and most over forty. Women predominate, perhaps three to one; and minority group members represent at least eighty percent of the American followers, although among the secretaries there is a higher percentage of majority group representatives. There are undoubtedly some who because of age and their long removal from the world would not venture to return to the larger community. There are possibly others who because of their investment in the properties of the movement are more financially secure than they would be were they to sell their share and attempt to establish an individual home. There are great economies in group ownership and maintenance and in wholesale feeding operations. The movement has always had high standards in property care and the same income outside the movement would not secure the pleasant living quarters or excellent food available in the Peace Mission.

There is a continuous recruitment into the movement and a very low attrition rate. Mother Divine and the secretaries seem to have been able to share in the charisma of Father Divine and to maintain the kind of voluntary cooperation which he evoked. Undoubtedly a degree of institutionalization or routinization of charisma, as Max Weber called it, is going on: the incorporation of the churches, the election of officers, the use of a lay lawyer, and the lack of emphasis on the drastic economic and political changes originally demanded by the Righteous Government Platform, are all evidences of this. But, at this point, it is my judgment after more than twenty years of observation of the Philadelphia community, it is still the conviction that Father Divine is God and that Mother Divine is his closest representative that maintains the group rather than the routinization which has occurred. Among the present followers there is no slacking in that conviction.

Notes

1. Robert Allerton Parker, *The Incredible Messiah, The Deification of Father Divine* (Boston: Little, Brown, 1937).
2. *Ibid.*, p. 23.
3. The *New Day*, April 18, 1940. This was occasioned by a newspaper criticism of a mission in Stratford, Connecticut. The *New Day* is the weekly newspaper published by some of the followers.
4. The *New Day*, April 28, 1956, p. 37 reprinted from 1936.
5. *Ibid.*, p. 37.
6. Bryan R. Wilson, *Sects and Society* (Berkeley: University of California Press, 1961), p. 10.
7. Robert Allerton Parker, *The Incredible Messiah, The Deification of Father Divine* (Boston: Little, Brown, 1937); John Hosher, *God in a Rolls Royce, The Rise of Father Divine* (New York: Hillman-Curl, 1936); Sara Harris, *Father Divine: Holy Husband* (Garden City: Doubleday, 1953).
8. The *New Day*, September 15, 1962, p. 11. Originally spoken March 15, 1946.
9. Until noted otherwise all the quotations which follow are from an interview with Mother Divine published in the *New Day*, December 10, 1966, pp. 21–22.
10. Reinhard Bendix, *Max Weber, An Intellectual Portrait* (Garden City, New York: Doubleday, 1960), p. 304.

Bibliography

Burnham, Kenneth E. "Father Divine, A Case Study of Charismatic Leadership." Ph.D. thesis, University of Pennsylvania, 1963.

Burnham, Kenneth E. *God Comes to America: Father Divine and the Peace Mission Movement* (Boston: Lambeth Press, forthcoming).

Cantril, Hadley. *The Psychology of Social Movements* (New York: John Wiley and Sons, 1941), pp. 123–43.

Fauset, Arthur Huff. *Black Gods of the Metropolis* (Philadelphia: University of Pennsylvania Press, 1944), pp. 52–67.

Harris, Sara. *Father Divine: Holy Husband* (Garden City: Doubleday, 1953).

Hoshor, John. *God in a Rolls Royce, The Rise of Father Divine* (New York: Hillman-Curl, 1936).

The *New Day* (weekly newspaper of the Peace Mission Movement), 1936–1969. Philadelphia: New Day Publishing Company.

Parker, Robert Allerton. *The Incredible Messiah, The Deification of Father Divine* (Boston: Little, Brown, 1937).

I have not depended on this bibliography for any facts in my presentation which is based on more than twenty years of personal observation, interviewing, a doctoral thesis and the *New Day*, which I know from observation is a completely accurate account of what is said and done by Father and members of the Peace Mission.

There have been three popular books written about the movement. I could not verify any of the biographical material given in them except the trial at Mineola, so I have quoted only that material. Parker's book, aside from the biographical material before 1914, seems to me to be accurate and fair. Hoshor exhibits much prejudice and stereotyped thinking about race, and I would not give it much credence. Harris reports conversations with members of the movement which my experience indicates it would have been impossible for her to have had. She presents hypotheses about the sexual hangups of the followers with which I do not agree. I believe this to be a much fictionalized account of the Peace Mission. It, like Hoshor, was not intended to be a scholarly work. Parker and Hoshor end with 1936. Harris observed in the early 1950's.

Fauset is a trained anthropologist and furnishes a comparison with four other minority group churches which were flourishing in Philadelphia in the 1940's. It is an accurate and scholarly account which advances theories of why such groups attract membership, and their function for minority group members.

Cantril is a social psychologist, describes a typical meeting in the 1930's, and advances a theory of the function of such groups for individuals. He gives a very accurate description of some of the earliest public meetings.

Some Notes on Arnold J. Ford and New World Black Attitudes to Ethiopia

Kenneth J. King

A few months before war broke out in Ethiopia in 1935, the American ethnologist, Carleton Coon, visited Addis Abäba. In the account of his abortive mission to measure Ethiopian skulls, he has left a number of observations on the small coloured American population of the country In particular he makes a tantalising reference to a black rabbi from the New World. According to Coon, this man was a British subject who had left Harlem in New York to seek out the famous Fälašas of Ethiopia, but, finding them inaccessible from Addis Abäba, had turned instead to carpentry during the day and banjo-playing at night. In fact along with another black from the New World he appears to have been one of the main attractions of the Tambourine Club, and to have beguiled its white patrons with Negro Spirituals and other pieces until it was closed down by the government for discriminating against local Ethiopian clients.[1] This present short article will attempt to throw more light on this allegedly militant black rabbi and, if possible, set him more generally within the larger perspective of New World–Ethiopian relations in the 1920s and 1930s.

A number of influences produced a New World black interest in Ethiopia after the Great War, the most potent of which was Garveyism. Marcus Garvey, founder and president of the Universal Negro Improvement Association, is generally thought to have used the word Ethiopia to mean the whole continent, and although this is certainly so in such usages as the "Universal Ethiopian Anthem," there is some evidence that he made a similar outreach to the historic empire as he did to President King's Liberia. A small mission of skilled blacks was apparently sent to Addis Abäba to investigate possibilities of colonisation, but seems to have met less enthusiasm than was anticipated.[2]

Although the UNIA's deputation failed to institutionalise links with north-east Africa, it succeeded in turning the minds of a number of individuals towards service there. Indeed, at the moment it appears as if rather more individual Garveyites went to Ethiopia than to Africa's other independent state. Despite greater inaccessibility, Ethiopia's antiquity and splendour exercised a stronger pull than the bourgeois and, to Garvey's mind, anti-African politics of the Americo-Liberian ruling elite. Certainly as soon as Garvey had broken openly with the Monrovia government, and exposed it as traitor to the Negro race, it would have been more natural for would-be emigrants to make for Ethiopia.

Garveyism obviously had a tremendous appeal to both the black Americans and West Indians in the States, but it does seem as if the majority of the emigrants to Ethiopia were West Indian like Garvey himself. Why this should be so is difficult entirely to understand. However, it should be remembered that many West Indians in North America had done a great deal of travelling already, both within the islands and over to Panama and Florida. When post-war America did not measure up to their hopes, some of them were prepared to move on. Undoubtedly they would not have gone unless they had caught Garvey's fundamental message of skilled service to Africa. But the immediate cause was often a chance contact with Ethiopian students in the States, or with the occasional Ethiopian delegation that came to Harlem in the late 1920s to solicit trained Negro colonists for Africa.[3] However, the black rabbi, already mentioned, seems to have been equally influential in projecting Ethiopia as the most appropriate destination.

This man was Arnold J. Ford. He was a Barbadian by birth. For a time he had taught music in the British Navy, and then was a clerk in Bermuda before moving to Harlem at the end of the Great War.[4] Here he was attracted by Garveyism, and for three years served as the musical director of Liberty Hall, Garvey's main meeting place. In this capacity he composed and directed many of the hymns that expressed the spiritual side of Garveyism. Some of these deserve attention because they in- capsulate the religious feelings of the group that would shortly come to Africa.

The main source for these attitudes is the twenty hymns of Ford's *Universal Ethiopian Hymnal*.[5] First of all, his general vision of Africa was not fundamentally different from that of such poets of the Negro renaissance as Langston Hughes and Claude McKay who were writing at this time. Africa was the promised land: ancient, bright and glorious; land of "pristine worth"; marked by its culture and its sages. From this perspective, Africa was seen as the Homeric Ethiopia, the "land where the Gods lov'd to be." Although Africa was thus paradise lost, from which the blacks went out to slavery and exile, and to which they must return, there is sometimes the suggestion that the tyrant's rod was felt not only in exile but in Africa itself. This had happened because Africa had slept; she had only to stir herself to be free.

Ford, following Garvey and other New World blacks, believed that the awakening of Africa was a major obligation upon the blacks of the diaspora. Moreover, he was sure that their efforts would soon succeed:

> O Africa awaken!
> The morning is at hand,
> No more art thou forsaken
> O bounteous motherland,
> From far thy sons and daughters
> Are hastening back to thee,
> Their cry rings o'er the waters
> That Africa shall be free.[6]

One reason for ascribing this redemptive role to New World blacks was the traditional one that they had been prepared for it through their exile and suffering. The Negro abroad had become for Ford, as for Blyden forty years earlier, the Christlike one, the "man of sorrows," refined in the fire of slavery for tasks in the motherland:

> O bright and glorious country
> From whence the Sons of God,
> Were called to foreign boundry
> To bear the chast'ning rod;
> Torn from thy blessed shelter,
> We all have suffered loss,
> Beneath the lash to welter,
> And made to bear the cross.[7]

Finally, Ford's imagery shares with other New World blacks the idea that the diaspora is parallel to the earlier Jewish exile from Jerusalem. This was no accident in Ford's case, because by the early twenties he had become the leading spokesman of the various sects of black Jews in Harlem. He was rabbi of the congregation of Beth B'nai Abraham, and knew his Hebrew. It is interesting to note that his Hymnal includes three or four entries that have been taken directly from the ancient Hebrew, and others of his own composition which have a strong Hebraic character. It is debatable whether Ford had articulated the theory held by later Harlem Jewish sects that the black diaspora was actually descended from Jacob.[8] Nevertheless, in the Universal Ethiopian Anthem he certainly suggests that Israel is almost interchangeable with the black community. Equally, in referring to New World blacks, Ford shares with the Harlem sectarians a scrupulous avoidance of the slave-given name of "Negroes," and a preference for such terms as: "sons of God," "Children born of love," "Pilgrims," "Ethiopian sons and daughters," or "Ethiop's children."

It must be stressed that men like Ford had become Jews long before they discovered the Fälašas. However, information about the Fälaša community was critical in verifying their convictions concerning black identity. It now looked plausible not only that blacks had been Jews, but also that they were "among the oldest families of the Jewish or Hebraic race upon the face of the earth."[9] The crucial connection was that at the same time as the black Jews of Harlem were becoming fully established, the plight of the Fälašas had aroused concern amongst white Jewish groups in Europe and America. One of the major links between the Ethiopian Jews and their white sympathizers was Jacques Faïtlovitch who, with his sister, had opened a school for them in Addis Abäba in 1924, and who often took Fälašas abroad with him to aid in fund-raising. It seems that on one of the American tours, Faïtlovitch was accompanied by Tamrat Emanuél (earlier a brief convert to Christianity). They contacted the black Jews of Harlem, possibly hoping for a ready commitment to the African cause.[10] They met Ford.

. The chance meeting, perhaps in 1929, seems to have determined Ford on emigration to Ethiopia. However, it is important to stress that ʹFord did actually go there in 1930, because his disappearance from the American scene at this time has led a number of scholars to connect his name with the mysterious figure of W. D. Fard, who is claimed to have founded the forerunner of Elijah Muhammad's Muslim sect in Detroit in the early 1930s.[11] Some plausibility for this hypothesis was lent by Islamic influences which Ford had revealed. His Hymnal is a very syncretic work, and amongst the Christian, Jewish and even the odd African traditional lyric, there are numerous references to Islam: "Father of all creation, Allah omnipotent," "Love is Allah's word," "Allah hu Akbar," and "God is love: from mosques and steeples ring the blessed news along." In addition, Ford was deeply concerned that Arab and Jew should live peacefully in Palestine.[12] But whatever his connection to Islam, he remained in Ethiopia from 1930 until his death by illness during the Italo-Ethiopian war. He appears to have been unable to maintain any significant contact with the Fälašas, and it is far from clear how his relations with Tamrat progressed once they had both returned from abroad. What is known is that he was interested in Ethiopian education, and seems to have taught music during the day and repaired musical instruments. It seems not unlikely that a man who could play some six instruments might also, as Coon suggests, have been a popular entertainer.

Ford was just one of a colony of New World blacks who began to arrive in Ethiopia between the Coronation of Emperor Haylä Sellasé and the outbreak of the war in 1935.[13] Too much should not be made of distinctions within the various New World groups, but it does seem, as was mentioned earlier, that the majority of the prospective settlers were from the West Indies. The West Indians appear also to have been more prepared than some of the Americans to make what adjustments were necessary to living in Ethiopia. Yet both communities were at various times the objects of discrimination; and in some cases, of gross mistreatment.[14] However, a good deal of work clearly would have to be done on individual case histories to evaluate the roots of this disenchantment, and to examine the attitudes of Ethiopians both educated and uneducated to the presence of New World blacks.

Such a study could produce a picture of the various American outreaches to Ethiopia, and the responses to them. First the period of the earliest adventurers such as Benito Sylvain from Haiti at the court of Menilek, with his plans for a pan-Negro organization. Then, in the wake of the Garvey era, a largish group of skilled technicians, many of them originally West Indian migrants to North America later recruited by Ethiopian delegations in the late 1920s. The vast interest in rallying to the defense of Ethiopia in 1935–36 has been sufficiently documented elsewhere, along with the effective British and American ban on the issue of travel visas to the many blacks applying for service with the Emperor.[15] Finally, with the restoration in 1941, a relatively small number of further New World blacks (perhaps twenty) managed to make their way over to Ethiopia, and take up various positions in education and other professions.[16] Today, however, only one or two families remain from the largest wave that came in the late twenties and early thirties, and it is interesting to note that amongst them is Mrs. Mignon Ford, widow of the rabbi. Together with two other West Indian women she started the Princess Zännäbä Wärq school in Addis Abäba in the early 1940s, and has continued its headmistress to the present.[17]

Among the many questions still outstanding about the New World blacks must be their religious commitments. Perhaps sufficient is known of Arnold Ford in the early period. But of many others it would be worth knowing whether they had participated in the Garvey-linked African Orthodox Church before they emigrated from America. Its primate, George McGuire, was also chaplain general to the Universal Negro Improvement Association, and he made much of the need to substitute black for white in the religious symbolism of his church. As West Indians were perhaps the major component in the African Orthodox Church in North America, it is not impossible that some of the emigrants to Ethiopia had had experience of a church that was radical in its approach to black religious nationalism, even if it was also greatly concerned about the legitimacy of its orders. Another question must be what, if any, was the interest amongst the returned blacks of the diaspora to Ethiopia's established Orthodox Church. The likeliest candidate for such interest would be Ford: but unfortunately all his hymns so far date from before 1926, when he was still anticipating the unity and freedom of Ethiopia's children at home and abroad. Liberty Hall had resounded with expectant verses in the mid-twenties. It would be fascinating to know what Ford and other Garveyites thought in the early 1930s once they had reached the "bright and glorious" country of their Harlem dreams:

O land of tropic splendor,
Of bright blue skies above,
To thee our best we tender,
O land of light and love.
Some day we'll know thy story,
We'll drink thy cup of mirth
Revive thine ancient glory
And bring the gods to earth.[18]

Notes

1. C. S. Coon, *Measuring Ethiopia and Flight into Arabia* (London, 1936), p. 137.

2. T. R. Makonnen, and K. King, *Memoirs of a Pan-Africanist* (forthcoming, 1972). Makonnen is himself an example of a West Indian from British Guiana who changed his name during the Italo-Ethiopian crisis. His cousin, David Talbot, who grew up in the same village of Buxton in B.G., emigrated to Ethiopia in the early years of the Second World War and is presently in the Ethiopian Ministry of Information.

3. For instance, Dr. Workneh Martin was in Harlem in November 1927 passing on the message that *Ras* Täfäri would welcome skilled artisans.

4. Interview with Mrs. Mignon Ford, Addis Abäba, July 26, 1970.

5. A. J. Ford, *The Universal Ethiopian Hymnal* (New York, Beth B'nai Abraham Publishing Co., n.d.), p. 17.

6. *Ibid.*

7. *Ibid.*

8. For a valuable description of the beliefs of the Harlem Jewish community, see H. Brotz, *The Black Jews of Harlem* (New York, 1964).

9. *Ibid.*, p. 22.

10. *Ibid.*, p. 49; also H. A. Stern, *Wanderings among the Falashas in Abyssinia* (London, 1968), introduction by R. L. Hess, p. xxx.

11. For instance, on the basis of popular report, Brotz (*op. cit.*, p. 12) gives the following account: "Ford, tiring of Judaism, emigrated in the early thirties to Africa where he became a Muslim and where he subsequently died. As this was in the midst of the depression, it is equally possible and even more possible that he emigrated not to Africa but to Detroit, and that the W. Ford or Farrad who founded the Islamic cult in that city and Arnold Ford were one and the same."

12. Interview, Mrs. Ford.

13. A useful account of the black American colony in the early thirties is J. Robbins, "The Americans in Ethiopia," *American Mercury*, xxix (May 1933), 63–69.

14. Coon, *op. cit.*, pp. 147–48.

15. See, for instance, R. Pankhurst, "Ethiopia and the African Personality," *Ethiopian Observer*, III (1959); also Makonnen and King, *op. cit.*, Ch. VI, "Into the Ethiopian Arena."

16. Dr. David Talbot, interview, July 1970.

17. *Princess Zennebe Worq School Silver Jubilee Anniversary* (Addis Abäba, 1966).

18. A. J. Ford, *op. cit.*, p. 7.

Racism, World War I and the Christian Life: Francis J. Grimke in the Nation's Capital

Louis B. Weeks III

The life and work of Francis J. Grimke bear recounting for at least two reasons: for their intrinsic value to the student of American Christianity, and also as a symbol of the tragedy and triumph of the black man in the United States. This study focuses primarily on Grimke's ministry in the face of American racism, and to a lesser degree on his reaction to U.S. involvement in the First World War. His contributions in those areas of involvement prove characteristic of the man's whole ministry. Historians have passed over Grimke's contributions all too quickly, pausing only to list his name alongside others who participated in the founding of the American Negro Academy or the National Association for the Advancement of Colored People.[1] Grimke, who did not seek personal recognition so much as he fought for a nation and a world devoted to Christian brotherhood, would not have minded the omission very much.[2] Now people need to hear his story and to reflect on his teaching, for Francis Grimke labored against difficult odds and sought to maintain Christian integrity in the face of myriad pressures to the contrary.

Forces today, however complex and strong, which call for individual and corporate resignation to the inevitability of racial strife, national militarism, and parochial religious attitudes, cannot be as pervasive or more compelling than those opposing Grimke. The years of his active ministry, from 1878 to 1923, coincided with the proliferation of Jim Crow laws in a concerted effort to institutionalize white supremacy.[3] On the international front, United States policy was characterized by differing responses to the nation's new role as a world power. Whether in dalliance with the prospects of insular imperialism or of "Good Neighborism," national foreign goals now appear to have been selfseeking and materialistic at their roots.

American churches concern with personal salvation and religious ex-
clusivism frequently obscured other, less selfish enterprises. And Negro
congregations seemed often most culpable, acceding to the dominance
of white institutions and ideas.[4] According to James Cone, the black
church in America "lost its zeal for freedom in the midst of the new
structures of white power." In this "era of endurance," when liberty
would only come in the hereafter, the black minister usually became
"a most devoted 'Uncle Tom,' the transmitter of white wishes." Thus,
Cone judges that "more than any other one person in the black community, the black minister perpetuated the white system of black de-
humanization."[5] Francis Grimke is an exception to that judgment.

As a minister Grimke chose to serve in Washington, D.C., certainly
a preeminent center of the rising black middle class. The classic study
by E. Franklin Frazier of the nation's *Black Bourgeoisie* centered on Washington, with its concentration of 90,000 Negroes and its "relatively large
professional class, including teachers in the segregated public school system,
doctors, dentists, and lawyers, and large numbers of Negroes employed
in the federal government."[6] The city offered an epitome of black "status
without substance." If, as Frazier determined, the Washington black
bourgeoisie sought escape in a netherworld of surrogate history and
delusions of importance, who could speak boldly in their midst of racial
integrity, of racist governmental oppression, and of the inherent inequalities
of the American quality of life? Francis Grimke could.

I

Born in Charleston, South Carolina, on 4 November, 1850, Francis
James Grimke was the middle son of Henry Grimke, a planter, and his
slave, Nancy Weston Grimke.[7] At the death of Henry Grimke, five years
later, the three boys—Archibald, Francis, and John—passed into the
guardianship of E. Montague Grimke, a half-brother and heir by primo-
geniture of the considerable estate. For several years the young heir
honored his father's wish to provide family and freedom for the younger
children; but when Francis was ten years old, the contemplated sale of
all the boys forced him to flee from the Grimke home. In due time the
youth suffered recapture, incarceration, and almost died of exposure in
the South Carolina prison. His mother rescued Francis, and nursed him
back to health. Then Montague sold Francis to a Confederate officer,
who made him a servant until the end of the war.

Free at last with the dissolution of the Confederacy, Grimke attended
the Morris Street School in Charleston, where Frances Pillsbury, the wife
of abolitionist Parker Pillsbury, served as principal. She observed his
remarkable abilities, encouraged him and his brother Archibald to enter
college studies, and sponsored their admission to nascent Lincoln Uni-

versity.[8] The brothers gained additional resources from Sarah and Angelina Grimke, feminists and abolitionist leaders, the sisters of Henry, who learned about their nephew and provided family and support for him.[9] Both Francis and Archibald graduated in 1870 from Lincoln, Francis the valedictorian of the class and Archibald as the third-ranking scholar. While Archibald soon entered Harvard Law School (he would become its first black graduate in 1878 and undertake practice in Washington),[10] Francis remained to study with the Lincoln faculty in their own law department. The following year he served as "financial agent" of the university, and for yet another year he attended the law school. In September, 1873, Francis transferred to Howard University's law department, where he continued his studies.

In Grimke's own words, it was while at Harvard that he decided "after due reflection," to turn his thoughts "toward the ministry." He entered Princeton Theological Seminary, which unlike the neighboring College of New Jersey, was open to blacks in the fall of 1878.[11] As a theological student, Grimke won the unqualified admiration of both seminary Professor A. A. Hodge, a guiding light in conservative circles of American Presbyterianism, and James McCosh, the president of the college and a director of the seminary. Professor Hodge labeled Grimke "a very able man, highly educated, of high character, and worthy of all confidence." President McCosh, even more effusive in praise of the young theologian, commented: "While here he convinced all the professors under whom he studied as a young man of a very high order of talent and excellent character." "I have heard him preach," McCosh confessed, "and I feel as if I could listen to such preaching with profit from Sabbath to Sabbath."[12]

From the evidence at hand, it is difficult to determine precisely the roots and reasons of Grimke's Presbyterianism. True, he had attended a Presbyterian Sunday School in Charleston, and Lincoln University, which was also affiliated wtih the church. During his sojourn at Howard, moreover, Grimke had attended the Fifteenth Street Presbyterian Church of Washington, D.C.[13] By whatever direction he came to his affiliation Grimke determined to accept the call of that same Fifteenth Street Presbyterian Church, and he entered into a pastoral relationship with that congregation directly from seminary.[14] For all his long and productive career—except for a recuperative interlude in Jacksonville, Florida, as minister of the Laura Street Church—Grimke remained pastor of a substantial black congregation in the nation's capital.[15]

Several months after his assumption of pastoral responsibilities, Francis Grimke also shared vows with Charlotte Forten, whom he married on 19 December, 1878. A remarkable woman in her own right, Charlotte was the granddaughter of James Forten of Philadelphia, a gifted businessman and organizer of black freedom throughout the difficult, early years of the nineteenth century.[16] Charlotte Forten, besides writing poetry and prose for the *Atlantic Monthly*, the *New England Magazine*, and other national periodicals, had served as a teacher and missionary during the Port Royal "Experiment" in educating newly freed slaves during and immediately after the Civil War.[17] For Francis Grimke she proved a constant helpmate and dedicated companion.[18]

If his home life remained idyllically Victorian, the same could not be said to characterize the public life of the Reverend Grimke. As a black clergyman in an essentially white denomination, as a black citizen in a nation dominated by white thinking. Grimke fought continually the insidious presence of political and religious racism. Throughout his life, although specific issues and the Christian response to each varied immensely, he remained consistently in favor of the full enfranchisement of black America.

As a Presbyterian, for example, Grimke sometimes participated in juridical and planning meetings and sometimes boycotted them, depending on the nature of the issue and the possibilities for constructive action. He declined to attend most of the meetings in Washington City Presbytery and of the Baltimore Synod because of the rank prejudice he discovered among his "brothers."[19] It was consistent for him to turn down the invitation issued October 1, 1918, by Rev. George G. Mahy of Philadelphia, Secretary of the General Assembly Committee on Evangelism, to meet before a regular synod convocation.[20] Grimke responded with a decided "No" to the request of Mahy, who had hoped "that together we may be able to strengthen the work of our Presbyterial Committee and stimulate the spiritual life of all our churches." Fresh from the effects of a recent Billy Sunday campaign in the nation's capital, Grimke urged the committee to think through its commitment to evangelism. Was it in fact giving support to efforts like those of Sunday, who seemed willing enough to allow the segregation, sometimes even the exclusion of blacks? "Until EVANGELISM as conducted by our assembly's Committee, and by the committees of other white organizations, means much more than it does today, I do not feel that a conference with such committees would be of any true value to me," he said. In Christian efforts at evangelism, not only do leaders fail to "call men to repent of this sin of racial hatred," but knowing converts are still racists, church folk welcome new members "with open arms, in express violation of the spirit and teaching of Jesus Christ." Grimke would avoid hypocritical evangelism and the meetings which supported it.[21]

Another such incident, one of several which appear of special significance only because they were the ones remembered in the collection of Grimke's writings, occurred with the "General Presbyterian Rally" of 1926 in Washington.[22] A banquet scheduled to initiate the fund-raising program would have excluded Negroes from attendance. Grimke and the officers of the Fifteenth Street Church objected strenuously, and an official of the presbytery met with the session to explain the action of the committee. Choosing not to attend even the meeting of his own session with the Presbytery's executive secretary, Grimke instead sent an impassioned appeal to the officers calling for their unequivocal stand against any encroachment on their human and Presbyterian rights. Finally the presbytery reconsidered its decision to employ such a segregated way of obtaining support for the fund drive, but an integrated dinner was out of the question so the hotel banquet was abandoned.[23]

If Grimke sometimes avoided meetings to attract interest and sympathy, he also chose on other occasions to attend for the same reasons. He served as a commissioner to the P.C.U.S.A. General Assembly of 1920, for example, in order to fight the proposed terms of union with the Presbyterian Church in the United States.[24] For several years a federal union of Reformed denominations had remained a subject of study and design. Many years before, in the Cumberland reunion debates, Grimke had circulated a list of arguments against such a union, and it had received the almost unanimous support of Negro leaders in the denomination.[25] Now he fought the reunion of southern and northern churches as a portion of the Protestant-wide "Plan of Union." The "Plan," weaker than organic union in its intent and already doomed by promised nonsupport from many of the presbyteries represented at the Assembly, did not fail because of Dr. Grimke's opposition. It does matter that Grimke chose to attend and fight the measure by his presence, to seek continued separation from southern and more blatantly racist power by active persuasion of representatives.[26]

While he stubbornly cut a solitary path among the predominantly white Presbyterians, Dr. Grimke nevertheless read and considered consistently and thoroughly the thoughts and ideas of Reformed churchmen. Presbyterian clergy, notably the eminent pastor of the New York Avenue Presbyterian Church, Wallace Radcliffe, numbered among Grimke's good friends.[27] He also read or corresponded with Clarence Macartney, Ian Maclaren, Murdock McLeod, and Sheldon Jackson among others.[28] In addition, he paid careful attention to the written proposals, reports, and minutes of the Presbyterian judicatories. Although his militancy often precluded publication of his thoughts in denominational periodicals, he continued to read several of them and to submit various articles for their perusal and refusal.[29]

His struggle with the Presbyterian Church, then, was a lover's quarrel of a man frustrated by his denomination's capitulation to American racism. But it was not just Presbyterians who failed to live up to Christian obligations. Grimke considered the Presbyterians as just a representative body of American Christians; and he took generally a pretty dim view of religion in the United States. "So far as the color line is concerned, white

American Christianity has been and still is absolutely rotten, utterly alien from the spirit and principles of the religion of Jesus Christ,"[30] Grimke declared. Time and again, he stated that incongruity of belief and action which racism evidenced. "Jesus came to break down the walls of separation and to make us brethren," he wrote, "but the American Church has been, and is now doing all in its power to produce the very opposite effect...."[31]

II

For Grimke, racism lay at the very core of American culture, and the Church reflected that sinful attitude. He preached, lectured, cajoled, and protested in behalf of an alternative to hate and divisiveness. In this ministry, Grimke took for his model Frederick Douglass; he associated with W. E. B. DuBois, and he attacked fellow Presbyterian, Woodrow Wilson.

Relatively early in his ministry, Grimke had met Douglass, although evidently he had already long admired the abolitionist leader.[32] For the *Journal of Negro History,* Grimke described the unusual coincidence of their first meeting. The young pastor went formally to pay respects to the redoubtable Douglass, who served as Recorder of Deeds in Washington.[33] The latter, a recent widower, looked up from his lunch and said, "I am thinking about getting married, and I want you to perform the ceremony." Grimke responded that he would be delighted.

In the pastor's own words, "On the evening set for the wedding, two carriages drove up to my door, 1608 R. Street, N.W., the bell rang and Mr. Douglass, Miss (Helen) Pitts, and Senator and Mrs. B. K. Bruce entered." With Charlotte and house guests Mrs. Stella Martin and her daughter Josie, Grimke joined in marriage Douglass and Miss Pitts, who happened to be white. Later Grimke chided critics of Douglass and his new wife. Although both black and white America objected strenuously, it was not the business of anyone except the parties involved. He did not hesitate to give his own views, that miscegenation "may not be a wise thing, in this country, in view of present conditions, but the right to marry if they want is inherent, God-given." Grimke also defended Helen Douglass against the character assassination attempted by both white and black groups.[34]

Interesting as it is to tell the story, it matters chiefly because Grimke's services at a crucial time, in a controversial situation, cemented his friendship with Douglass and reinforced his admiration of the "formidable reformer." Their personal camaraderie, however, proved just icing on the cake. Grimke many times spelled out what Douglass symbolized to all black people, and he spared no superlatives in the description. For assembled school children, he compared Douglass with others of "the most illustrious men of a century" and found him the most noteworthy. To Negroes he represented even more than the "American flag."

The Stars and Stripes mean a great deal to white Americans, they go into ecstacies over the flag; nothing seems to delight them more than to wave "Old Glory," as they call the flag; and, that is the way I feel about this man, I always like to hold him up, and wave him before the eyes of the Negro youth of our land.... For the flag has not always been the symbol of liberty and fair play, it has not always stood for human rights: it has stood for the rights of white men, and for Anglo-Saxon supremacy, but not for the rights of man as man, as was true of this man.[35]

Some years earlier, and for an adult audience, he delivered a full length address on the man. Grimke minced no words. He called Douglass "the greatest representative of the colored race that this country has yet produced."[36] He recited personal memories and collected impressions attesting to Douglass' physical winsomeness, his intellectual prowess, his moral character, and his sterling reputation. Grimke also listed and spelled out contributions Douglass had made to the struggle for equality by American black people: his unforgettable oratory, expressing by his "magical voice" and his use of the right word the needs of black America; his incessant work, whether surreptitiously on the underground railway or above ground with his unselfish devotion to every worthy cause; his influence among whites in government, enabling new opportunities for Negro soldiers; his unflagging insistence on the ballot for all Americans, which had yielded the vote and general enfranchisement for ex-slaves.[37] In the name of Douglass, Grimke put forth his dream that a day would come "when black and white shall clasp friendly, in the consciousness of the fact that we are all brothers, and that God is the Father of all of us."[38]

Such hagiography and unadulterated optimism Grimke reserved almost for Douglass alone. He supported other leaders of American black liberation, especially W. E. B. DuBois. For DuBois, however, Grimke managed some harsh words:

Men like DuBois, when they speak on economics, or on the civil and political rights of the Negro as an American citizen, speak with authority and may be safely followed; but when it comes to religion and morality, they are sadly in need of guidance themselves. They are far, far out of the way as tested by the Word of God and the ideals and principles of Jesus Christ. Their views are distorted, perverted, erroneous. To follow them is to be misled, to be facing in the wrong direction. Not being right themselves, they are incapable of pointing out the way to others. No leaders are so dangerous as those who have perverted views on religion and morality.[39]

With such a scathing critique of the man's religion, a reader might suspect Grimke of piecemeal support of the radical DuBois' program for equalization of black opportunity in America. Although he had earlier been a rather close acquaintance of Booker T. Washington, and although he had journeyed several times to Tuskegee Institute as a visiting lecturer, Francis Grimke attended the summit meeting of Negro America in New York, 1904, as a critic of the "Tuskegee Machine."[40] Likewise, with brother Archibald, Grimke participated in other "radical" ventures such as the Niagara Movement which DuBois headed.[41] The brothers Grimke, like DuBois himself, considered Washington's "Middle Way" in fact a capitulation to white racist forces in America.[42] The public records show not Grimke's quarrel with DuBois but his solidarity with his fellow black man. Until well into the time of Grimke's declining health in 1934, general statements such as approval of DuBois' "Credo," his *Souls of Black Folk*, and his contributions to ending racism, remained characteristic of Grimke's appraisal of the Harvard graduate.[43] Grimke opposed racism. He favored any ally who sought to reduce its power.

For a brief time Grimke thought he would find in the person of Woodrow Wilson a powerful ally for combating racism. Wilson's election to the presidency coincided with a reprint in the *Expositor* of his scholarly argument on "The Importance of Bible Study." Grimke read Wilson's words and responded warmly:

> Washington, D.C., November 20, 1912
>
> Dear Sir:
> I am a colored man ... You may not know it, but the triumph of the Democratic Party has always been attended, more or less, with a sense of uneasiness on the part of colored people for fear lest their rights might be interfered with. It is unfortunate that the ascendency of any party in this country should seem to any class of citizens to imperil their rights. But such, unquestionably, is the feeling of the great majority of the colored people, induced by what has been the general attitude of the Democratic Party toward their rights as citizens.[44]

Grimke confessed that he too had "shared, somewhat, this feeling." Now, however, the pastor had read Wilson's address to a "body of Sunday School teachers." He declared to the President-elect, "I cannot tell you how greatly it has relieved my mind."

> ... I said to myself, no American citizen, white or black, need have any reasonable fear from the Administration of a man who feels as he does, who believes as he does in the word of God, who accepts as he does, without any reservation, the great, eternal, and immutable principles of righteousness for which that Word stands. ... It is a comforting thought, especially to those who are struggling against great odds, to know that the God of Abraham, of Isaac, and of Jacob—the God that the Bible reveals, is on the throne, and that under Him, as his vice-regent, will be a man who has the courage of his convictions, and who will not falter where duty calls.[45]

Grimke closed with words of "earnest prayer" for Wilson's incumbency—prayers which Grimke must have considered unanswered in light of subsequent events. Wilson keenly disappointed Grimke by acceding to cultural norms in his appointments of positions in government. The President allowed extension of the nation's "color line" into the very departments of government, and by generally showing his "Southern" bias in matters of black and white. Grimke protested:

Washington, D.C., September 5, 1913

Dear Sir:

As an American citizen I desire to enter my earnest protest against the disposition, under your Administration, to segregate colored people in the various departments of the Government. To do so is undemocratic, is un-American, is un-Christian, is needlessly to offend the self-respect of the loyal black citizens of the Republic. We constitute one tenth of the population, and, under the Constitution, have the same rights and are entitled to the same considerations as other citizens. We had every reason to hope, from your high Christian character, and from your avowal of lofty principles prior to your election, that your accession to power would act as a check upon the brutal and insane spirit of race hatred that characterizes certain portions of the white people of the country. As American citizens we have a right to expect the President of the United States to stand between us and those who are bent on forcing us into a position of inferiority. Under the Constitution, resting upon the broad foundation of democratic principles as embodied in the Declaration of Independence, there are no superiors and inferiors. Before the law all citizens are equal, and are entitled to the same consideration. May we not expect,— have we not the right to expect, that your personal influence, as well as the great influence which comes from your commanding official position, will be thrown against what is clearly, is distinctly not in accordance with the spirit of free institutions? All class distinctions among citizens are un-American, and the sooner every vestige of it is stamped out the better it will be for the Republic.

Yours truly,

Francis J. Grimke.[46]

III

Initial suspicions had been confirmed, and Grimke confessed that odds against the black American were as great as ever. He voiced a lonely protestation against American involvement in the "Great War," which Wilson's administration waged despite its campaign slogans to refrain from entering the fray.

Dr. Grimke protested sharply the involvement of America's black population in what was essentially a war "to insure white supremacy throughout the world." He confided to his *Journal* the bitterness and humiliation which the United States war effort engendered in him:

April 16, 1918

I saw, a few days ago, on Pennsylvania Avenue over one of the moving picture theatres this inscription: "SHALL HUMANITY RULE OR THE SAVAGE?" The white people of this country seem to be greatly concerned as to whether humanity or the savage is to rule in other lands, but utterly indifferent as to which rules in this. The exhibitions of savagery that are constantly taking place in this country they are perfectly willing to have go on, since the victims are colored people; are perfectly willing to have the savage rule so long as he doesn't rule over white people. A white savage, showing his savagery to darker races, is not objectionable. It is only when shown to whites that it is to be condemned. That shows, as clearly as anything can, that the whites are nothing but savages themselves; that they are still on a very low plane of moral development.[47]

White presumption, not thinking of "darker and weaker races, but only of the whites and of their interests," concerned Grimke very much. The thought of black presence in the Army of the United States, that "some have already gone over to lay down their lives as representatives of this government on a foreign soil, and yet not one of them could enter a single restaurant, eating place, or hotel on Pennsylvania Avenue and get a sandwich, or a glass of milk, simply because of the color of his skin," filled the pastor with bitterness and hostility. He secretly admired the blacks who chose to die in America in revolt against racism here rather than submit to the hypocrisy of American "making the world safe for democracy."[48]

"Dying here in defense of democratic principles is just as honorable as dying on a foreign soil," he concluded in reflection on the death of a young black man from Louisville, Kentucky, in a racial incident at Camp Merrit, New Jersey, and on the execution of thirteen black soldiers in Houston, Texas. Having equalized the honor due each, Grimke went a step further, "The greatest enemies to true democracy are not in Germany or Austria, but here in the United States of America."[49]

Although he evidently kept his most critical thoughts to himself, Grimke did not hesitate to confirm in public what he expressed in private. Several times he refused to support the drive to sell bonds underwriting America's mobilization efforts. Again, he wrote a complaining letter to the U.S. Employment Service of the Department of Labor; the government sought to limit blacks from all but the most menial jobs relating to national defense. He did not mince words, objecting to the "unwarrantable assumption" that the Negro was inferior and declaring that the public circular of regulations "is an insult to every self-respecting Negro." Grimke confessed his own hesitation in writing, but he felt impelled to do so by his own personal self-respect and by his sense of justice in behalf of fellow blacks.[50] So, during the time of America's war involvement, Grimke objected strenuously to black presence in its support.

When the war finally came to an end, Grimke sincerely rejoiced along with everyone else in America at the return of the troops. In an address delivered 24 November 1918, he enumerated several reasons for his exaltation: the end of dying needlessly for women, children, and even for combatants; the victory of the Allies, who, if they proved seldom more democratic or humane than their opponents, at least did not initiate the war; the demise of the great European autocracies; the promise of better things to come, especially a "higher type of Christianity than at present prevails," which would benefit the "darker and weaker races of the world."[51]

At one point Grimke quoted extensively from a work by Harry Emerson Fosdick, *The Challenge of the Present Crisis,* but he chose Fosdick's stirring plea for God's condemnation of all warfare.[52] More personally, the Washington pastor reflected that "there is no difference, or very little, between the Central Powers and the Allies" insofar as both *consortia* really sought "to make the world safe for white supremacy." Even in American victory, Grimke's rejoicing showed his decided ambiguity of feeling. It raised as many questions as expressions of thanksgiving.[53] Why does the Democratic administration of Woodrow Wilson patronize only white power groups?[54] He wondered if blacks had done their cause good or harm by fighting for America. He surmised that they "certainly have not been fighting to make [the world] safe for true democracy—for democracy in any adequate or worthy sense of the term." Would the Allies continue to ignore in barbarous fashion the rights of man? Was American selfishness— white selfishness—at the root of intervention?[55]

Only the probability of an emergent "super-man of the future," no longer of the German type "nor of the contemptible little type that we find here in America, assuming and acting upon the theory that under a white skin is to be found anything worthy of respect." No, the super-man of the new day would be "of the Christ-like type"; and the super-nation of the future would be a new "Commonwealth of Israel":

> The super-nation of the future is not to be the German nation, nor any of the existing nations, but the Commonwealth of Israel— the Church of the living God, purified, cleansed, Spirit-filled, God-centered, meek and lowly, girded with strength, and arranged in beautiful garments of righteousness.[56]

IV

At least twice again, though in more tempered speech, Grimke re-affirmed his opposition to American preoccupation with the war and the truce in Europe while ignoring conditions of oppression at home. For a Christmas message in 1918, repeated for returning soldiers in April, 1919, he spoke in favor of the "Prince of Peace" as the *exemplum omnium* for the gospel of love.[57] It would replace the gospel of hate which thus far yielded a domestic war more terrible than the recently concluded World War. This gospel of love, this Prince of Peace, Grimke offered as the cure to war and racism alike.

Solutions to the problems of racism and war, to every other human quandary as well, could only be found in adherence to the Christian faith. Grimke meditated on its superiority to other religions and ideologies of mankind. It was, for him, not only a "high type of religion: but the highest, the best, the noblest that has ever appeared among men."[58] Christianity more than any other way of life could remake individuals and societies into loving persons and communities. It established "home betterment," and also enabled "a great, permanent, and ennobling civilization." Most important, Grimke asserted that the Christian faith brought eternal salvation to those who professed it, a reward immeasurable by human standards.

The life, death, and resurrection of Jesus Christ remained at the fulcrum of Grimke's interpretation of the Christian faith. Through the "transforming power of Jesus Christ," men could follow Christian principles and live for higher goals than personal selfishness or racial supremacy. At times Grimke spoke of the "friendship" Christ affords:

> Jesus Christ came into the world as the friend of man—not white men, nor black men, nor yellow men, nor red men, nor brown men, but of man—of men of all races, classes, conditions.... The friend, above all others, that we need, is Jesus Christ.... It is a friendship that is a steadily uplifting force—a force which always beautifies, always ennobles. Out of it nothing ever comes but good. If we grapple him to our souls with hooks of steel, our course will be like the shining light that groweth brighter unto the perfect day.[59]

At other times, Grimke chose to employ the term "peace" as the gift of God in belief of Jesus. The Christian religion, he maintained, can "beget within us an inward peace that no outward conditions can disturb."[60] On still other occasions, the all-encompassing result of faith he described in models of beatitude.[61] Whatever the way of describing its results, the Christian faith remained for Grimke the answer to all the world's problems.

The Negro in America needs to hear of the meaning of the Christian faith, Grimke declared. The white man has the greatest need of it. The great majority of whites, he claimed, "are pagans" in regard to their treatment of blacks: "They live entirely outside the pale of Christian ideals and principles." In their neglect of the "brotherhood of man" and in their misunderstanding of the meaning of the church, whites worship a "Baal-spirit," which must be "rooted out" before true redirection in world history can occur.[62]

Such enterprises as world missions, temperance movements, truly open Sunday Schools, and "Christian Endeavor," Grimke supported completely.[63] Other institutions, like the Y.M.C.A., the home missions societies, and the ecclesiastical hierarchies, had the potential at least of Christian service; and he sought their purification.[64] Each particular enterprise, however, he measured by Christian standards of brotherhood and "character."

But it was really the Christian faith, in biblical terms, that Grimke professed and preached. He felt so strongly about its value that he risked presumption to proclaim it. To Pinckney B. S. Pinchback, ex-Governor of Louisiana and the elected Senator from that state who never was permitted to serve, Grimke wrote a letter of "witness."[65] "Soon the end of the earthly pilgrimage must come," he declared. Embracing the traditional language of the "soul-saver," the pastor claimed in corporate terms: "We cannot go into eternity with our sins unrepented of and hope for any good. The blood of Jesus Christ alone cleanses from sin." He closed with yet another admonition. "Don't allow life to pass without making the great surrender of yourself to Jesus Christ. I am, Your sincere friend, Francis J. Grimke."[66]

Had Grimke received a different tradition, or had he made a habit of such personal evangelism, one might suspect that his rhetoric merely adopted a conventional vernacular in which the minister had an "upper-hand" over others. But the uncharacteristic language for Grimke and the reply from Pinchback attest to simple Christian sincerity and to genuine concern for the black politician. Pinchback wrote to Grimke, "Your esteemed favor of the 28th ult. was duly received, contents noted and fully appreciated." He called Grimke's admonition "timely and pertinent." Grimke's words did help the man.[67] Whatever their outcome, they testify to Grimke's own appraisal of the Christian faith as utterly necessary for all.

During the height of Grimke's productivity, the minister made concerted efforts to spell out for his congregation the meaning of the faith for Christian nurture.[68] Although he did not outline an entire theology in these series of sermons, Grimke did manage to list a number of categories of nurture. Together they assist in delineating his theology.

Many of the categories which Grimke urged upon parents and church members in rearing children appear culturally defined. For example, "purity," Grimke took to mean pre-marital virginity and the total covering of one's body in respectable clothing. He decried prostitution, adultery and fashions revealing "bare arms and half naked bodies." "If they are properly trained," he asserted, children will grow up pure and there "will be no low necks, greatly abbreviated skirts and transparent stockings." Nowhere in the section on "purity" did the pastor explore the meanings of the word with regard to motivation, social institutions, or any of the other "deadly sins" such as pride, envy, or greed.[69]

Purity was not the only area of Christian growth that Grimke interpreted narrowly. He maintained also that being neat, polite, and punctual were necessary Christian attributes; and he spelled out their implications in the education of children in the faith. Again, he encouraged industriousness and frugality as indispensable ingredients for Christian growth. In each case Grimke limited the term to its rather constricted, indeed, "Victorian" interpretation. On the other hand, Grimke urged parents to raise their children, and to live themselves, in a spirit of unselfishness. In the amount of attention and space he devoted to this category, Grimke clearly demonstrated that unselfish behavior was more important than dress or social grace.[70]

In addition, he encouraged families to instill in children a sense of justice, "the recognition of the fact that other people have rights which we are bound to respect."[71] Under this rubric, he subsumed a discussion of stealing and dishonesty; but it remained justice more than property which Grimke respected, certainly not a typical expression of the mores of his day.

Character, more than any other attribute, Grimke sought to instill in would-be believers. An all-embracing mark of the Christian life, character included for him elements of piety and ethics. He advocated "character" for white and black alike. "What we need most of all is character," he told fellow blacks at the 1892 meeting of the Ministers' Union in Washington, D.C.[72] Proceeding to explain that he did not intend to deprecate wealth, education or sagacity, for all these things were important, he nevertheless saw character as the "moral base" of all other pursuits. "Put that first," he exhorted, "make righteousness the basis of life; enter into the kingdom of God. . . ." Character meant integrity, humility with pride, conscience with life, and a willingness to pursue the life Christ sets forth without regard for the costs. It was character, more than all else, which Grimke sought for himself; and it was character which enabled him to stand as his own man.

Retracing the life and theology of Francis Grimke appears easier than categorizing the man himself. Roi Ottley, in his pioneering study of the *Black Odyssey*, refers in passing to Grimke and calls him a "bishop."[73] Ottley missed somewhat in his characterization, because, while Grimke technically was bishop to the session of his congregation, he never commanded the ecclesiastical power historically associated with that title. Even if he spoke for a large portion of black Presbyterians, Grimke remained more a prophet than a mitred politician. His was more a voice "crying in the wilderness" against oppression of blacks by Church and civil authority than it was an exercise in *ex cathedra* leadership.

Members of his own congregation sometimes called their pastor the "Negro Puritan."[74] Carter Woodson, in his biographical sketch of the man, employed the term "Black Puritan," and said that it too had been a label for Grimke through the years.[75] Thus when Clifton Olmstead, contributing a portrait of Grimke for a sesquicentennial anniversary volume of Princeton Seminary, asked "What manner of man was Dr. Francis James Grimke?" he replied to his own question: "To the present writer, Dr. Grimke was a Negro Puritan. . . ."[76] Perhaps such a characterization is partially justified, for Grimke did reckon "duty" to God and fellow man among his determinative drives.[77] Again, he remained constantly responsive to the guidance of a sovereign God, and to the power of a risen Christ. Moreover, his religion "spilled over" into all of life, so that he reflected theologically on all experience and human relations.[78] These traits do mark Grimke as a participant in some Puritan ethic. But they do not seem to point to the core of his life and contributions, for "Puritanism" is certainly a designation of a western, particularly white, tradition. And Grimke, though son of a white as well as of a black parent, seized on the heritage of his blackness and pronounced it "Beautiful."

The man really defies any attempt to pigeonhole his life and work. He proved a Christian of his day, a prophet of black consciousness, and a pastor by profession. Nevertheless, by refusing to accept either cultural definitions of the limits of Christianity and by facing capitulation wherever it impinged on human rights, Grimke remained a singular personality.

Notes

1. See John P. Davis, ed., *The American Negro Reference Book* (Englewood Cliffs, New Jersey: Prentice Hall, 1966), 558; Herbert Aptheker, *A Documentary History of the Negro People in America* (New York: Citadel, 1951, 1969), 765, 915. Note that Saunders Redding, *They Came in Chains* (Philadelphia: Lippincott, 1950), John Hope Franklin, *From Slavery to Freedom* (New York: Knopf, 1956), Nathaniel Weyl, *The Negro in American Civilization* (Washington: Public Affairs, 1960), Lerone Bennett, *Before the Mayflower* (Chicago: Johnson, 1964), and *Eyewitness, The Negro in American History*, by William Katz (New York: Pitman, 1969), uniformly ignore Grimke, as do general works on American History. The situation will be improved with the publication of Henry Ferry's Yale dissertation, "Francis James Grimke: Portrait of a Black Puritan" (1970, Copyright 1971). Ferry reconstructs Grimke's personal history. The biographical study is an excellent one wrought from a variety of sources.

2. Francis J. Grimke, *The Works of Francis James Grimke*, edited by Carter G. Woodson (Washington: Associated Publishers, 1942), in four volumes. See Vol. III for Grimke's emphasis that "it is the work, not the workman that it is important to keep alive." Thus he refused the suggestion of a friend to provide an autobiography or to commission a biography. "If I have helped anyone to appreciate even in small degree the significance of life . . . I am glad of it, am profoundly grateful." He only regretted "that it could not have been far greater." 609.

3. C. Vann Woodward, *The Strange Career of Jim Crow* (New York: Oxford, 1955, 1966), 67–192. Cf. Rayford W. Logan, *The Betrayal of the Negro* (New York: Macmillan, 1965), 125 ff.

4. E. Franklin Frazier, *The Negro Church in America* (New York: Schocken Books, 1963), 29–86, pointed to the subservience of the black churches. Both Joseph Washington, *Black Religion* (Boston: Beacon, 1964), *passim*, and James Cone, *A Black Theology of Liberation* (Philadelphia: Lippincott, 1970), 236, agree in essence with the consideration of that era in black churches as a time of "Decline and Fall." See Allen Weinstein and Frank Gatell, eds., *The Segregation Era* (New York: Oxford, 1970), part III, for the wider use of the expression.

5. James Cone, *Black Theology and Black Power* (New York: Seabury, 1969), 105, 106.

6.. E. Franklin Frazier, *Black Bourgeoisie* (Glencoe, Illinois: Free Press, 1957), 196–99.

7. A thumbnail sketch of keen insight is available in August Meir, *Negro Thought in America, 1800–1915* (Ann Arbor: Michigan Press, 1963), 223. More extensive biographies appear in William Simmons, *Men of Mark: Eminent, Progressive, and Rising* (Cleveland: Rewell, 1887), 608–12, and in an obituary in *Journal of Negro History*, 23 (1938), 133–36. Ferry, *op. cit.*, is unsurpassed.

8. See Carleton Mabee, *Black Freedom* (London: Macmillan, 1969), for just one recent history of the movement in which Pillsbury moved as a vital participant. On Mrs. Pillsbury, see D. B. Pillsbury, *The Pillsbury Family* (1898).

9. See Gerda Lerner, *The Grimke Sisters of South Carolina* (Boston: Houghton Mifflin, 1967), 359–66 for one account of their contribution to the welfare of the brothers.

10. A brief summary of Archibald Grimke's life, together with a selection from his work, has been included in *Negro Social and Political Thought, 1850–1920*, edited by Howard Brotz (New York: Basic Books, 1966), 464–80.

11. At Least Carter G. Woodson made this observation as an aside in Grimke, *Works*, IV, 136. Note the letter to Grimke from G. F. Miller, a student at the seminary on November 4, 1914, complaining strenuously of the seminary's attitude toward blacks.

12. October 18, 1879, letter from A. A. Hodge to Theodore Cuyler, a Presbyterian pastor in Brooklyn, in Grimke, *Works*, I, x; a simultaneous letter from James McCosh, and another from McCosh dated February 10, 1881, in Grimke, *Works*, I, x f.

13. *Ibid.*, I, 526.

14. Rev. John F. Cook had first led the Fifteenth Street congregation, which had been founded in 1841.

15. *The Journal of Negro History*, 23 (1938), 134, calls it the "Laurel Street Church," and *Minutes of the General Assembly*, Presbyterian Church, U.S.A. (1888), names the "Third Presbyterian Church" of Jacksonville. At any rate, Grimke served that congregation from October 1885 until early in 1889. In 1891, he turned down a call from Biddle University to become "Professor of Christian Evidences and Mental and Moral Philos-

ophy." He also refused the presidency of Howard University, at least according to one account. He did accept Lincoln's proffer of a doctorate in divinity, June 5, 1888.

16. For James Forten's 1813 speech on civil rights, together with some brief remarks on his life, see Carter G. Woodson, *Negro Orators and their Orations* (Washington: Associated Publishers, 1925), 42 ff.

17. See *The Journal of Charlotte Forten*, edited by Ray A. Billington (New York: Collier, 1961). For her participation in "Gideon's Band" for the Port Royal Experiment, see Willie Lee Rose, *Rehearsal for Reconstruction: The Port Royal Experiment* (New York: Vintage Books, 1964).

18. See Billington, introduction to Forten's *Journal*, and Grimke, *Works*, III, *passim*.

19. He declined especially the "country meetings" of the groups, where he felt discrimination most keenly. But he maintained interest and informed opinions on the various projects the judicatories undertook. See Grimke, *Works*, IV, 115 ff.

20. *Ibid.*, 225.

21. *Ibid.*, 225, 226.

22. *Ibid.*, III, 156, 157. See also IV, 127, 144.

23. *Ibid.*

24. For a resume of the General Assembly, see *The New Era Magazine*, 26 (1920), 502–15.

25. See Lefferts A. Loetscher, *The Broadening Church* (Philadelphia: University of Pennsylvania Press, 1954), 101. Grimke had attended the 1904 General Assembly and spoken against the PCUSA/Cumberland Church merger. See *Minutes* (1904).

26. Among others, his friend Wallace Radcliffe also attended the meeting.

27. Grimke, *Works*, I, xvii.

28. *Ibid.*, III, 187, 257, 193, 15–17.

29. *Ibid.*, IV, 126.

30. *Ibid.*, III, 352.

31. *Ibid.*, IV, 192.

32. Frederick Douglass (1817?–1895), black abolitionist and reformer, traveled extensively and spoke frequently to audiences all over the North. His high visibility, together with his stunning presence, became a model for many blacks—not just for Grimke. See *Life and Times of Frederick Douglass*, written by himself (London: Collier-Macmillan, 1962), based on the revised edition of 1892.

33. Grimke, "The Second Marriage of Frederick Douglass," *Journal of Negro History*, 19 (1934), 324–29.

34. *Ibid.*, 325, 326, and I, 71–80.

35. *Ibid.*, 65. The speech is dated February 14, 1908.

36. March 10, 1898, in *ibid.*, I, 34.

37. *Ibid.*, 36–53.

38. *Ibid.*, 54.

39. *Ibid.*, III, 465. W. E. B. DuBois (1868–1957) pioneered in the study of sociology and in the militant struggle fof black enfranchisement in Amer-

ica. His *Souls of Black Folk* (1903) called on the Grimkes for assistance in the repudiation of Washington's racial strategy, a point explained in F. L. Broderick and August Meier, eds., *Negro Protest Thought in the Twentieth Century* (New York: Bobbs-Merrill, 1965), 37, 40.

40. Grimke, *Works*, IV, 89–90. In a confidential memo to Grimke, dated December 28, 1903, DuBois laid out the various principles which anti-Washington men would seek in the meeting; among them, equal civil rights, equal ballot opportunity, equal educational promise, and the right to disagree with the pro-Washington forces. DuBois counted only Clement Morgan, a black attorney from Cambridge, Massachusetts, another lawyer and Chicagoan, E. H. Morris, F. L. McGhee from St. Paul, the redoubtable Kelly Miller, Grimke, and himself as being decidedly anti-Bookerite among the leadership chosen for the conference.

41. On the Niagara Movement, see Elliott Rudwick, *W. E. B. DuBois: A Study in Minority Group Leadership* (Philadelphia: University of Pennsylvania Press, 1960), 94–120.

42. A fine insight into the nature of the differing strategies is provided in *The Negro Problem* (New York: James, 1903, reprinted 1969, Arno Press and the New York *Times*) where both Booker T. Washington and W. E. B. DuBois spell out their views in articles.

43. Grimke, *Works*, I, 367, 398.

44. *Ibid.*, IV, 129.

45. *Ibid.*, 129 f.

46. *Ibid.*, 133 f.

47. *Ibid.*, III, 44.

48. *Ibid.*, 45–50.

49. *Ibid.*, IV, 197.

50. *Ibid.*

51. *Ibid.*, I, 573.

52. Grimke, *Works*, I, 560, 561. Harry Emerson Fosdick (1878–1969) had resigned from Montclair, New Jersey, church to serve in the war as a chaplain. His *The Challenge of the Present Crisis* (New York: Association Press, 1918) mixed with condemnation of war the rationale for involvement in the "Great War."

53. Grimke, *Works*, I, 563.

54. Grimke remained extremely critical of Woodrow Wilson for his hypocrisy toward blacks, and he thought the President all the more guilty of double-dealing for his pre-election promises which subsequently went unheeded. See Grimke, *Works*, I, 178 f., 505, 559–77.

55. *Ibid.*, I, 564 f.

56. *Ibid.*, 576.

57. *Ibid.*, I, 577–96.

58. *Ibid.*, IV, 401.

59. *Ibid.*, III, 75.

60. *Ibid.*, 313.

61. *Ibid.*, 431–33.

62. *Ibid.*, II, 291–333.

63. *Ibid.*, 471–82, 494–600.

64. At least he presented this opinion in more hopeful times.

65. *Ibid.*, IV, 171.

66. *Ibid.*, 171 f.

67. *Ibid.*, 179.

68. Grimke, *Works*, II, *passim*, especially pp. 1–20.

69. *Ibid*, II, *passim*.

70. Grimke, *Works*, II, 97–99.

71. *Ibid.*, 73.

72. *Ibid.*, I, 223–33.

73. Roi Ottley, *Black Odyssey* (New York: Scribner's, 1948), 279.

74. Grimke, *Works*, IV, 204.

75. Woodson, introduction to Grimke, *Works*, I, XIII.

76. Clifton E. Olmstead, "Francis James Grimke, Christian Moralist and Civil Rights," in *The Sons of the Prophets* (Princeton: University Press, 1963), 175. Olmstead did not credit either members of Grimke's congregation or Woodson. Worse, Olmstead took a dim view of Grimke's criticism of Wilson, Booker T., and the Presbyterian Church. Thus he concludes Grimke's contribution as chiefly a negative one. By the same token Henry J. Ferry's work (reported in *Journal of Presbyterian History*, XLIX, 1971, 183, 184) reverts in title to the "Black Puritan" employed by Woodson. His excellent article, "Racism and Reunion: A Black Protest by Francis James Grimke" (*Journal of Presbyterian History*, L, 1972, 77–78), reports and interprets the events immediately surrounding the PCUSA/Cumberland Presbyterian Church merger of 1904–1905, with emphasis on Grimke's opposition.

77. Grimke spoke very frequently of the "duty" of parents (*Works*, II, 42, 49 f.), of all Christians (58–90), of spouses (191) and of all people.

78. So much so that Olmstead, for example, characterized Grimke's faith as "a way of life" (*Sons of Prophets*, 175).

Gordon Blaine Hancock:
A Black Profile from the New South

Raymond Gavins

Black leadership is an essential part of the Afro-American experience. It consists of individual and collective contributions to black uplift, including black spokesmen, community organizations, protest movements, and race relations.[1] Careful inquiry into its dynamics should richly illuminate our understanding of the programs, ideologies, and tactics black leaders employed in the past and, to a great extent, advocate in the present. In the New South, particularly in the age of segregation,[2] black leadership is one window through which historians can view black responses to oppression.

Traditionally, biographers of black leaders have singled out men and women of indisputed national reputation, a few black heroes and heroines esteemed the most outstanding representatives of their race.[3] Lesser known members of the black vanguard, until recently, have been obscure. To achieve broader perspective on the perils and prospects of black leadership, however, it is imperative that we study more of the latter, who have stood perhaps too long in the shadows of the former—the Great Negro Leaders. Studies of significant minor figures can provide new data for the portfolio on how black leaders function.[4] By documenting what black spokesmen of varying persuasions, at a given time and place, were feeling, thinking, saying or doing, these studies will permit a fuller interpretation of the black struggle against caste. In an attempt to fulfill a small portion of the larger task, this paper is concerned with a Southern black leader who has not received much attention. Gordon Blaine Hancock was an educator, clergyman, journalist, and interracialist in the period from 1920 to 1954.[5] Although he formulated certain basic assumptions about black-white relations prior to 1920, his racial ideology crystallized in the context of the crisis which followed. During this time currents stirred by depression, recovery, war, and postwar demands for integration rigorously tested the fabric of black life and leadership in the South and nation.

An early awareness of black deprivation and a strong sense of racial responsibility motivated Gordon Blaine Hancock to become a champion of the Negro's cause. Born June 23, 1884, in Ninety-Six township, Greenwood County, South Carolina,[6] he grew up in an era when the Palmetto State maintained "the subordination of the Negro by a caste system based on race under which black and white seldom came into personal contact except in the relationship of employer and laborer."[7] A visitor to Ninety-Six in Gordon's boyhood days would have found no signs of a trend toward industrial and commercial development. The worn-out post office and train stop were its most important contacts with the outside world. This township in contrast to Greenwood, the county seat about fourteen miles away, which had mills, stores and a newspaper, remained rural and a bastion of white supremacy.[8] The economic status of blacks in Ninety-Six and its environs was deplorable. A farm area, with cotton as the cash crop, in 1900 it had 2,395 residents, of whom 1,545, or 65 percent, were Negroes. Greenwood County, reporting a comparable ratio, had a population of 28,343 of whom 18,906, or 66.7 percent, were Negroes.[9] In addition to farming or sharecropping most black men worked as wage hands while black women were primarily domestics.[10]

Blacks suffered not only economic captivity but political and social isolation as well. Denied equal rights and excluded from politics, they turned to their own institutions for a meaningful existence. Despite poverty, black families were generally stable. A network of supportive relationships, rooted in the churches and fraternal clubs, kept desertions, illegitimacy and crime low. Unlike the cities of Charleston and Columbia, the county did not have a burgeoning black intellectual and professional elite. Leadership usually came from a handful of ministers and teachers, frequently poorly trained, who rejected class distinctions and identified with the masses.[11] If blacks knew their place, they did not always stay in it; nor did they accept injustice without complaint. Race relations, though invariably paternalistic, were strained by an endemic violence. Throughout the 1890's, lynchings increased in the county and state, partly a consequence of populism and, after 1895, black disfranchisement.[12] For example, an undetermined number of blacks died in the infamous Phoenix Riot in November of 1898 near Ninety-Six, precipitated by a dispute between Democrats and Republicans over black voting rights. For several days an armed white mob, allegedly searching for "niggers" who had signed an affidavit to vote, moved into black neighborhoods, butchering all who resisted. Because of conflicting and insufficient reports and the wide area over which the mob ranged, no one ever knew the precise number of victims.[13] But the fear born of this ordeal smothered open political aspirations in the black community.

This closed society had a powerful influence on Gordon. As he later recalled, three incidents sparked his consciousness of color: hearing white ruffians in a country store voice "their low opinion of niggers"; having his parents angrily rebuke him for playing with a white boy; and trudging "down the same dusty road" with white children to a separate school.[14] At the age of fourteen when the Phoenix Riot broke out, Hancock noted in an autobiographical sketch that "it caused great travail and trembling among the Negroes." One black man was "shot to death on the main road." he said, "and no Negro in Ninety-Six went to town for weeks."[15] Benjamin E. Mays, former president of Morehouse College, lived in Epworth at the time, ten miles from Ninety-Six. He described the Phoenix episode as his "earliest memory," recollecting that a crowd of white men carrying rifles "cursed my father, drew their guns and...made him take off his hat and bow down to them several times."[16] For Hancock and Mays, two precocious youths, the shock of mob violence had lasting effects. Memories of that fateful November in 1898, no doubt, undergirded their eloquent appeal for nonviolence more than a generation later.

Hancock's family ties represented a protective medium against the hostile environment. Anna Mark, his mother, was born in slavery in 1863. One of twelve children, she attended freedmen's schools after the Civil War and at age sixteen, encouraged by her yankee mentor, passed the county examination to become "the first colored teacher in Ninety-Six." She married Robert Wiley Hancock in 1881, and bore him two children, Edith and Gordon. While still a young woman in 1886, she died suddenly, probably from poor health and exhaustion. Born in 1862, to free mulatto parents, Robert, by strength of courage, enrolled in Benedict College in Columbia, South Carolina. By 1882, he had accepted the pastorate of First Baptist Church in Parksville and established a school in Flint Hill, each within commuting distance of Ninety-Six. After Anna's death, he married Georgia Anna Scott, daughter of a sharecropper. A fine stepmother to Edith and Gordon, she gave birth to four girls and two boys. "She was unlearned," Gordon said to a friend in 1934, "but she taught me in the ways of the Master." In 1902, the Reverend Hancock, who taught his children that faith in God, knowledge and self-reliance were prerequisites for life, died of a heart attack, "stricken in his pulpit." Georgia Anna, who tried hard to console Gordon, died in 1906.[17]

In 1902, Gordon Hancock passed the county teacher examination. For two years as schoolmaster in China Grove and Edgefield, twelve and five miles from home respectively, he encountered dilapidated buildings, two-month terms, too few books, inadequate instruction, indolence, underpaid teachers, and general invisibility. To undermine such invidious conditions, he urged blacks to consolidate their limited resources. At China Grove he circulated a petition, raised money, and had the term extended to five months,[18] no ordinary feat in a decade when state "school expenditures had risen from $2.75 to $3.11 per capita for whites, while dropping from $2.51 to $1.05 for Negroes."[19] Following his father's example, in 1904, he enrolled at Benedict College, a liberal arts school founded by white Northern missionaries after the Civil War, in Columbia, seventy-five miles from Ninety-Six. Working part-time to pay his expenses, he studied three years in the academy before completing his A.B. in 1911 and B.D. in 1912 summa cum laude, excelling in philosophy, history, religion and rhetoric. "The struggle to get an education was the best part of my education," Hancock stated reminiscently in 1959. "I had the good fortune to earn every dollar of it."[20]

Ordained for the ministry in 1911, Hancock became pastor of Bethlehem Baptist Church in Newberry, not far from Columbia. That same year he married Florence Marie Dickson, a middle class young woman he met at Benedict. Not much can be said of the church, except that it had a membership of "over 1,200 souls" and that gospel preaching was its central attraction. His wife who was born July 31, 1893, grew up in Society Hill township, Darlington County. Joseph Samuel Dickson, Sr., her mulatto father, ran a mercantile business, owned large tracts of farm land, and employed more than fifty black and white tenants. Florence Marie attended Browning Home, an exclusive elementary school for girls in Camden, before entering the academy of State College for Negroes in Orangeburg. She transferred to Benedict in 1908, received a diploma in 1910, and taught home economics. Sheltered from hardship, ambitious, cultured, she harbored beneath her loftiness sympathy for the downtrodden and a passion for thrift, qualities which endeared her to Gordon Hancock for almost sixty years.[21]

In 1912, the South Carolina Negro Baptist Convention's board of trustees named Hancock principal at Seneca Institute, a three-hundred pupil coed boarding school in Seneca, South Carolina. Hancock, anxious to upgrade it, quickly made the institution solvent through extensive fund raising. By 1916, he had constructed Dunbar Hall, a three-story classroom and dining building which cost $20,000. During a six-year tenure he accelerated the pre-college curriculum, and supplemented Sunday vesper services with required evening study hours, and developed a merit system.[22] At Seneca, moreover, Hancock stressed black pride, self-help and Christian character which were themes in his later preachments and hallmarks in the age of accommodation. Negroes, he agreed, should cast down their buckets in learning vocational skills, acquiring property, and cultivating white good will, but not at the expense of manhood. Still, he believed that the burden of Negro uplift rested heavily on the shoulders of highly educated leaders, a Talented Tenth. His synthesis came from intellectual exposure. He never met Washington, but he read *Up from Slavery*. Although he did not meet DuBois until 1928, he knew about the scholar's attack on "Mr. Booker T. Washington" and had seen one of the Atlanta University

Publications, which stimulated his initial interest in studying sociology.[23]

Seneca served as a proving ground. In visiting neighboring white schools and approaching white merchants, usually unsuccessfully, he made his first wavering steps toward interracial cooperation. He made Seneca Institute an experiment in "upward striving," concluding that blacks, while open to sympathetic white support, must ultimately sustain their own institutions. He also proposed that "color prejudice" was the fundamental reason for "the Negro's proscribed and disadvantaged status." From these motifs he would piece the mosaic of his thought. In 1914, he travelled to England, Ireland, Scotland, Wales, France, Italy and Switzerland, a tour financed by the Baptist Convention. Far from the provincialism of South Carolina he saw a different world, fear-ridden nations on the brink of war. Disturbed, he returned to Seneca more determined than ever, he said, "to further the emancipation of my stricken race." As could be anticipated, diehard whites considered his speeches "on the subjugation of the lowly Negroes" abrasive. Sometime in the spring of 1918, following his talk to a local black congregation, word came that he would be lynched, not a distant possibility in the racist milieu of World War I. Frightened, he ran. Hancock, however, always concealed the threat on his life. "Gordon never wanted anybody to know because he was afraid of being called a coward, but I will never forget it," Mrs. Hancock revealed. "My husband was a marked man. That very night we took the train to Columbia." With the assistance of his former professors, who were Colgate men, he applied to Colgate University in Hamilton, New York, anticipating the day when he would resume the work he left behind.[24]

Despite his two degrees from Benedict, Hancock entered Colgate in 1918, as a junior. Thirty-four and disciplined, he performed exceptionally well, finishing another A.B. in 1919, and B.D. in 1920. As a seminarian he held the coveted Smith Scholarship, became class vice-president, and delivered the valedictory. Liberal divinity studies enlarged his perspective on the role of organized religion in solving human problems. In his opinion, Christians were custodians of society and ministers to man's temporal and spiritual needs. Theologically, this philosophy complemented the "social gospel" of the black church which was exemplified in his father's ministry.[25]

The real meaning of Colgate lay in its effects on Hancock's racial attitudes. Hamilton was lily-white. The Census of 1910 reported no Negroes among its 1,689 residents. Only four Negroes were there in 1919, the Hancocks and the Parkers, a couple also affiliated with the University. Never before had Hancock lived so close to whites. Sensitive but not timid, he moved in a twilight zone between uncertain tolerance and forced isolation, openly avoided by Southerners and kept at a respectable distance by Northerners. "I deplored the fact that no Negroes were to be found at Colgate," he said in 1944. "I was not surprised, however, for I knew about President Cutten's attitude toward Negroes." The professors were polite, if condescending, and some quite congenial. "Several of Gordon's teachers had us in their homes on certain occasions," his wife stated, "but I don't think the Parkers were ever invited out." Although his experience in South Carolina made him skeptical of white people, it is probable that the few unprejudiced whites he met at Colgate softened his suspicions. "Some of my high opinion of white men and my indisposition to curse out the whole lot because a few are lynchers is based largely on the fact of the fine men I met at Colgate," he confided. "I have outlived hatreds. I am free to respect and love all men."[26]

On the basis of his excellent scholarship Hancock matriculated at Harvard in 1920. A graduate fellow in sociology, under the direction of Professor James Ford, he completed the Master of Arts degree in August 1921. His thesis, "The Interrelationship of the Immigrant and the Negro Problem," examined Irish-Negro antagonisms in Boston. The Negroes, Southern born, ignorant and poor, arrived in large numbers during World War I in search of economic opportunity. The Irish, Catholic white and working class, came largely a generation earlier, secured jobs, and resented the Negro newcomers. What made them hostile was not the issue of social equality, he said, as much as employer use of Negroes to break strikes and depress wages.[27] Hancock had expressed an interest in sociology since his days at Seneca. More immediately, in the wake of postwar riots, he began pondering the socio-economic causes of racial conflict. "I wanted to earn a degree from a school known around the nation," he averred. Unquestionably prestigious, Harvard became a leader in the emerging field of sociology, surpassed in the 1920's only by Chicago and Columbia Universities. In an era of intense black intellectuality, radiating from the Harlem Renaissance, a militant Negro press, and developing Negro colleges, Hancock became a spokesman for black sociology at Harvard. On this foundation he became an articulate and outspoken analyst of black urbanization and economic development. After 1921, in spite of other commitments, he continued at Harvard. He took required courses for his doctorate in the summers, 1922–1925, and did post-graduate work in 1937 and 1938, at Oxford and Cambridge. But he never finished the degree. In 1939, his old adviser wrote to him: "As for the question of . . . your work for the Ph.D. degree, I cannot help feeling that you have already attained a distinction beyond that which the degree would confer. I still think your greatest contribution can be made in preparing some publishable study in the field of race problems."[28]

Soon after earning his Master of Arts degree, Hancock accepted a professorship at Virginia Union University in Richmond, Virginia, where he took up his duties in September, 1921. Three factors that made Union attractive were a reputable liberal arts and theological program, the development of a department of economics and sociology, and location in a booming center of the upper South, providing a laboratory for racial research. "I came here deliberately after turning down a thirty-five hundred dollar job on the theory that educated Negroes born in the South should not run away and leave the submerged Negro to fight it out as best he can," he declared in 1948. "When I came to Virginia Union I was getting only twelve hundred dollars as salary."[29] For more than three decades, until his retirement in 1952, Hancock was part of Virginia Union's development. In 1921, its five gray granite buildings, artistically spaced on sixty-five acres, faced North Lombary Street in the former Confederate Capital. A brick tower, later added to the campus scenery, overlooked the homes and businesses of the colored bourgeoisie lining Clay Street, the black ghetto off Jackson Street known as Jackson Ward, and the white downtown commercial district along Broad Street. A faculty of twelve in 1921, included five white members. By 1952, the fifty-six people in administrative and faculty positions were almost all black. The endowment had increased from $205,000 to $1,015,596. Student enrollment increased from 223 to 805, 75 percent of whom earned all or part of their expenses. Sixty Unionites received doctorates in the 1910–1950 interim, while others were nationally ranked in the professions. Professors such as Gordon B. Hancock, sociologist, Miles Mark Fisher, folklorist, Arthur P. Davis, literary specialist, and Rayford W. Logan, historian, gave the school a scholarly image. For Hancock, this small black university—its fabric interwoven with bourgeois standards of respectability and success—proved amenable to a vigorous focus on race.[30]

No city could have provided more economic and social data for study than Richmond. Between 1920 and 1950, its population mushroomed from 171,667 to 230,310. It was second only to Atlanta as the fastest growing metropolis below the Potomac and "the real seat of empire for the tobacco industry of the world." The black population in Richmond increased from 54,041 in 1920 to 72,996 in 1950. Blacks represented the main source of cheap labor and were strictly segregated and relegated to a lower caste. Still, a proud black community existed behind the wall of segregation. John Mitchell, editor of the Richmond *Planet* and head of Mechanics Savings Bank, and Maggie L. Walker, president of Saint Luke Savings and Trust Company, represented a minute but dominant Negro upper class, based on free ancestry and white paternalism. In the 1920's, because of a continuous black influx, the old line leadership gradually gave way to an upward mobile group of professional and business men dependent on the Negro market. These professional and business men usually belonged to the First African, Ebenezer and Moore Street Churches and were members either of the Urban League, the NAACP or graduates of Virginia Union. Most blacks, in any case, remained in poverty. Three-fourths occupied rental housing, and half lived "at or below the line of minimum subsistence" in 1930.[31]

The Richmond setting was the backdrop against which Hancock rose to prominence. In 1921, he organized the Department of Economics and Sociology at Virginia Union; in 1940, he became dean of the seminary. According to a 1969 Colgate University citation, "His course in race relations is believed to have been the first of its kind offered by any institution in America." He authored more than twenty publications in journals, anthologies, and public affairs periodicals. Benedict College honored him with the Doctor of Divinity degree in 1925, when he accepted the pastorate of Moore Street Baptist Church. He was one of Richmond's most influential black ministers, when he retired from this church in 1963 with a membership of approximately 3,500. A member of the Richmond Negro Welfare Survey Committee. Hancock wrote most of the section on economic status for the final report, published in 1929 as *The Negro in Richmond, Virginia*. He contributed articles to the Richmond *Shepherds' Voice* and *St. Luke Herald* from 1925 to 1929, and he originated and popularized the idea of the "Double-Duty-Dollar." He joined the Associated Negro Press, contributing a regular article, "Between the Lines," which appeared in 114 Negro newspapers throughout the country. The Norfolk *Journal and Guide*, Virginia's largest black paper, featured his column weekly. Between 1929 and 1969, he wrote over 2,500 press releases comprising thousands of written pages.

With a gift of $10,000 from Mrs. Francis J. Torrance, a wealthy white Pennsylvania matron, Hancock founded the Torrance School of Race Relations at Virginia Union in 1931. Until its demise in 1938, the school promoted discussion and fact-finding concerning race relations. A trustee of the Richmond Urban League, Hancock served simultaneously on the boards of the Virginia Commission on Interracial Cooperation, the Richmond NAACP, Crusade for Negro Voters, Memorial Hospital, the Community Chest, the Council on Human Relations, the Protestant Ministers Association, the Lott Carey Baptist Convention, and the Palmer Memorial Institute in Sedalia, North Carolina. The only black appointed to President Hoover's Housing Commission, Hancock also participated in the 1932 New York Conference on Unemployment, a blue ribbon meeting of thirty-one economists who proposed a program of emergency public works. Between 1931 and 1945, he spoke to hundreds of social action groups and lectured at more than fifty colleges and universities, North and South, black and white, including Columbia and Princeton. When he delivered "The Color Challenge," his much heralded keynote speech before the 1939 Baptist World Alliance in Atlanta, he had become one of the most outstanding black spokesmen in the South. During World War II, he coordinated and directed the historic Durham Conference of Southern black leaders, resulting in the establishment of the Southern Regional Council. The Richmond *Times-Dispatch* named Hancock to the Virginia Honor Roll in 1944. Ten years later, at seventy, he was still active in ten community, four fraternal, and twelve professional organizations. After the *Brown* vs. *Topeka Board of Education* decision in 1954, he preached, travelled, and deplored the South's resistance to desegregation; he was dwarfed, nevertheless, by younger and more militant blacks. Belonging to a disappearing generation of older "race men," he epitomized the values of an earlier leadership which made mass protest possible. Virginia Union and Colgate Universities conferred honorary doctorates upon him in 1962 and 1969. He died in July 1970.[32]

Although his pronouncements overlapped, there were four organizing themes in Hancock's ideology: namely, efforts to analyze the race problem scientifically, words to inspire blacks to look beyond their circumscribed plight, schemes to promote black self-help and solidarity, and steps to improve interracial relations.

He defined race in social rather than genetic terms. "The color question is a social problem and, as such, is not essentially different from any other social problem," he stated; "and by reason of this fact, it responds to the same processes of adjustment or maladjustment." Wearing the mantle of learning, he based his views on "the calm, deliberate and dispassionate consideration presupposed in the scientific approach to... race relations." The study of the Negro and his interaction with whites, he believed, should be an integral part of black education. Otherwise, young blacks could not successfully meet the challenge presented by the white world. In a spirit combining the academic contributions of W. E. B. DuBois and the practical wisdom of Booker T. Washington, he taught Virginia Union students that "races vie in a fierce struggle for existence." Discrimination against the Negro not only denied him opportunity and "a man's chance" but threatened his "economic survival." Black illiteracy, unemployment, and poverty were its products, and so were high rates of crime and illegitimacy. As he put it, "Negroes are too often the victims of an iniquitous system and the system, not they are the blame." His lectures were filled with statements about "the ghastly spectre of mob violence" and "the many lynchings in the South." He said that the "black exodus," partly a reaction to disfranchisement and impoverishment, foreshadowed a more uniform distribution of the black population. "The problem will be scattered throughout the country," he suggested, "and a scattering of the problem is a phase of the solution." Notwithstanding the lure of the city, he thought better health, land-ownership, and family life in rural areas outweighed the submarginal existence of most urban blacks. He popularized these ideas under the caption of "Back to the Farm." Since white labor unions excluded blacks, he argued that blacks should either become scabs or organize their own unions.

When the demand that white administrators and professors be replaced by competent blacks swept black colleges in the 1920's, Hancock dissented. "Whites might be rejected because they are incapable or unsympathetic or condescending, but not because they are white." A color argument, he feared, would boomerang on the Negro. While he did not openly attack segregation, he insisted that Union students "reject the notion of racial inferiority." He analyzed West African art, ethics and politics in 1923, and found "no sanction in history or archaeology" for the thesis that blacks were a people without a culture or a past. In a 1926 statistical survey of commercial advertising and crime, he pointed out that when the masses cannot earn money to buy the goods widely advertised, they become desperate and form "a dangerous segment in society." Subsequent studies of black welfare, urbanization, and labor prompted him to conclude that an inferior economic status underlay most black social problems, including poor health, early death, dilapidated housing, and dependency. Throughout the 1930's he warned that racial competition and conflict in the cities—heightened by depression, automation, and unionization—dimmed black prospects for regular employment, higher wages, increased education, and technical advancement. He maintained that the Negro lived in "economic captivity," confined to domestic and unskilled jobs. In all, though his critics claimed he was more the propagandist than the scientist, Hancock proved himself a forceful contributor to what DuBois called "the collection of a basic body of fact concerning the social condition of American Negroes, endeavoring to reduce that condition to exact measurement whenever or wherever occasion permitted."[33]

Hancock drew a shocking portrait of blacks, finding them disunited, poor, weak, and discontented, causing contemporaries to dub him as the "Gloomy Dean." "What the race needs is . . . general improvement among the Negro masses," he said. "Not only is the Negro hard pressed in his battle for social recognition but he is sorely pressed in his battle for bread." On another side, he seemed more the confident counselor than the pessimistic analyst. Never without hope for a brighter tomorrow or the faith that empirical truth would inevitably destroy race prejudice and fear, he urged black people to look beyond the blocked horizon. "If the Negro could survive nearly three hundred years of wretched slavery and live to become a citizen in the land of his enslavement, greater things are still possible," he contended, noting that time and democracy were on the black man's side. "Common sense would dictate . . . the impossibility of keeping the Negro quiet with a sub-citizen status when all history and all education are built around full citizenship and the ideologies thereof." He called for psychic, if not physical, resistance to oppression. "Struggle is the law of life and the emblem of progress is not a palm branch but a tomahawk," he declared to Hampton graduates in 1929, challenging them to think in ultimate terms. "The Negro finds himself forced to fight and must fight with his hands tied behind him." In Hancock's view, no institution could better sustain blacks than their church. "The Negro church is of such vital importance that nothing the race has set afoot can survive without the support of the Negro church," he testified on one occasion. For it buttressed blacks in "organizing for self-help and mutual protection and in working out their own salvation." While he asserted that Christianity held "survival value" for the race, he spoke out against both excessive formalism and emotionalism in black religious life. "The Negro needs a social gospel," he said, offering his own version from the pulpit and press. "All around us are numberless opportunities to help, to encourage, to inspire, to enthuse, to contend and to conquer," he cried in a typical Moore Street sermon. "When we consider how far behind the Negro is running in the race of life ... our service is the chiefest aim of living." In one column he hammered out his teachings in moving cadence: "Vote consciousness, dollar consciousness, land consciousness, job consciousness, and character consciousness constitute the ideals of the Negro salvation. To cast an intelligent ballot, to make the dollar do double duty, to own some land, and to be somebody is our only way out."[34]

But inspiration alone could not uplift the Negro. "Minority groups must predicate their survival on strategy even as majorities predicate theirs on strength," he said. One part of his program included pressuring government to safeguard Negro rights. The black vote, petitions, press, and interracial conferences served as means to that end. The results were consistently negative, however, mainly because blacks were not "a powerful political and economic interest group that the government could not afford to ignore."[35] Frustration over this problem caused Hancock to vacillate on the New Deal. Normally an independent, he actively campaigned for "Roosevelt and relief" in 1932. He applauded the Civilian Conservation Corps for accepting some 2,000 Virginia blacks by 1934, the Homestead Project in Newport News, the National Youth Administration scholarships for Negro Youth, the Public Works Administration construction sites in Norfolk, Hampton and Richmond, the Works Progress Administration and the benign friendship Eleanor Roosevelt displayed toward blacks.[36] He openly criticized segregation, the denial of Agricultural Adjustment Administration benefits to black farmers and wage laborers, and the National Recovery Act minimum pay scales which were either unenforced or resulted in thousands of black dismissals. Alarmed that blacks in the lower brackets of labor, including domestics, were refused social security, he joined the militant Joint Committee on National Recovery, composed of more than twenty Negro organizations, which met at Howard University in May 1935. He reported in a paper before the body that blacks had been given some relief but were not receiving jobs in proportion to their numbers and needs. He ended on a critical note: "Relief can never be a desirable substitute for economic opportunity." The political race baiting of Southern Democrats and the unwillingness of Franklin Delano Roosevelt and liberal elements in the South to back the anti-lynching bill of 1935 quenched his New Deal spirit. Although he rejected Communism because it did not attack the color line and was essentially atheistic, he created a furor in 1936, shortly after the three-day meeting of the National Negro Congress in Richmond, when he announced to a white congregation: "You white people have been offering the Negro for a long time Christianity without his rights; now there come movements offering him rights without any Christianity. Which do you think he is going to take?" Because the Roosevelt Reconstruction had overlooked the Negro, he stated in 1939: "Unemployment is still the No. 1 Negro Problem."[37]

The most fundamental part of the Hancock program consisted of the Double-Duty-Dollar and self-help. In short, he emphasized a network of concepts revolving around thrift, industry, respectability, self-dependence and solidarity which seemed to have a particular relevance in the Hoover-Roosevelt drought. "The Negro must rely more and more upon himself for his own employment," he told a massive black audience at Durham's Tidewater Fair in 1933. "We have little except our labor with which to trade in the open markets. . . . If the demands for our labor are decreasing —and they are—we must stimulate that demand or create markets of our own." When a Negro buys from the Negro grocer, Hancock suggested, "he not only gets a loaf of bread but helps to make a place of employment for some aspiring Negro. His dollar does double duty." In turn, the Negro grocer might patronize other Negro professionals. "The question," he continued, "is whether the Negro who possesses this dollar shall return it immediately to the white man or will he let other Negroes use it." Although he coined the Double-Duty-Dollar phrase in the early 1920's, it related in purpose to the "Jobs for Negroes," "Don't Buy Where You Can't Work," "Buy Black" campaigns of the 1930's, all efforts to promote racial uplift through economic solidarity or what DuBois called in 1934, a group economy.[38] Certain scholars have pointed out that the doctrine of black support for black enterprises could be used opportunistically by entrepreneurs who were more interested in advancing themselves than the exploited masses,[39] but Hancock framed his scheme in terms of improving the economic standing of the black community as a whole. Responding to columnist George Schuyler of the Pittsburgh *Courier* and sociologist Ira Reid, two of his critics, he said that while Negro business at the time could not create enough jobs to wipe out unemployment "self-help . . . is the only logical course for the Negro," a move in the right direction "using the little-by-little method." As for the charge that the Double-Duty-Dollar ideal perpetuated the segregation which he professed to detest, Hancock replied: "Racially speaking, we oppose segregation, but economically speaking it forms the basis of our professional and business life. There is nothing at present to indicate that there is the slightest change in this bi-racial attitude." His pragmatic approach to this problem was the crux of his ideology. Full citizenship and self-sufficiency were not necessarily incompatible, only different avenues to Negro equality. More a pluralist than a nationalist-separatist, he wanted the doors to black participation in society fully opened and simultaneously crusaded for black self-development along social, economic, political, and cultural lines. If he hailed the New Deal and later gave it low marks on the test of race, castigated lynching and the white primary, or pushed for the equalization of teacher salaries in Virginia and the South, he also called out to the Negro in eloquent redundancy: hold your job; save your money; live within your means; protect your health; educate your children; respect your race; support your church; cast your vote; buy black; and get some land.[40]

Hancock's advocacy of interracial cooperation, including his denunciations of prejudice, disclosed an irrefutable reality. Blacks could not build a viable group economy or achieve first-class citizenship without white tolerance. It was his hope, therefore, that progressive black and white leaders, working jointly and within their own communities, would resolve race conflict, create an enlightened public opinion, and foster ethnic understanding. The church, the Torrance School of Race Relations at Virginia Union, and the Interracial Commission were only organizational means to those ends. Using appeals to conscience, Hancock vindicated the black man's cause. White Christianity, in his view, had to annul its marriage with racism. "There is in fact nothing to set the church apart as a leader in attacking the evils of the present social order," he stated in 1928. "Either Christianity must crush prejudice, or it will itself be crushed." Like-minded a decade later, he told the Baptist World Alliance: "White prejudice is a threat against the integrity of organized religion and the church. . . . This world must be brotherized or it will be brutalized. The church must accept this challenge or seal its own damnation." If brotherhood in the teachings of Christ provided the theological rationale of his message to white churchmen, the need for a moratorium on hate, discrimination, and mob violence backed his pleas to others. In 1935, he stated, "The greatest trouble with the South today is not its unyielding traditions but the lack of men and women with sufficient moral courage to take the first step." "Paternalism will not reach the seat of the interracial troubles in the South and nation; nothing short of fraternalism will do it." He recognized most whites' unwillingness to enter into fraternal partnership with blacks, however, submitting that few did not harbor "the superiority complex for which the average Southern Negro has contempt." Yet, he expressed admiration for the minority of whites who attempted to "implement their often carefully concealed notions of fairness and justice." These liberals, he said, "afford an invaluable liaison between the Negrophobes and the Negroes that saves the situation from threats of total loss."[41]

Although amalgamation and segregation were the Achilles' heel of

this tenuous black-liberal alliance, Hancock spoke out frankly on both
issues. "The Negro is not asking, begging, nor praying for amalgamation,"
he noted angrily in a column for the Richmond *News-Leader*. "What the
Negro wants is not the hand of the white man's daughter in marriage,
but a man's chance and simple justice." At Princeton University in 1934,
he said that even if circumstances permitted intermarriage, the Negro
would still preserve his racial integrity. "A people with an ideal and with
pride does not want to mix considerably with other groups," he stated.
Addressing a Randolph-Macon College audience in 1938, he warned:
"Segregation means death to the Negro race. It is a form of elimination
that must be terminated if the Negro is to survive." That he seldom
said when or how segregation should be eradicated brought him scorn
from some members of the Black community. "Just because the Southern
Negro may be somewhat restrained in his deliverance is no proof that
he lacks manhood," Hancock said. "The only reason any Negro ever lived
in the South and departed alive was due to his ability to compromise."
But he remained bold. "If being white consists so largely in trying to
humiliate and subjugate the non-white world . . . then being white has
become a dangerous, deadly, diabolical thing," he declared to a dismayed
Richmond Ministerial Alliance in 1939. The same year, reflecting his own
frustration over the failure of the NAACP to gain support for the Costigan
anti-lynching bill, the New Deal racial debacle, and the outbreak of
World War II, he exploded: "Negroes who are segregated and relegated
and aggravated and exploited and subjugated and dominated and repudiated are expected to have more crime. . . . To make it appear that Negroes
without a chance can equal whites with a chance is bologna!"[42] Taken as
a whole, such pronouncements indicate that Hancock pursued more than
paternalistic amity between the races or the guilt-ridden sympathies of
white liberals. Rather, they document his deep involvement in the un-
glamorous business of trying to change racial attitudes, the *sine qua non*
of social justice.

Pulled between the fight for democracy abroad and the chains of his
race at home, Hancock set the stage for the wartime departure in
Southern interracial cooperation. In 1941, he wrote an article condemning
"the all-too-frequent riotous outbreaks here and there about the country."
In February 1942, Hancock met with Jessie D. Ames, field secretary of
the Southern Interracial Commission, at the Richmond Colored YMCA,
where they agreed to coordinate separate conferences on race relations,
draft proposals, and jointly implement them. Hancock, editor P. B. Young
of the *Journal and Guide*, historian Luther P. Jackson of Virginia State
College, and a few others caucused at Virginia Union on June 30, 1942.
They decided to convene the Negro meeting in Durham and restrict
attendance to Southern blacks, fearing that otherwise their statement might
be dismissed "as just a petition of Northern agitators." Of the seventy-five

leaders invited, fifty-seven showed up at North Carolina College, October 20, 1942, Charles S. Johnson, Benjamin E. Mays, Horace Mann Bond, C. C. Spaulding, and Charlotte Hawkins Brown among them.[43] They named Young permanent chairman, Jackson secretary-treasurer, and Hancock director. Thirty-four were educators; the remaining twenty-three were ministers, editors, civic workers, businessmen, and labor officials. At least twenty-two were members of the Interracial Commission, and their presence in Durham might well have been a black mandate for a new organization. "We need not cringe or crawl, tremble or truckle, or even tip-toe," Hancock assured them. "We are proposing to set forth ... just what the Negro wants and is expecting of the post war South and nation." The conference report, released to the press in December of 1942, "opposed ... the principle and practice of compulsory segregation" in low-key but forcefully outlined black employment, welfare, education, and civil rights grievances.[44]

On April 8, 1943, one hundred and thirteen white Southerners, headed by influential liberals such as Howard Odum, Virginius Dabney and Ralph McGill, gathered in Atlanta. While pledging their "sincere good will and desire to cooperate," they reaffirmed their faith in the separate but equal doctrine. Hancock, calling privately on Dabney afterwards, complained that the whites should have rejected segregation in principle even if they were constrained to accept it in practice. Just how far apart the two groups really were became clearer in the June 16, 1943 Richmond Collaboration Conference which Hancock almost foiled by insisting that the meeting be held under open seating arrangements. Nearly sixty people attended that uncertain conclave at Grace Covenant Church, thirty-three of them black. In a keynote speech, Hancock said that Southern black leadership "can be strengthened or strangled." He said the white South "must not table every motion for Negro advancement," and he warned of "the grave danger in going too slow." M. Ashby Jones of Atlanta then took the floor and "rebuked him for going too far." Feelings ran high on both sides, and the gathering fell into verbal conflict. Only the timely intervention by Odum prevented a black walkout. The purpose of the Southern Regional Council which the two groups formed, as stated in the charter of January 1, 1944, was "to achieve through research and action programs the ideals and practices of equal opportunity."[45]

Critics immediately plunged the Council into turmoil, claiming that it wanted to do a new job with an old ideology. Lillian Smith and J. Saunders Redding scored its failure to repudiate Jim Crow and questioned its sectional approach to a national problem. Some participants resigned in disgust, but Hancock remained with the Council, pressing for "a more aggressive attitude." In 1948, he wrote, "I believe that we could go much farther and much faster without the great calamity the white leadership seems to fear so terribly." Hancock welcomed the "Civil Rights Revolution" of the fifties and sixties, viewing it in 1968, as "the most constructive departure in race relations since the emancipation of the Negro."[46]

"For over a half century, long before the civil rights breakthroughs of the sixties," stated the *Journal and Guide,* "Dr. Hancock and a handful of courageous colleagues ... braved economic reprisals, personal threats and all sorts of evil handicaps in the battle against racial discrimination." Partly because they were primarily local figures, Gordon B. Hancock, P. B. Young, Luther P. Jackson, Charles S. Johnson, Benjamin E. Mays, Horace Mann Bond, and others did not enjoy national popularity. Little is said of them in black histories and race relations studies, except that they issued the Durham Manifesto in 1942. A cadre of intellectuals and professionals, they emerged in the twenties and struggled in the thirties and forties. Collectively, they were the most important black spokesmen in the South between the death of Booker T. Washington and the rise of Martin Luther King, Jr. Hancock is significant not only for his individual contributions but because he is a microcosm of that group. Influenced by a tradition of upward striving, he pursued a career which took him to such academic institutions as Benedict, Seneca Institute, Colgate, Harvard, and Virginia Union. Among the hundreds he inspired to excel were Abram L. Harris, Henry A. Bullock, Spottswood W. Robinson III, Samuel D. Proctor, and T. Arnold Hill.[47] An early black sociologist, his perspectives on black welfare, education, migration, urbanization, labor, unemployment, and ethnic relations anticipated the scope of current black social research. Moore Street Church, Richmond Memorial Hospital, the Community Chest, and the local Urban League remain monuments to his indefatigable ministry and civic service. By insisting that the church wage war against prejudice and work for racial up-lift, he spaded valuable ground for the seeds of contemporary black theology. The Double-Duty-Dollar philosophy, which Hancock popularized in the Negro press, became a rallying cry for black economic solidarity in the three decades after World War I. A dynamic speaker, he preached black self-help and interracial cooperation. His ambiguity on segregation reveals the limitations imposed upon black leadership in the South where the practice was pervasive and allies to fight it so few. He used moral suasion although the prerequisite for change was political power—an essential denied Southern blacks in his day. A co-founder of Southern Regional Council, he helped to engineer its transition from interracial cooperation within the biracial framework to integration. It is today the leading organization working for desegregation and peaceful social change in the South. Neither an accommodator nor a radical, Hancock was a tough moderate during a generation when race pride and indomitable will enabled blacks to survive.

Notes

1. The character, functions, and problems of black leadership are best conceptualized in two memoranda by Ralph J. Bunche: "The Programs, Ideologies, Tactics, and Achievements of Negro Betterment and Interracial Organizations," 743 pp. (June, 1940), and "A Brief and Tentative Analysis of Negro Leadership," 216 pp. (September, 1940), microfilm, Carnegie-Myrdal Study of the Negro in America, Duke University Library, Durham, North Carolina. Philosophies are cogently analyzed by Oliver C. Cox, "Leadership Among Negroes in the United States," in Alvin W. Gouldner, ed., *Studies in Leadership* (New York: Harper and Brothers, 1950), pp. 228–71; and August Meier, *Negro Thought in America 1880–1915* (Ann Arbor: University of Michigan Press, 1963).

2. See especially George B. Tindall, *The Emergence of the New South 1913–1945* (Baton Rouge: Louisiana State University Press, 1967), pp. 143–88. New South, as employed in this article, is inclusive, embracing the post-Reconstruction period, the era of segregation, and the years since World War II.

3. This refers to the overemphasis in Afro-American biography on national types such as Frederick Douglass, Booker T. Washington, W. E. B. DuBois, Mary McLeod Bethune, and, more recently, Martin Luther King, Jr.

4. Local black leadership is discussed in Daniel C. Thompson, *The Negro Leadership Class* (Englewood Cliffs, New Jersey: Prentice-Hall, 1963). Richard Bardolph mentions a good many lesser known leaders, including several from the South, in part three of *The Negro Vanguard* (New York: Vintage Books, 1959), pp. 275–462.

5. The selection of Hancock is based on Raymond Gavins, "Gordon Blaine Hancock: Southern Black Leader in a Time of Crisis, 1920–1954" Unpublished Ph.D. Dissertation, University of Virginia, 1970).

6. G. James Fleming and Christian E. Burckel, ed., *Who's Who in Colored America* (Yonkers-on-Hudson, New York: Christian E. Burckel and Associates, 1950), pp. 236–37. Postal Route Map of South Carolina, U.S. Post Office, September 1, 1944.

7. George B. Tindall, *South Carolina Negroes 1877–1900* (Baton Rouge: Louisiana State University Press, 1952), p. 302.

8. The description of Ninety-Six is derived from Benjamin E. Mays, *Born to Rebel: An Autobiography* (New York: Charles Scribner's Sons, 1971), pp. 1–21.

9. U.S., Bureau of the Census, *Twelfth Census of the United States: 1900. Population*, 1,350.

10. U.S., Bureau of the Census, *Negro Population in the United States 1790–1915* (Washington, D.C.: Government Printing Office, 1918), p. 746.

11. Mays, *Born to Rebel*, pp. 22–34; Tindall, *South Carolina Negroes*, pp. 282–90.

12. Tindall, *South Carolina Negroes*, pp. 233–39.

13. *Ibid.*, pp. 256–59. Tindall reports that five blacks were killed, discounting newspaper accounts whose estimates were usually larger but based on rumor.

14. Quoted in Bardolph, *Negro Vanguard*, p. 171.

15. Autobiographical Reflections, n.d., Gordon Blaine Hancock Papers, Richmond, Virginia. Mrs. Hancock stated, "Gordon always talked about Phoenix and the lynchings. He said Negroes were tied to logs and whipped, and several of them died." Interview, August 16, 1973, Richmond, Virginia.

16. Mays, *Born to Rebel*, p. 1.

17. Autobiographical Reflections, Hancock to Mrs. Francis J. Torrance, July 27, 1934, Hancock Papers.

18. Autobiographical Reflections, Hancock Papers.

19. Tindall, *South Carolina Negroes*, p. 216.

20. Quoted in Bardolph, *Negro Vanguard*, p. 172.

21. Autobiographical Reflections, Hancock Papers. Interview with Mrs. Hancock, August 16, 1973.

22. Autobiographical Reflections, Hancock Papers.

23. *Ibid*. That book by DuBois was *Efforts for Social Betterment among Negro Americans*, Atlanta University Publication no. 14 (Atlanta: Atlanta University Press, 1910).

24. Autobiographical Reflections, Hancock Papers. Interview with Mrs. Hancock, September 23, 1972.

25. See Hancock, "The Challenge to Christianity Today," *Home Mission College Review*, I (March, 1928), 25–29.

26. Interview with Mrs. Hancock, September 23, 1972; Hancock to Judge Orrin Judd, March 13, 1944, Hancock Papers.

27. Miles Mark Fisher, ed., *Virginia Union and Some of Her Achievements* (Richmond: Virginia Union University, 1924), p. 11. Interview with Gordon B. Hancock, March 7, 1969.

28. Bardolph, *Negro Vanguard*, pp. 317–18; Robert E. L. Faris, *Chicago Sociology 1920–1932* (San Francisco: Chandler Publishing Company, 1967), pp. 123–33; Autobiographical Reflections; James Ford to Hancock, November 2, 1939, Hancock Papers.

29. Hancock to John M. Ellison, October 16, 1948, Hancock Papers.

30. Hancock, "Supplementary Facts Pertaining to the Centennial Issue of the Virginia Union Bulletin" (mimeographed), 1966, Hancock Papers; *Annual Catalog, 1919–1920* (Richmond: Virginia Union University, 1920); Mary Irwin, ed., *American Universities and Colleges* (Washington, D.C.: American Council on Education, 1952), p. 977; and Horace Mann Bond, Centennial Address, February 12, 1965, copy in William J. Clark Library, Virginia Union University, Richmond, Virginia.

31. U.S., Bureau of the Census, *Fourteenth Census of the United States: 1920. Population*, III, 1074; U.S., Bureau of the Census, *Seventeenth Census of the United States: 1950. Population*, I, 46; *Richmond City Directory 1921*, pp. 6–8; Walter B. Weare, *Black Business in the New South* (Urbana: University of Illinois Press, 1973), pp. 12–16; and Federal Writers' Program, *The Negro in Virginia* (Hampton: The Hampton Institute, 1940), pp. 335–52.

32. Citation, Colgate University Convocation, September 25, 1969, honoring Hancock with the Doctor of Laws degree; Hancock, "Back to Benedict: An Abbreviated Account of My Stewardship"; Brochure, "The Francis J.

Torrance School of Race Relations in Virginia Union University"; Speech text, "The Color Challenge," 1939, Hancock Papers. Negro Welfare Survey Committee, *The Negro in Richmond, Virginia* (Richmond: Richmond Council of Social Agencies, 1929).

33. Hancock, "Race Relations in the United States: A Summary," in Rayford W. Logan, ed., *What the Negro Wants* (Chapel Hill: University of North Carolina Press, 1944), pp. 217–47; Syllabi, Economics 204, Sociology 1, and Race Relations; *Union-Hartshorn Bulletin*, XXIII (January, 1923), 5–14, Hancock Papers; Hancock, "Three Elements of African Culture," *Journal of Negro History*, VIII (July, 1923), 284–300; "The Commercial Advertisement and Social Pathology," *Social Forces*, IV (June, 1926), 812–19; "When the Manna Faileth," *Opportunity*, VI (May, 1928), 133–35; and W. E. B. DuBois, "My Evolving Program of Negro Freedom" in Logan, ed., *What the Negro Wants*, p. 46.

34. Clippings, *Shepherd's Voice*, January, 1926; *St. Luke Herald*, February 2, 1929; *Journal and Guide*, May 13, 1939; and January 6, 1945, Hancock Papers. Hancock, "Race Relations," in Logan, ed., *What the Negro Wants*, pp. 220–23; and "Thinking in Ultimate Terms," *Southern Workman*, LVIII (July, 1929), 291–97.

35. Raymond Wolters, *Negroes and the Great Depression* (Westport, Connecticut: Greenwood Publishing Corporation, 1970), p. 384.

36. Clippings, *Journal and Guide*, October 22, 1932; November 12, 1932; November 19, 1932; March 21–April 11, 1934; and March 9, 1935, Hancock Papers.

37. *Journal and Guide*, April 15, 1935; November 14, 1936; and August 26, 1939; Federal Writers' Program, *Negro in Virginia*, p. 261.

38. Hancock, "The Changing Status of Negro Labor," *Southern Workman*, LX (August, 1931), 351–60; "The Double Duty Dollar," an Address by Gordon B. Hancock on Educational Day, Tidewater Fair, Durham, North Carolina, October 20, 1933, in Rare Virginia Pamphlets, University of Virginia Library, Charlottesville, Virginia. "The Double Duty Dollar in Principle and Practice," Hancock Papers; and John H. Bracey, Jr., "Black Nationalism Since Garvey," in Nathan Huggins, Martin Kilson, and Daniel Fox, eds., *Key Issues in the Afro-American Experience*, II (New York: Harcourt Brace Jovanovich, 1971), pp. 262–66.

39. See August Meier, "Negro Class Structure and Ideology in the Age of Booker T. Washington," *Phylon*, XXIII (Fall, 1962), 258–66, for an overview of the problem; and Abram L. Harris, *The Negro as Capitalist* (Philadelphia: American Academy of Political and Social Science, 1936), pp. 177–83, as an example.

40. *Journal and Guide*, June 10, 1933; February 22, 1936; October 16, 1937; and January 13, 1945.

41. Hancock, "The Challenge to Christianity Today," p. 29; "Orthodox Christianity: Does it handicap Negro progress?" *The Messenger*, July 5, 1927; Speech texts, "The Color Challenge," 1939; "Two Master Plans of Rebuilding the Social Order," 1935, Hancock Papers. Hancock, "Race Relations," in Logan, ed., *What the Negro Wants*, p. 226.

42. Clippings, *News-Leader*, n.d.; *Journal and Guide*, June 3, 1939; January 30, 1943; and March 17, 1945, Hancock Papers.

43. The article was published in December, 1941, and reprinted by CIC as "Interracial Hypertension" in July, 1942; Hancock, "Writing a 'new Charter' of Southern Race Relations," *New South*, XIX (January, 1964), 18–21; Ames to Hancock, March 12, 1942; Young to Hancock, May 26, 1942; July 5, 1942, and clipping, *Journal and Guide*, May 23, 1942, Hancock Papers. Johnson was director of Social Sciences, Fisk University; Mays, president, Morehouse College; Bond, president, Fort Valley State College; Spaulding, president, North Carolina Mutual Life Insurance Company; and Brown, president, Palmer Memorial Institute, Sedalia, North Carolina.

44. Official Program, "Southern Conference on Race Relations, Durham, North Carolina, October 20, 1942" (mimeographed); "Statement of Purpose"; and Conference Report, unpublished version, in Hancock papers.

45. "Statement of Conference of White Southerners on Race Relations," Atlanta, Georgia, April 8, 1943; "Resolutions of the Collaboration Committee, Richmond, Virginia, June 16, 1943; copy of "The South's Greatest Vision," keynote address delivered by Hancock, June 16, 1943, in Hancock Papers; Odum to Jackson Davis, June 19, 1943. Howard W. Odum Papers, University of North Carolina Library, Chapel Hill, North Carolina.

46. Lillian Smith, "Addressed to White Liberals," *New Republic*, CXI (September 18, 1944), 331–32; J. Saunders Redding, "Southern Defensive I," *Common Ground*, IV (Spring, 1944), 36–42; Guy B. Johnson, "Southern Offensive" (Summer, 1944), 89–90; J. E. Blanton to Hancock, June 7, 1944; Hancock to Blanton, June 14, 1944; Hancock to Lillian Smith, June 24, 1944; Hancock to Dabney, November 15, 1948; and Hancock to the author, May 26, 1968, Hancock Papers.

47. *Journal and Guide*, August 8, 1970. Abram L. Harris became an economist; Bullock, an educator and the first black professor at the University of Texas; Robinson, civil rights lawyer and now a Federal Judge; Proctor, college president and now Distinguished Professor at Rutgers University; and Hill, one of the prime architects of the development of the National Urban League.

George Edmund Haynes:
Advocate for Interracial Cooperation[1]

Samuel K. Roberts

A biographical statement is in a very real sense a social document, for each man's life is a testament to the verve and social dynamics of his age. So it was with George Edmund Haynes. Sociologist, Congregational churchman, and civil rights activist, Haynes throughout most of his eighty years charted an illustrative career in the field of race relations in America during the often turbulent first half of the twentieth century.

This essay will delineate the major influences in the formation of his social theory and vision for racial harmony in America. First, his ideological perspective with regard to what he perceived to be the proper way to achieve race improvement will be discussed. The point of departure for this discussion will be his early education at Fisk University. Secondly, his introduction to the science of sociology occasioned by studies at Yale University under the eminent American sociologist, William Graham Sumner, and the subsequent application of sociological insights to proposed solutions of racial conflicts will be discussed. Related to the sociological influence in Haynes' profile was also his preoccupation with the economic problems brought about by inequities between the races. Specifically, his enrolling in the New York School of Philanthropy in 1908 immersed him in the urban economic problems encountered by blacks in America's largest city. Economic problems would continue to intrigue Haynes during the First World War, culminating in his mobilizing the Commission on Race Relations to meet some of the more chronic conditions among blacks during the Great Depression.

Next, this essay will present a profile of Haynes, the churchman. His theological orientation will be traced as it evolved from his divinity studies at Yale Divinity School during the spring of 1905 and subsequent work with the Colored Men's Division of the Y.M.C.A.

Finally, the social ethic of George Haynes will be discussed. This ethic came to be a blend of informed social observation, some principles of social psychology, and the notion of brotherhood inherent in the Christian faith.

1

George Edmund Haynes was born on May 11, 1880, in Pine Bluff, Arkansas. Indications are that the elder Haynes supported his family as a laborer; thus the family was somewhat typical of the black families found in post-Reconstruction Arkansas. Before young George had reached the age of ten, the father had passed on, leaving the care of the boy and his younger sister, Byrdie, in the hands of his mother. Haynes was blessed in that his mother felt that the care of her children included what to her seemed the key to breaking the imposed shackles on blacks: education. With a zeal characteristic of so many of the first generation freedmen, she endured what must have been considerable personal privations in order that the two children receive schooling. Such difficulties were caused in part by the discriminatory patterns in the state educational program. In Arkansas the protagonists of erstwhile Confederate rule very soon after the war went to great efforts to make sure that the social conditions between the races as nearly as possible approximated ante-bellum days. One way of insuring that this be accomplished was to discourage as much as possible education among the blacks. Thus in 1867 Arkansas passed a law which established a system of free education for whites only. If black males could pay a special tax of $1.25 per year, they could have their own "public schools."[2] It was thus under such burdens that George Haynes was sent to the little one-room "public" school for black boys and girls to learn his three R's. After the educational opportunities in Pine Bluff had been exhausted, the family moved to Hot Springs, where facilities were somewhat greater.[3] Yet even the educational opportunities in Hot Springs were not sufficient to quench the thirst for learning in young Haynes. In 1895 at the age of fifteen he left Hot Springs and enrolled in the Agricultural and Mining College at Normal, Alabama. After finishing the basic courses offered there he realized the limitations of the school and returned to Arkansas to prepare to enter Fisk University's High School as a prelude to college. Coincidentally with the burning passion for learning being fired in these years, young Haynes was introduced to the pulse of urban life. In the summer of 1893 he had a chance to go to the World's Columbian Exhibition in Chicago. Many years later Haynes wrote that this excursion "opened my eyes to big city life."[4] His peregrinations about the city and the grounds of the Fair no doubt introduced him to the more vocal, articulate and civic-minded blacks of the urban North. Thus the "exposure to the animated social life of Chicago stirred up dreams and ambitions in the mind of the young Haynes."[5]

Upon entering the Fisk University High School in 1896, Haynes immediately plunged into studies designed to prepare him for the college regimen. Fortunately, his penchant for liberal arts found a compatible milieu in the school's curriculum. Fisk, like many of the higher educational institutions founded by Northern religious philanthropy, held the position that one of the ways of dispelling popular beliefs about the inherent intellectual weaknesses of blacks would be to encourage its students to master the culture of American society.[6] The university's students, viewed as future leaders of their race, were expected then to learn the subtleties of Western culture and to develop an appreciation for the cultured life. Hence, the emphasis in the curriculum was on classical studies and the humanities, as opposed to industrial arts. Thus Haynes took three years of Latin and Greek literature and grammar, rhetoric, and elocution. In the field of history his courses wandered over the development in the affairs of Russia, England and America. Rounding off this preparatory program were courses in the natural sciences as well as plane and solid geometry.

Entering the university proper in 1899, Haynes continued his studies in the classics, especially courses in Roman and Greek civilization, mainly to acquire "an understanding of the art, literature, history, and geography of the two ... great cultures which left so much to us."[7]

This immersion in the study of classical cultures provided in part for him an early answer to the problem of cultural or race progress of a people. In a valedictory message to his fellow graduates of Fisk in 1903 he declared that "every race or nation that has gained a place of high virtue and power has done so through the sacrifice of its best and brightest men and women."[8] Furthermore, "... this class of the race must sacrifice itself to uplift the rest of the race."

There was stirring in the young Haynes what may be called an elitist outlook, but an elitism which assumed the burdens of laboring for the less lettered and less gifted of the race. Station acquired through educational striving demanded self-sacrificing service. This posture would come to full height when in addressing graduates of Florida A. & M. College in 1936 he admonished his young listeners to avoid one danger of learning—estrangement of the masses. Characteristically summoning scientific findings to back up assertions, he cited the latest discoveries in educational psychology to warrant his claim that "probably for the first time in history we see solid scientific foundations for our dreams of democracy. The masses may be educated."[9] Citing his own experience in speaking in the Public Forum Series,[10] he assured the graduates of the possibility of "lifting the intellectual vision and firing the aspirations of the common man and woman whenever we bring to them the values of truth, of beauty, and of goodness in such forms that they may understand, enjoy and use."[11] His hearers were finally warned that "the test will be how well you identify yourselves with the common people and how you induce them to follow you and the higher things of living and life which you have learned."[12]

Though he qualified for inclusion in DuBois' "talented tenth," Haynes still considered himself tied to the destiny of the farmers whose lives were linked to the soil of Arkansas and other states in the South. This ambivalence would later prove to be an advantage, enabling him to move with some degree of ease equally among the sharecroppers whom he exhorted to "own a piece of land" and also among the more refined circles of academia.

But there is another dimension in which this early elitism was certainly couched. This dimension was his personal alignment to various currents within the stream of black leadership at the turn of the century. As a college student during this period he could not have escaped the awareness of the ideological cleavage among the leaders of the race over the exact route toward "uplifting the race." The Tuskegee School, whose posture was exemplified by its President, Booker T. Washington, held that the best way to ameliorate the status of Afro-Americans was to develop a class of artisans, petty bourgeois, and farmers whose corporate economic worth would be indispensable to American society. Civil rights and arguments over social equality were for this school ethereal issues whose essential substance would in the final analysis be worked out in the marketplace. DuBois and other like-minded intellectuals, for the most part in the North, challenged Washington's formula and insisted that civil rights and social equality be figured in the resolution of the "race problem."[13] Being basically mild-mannered in temperament and having an aversion to precipitous behavior, George Haynes' own views with regard to "uplifting the race" attitudes toward whites lay somewhere in the middle between those two camps.[14] In the wake of the "bloody summer" of 1919 Haynes contributed an article to the magazine *The Public* in which he sought to analyze the various attitudes which obtained in the national black community with respect to the pace of achieving civil rights. The typology he formed categorized three groups: the left wing, center, and the right. Of the left wing, being the "most recent in origin and having very radical and revolutionary tendencies, there is considerable evidence that it is being definitely developed by the radical and revolutionary white socialists."[15] In what was most probably an attempt to cast aspersions on this segment of the black leadership by raising the unpopular association with Soviet Marxism, he indulged a bit of hearsay by venturing to say that "there is belief in some quarters that out and out Bolshevist propaganda is being attempted among them."[16] Of Radicalism, especially the variety which smacked of either foreign influence or that in which blacks were allegedly used to further the designs of radical whites, Haynes would be a life-long foe. While he could concede that "revolution, and war are understandable human responses to hatred, brutality, exploitation and outrage," he insisted that "if there is one thing that history shows clearly, it is that no progress has been built upon hatred and violence, revolution and war."[17]

Yet there were times when Haynes uttered statements that in the context of the given forum could be considered genuinely radical at the time. Frequently he was forced to assume such a position when statements by those whom he regarded as presumptuous whites forced him to take a counterstance. For example, when the Home Missions Council published its report for 1921 it was obliged to include as a part of it Haynes' rejoinder to some of the statements written by the chairman of the council, George R. Hovey. The report of the Council took a dim view of any radical movements among blacks. It especially castigated the Garvey movement, terming it a "largely inflated and unstable affair." Segments of the black press, notably papers such as the *Messenger*, the Chicago *Whip*, and the *Defender*, exhibited in the view of the Council "at times a bitterness somewhat out of harmony with . . . the general trend of Negro journalism."[18] Hovey, speaking for the Council, went on to declare that:

> The Negro does not look to Russia for his ideals. He looks to the best of essential Americanism and patiently dares to pin his faith to the principles of the preamble and amendments of the Constitution.[19]

Hovey concluded that the churches should take note of these developments within the black community for the reason that "it [the black radicalism] forces upon the Protestant church the necessity of freshly realizing the places of sane religious inspiration and right spiritual leadership."

One can almost feel Haynes bristling upon hearing this analysis of the current black radicalism. In his section of the report, entitled simply, "The Negro," he lays the basis for his rejoinder by stating that "there is a growing inner race consciousness among Negroes of what it means to be free."[20] That consciousness is being expressed in two ways: "first, in a new sense of their own worth and their own dignity as a people." Secondly, "there is a change in attitude toward white people." Although he carefully qualified what was to follow in his statement by indicating that he would "try to speak, not my view, but what I can sense is going on in the minds of Negroes of all grades of intelligence in all parts of the country," Haynes obviously shared somewhat in this new consciousness. Of this mood and of blacks in general, he said:

> They are coming more and more to ask and more and more to feel that they are not going to take the word or the appearance of things so far as the attitude of white people is towards them.

> In other words, there is more of a tendency to be suspicious of white people and demand proof that individuals among them are different from the ordinary individuals with whom Negroes come in contact from time to time.[21]

Similarly, while far from being a Garveyite, he defended the Garvey movement as the embodiment of black suspicion of whites as well as the resurgence of race consciousness and pride:

> One of the main points of this movement is to challenge the sincerity of white people as they come in contact with colored, to question the attitude of great numbers of the white world....[22]

Yet Haynes could in no way be considered a thorough radical. Generally he tended to discourage violent disruption of the fabric of society, preferring more reserved but firm means of social change.

Haynes, sympathetic in some respects with the posture of what he called the right wing of black leadership, could not give it unreserved approval either:

> ...the right wing believes in full justice, manhood rights and full American opportunities for the Negro American but still clings to the methods of conciliation, the preaching of cooperation, with a policy opposed to militant methods.[23]

The flagrant lynching of blacks and attacks on their personal property "are arousing the majority of the Negro people to a race consciousness" which will not augur well for the right wing faction. In fact, this faction's days are numbered for "whether the conciliatory school wills it or not, the logic of the hour appears to the majority of Negroes to favor the militant methods and policies of the 'center.'"[24] Furthermore, "...the time for heated debate over the so-called 'race problem' is passed. The time for action to make democracy safe for every American, black and white, has arrived."[25]

It was in the center apparently that Haynes wished to place himself, although much of his later program and philosophy with the Commission on Race Relations would reflect a "right wing" position as he had defined it in 1919. However, his analysis of the "center's" position retained enough breadth so that he could feel comfortable counted among its number. The "center" for Haynes, was not merely a conveniently constructed ideological half-way house; rather it was in the center that he could display a fierce independence of both extremes. A bit of this temperament was revealed thus:

> What we have said and continue to say to the Communistic radical on the one hand and the Fascistic baron on the other is that revolution, mobs or violence never settled any human problems and will not settle them.[26]

Moreover, in the "center" Haynes saw himself as one of the "spiritual descendants of the aggressive abolitionists" who are "believers in the best in American institutions and governmnet."[27] They are "hotly and actively agitating against all forms of color discrimination and injustices and are committed to a program of uncompromising protest."[28]

There were times, however, when Haynes' "protest" did have unfortunate hues of compromise. In 1924 when the Federal Council journeyed to Atlanta for its Quadrennial Meetings the degree to which he would go to protest an issue was put to a test. John J. Eagan, one of the Southerners who prevailed upon the Council to come South that year, assured everyone that if some of the sessions were held in First Presbyterian Church where he was an elder, no segregation in seating facilities would be practiced. As Eagan had considerable influence in the church, his assurances were made good and the delegates were not segregated by race. However, for its public service on the Sunday of that week, it was obvious that First Church would not accommodate the expected crowd. The City Auditorium was thus chosen, where by city ordinance blacks and whites would have to be segregated. The desire to expose as many Atlantans as possible to the Council's worship service outweighed any sensibilities against segregation. But all was not calm. Local black civic and religious leaders boycotted the service rather than sit in the balcony. Yet Haynes attended, no doubt with the conviction that more good would come in the long run from the Council through patient work within its system than through attacks against it.[29]

There was thus in George Haynes an ideological profile which reflected the inner ambivalence of a man responding to the difficult problem of charting the best course for black America in the early decades of the twentieth century. That tension never was fully resolved. He was not a protestor but viewed himself as an architect whose task was to build lasting structures for interracial harmony. Though generally admired and respected by acquaintances and associates for his work in the field of race relations over the years, most reminiscences of the man reveal the impression that he "took mainly a mediating position"[30] between the races rather than a more vigorous crusade characteristic of some more radical leaders of his day. However, a life and career with the longevity and breadth as that of Haynes' was bound to reveal some inner tensions and open contradictions. But all in all, it may be said that "he led an active, important, and fruitful life ... to bring to the churches the insights of the social sciences,"[31] and to impress upon them their responsibilities in the area of race relations in America.

2

George Haynes became in his lifetime a respected sociologist in American academic circles. This "conversion" to the discipline of sociology, as he was to later term his experience, took place when he entered Yale University in the fall of 1903 to work toward a Master's degree.

Yale University in the opening years of the new century, while not blatantly hostile to blacks, did not take it upon itself to openly welcome them there either. During the period from 1900–1904 only nine blacks graduated from Yale, while in one year alone, 1904, the total student body of the university was 3,000. Often upon arriving at Yale black students met a pervasive suspicion as to their chances of success, no doubt reflecting a general condescension toward the viability of Southern black schools and also a feeling that blacks were intellectually inferior anyway. As his memoirs indicate, Haynes' admission to Yale was under such a cloud of skepticism relative to his own chances for success. He writes that when he showed interest in registering for a course in Experimental Psychology, the professor told him, "You graduates from these southern Negro colleges have not had adequate training to meet the strenuous requirements of graduate courses at Yale.[32] Young Haynes replied that he only wanted the opportunity to study and do the work. Faced with the challenge, he buckled down to his studies. Leaving no time for sports or recreation, he took upon himself a regimen of "studying seven days a week."[33] During this year he took courses in Genetic Psychology, Experimental Psychology, Political Philosophy, Philosophy, and a course in Ethics and Epistemology. The close regimen was rewarded, for at the close of the year he was called in by the Dean and informed that the handicap with which he entered Yale had been overcome and that he would be awarded the Master of Arts degree at the June commencement, 1904.

During this academic year the area of work which held the most fascination for Haynes was a course on the relatively young science, sociology, or "societology" as it was termed by the professor, the eminent sociologist William Graham Sumner. It was Sumner who actually chanted the incantations during Haynes' "conversion" to the discipline.[34] As a graduate student in a seminar composed of undergraduates and graduate students, Haynes received special attention from Sumner. After becoming very close to Albert G. Keller,[35] an assistant to Sumner, Haynes was brought into an even closer contact with Sumner, "who occasionally invited us to his home where he talked more intimately about his methods."[36] It was during these fireside discussions in the Sumner home that Haynes learned much of sociology. Although there was much in Sumner's thought that was inimical to Haynes,[37] the pupil credited his teacher with having taught him the basic principles of social life "that I have used and tested through many years of teaching, research and experiment in social welfare."[38] Haynes remembered five principles which he learned from Sumner. These five principles had to do with, first, the perpetuation and survival of the populations of societies; secondly, the self-maintenance of the society in all of its physical and mental activities for securing food, clothing, and shelter; third, the controls that a society institutes through its machinery of political operations in the family, the clan, the tribe and the nation; fourth, the acculturation process of society which transmits its tradition, wisdom and philosophy from one generation to another; and finally, the religious notions, beliefs, superstitions and ghost-fears which vibrate in a society.[39] Helpful also for Haynes was Sumner's concepts of *folkways* and *mores*. By folkways Haynes understood Sumner to mean "the habits and processes of individual beliefs" while mores served as "sanctions for the rightness or wrongness of the folkways."[40] Another important concept Haynes learned from Sumner was the "method of dispassionate analysis, classification, comparison and inductive conclusions in the field of human affairs and in the study of mankind."[41] Haynes remembered vividly how Sumner "taught us to subject any notions to rigorous tests of the facts," and how he "blasted the appeals to the supernatural or to authority or reliance on hunches and intuition and deductive logic." One final idea which he was to employ extensively in his later work was attributed to Sumner. This was the notion that pleasurable and unpleasurable experiences attended societal groups in their activities, out of which grew folkways "which arise from their efforts to avoid the unpleasurable and to secure the pleasurable in satisfying their needs." Haynes remembered Sumner emphasizing:

> ... these actions to avoid unpleasant experience and to obtain pleasurable experience in one group or generation become habitual and regulated and take on the nature of a social force for other groups and succeeding generations.[42]

Haynes did very good work under Sumner at Yale, so much so that five years after leaving the school his old teacher could write an unqualified recommendation for him:

> Yale University
> 4/28/09
> I am very glad to testify that Mr. Geo. E. Haynes distinguished himself while a student of Sociology under me, by the zeal and success with which he did the work. I shall be glad to answer any inquiries about him.
>
> W. G. Sumner[43]

The purpose of this recommendation was to aid his former pupil in entering what was then known as the New York School of Philanthropy in the fall of 1909. Haynes brought his theoretical understanding of the dynamics of sociology to an institution which itself was seeking its own peculiar corporate style in coping with the social problems of New York City. The approach of the school owed its existence in part to a theme which had been sounded a little over a decade before by a professor of social work, Albert O. Wright, at the National Conference of Charities and Correction in 1896. At this conference Wright spoke on the subject, "The New Philanthropy." Wright characterized this "New Philanthropy" as one whose aim was to improve the very conditions which older forms of charities had sought to ameliorate. It seeks to bring theoretical understanding of society and practical dimensions into a closer relationship:

> . . . on the philosophical side it studies causes as well as individuals. On the practical side it tries to improve conditions. . . . Philanthropy is thus raised to the rank of a science and the practical and theoretical are yoked together.[44]

While enrolled in the school, Haynes was supported financially by the Bureau of Social Research.[45] This Bureau had a two-fold purpose: to train investigators for the ever widening field of social activity and to study current social problems. One of those problems which early caught the eye of Haynes was the phenomenon of heavy migration of blacks into the city. Haynes' research project brought him into close contact with the hard realities of the economic plight of blacks in the city. His study was so impressive that he was encouraged by Dr. Samuel McCune Lindsay, the director of the school, to expand it. This expanded study became his doctoral dissertation which he submitted to the faculty of Columbia University in 1912, becoming in this year the first black man to take the Ph.D. degree at Columbia. His dissertation was later bound and issued as a published book. Entitled "The Negro At Work in New York City," the study revealed that blacks were drawn to the city by the same forces that attracted whites. Haynes' main thesis in this work was stated thus:

> . . . the Negro, along with the white population, is coming to the city to stay; . . . the problems which grow out of his maladjustment to the new urban environment are solvable by methods similar to those that help other elements of the population.[46]

Haynes marshalled an array of census figures which showed that quite to the contrary of public opinion, black migration to the big cities was just as vigorous as that among whites. The reasons for this migration were both negative and positive. Among the negative factors was the fact that blacks were divorced from the land in the South, a condition occasioned by several factors: soil erosion, anti-Negro terrorism, the inequities of the sharecrop practice, and the plague of the boll weevil. Viewed a bit more positively, the cities, those of the South and later on those of the North, held for the southern black a hope for a different kind of life, even one of plenty and success.[47] Haynes uncovered other factors which accounted for the migratory wave of blacks to the cities: legislation which tended to favor urban living as opposed to rural residence through the provision of more schools and recreational facilities. The presence of relatives in cities also was a big drawing factor; a general restlessness on the part of many of the southern Negro peasantry was also revealed through interviews Haynes conducted with blacks in New York City. Haynes' work thus broadened the geographical base of what was still termed the "Negro problem." He offered conclusive proof that it was not merely confined to the South but by now was being an urban and Northern issue. The "problem" as he saw it had thus essentially economic perimeters: blacks discriminately treated in the South sought a better life in the North, thus creating strains on the available jobs in these urban centers. It is this dialectic that so intrigued Haynes that he felt it to be "fundamental to the relations of whites and Negroes in America."[48]

While he was engaged in the research at the School of Philanthropy, he was hired by the Committee for Improving the Industrial Condition of Negroes. This Committee had been formed in 1903 when William H. Baldwin, president of the Long Island Railroad, called a meeting of interested white and black social activists to discuss the economic plight of blacks in New York City. At the meeting were W. E. B. DuBois; Felix Adler, of the Ethical Culture Society; William Brooks, pastor of St. Mark's Methodist Church in Harlem; George Foster Peabody; and Dr. William Bulkley, the first black principal in the consolidated New York City school system.[49] Bulkley organized classes for adults as well as children on various subjects of practical worth: hygiene, nutrition. He also established an evening school for commercial and vocational training for young adults. Haynes' work with the CIICN included interviewing graduates from Bulkley's school and assisting in their placement in actual jobs. Naturally in the course of securing these positions, he came into close contact with the employers, mainly white, with whom he had to deal to negotiate slots for black workers. At about this time, Haynes gained familiarity with another group which was working in the general area of improving economic conditions among blacks in New York City. A Miss Frances H. Keller, observing how many young and inexperienced black girls were lured to the city and then forced into prostitution, resolved to offer these girls some protection. She and a group of friends formed the Inter-Municipal Committee on Household Research which later became the National League for the Protection of Colored Women.[50] At points the leadership of this committee and the CIICN were virtually interchangeable, so close were the social service circles in New York at the time. In this group was Mrs. Ruth Standish Baldwin, widow of William H. Baldwin. Although she and her husband could never come to advocate complete racial equality, her Quaker heritage provided her with a strong sense of social involvement and moral outrage at injustices done to blacks. Soon Haynes began to realize the limitations of the Committee for Improving the Industrial Condition of Negroes. Similarly, Mrs. Baldwin began to have reservations about the efficacy of the League for the Protection of Colored Women. In their mutual anguish over these existing methodologies and programs they organized a meeting on May 19, 1910, at the New York School of Philanthropy, out of which was born the Committee on Urban Conditions Among Negroes. This Committee was the immediate forerunner of what is known today as the National Urban League.[51]

When Haynes was invited to return to his undergraduate alma mater as a professor of sociology in 1911, he carried with him the intense desire to impart to younger men and women of Fisk the principles of social science in hopes of preparing them for service within the community. Thus simultaneous with his teaching duties at the university was his establishment of a training program for Urban League Staffers. The program came to be known as the Bethlehem House Program because of the name of the building in which it was housed. He enjoyed the esteem of his colleagues on the faculty and the students whom he taught in social science courses.

Haynes continued to develop his skills and talents in the social sciences while teaching at Fisk. In 1918 his expertise in the area of economics and labor conditions among blacks was rewarded when he was summoned to Washington to become a special advisor in the United States Department of Labor. The Department of Labor had become increasingly aware of the problem of migration of blacks and its effects on the economic conditions of both the South and the North. In 1916 farmers in the South complained to Department officials that they were losing their labor supply to Northern railroads.[52] When the World War came, the problem for these Southern landholders and farmers was intensified all the more. But there were other sufferers in this drama. Looking back at the problem Haynes analyzed it from the perspective of the black workers in the urban center:

> . . . the Negro workers who had been turned into the plants of the North faced the necessity of performing efficient work in the minimum of time, of adjusting themselves to northern conditions and of becoming fixtures in their particular line of employment or becoming "floaters."[53]

Yet the nation needed desperately the black labor force which economic conditions in the South had displaced. In view of these perplexing questions, the Secretary of Labor, William B. Wilson, decided to create a position of Advisor on Negro Economics to work within his office. The title was to be Director of the Department of Negro Economics. Wilson telegraphed Haynes on April 15, 1918, asking that he come to Washington to confer on the issue of black wage earners.

After securing the approval of the Fisk administration, Haynes accepted Wilson's call to fill the position as Director of Negro Economics. On May 1, 1918, the day Haynes was officially sworn in as director, the Bureau of Negro Economics was officially opened and charged with the task of providing advice "to the Secretary of Labor and the Directors and chiefs of the several Bureaus and Divisions of the Department on matters relating to Negro wage earners, and cooperation between Negro wage earners, white employers, and white workers in agriculture and industry."[54] Wilson gave strict instructions that the advice of the Director of Negro Economics was to be secured before any work dealing with blacks was undertaken, and that he (Haynes) be kept advised of the progress of such work so that the Department of Labor might have, at all times, the benefit of his judgment.

The Bureau began its work by outlining three types of activities it would use to deal with the problems. First, it would organize cooperative committees of white and black citizens in the various states and localities where problems between workers across racial lines were most acute. Secondly, it proposed the development of a publicity or educational campaign which hopefully would create good feelings between the races. Finally, it would appoint black staff workers in the states and localities to implement these plans. Haynes and his staff realized the enormous obstacles which would be encountered in implementing such an undertaking. For example, there would be the difficulty of forestalling a strong feeling of suspicion on the part of blacks which grew out of past disappointments in racial and labor matters.[55] At the same time the young Bureau chief and Secretary Wilson realized that feelings of hostility among whites, in the North and South, would possibly be raised. Against both of these potential sources of hostility and detraction, the Bureau posited three "cardinal facts" as guidelines in the task it was undertaking. The first "fact" was the realization that the two races were "thrown together in their daily work, and that the majority of the employers and a large number of the employees having relations with Negro employees were whites." The second "fact" recognized that while "the problems are local in character . . . the people in these communities need the vision of national policies, plans and standards to apply to their local situations." Finally, "any plan or program should be based upon the desire and need of cooperation between white employers and representatives of Negro wage earners, and wherever possible, white workers."[56]

With these understandings in the area of policy and purpose laid down, Haynes and his Bureau launched a whirlwind tour of cities where problems among black workers demanded the most pressing attention. Informal interviews and local conferences were held. These local meetings and discussions of issues spawned a desire to meet over conference tables on a state-wide level in various places. Thus on June 19, 1918, the governor of North Carolina, T. W. Bickett, called the first bi-racial meeting in that state to consider labor problems between blacks and whites. Haynes, who had worked closely with state authorities in setting up the Conference, came and outlined the plans of the Department of Labor which hoped for "increasing morale and efficiency of Negro workers."[57] At the close of the meeting Governor Bickett appointed a temporary committee which drafted a constitution providing for a State Negro Workers' Advisory Committee and for the organization of local, county, and city committees. This plan, later modified, served as a model for other states which in the next six months were set up. Another southern state soon followed the lead of North Carolina. On July 16, 1918, Florida's governor, Sidney Cotts, called a bi-racial meeting at Jacksonville. Similarly from this conference there came forth a State Negro Worker's Advisory Committee which was composed of whites and blacks under the auspices of the State Council of National Defense and the U.S. Employment Service. Four days before this meeting in Jacksonville, the Southern Sociological Congress met at Gulfport, Mississippi, and sponsored a bi-racial meeting to which Dr. Haynes was invited. As a result of the meeting, to which 200 whites and 75 blacks had come, another state-wide organization similar to the North Carolina plan was instituted.[58]

At the end of the first six months of the existence of the Bureau of Negro Economics, under Haynes' direction, Negro Workers' Advisory Committees in states, counties, and cities numbered almost 225 in 11 states. The total membership numbered more than 1,000 appointees.

The Bureau continued its work throughout the remainder of 1918 but by the time the new federal budget was being drawn up for fiscal year 1919–1920, signs of trouble began to appear on the horizon. The federal budget passed in May of 1919 revealed that some services and expenditures carried by the Labor Department in the war reconstruction effort would be eliminated or seriously curtailed. The appropriations for the U.S. Employment Service had been so severely cut that the State Supervisors of Negro Economics in the eleven states where they were operating would have to be eliminated.[59] The future of the Bureau of Negro Economics appeared even more bleak. Many Congressmen could no longer see any usefulness of the Bureau as the nation sought to restore itself after the Great War. Consequently, the proposed federal budget for the next fiscal year, 1919–1920, revealed that budget items for the Bureau had been eliminated altogether. A somewhat alarmed Haynes appeared before the Senate Finance Committee to argue for the continuance of the funds for the Bureau. He was assured by the then Republican Senator from Ohio, Warren G. Harding, that some of the items would be restored,[60] but the Bureau as it was constituted in the year gone by was to be a thing of the past. Secretary Wilson desired to carry on as much work of the Bureau as possible, asking Haynes to continue his work on a per-diem basis for a few days out of each month. This arrangement continued for the balance of the year.

When Warren G. Harding was inaugurated as the 29th President of the United States on March 4, 1921, Haynes' connection with the Department of Labor was soon to be severed. Quite naturally, Harding brought into office with him a virtual new slate of Cabinet members and heads of various governmental offices. His designation for Secretary of Labor in turn was obliged to appoint a new man as Director of Negro Economics. While the new Secretary was quite sympathetic with Haynes' desire to remain on in the capacity, he explained that his hands were tied politically, that he owed a political debt to the National Republican Committeeman from Kentucky who had his own candidate for the post. Haynes prevailed upon his Senator from New York, James W. Wadsworth, to intervene on his behalf, explaining to the Senator that he did not desire the position purely for personal gain, but because he feared for the fate of the programs he had begun among black wage earners. Wadsworth intervened, but to no avail.[61] Haynes subsequently tendered his resignation as Director of Negro Economics.

It was probably quite fortuitous that Haynes was relieved of his duties within the Labor Department during the summer months of 1919 for he was then free to enter into the service of the cooperative church movement in America, specifically, the work of the Interchurch World Movement. This movement had been launched on December 17, 1918, by a conference of executives of denominational boards. Ralph E. Diffendorfer of the Foreign Missions Board of the Methodist Church was also Secretary of Survey and Program of the Interchurch World Movement. On September 22, 1919, he telegraphed Haynes and invited him to join the staff to help in preparing a study on "all matters affecting the welfare of Negroes in the U.S."[62] Haynes accepted the invitation and became a member of the survey staff, entering into the mainstream of religious and church circles. Here he was asked to use his skill in social science and social research for discerning the peculiar task the Church had before it with regard to black America. He was simultaneously doing some research work for the Home Missions Council.[63] Yet one must go back almost fifteen years while Haynes was still a graduate student at Yale University to discover the first stirrings of the committed churchman he was to become.

After finishing his graduate work at Yale in the spring of 1904 many of Haynes' teachers and friends urged him to enter the Christian ministry as a profession. Notable among these friends was the Rev. E. F. Goin of the Dixwell Avenue Congregational Church of New Haven. Haynes had been affiliated with this church during his student months doing Youth and Sunday School work. But the question of entering the ministry was not as definite in Haynes' mind as it was in Mr. Goin's. Like so many of the young blacks who had been exposed to higher education during this period, he tended to look critically at the life style and demeanor of the typical black clergyman, who very often had not had exposure to serious theological training. It is doubtful whether Haynes believed in the integrity of the "call" as a means for entrance into the ministry. Hence, there was no way to easily resolve the issue because he "did not know enough about religious theory to have background for an independent decision."[64] To acquire the basis to make such a decision Haynes decided to enter Yale Divinity School. He applied for and received a scholarship with the option to take courses in the Graduate School. The first semester of the 1904–1905 school year went very well academically. Financially, he was able to keep fairly above water. However, in February of 1905 misfortune hit the Haynes household back in Hot Springs, Arkansas. A fire raged over a good portion of the city consuming the house where Haynes had spent part of his boyhood. He scraped up enough money to rush to his mother's side only to find her living in a tent with other homeless victims of the fire. She insisted that he return to Yale and finish the academic year, which he did. But Haynes was never to pursue his theological studies again. His younger sister Byrdie was now ready to enter Fisk's preparatory school and would naturally need his financial support. After thinking the matter over, he decided that "it would be wiser for me to drop out of the Graduate School than to have her to give up college."[65] Fortunately he had been offered a position with the Colored Men's Division of the YMCA by William A. Hunton, Senior Secretary of the Division, after he had taken his Master's degree the previous year, but had at that time turned it down in favor of pursuing theological studies. However, the family financial crisis forced him to reconsider this offer and the help he could be to his sister. He decided to accept the position as Field Secretary with the Division. After spending the summer pastoring the little mission Congregational Church at Haverhill, Massachusetts, Haynes reported to the Division headquarters in Atlanta on September 1, 1905.

By the time Haynes joined them, Hunton and his associate, Jesse E. Moreland, had become swamped by what was coming to be an enormous network of YMCA local affiliates. In 1905 there were more than 116 associations with more than 8,000 members divided into two sections, city and student. There were forty-three college associations and seventeen city associations and the field was growing.[66] Haynes was brought to the Division to help strengthen ties between the associations in the field and the Division office in Atlanta, some of the former not having been visited in three years. Thus it was that he took to the railroads, characterized by strictly Jim Crow facilities, and to other uncomfortable conveyances such as buggies and wagons, visiting and exhorting local associations in the principles of the YMCA and helping with organizational problems. In spite of this physical discomfort and other deprivations he encountered, Haynes nevertheless "found evidence of the Holy Spirit in the enlarged vision and greater efficiency of my work and as a beginner in Christ's work for the world."[67] Of the Holy Spirit, he "could not have hoped for better companionship and guidance."[68]

It was thus during these years with the YMCA that the content of Haynes' religious and theological views began to take shape, as well as his understanding of the possibilities that lay within the Christian faith for establishing racial harmony. Hunton and Moreland exerted a strong influence on the young Haynes. He wrote of them in his *Memoirs*:

> My first year of association with these two sincerely deeply religious men was a great blessing to me as a young graduate stepping out into the tangled world of that pre-war period and working along the interracial front.[69]

Yet there would emerge within Haynes' religious sensibilities the desire to *act out* religion rather than have it remain a private, personal regenerative affair. No doubt two factors figured into this emerging posture. First, there is a hint of rebellion within Haynes against the popular notions of religion as it was conceived and practiced among his associates during this period. Secondly, the Social Gospel movement was moving toward the pinnacle of its influence in the American theological scene during the 1910's. Shades of his rebellion may be seen in a letter that he wrote to Dr. Moreland in 1916:

> Let me assure you that the Bible and prayer are still a part of my routine and that my intense interest in the young men and the YMCA grows as the years go by. In frankness, however, I should say that as it goes on, my religious development leads me less toward discussion and more toward a burning desire to act and do something to make the community and people with whom I live happier and better. In a word, the doing of Christ's will and the bringing of His Kingdom are becoming more and more a practical everyday matter.[70]

Haynes' views on religion and society put him in some respects within the Social Gospel movement of American Protestantism, especially that part of the movement which saw the close relationship between national directions and the implications for the ethical mandates inherent in the Gospel. The conceptual tool for such a union of ideals was of course the Kingdom of God. Having its roots within the character of American history, within the Social Gospel, the "hope of the Kingdom had blended with the democratic ideal in the foundation of the republic and its later equalitarian aspirations."[71] Haynes echoed such a hope, though specifically in the area of measuring racial harmony with democratic sensibilities of America. "The Christian ethic must change this rampant racial egotism for the sake of saving civilization and for the sake of the Kingdom of God."[72] Before the Federal Council of Churches he declared in 1920 that "the acid test of our national Christianity and our professed sympathy with other darker races was in our treatment of the Negro at home."[73] Indeed, taking seriously the love ethic inherent in the Christian faith is "sound social and democratic principle as well as a religious ideal."[74]

Both of these influences produced in Haynes a religious posture which put him squarely within the liberal tradition of American Protestantism. His academic training in the principles of social science produced in him an affinity to the tentativeness and openness of the liberal spirit. His theological studies and introduction to biblical criticisms made him comfortable in the liberal posture. Finally, his classical training in the great cultures of the world, the observations incurred in social research led him to embrace a further characteristic of the liberal spirit: the essential unity of mankind.[75] In a reply to the *African Methodist Episcopal Zion Quarterly Review*'s request to submit a series of articles on three remedies within the Christian faith to racial problems, he listed at the outset what he saw as six principles of the Christian faith:

1. The infinite value of the individual person as a child of God, the heavenly Father of all men.

2. The consequent unity and oneness of mankind.

3. The use of persuasion, understanding and good will as the instrument for adjusting all conflicts of interests in relations of persons, groups, and nations.

4. The condemnation of violence and force as a futile instrument for adjusting human relations.

5. The ideal of justice as an evaluation and adjustment of the relations of one member of society to all other members.

6. Love as the dynamic power of moving mankind toward the Great Society visualized in the Realm of God.[76]

In addition to this understanding of the Christian faith, Haynes also saw some definite possibilities in religion per se for solving social ills. He interpreted the phenomenon of religion from a psychological point of view.[77] From the general observation that religion deals with the emotional side of life he ventured other aspects of the phenomenon. It was basically an "experience which involves the integration of personality with itself and the relations between personalities."[78] Divine-human contacts were interpreted by Haynes as "the harmonizing of human personality with the Divine or Ultimate Personality." Religion, therefore, involves the relationship between the microcosm (the totality of individual experience) and the macrocosm (the totality of all experience).

The problem for Haynes, however, was the role of organized religion in "adjusting" social ills, specifically racial conflicts. His overall view of religion was consequently quite functional. Religion, especially in its organized forms, was most internally viable when it accomplished something in the area of social relations. "Christian religion should remove old maladjustments," repeated Haynes on many occasions. The prejudices one race felt for another, the proclivities toward discrimination, the resulting political and economic inequities, all existed because of social maladjustment caused by the perpetuation of noxious values. The corrective for this situation is religion: "The effectiveness of religion as a functioning force in interracial adjustment depends upon the embodiment in the religious culture of the desirable mores which makes for the welfare of all the personalities involved."[79]

George E. Haynes' social ethic and method for social change in the area of race relations grew out of two factors: 1) his understanding of the dynamics in the social history of the races in America, and 2) the enormous potential within the Christian faith, understood in social psychological terms, for bringing the races together. From these two factors came the principal element in Haynes' social ethic: the ideal of interracial cooperation.

George Haynes was an astute historian of the relations between whites and blacks in America. In reflecting on this history he was influenced by the idea of "consciousness formation through environment" as one of the crucial factors which could explain the relations between the whites and blacks of America in the periods after the institution of slavery. From the economic advantages of using slave labor, and the socially depraved condition of blacks during and after slavery came a reinforcement of the belief in the inherent inferiority of blacks and the supposed superiority of whites.[80]

> ... the doctrine of superiority-inferiority is a belief rationalized out of conditions and experience to justify the whole existing serf system from plantation to factory, from courtroom to legislature, from school and colleges to churches and community life.[81]

What emerges is an American caste system which locks racial groups in set social patterns based on race and reinforced by past experiences. This caste system is anchored by the superior attitude of whites and to a certain extent by the assumed inferior attitude held by some blacks.

> These powerful attitudes of persons are largely produced by the behavior patterns of the family and the community, which have grown up through generations. From childhood these patterns mold

the emotions and the thinking of individuals of both the white majority and colored minority racial groups. The attitudes and behaviors of persons of all racial groups are so set by such conditioning that few can lift themselves by their bootstraps out of the slough of their prejudices and unfriendly practices.[82]

It is for this reason that Haynes was convinced that both races are hurt by the attendant "ills of a caste society"[83] and are bound by the customs and inferior-superior attitudes. This segregated society is a divisive one, separating and isolating people "in their thinking, in their living and working conditions, and in community relations." Segregation is also harmful in the areas of mental and physical health as well as causing such inequities as discrimination in employment and educational opportunity, in housing and health facilities, and in the exercises of civic rights and privileges.

There are various phenomena which have catalytic functions for the development of these interracial experiences, which fundamentally are unpleasant thus making members of opposite races equally repugnant.

Such painful experiences are of greater frequency when and where migrating populations are making new contacts or where economic or other community conditions are rapidly changing and where the economic, educational, political or other status of impinging racial groups are being relatively altered.[84]

Such migratory patterns were some of the major causes of the Chicago Riot of 1919. Rumor and imagined events may also perpetuate unpleasant experiences between the races. Posterity may also have the dubious benefit of these experiences through communications media: film, radio broadcasts, novels. In this category may fall, for example, the controversial film, D. W. Griffith's "The Birth of a Nation."

It follows then, at least according to Haynes' view, that interracial harmony may be brought about if *positive* interracial experiences are produced between individuals or between groups.

Individual and group contacts also give pleasant emotional experiences that are the bases for friendly attitudes and cooperative habits or patterns or action. . . .[85]

In this regard, Haynes relied to a great extent on the outcome of cases-in-point in which racial intolerance had been oevrcome because of pleasant contacts across racial lines. Most examples used by Haynes displayed an incredibly optimistic view of the capacity of whites to change their prejudices,[86] underlying what might be judged to be a naive estimation of the racial barriers erected by prejudice. Yet he was aware of the limitations of the person-to-person approach in achieving interracial harmony. "The person-to-person contact necessarily must affect enough individuals within a group to change the group folkways and mores."[87] Thus in the final analysis his hopes for entire racial groups shedding their past emotional and prejudicial entanglements was still based on individual regeneration. However, Haynes was convinced that much could be achieved, largely because of his belief that corporate attitudes are but the amalgam of individual attitudes. Thus he could favorably cite the "pleasurable" contact between the races at an art exhibition of Negro artistic works as an example of group attitudes changing as a result of individual changes:

> It is not possible to estimate the total emotional experiences of these thousands of white people who viewed these works of art. However, it can be estimated positively from the expressions of hundreds of them that the experience was pleasurable and that friendly cooperative reactions followed.[88]

The church has a special role in solving the interracial problem. First, Haynes envisioned the work of the church to be generally "to promote the ideal of brotherhood in race relations . . . on the basis of understanding and brotherly cooperation."[89] Furthermore, it is within the walls of the church that the institution can be a "light unto the nations." In contrast to the community pattern of segregation, "church programs should be based upon integration of groups."[90] The church is charged with the task of proposing alternative values to the ones which have fostered the segregated society. It has an educational task; indeed the church is charged to promote a pedagogy of morals in the community:

> Organized Christianity deals with certain values in relations between personalities which have developed out of past experience of groups and through the intuitive vision of wise and good leaders. In the growth of the attitudes and habits of action, standards of value for both attitudes and action develop. Christianity has sought to preserve those that foster highest human welfare and seeks to relate personalities to them in their group relationships.[91]

The church, having understood the values it must uphold, must:

> . . . hammer home the Christian values just opposite to the racial superiority myth. . . . The churches have the tremendous task of pressing this view and thus changing the attitudes of millions of their members from hostility, suspicion and exploitation toward the members of other racial groups to Christian attitudes.[92]

At the same time, the churches also can help in ameliorating the conditions of oppressed races whose debased status further feeds the myths of superiority held by other races in the society. Haynes presented a practical program for the churches in his study, "Negro New-Comers to

Detroit" in 1918. Noting that the economic conditions of blacks in Detroit were critical because of the great migrations of unskilled labor from the South and the scarcity of jobs, Haynes posed the question to the churches:

> ... how may the Christian church through its members and organizations so extend its service to these people as to help them make the necessary adjustments not only in such concrete needs as employment, housing, recreation, health, but also in obtaining a firm hold upon those ethical and religious ideals which will make them an asset and not a liability to the community into which they have come?[93]

He went on to propose that the churches of Detroit initiate night school sessions in vocational education, tutorials in English, lectures on work habits, and referral services for jobs.

Given the psychological matrix and understanding of the formation of values which were antithetical to racial harmony and the churches' responsibility in the area of teaching alternative values, the doctrine of cooperation was bound to emerge as the central element in the social philosophy of George E. Haynes.

Interracial cooperation and its attendant agenda of cross-racial education, mutual aid projects, and the like may be first seen in the life of Haynes when he started work with the YMCA in 1905. A short time after joining Hunton and Moreland in the work there, the three of them were approached by a young white secretary of the International Commission of the "Y," W. D. Weatherford, for consultation on what might be done on the issue of race relations in the South.

Haynes joined the three men in discussion on the issue over a period of several months. After overcoming some initial trepidation ("he [Weatherford] seemed rather afraid of us"),[94] they arrived at the consensus that "a study of Negro life prepared for Southern white college students would be the best approach."[95]

During the decade before he came to the Federal Council of Churches other contacts with persons involved on the interracial front contributed to his belief in the soundness of interracial cooperation as the best solution to the race problem. A review of Haynes' correspondence during the 1910's is quite illuminating. He must have been encouraged by the news from a Miss E. E. McClintock of the University of Chicago, who in reporting on her work in the South could say, "In my home town of Columbia, South Carolina, we have been able to get good results by cooperation."[96] The fact that there were evidently organizations in the nation whose expressed purpose was to foster interracial cooperation also was significant in the formation of his own views. One such organization was the Cooperative Educational Council of Springfield, Ohio. Its founder and secretary, Z. W. Mitchell, carried on a long and extensive correspondence with

Haynes while the latter was a professor of sociology at Fisk University. Mitchell, after reading one of Haynes' monographs on black migration[97] from the South to Northern urban centers and the attendant problems of that phenomenon, wrote Haynes suggesting that they share methods each had used to combat the problem.[98] The stated purpose of the Cooperative Educational Council was printed on its rather impressive letterhead. Its purpose was "to improve the Living Conditions of the Masses of Colored People; to encourage closer cooperation between the White and Colored Races; and to promote thrift, economy, and enterprise among Afro-Americans.[99]

It is difficult to determine the exact degree to which Haynes was influenced by this organization or other people who like him were intensely interested in interracial cooperation. However, with George Haynes this quite simple formula became the conceptual tool around which his ethical sensibilities as well as his observation in social psychology coalesced. This coalescence can be seen quite clearly as he describes the process of inter-racial cooperation:

> Whenever members of different groups are helped to do something together two things are accomplished: They act cooperatively across racial distances and contact is established under conditions where the experience is pleasant. The emotional effect is beneficial and frequently leads to further contact in group meetings and actions for mutual ends.[100]

But aside from the purely utilitarian aim of interracial cooperation, this act is in and of itself ethically viable. In speaking further of the dynamics which obtain when two racial groups engage in cooperation, Haynes further explained:

> The particular things they do together are of less importance than that they meet and act together.[101]

From the doctrine of cooperation came a method of "adjusting" racial conflicts that Haynes would implement through the mechanism of the Federal Council of Churches' Commission on Race Relations, for which he served as Executive Director from 1922 to 1947. A natural structural element in the doctrine was what he termed the "method of conference" or "trying to think through and deal peacefully with serious situations by palaver instead of fighting."[102] Haynes saw "survey and study of the facts as a process that should go hand in glove with con-ference and discussion," but he added that "one of the drawbacks of interracial cooperation is that even when men meet and confer they are not willing to face facts."[103] Thus there was always in his method a need to *document* the nature and scope of discrimination or interracial conflict.

Finally, he hoped that action would ensue, based on cognizance of the facts, and on the mutual reinforcement of positive values among racial groups. The type of action Haynes envisioned would range from protest against discriminatory practices to joining efforts in economic empowerment for Afro-Americans.

Haynes would in the years of his work with the Commission on Race Relations incur many challenges to the soundness of his theory and program, within and without the Federal Council. He and the Commission would quietly initiate programs to encourage black sharecroppers to own a piece of land as well as help nurture the artistic sensibilities of the race. His voice would be heard among those who sought justice for the Scottsboro Boys as well as those who called for calm and amelioration of social ills during the fierce urban disturbances in Detroit and Harlem in the 1940's. Through it all, he remained undaunted in his belief that within the riches of the Christian faith lay solutions to interracial problems.

On December 19, 1946, the Federal Council paid an official and warm tribute to the man who had guided its Commission on Race Relations for a quarter of a century. After receiving a Hamilton watch as a token, Haynes was asked to say a few words to his old friends and colleagues. In so doing, he stated again his hope that the churches would do their part in the great task of bringing to America an era of true interracial harmony and justice:

> We see in the future a most challenging unfinished task for the churches to implement their decisions in the various lines in which they have set goals; in renouncing the pattern of segregation; in a continual crusade for a lynchless land; in a new effort for legislation against racial discrimination in employment and all lines of human endeavor; and in general increased service to local churches and communities to meet their own racial situation and put into action remedies that will assert the sufficiency of Christianity as a solution.

It is perhaps the relentless struggle of George Edmund Haynes and his Commission on Race Relations to achieve true interracial justice that many will come to view as a worthy legacy to the American Church and its people.

Notes

1. In this essay the writer proposes to present only the events and developments in the life of George Haynes which were crucial in the formation of his social ethic and his understanding of the relations and tensions between the races. A more detailed study is found in a recent dissertation by Dr. Daniel J. Perlman entitled "Stirring the White Conscience: The

Life of George Edmund Haynes" (unpublished dissertation, New York University, 1972). Another dissertation by Nancy Joan Weiss, "Not Alms But Opportunity: A History of the National Urban League" (Cambridge: Harvard University Press, 1968), also presents some biographical material on Haynes, who was one of the founders of the Urban League.

2. John Hope Franklin, *Reconstruction After the Civil War* (Chicago: University of Chicago Press, 1961), p. 46.

3. George E. Haynes, *Memoirs*, Section II, p. 6. Before his death in 1960 Haynes had begun to respond to the often posed request that he write the memoirs of his life. Upon his death, however, the task was only about three quarters completed. The typewritten manuscript was consulted throughout 1972–1973 at his Mt. Vernon residence through the gracious cooperation of his widow, Mrs. Olyve Jeter Haynes. Other material consulted at the Haynes residence in Mt. Vernon will be designated MVF (Mt. Vernon Files).

4. George E. Haynes, *Memoirs*, Section III, p. 5.

5. Daniel J. Perlman, "Stirring the White Conscience: The Life of George Edmund Haynes" (unpublished dissertation, New York University, 1972), p. 2.

6. See H. Paul Douglas, *Christian Reconstruction in the South* (Boston: Pilgrim Press, 1909).

7. George E. Haynes to President George Gates of Fisk University, August 2, 1910, MVF.

8. George E. Haynes, "The Lamp of Sacrifice," *Fisk Herald*, March, 1903, MVF. An earlier Fisk graduate of the class of 1888, W. E. B. DuBois, had sounded a similar note in an essay of 1897 when he called for the establishment of a Negro Academy which would be an intellectual clearing house among blacks comprising "something of the best thought, the most unselfish striving and the highest ideals." From "The Conservation of Races," in *Negro Social and Political Thought, 1850–1920*, ed. Howard Brotz (New York: Basic Books, 1966), p. 490.

9. George E. Haynes, "What Price College Education," commencement address delivered at Florida A. & M. College, May 28, 1936. Reprinted in *Florida A. & M. Quarterly Journal* (April–July, 1936), MVF.

10. The Public Forum series was an adult education effort sponsored by national civic groups during the period 1932–1935. Haynes served as a volunteer lecturer on the social sciences.

11. George E. Haynes, "What Price College Education."

12. *Ibid.*

13. While Washington was doubtlessly throughout his career an accommodationist, a revisionist view of his career notes how he surreptitiously financed challenges to the grandfather clause, denial of jury service, Jim Crow conveyances, and peonage. See Louis R. Harlan, "Booker T. Washington in Biographical Perspective," *American Historical Review*, 75 (October, 1970), 1581–1599. See also Harlan's fuller work on Washington, *Booker T. Washington: The Making of a Black Leader, 1856–1901* (New York: Oxford University Press, 1972).

14. For discussions of the battles between the followers of Washington and the anti-Bookerites, see August Meier, *Negro Thought in America, 1880–*

1915 (Ann Arbor: University of Michigan Press, 1963), pp. 171–89 and *passim*; see also Lerone Bennett, *Confrontation in Black and White* (Chicago: Johnson Publishing, 1965), pp. 95–113.

15. George E. Haynes, "What Negroes Think of Race Riots," *The Public*, August 9, 1919.

16. Although he never explicitly identified these radical groups, Haynes probably had in mind the African Blood Brotherhood and the Star Order of Ethiopia, commonly known as the Abyssinians. The Brotherhood was started in 1919 by a Jamaican from St. Kitts named Cyril V. Briggs. Briggs was a brilliant writer and polemicist. Landing a job as a reporter for the *Amsterdam News* in 1912, he became editor in less than two years, only to be sacked by the newspaper publisher in 1917 for writing an editorial critical of Woodrow Wilson's failure to include native American blacks in his scheme for self-determination of national peoples.

The Brotherhood viewed itself as a community defense group, ferreting out and acting upon charges of police brutality and other alleged mistreatments of blacks by whites in black communities. The Brotherhood claimed a major role in defending the black community during the Tulsa Riots of 1921 when marauding whites attempted to roam at will throughout Tulsa's Northside. The Brotherhood's newspaper, *Crusader,* subsequently brandished the slogan "Remember Tulsa" in a fund-raising issue as a reminder of the group's tactics.

Briggs was enamored with the Bolshevik Revolution and its vision of solving the nationalist problem for races and ethnic groups in Russia. Many other leaders of the Brotherhood were attracted to Russian Communism. Briggs tried to link up with Garvey's movement but the latter would have nothing to do with the Brotherhood because of its closeness with white Radicals. By the mid-1920's the Brotherhood had just about ceased to exist.

The Star Order of Ethiopia and Ethiopian Missionaries to Abyssinians was formed in the spring of 1919 mostly by former Garveyites. The group came into the public light in 1920 through a bizarre incident in Chicago involving its leader, Grover Cleveland Redding. Redding, claiming to be from Ethiopia, but in reality a native of Georgia, mounted a white stallion and led a recruitment parade through sections of Chicago culminating on the black Southside. There he produced an American flag, poured gasoline on it and set it ablaze. For a spectacular finish, he riddled the charred remains of the flag with a few bullets. Two white policemen tried to intervene but retreated to seek reinforcement when threatend by Redding's followers. A subsequent confrontation occurred in which two policemen were killed and six were wounded. Redding also had a grandiose plan of sending an armed train into the South to liberate certain areas. However, after the Chicago incident he was tried for murder and finally executed. See Theodore G. Vincent, *Black Power and the Garvey Movement* (Berkeley: The Ramparts Press, 1967).

17. George E. Haynes, "What Price College Education."

18. Home Missions Council and Council of Women for Home Missions, *Annual Report* (New York, 1921), p. 6, MVF. The *Messenger* was begun in 1917 by A. Phillip Randolph and Chandler Owen and reflected their socialist philosophy. The *Whip* and *Defender* have been commonly considered organs produced by the black bourgeois element. Somewhat constricted by indirect censorship because of white advertisers, these papers tended to

present the more popular or spectacular news in the black community. Yet the *Whip* showed an admirable degree of bravery on most social issues, given its dependence on white advertisers. Its endorsement of Sufi Himid's economic boycotts against the discriminatory practices of some firms resulted in decreased revenues from advertisers so much that it had to cease publication in 1932.

19. *Ibid.*, p. 6.

20. *Ibid.*, p. 13.

21. *Ibid.*, p. 14

22. *Ibid.* Haynes misread Garvey's motives and position. For Garvey, suspicion of whites was not a real issue. He was convinced of white America's intent to preserve the nation as a "white man's country" in which there would be no room for black assertion. Garvey's perception of the race problem in America was decidedly dualistic; the white and black races were naturally inimical to each other. Thus it seemed to Garvey that the white man was most sincere when he admitted his desire that the black quit America for another land. In this regard Garvey and the Ku Klux Klan, the Anglo Saxon Clubs which were prominent in the 1920's came to be strange bedfellows indeed. See *Philosophy and Opinions of Marcus Garvey*, compiled by Amy Jacques Garvey (New York: Augustus M. Kelley, 1967), originally published by Amy Jacques Garvey in 1923.

23. George E. Haynes, "What Negroes Think of Race Riots."

24. *Ibid.*

25. *Ibid.*

26. George E. Haynes, "What Price College Education."

27. George E. Haynes, "What Negroes Think of Race Riots."

28. *Ibid.* The "center" would specifically include groups such as the NAACP and the National Urban League. A case also could be made that A. Phillip Randolph would fit into this category notwithstanding his socialist orientation. The fact was that Randolph's constituency was composed of either activist, establishment types or the men for whom he was advocate, the railway porters who never exhibited the impatience typical of the left-wing radicals. Toward the middle 1920's Randolph had ceased affiliation with the Industrial Workers of the World, the Russian Bolsheviks and the American Communists. He and Haynes denounced radical exploitation of the Scottsboro Case in the 1930's. Both denounced the direction of the National Negro Congress in the latter 1930's with Randolph finally resigning as president in 1940.

29. Interview with Samuel McCrea Cavert, July 23, 1973.

30. The Rev. William Lloyd Imes to Samuel K. Roberts, January 26, 1973. A similar impression was recalled by Dorothy I. Height in an interview on December 27, 1972.

31. The Rev. William Lloyd Imes to Samuel K. Roberts, January 26, 1973.

32. George E. Haynes, *Memoirs*, Section V, p. 7, MVF.

33. *Ibid.*

34. George E. Haynes, "What Sociology is About," speech delivered in 1911 before the Fisk University student body, MVF.

35. Keller later pursued a brilliant teaching career at Yale in the course of

which he remained a disciple, expositor and editor of Sumner's thought and writings.

36. George E. Haynes, *Memoirs*, Section V, p. 9a, MVF.

37. Sumner fiercely upheld a belief in laissez-faire, as it could be applied to relations between classes in society; cf. *What Social Classes Owe to Each Other* (New York: Harper and Bros., 1903). Sumner understood society to be an "organism" which resisted artificially induced modifications. Thus social reforms were senseless in his estimation. While he did support public education, Sumner opposed all poor laws, regulations for working hours and conditions, and the activities of labor unions. He also resisted notions of equality between the white and black 'races and opposed suffrage for blacks. When asked if in his estimation Jefferson was thinking about blacks when he declared that "all men are created equal," Sumner replied that Jefferson "was not talking about Negroes," quoted in Thomas F. Gossett, *Race: The History of an Idea in America* (New York: Schocken Books, 1963), p. 154.

38. George E. Haynes, *Memoirs*, Section V, p. 9b, MVF.

39. *Ibid.*

40. *Ibid.* Sumner's exact definition of folkways centered around the notion that they were universal, uniform ways of satisfying needs in cultures; cf. *Folkways* (Boston: Ginn, 1906), pp. 2–3.

41. George E. Haynes, *Memoirs*, Section V, p. 9b, MVF.

42. *Ibid.*, p. 9c.

43. William Graham Sumner, "To Whom It May Concern," photostatic copy, MVF.

44. Albert O. Wright, "The New Philanthropy," in *Proceedings of the National Conference of Charities and Correction* (Boston, 1896), quoted in Elizabeth G. Meier, *A History of the New York School of Social Work* (New York: Columbia University Press, 1954), p. 5.

45. Daniel J. Perlman, *op. cit.*, p. 55.

46. George E. Haynes, *The Negro At Work in New York City: A Study in Economic Progress* (New York: Columbia University Press, 1912), p. 14.

47. Haynes, *The Negro At Work in New York City*, p. 30.

48. George E. Haynes, *Memoirs*, Section IV, p. 53, MVF.

49. Daniel J. Perlman, *op. cit.*, p. 62.

50. *Ibid.*, p. 56.

51. Daniel J. Perlman, *op. cit.*, pp. 66–67. Although Haynes was one of the early leaders and guiding voices of the League, the increasing rivalry of other officers as well as his physical estrangement from the New York headquarters while teaching at Fisk University eventually brought about an erosion of his influence in Urban League policy matters. By 1917 virtually all official ties between Haynes and the League had been severed.

52. *The Anvil and the Plow: A History of the U.S. Department of Labor* (Washington: Government Printing Office, 1921), p. 31. The immediate precipitous events in the South which occasioned the mass migrations of blacks could be traced to the severe labor depressions of 1914 and 1915 during which wages plummeted to as low as 75¢ per day and less. The boll weevil plagues of 1915 and 1916 aggravated the situation by dis-

couraging anyone who had hopes in cotton production from staying in the South. Floods in the summer of 1915 left many blacks homeless and sent many looking for homes elsewhere in the nation. See John Hope Franklin, *From Slavery to Freedom* (Chicago: University of Chicago Press, 1947), p. 472.

53. George E. Haynes, *The Negro At Work During the World War and During Reconstruction: Statistics, Problems and Policies Relating to the Greater Inclusion of Negro Wage Earners in American Industry and Agriculture* (Washington: Government Printing Office, 1921), p. 11.

54. *Ibid.*, p. 12.

55. Suspicions were justified. Attitudes of organized labor toward black workers from the 1880's on had ranged from mildly hostile to rank exploitive. It is true that Samuel Gompers, head of the American Federation of Labor, did take to task some unions (e.g., the National Association of Machinists, the Brotherhood of Locomotive Firemen) who excluded blacks, but he did so because of their *written constitutional* proscriptions. Furthermore, his campaign to include blacks in the A.F. of L. was based more on enlightened self-interest than anything else, fearing that lest they be included unscrupulous employers would use them as strikebreakers and pawns against labor. Gompers progressively began to entertain more and more racist explanations of the conditions of black workers, assigning their lack of skills to generic limitations, their working for lower wages to innate happiness. By 1902 the A.F. of L. abandoned even the formality of equal status in that organization for black workers. See Bernard Mandel, "Samuel Gompers and the Negro Workers, 1886–1914," *The Journal of Negro History*, XL (1955), pp. 34–60.

56. George E. Haynes, *The Negro At Work During the World War and During Reconstruction*, p. 13.

57. *Ibid.*, p. 14.

58. *Ibid.*

59. George E. Haynes, *Memoirs*, Section XI, p. 2, MVF.

60. *Ibid.*

61. *Ibid.*, p. 78.

62. Telegram from Ralph E. Diffendorfer to George E. Haynes, September 22, 1919, MVF.

63. This research work resulted in a published monograph on migration patterns of Southern blacks to Detroit entitled, "Negro New-Comers to Detroit, Michigan—A Challenge to Christian Statesmanship: A Preliminary Survey" (New York: Home Missions Council, 1918).

64. Haynes, *Memoirs*, Section V, p. 9, MVF.

65. *Ibid.*, p. 11.

66. W. A. Hunton, "The Colored Mens' Department of the YMCA," in *The Voice of the Negro*, I (June, 1908), p. 391, quoted in Daniel J. Perlman, *op. cit.*, p. 40.

67. Annual report of George E. Haynes to the International Committee of the YMCA, Colored Men's Department, August 31, 1906–June 17, 1907, quoted in Perlman, *op. cit.*, p. 42.

68. *Ibid.*

69. Haynes, *Memoirs*, p. 15, MVF.

70. George E. Haynes to Dr. J. E. Moreland, June 2, 1916, MVF.

71. John Dillenberger and Claude Welch, *Protestant Christianity* (New York: Charles Scribner's Sons, 1954), p. 243.

72. George E. Haynes, "Basic Problems and Christian Ideals in Race Relations," Lecture No. 2, Middlebury Convocation, Middlebury, Vermont, September 17, 1931, MVF.

73. Editorial, *Federal Council Bulletin*, January, 1921, p. 3.

74. George E. Haynes, "Some Effects of the New Radicalism on the American Scene: The Remedy in the Christian Religion," *AME Zion Quarterly Review*, LII (October, 1942).

75. See Dillenberger and Welch, *Protestant Christianity*, chap. IX.

76. Haynes, "Some Effects of the New Radicalism on the American Scene: The Remedy in the Christian Religion."

77. During the summer of 1907 Haynes worked and studied in the psychology laboratory of Dr. James Angell at the Summer School of the University of Chicago. Of Angell, Haynes wrote in his *Memoirs* that from the labors and studies in that laboratory would develop a life-long association "on questions of interracial adjustment and civic life."

78. George E. Haynes, "The Function of Organized Religion in Interracial Adjustment," speech given at the Institute of Race Relations, Swarthmore College, July 19, 1933, MVF.

79. *Ibid.* For a slightly different view held by another black thinker on the function of religion in solving racial crises, see Kelly Miller's essay, "Religion As a Solvent of the Race Problem," in *Radicals and Conservatives and Other Essays on the Negro in America*, ed. Phillip Rieff (New York: Schocken Books, 1968; first published in 1908).

80. George E. Haynes, *The Trend of the Races* (New York: The Council of Women for Home Missions and the Missionary Education Movement of the United States and Canada, 1922), pp. 11–12.

81. George E. Haynes, "The Crux of the Interracial Problem in America," reprinted in the *Interracial Review* (July, 1937); Haynes, *The Trend of the Races*, chap. II.

82. George E. Haynes, "The Unfinished Interracial Task of the Churches," reprinted from the *Journal of Religious Thought* (Autumn–Winter, 1945).

83. Haynes, "The Crux of the Interracial Problem in America."

84. George E. Haynes, "Some Psychological Factors in Education in Interracial Attitudes," speech before the Institute of Race Relations, Swarthmore College, Swarthmore, Pennsylvania, July 19, 1933, MVF.

85. *Ibid.*

86. On one occasion speaking to students at the Swarthmore Race Relations Institute, he cited the case of a white man who objected strenuously when it was proposed that a Negro man share a Pullman compartment with him. The white man, becoming ill during the night, was treated by the very black man whose company he earlier had spurned. The next morning, upon recovering, an erstwhile racially intolerant white man invited the black to breakfast.

87. Haynes, "Some Psychological Factors in Education in Interracial Attitudes."

88. *Ibid.* The works of art Haynes referred to were those which formed what was possibly the first touring exhibition of artistic works by Afro-Americans in the twentieth century. The Commission on Race Relations began in 1925 a program to recognize superior achievements by blacks in a number of fields of endeavor, among them Business and Industry, Literature, Music, Fine Arts, Religious Endeavor, Science, and Invention. Called the William E. Harmon Awards for Distinguished Achievement Among Negroes, this program was a notable gesture from the religious community in recognizing the "New Negro" of the 1920's Renaissance. Beginning in 1928, eighty-seven paintings and works of sculpture by black artists were exhibited at International House in New York City. By 1931, this number had climbed to thirty-one. In 1929, the standing committee on Negro Achievement selected sixty-four paintings from the exhibition and sent them on a nine-city tour. Between this time and 1931 twenty-five cities were visited allowing approximately 75,000 persons to view these works of art.

89. From a Department of Race Relations flier, ca. 1930, entitled "Origin and Purpose of the Department of Race Relations," National Council of Churches Archives, New York City.

90. Haynes, "The Unfinished Interracial Task of the Churches."

91. Haynes, "The Function of Organized Religion in Interracial Adjustment."

92. Haynes, "The Unfinished Interracial Task of the Churches."

93. George E. Haynes, "Negro New-Comers in Detroit, Michigan—A Challenge to Christian Statesmanship: A Preliminary Survey" (New York: Home Missions Council, 1918).

94. Haynes, *Memoirs*, Section V, p. 14, MVF.

95. *Ibid.* Weatherford went on to chart an illustrious career in race relations research. Perhaps his best work was in collaboration with Charles S. Johnson, *Race Relations, Adjustment of Whites and Negroes in the United States* (Boston: D. C. Heath, 1934).

96. Miss E. E. McClintock to George E. Haynes, August 7, 1916, MVF.

97. Quite possibly, George E. Haynes, "The Movement of Negroes From the Country to the City," *Southern Workman,* XIII (April, 1913).

98. Z. W. Mitchell to George E. Haynes, December 16, 1916, MVF.

99. From the letterhead of the Cooperative Educational Council. Above the Statement of Purpose was a picture of a white man and a black, both dressed in conventional business suits, their hands resting on four books which were entitled: Cooperation, Morality, Integrity, and Education. Atop the four books was the statue of Justice—blindfolded. The foundation on which all rested was a pedestal in which a motto was inscribed: "Cooperation—the Foundation of the solution of the Race Problem."

100. George E. Haynes, "The Unfinished Interracial Task of the Churches."

101. *Ibid.*

102. Haynes, "What Price Interracial Cooperation."

103. *Ibid.*

James Theodore Holly (1829-1911)
First Afro-American Episcopal Bishop:
His Legacy to Us Today

*J. Carleton Hayden**

His Vision

The purpose of this essay is to discuss the continuing significance of James Theodore Holly, the first Afro-American to be consecrated to the episcopate by the Protestant Episcopal Church and one of the nineteenth century's leading architects of Pan-Africanism as shown by his ideology and achievements in Haiti.

Holly is significant first because of the greatness of his vision. History is made by men with a vision, a conceptualization of the "is" and the "ought" and who labor to bring into actuality the "ought" from the "is." In Proverbs, we read "where there is no vision the people perish."[1] The great black champions were men of prodigious vision, men who dared to dream: Richard Allen, Nat Turner, Booker T. Washington, Marcus Garvey, Elijah Mohammed. They all began with very little, amidst a people poor and oppressed but they had a vision. Of such a one was Dr. Martin Luther King, Jr. who dared to dream that one day in America the nation would practice its creed that "all men are created equal," that one day the children of slaves and of slaveowners would live in brotherhood, that one day his four children would be judged not by their color but by their character. Dr. King dared to share the dream of the prophet Isaiah:

> I have a dream that one day every valley shall be exalted, every
> hill and mountain shall be made low, the rough places will be

*I wish to acknowledge assistance from Mr. Larry E. Cody and a grant from the Howard University Faculty Research Program in the Social Sciences, Humanities, and Education.

made plain, and the crooked places will be made straight, and
the glory of the Lord shall be revealed, and all flesh shall see it
together.[2]

Bishop Holly too had a vision, a vision of the greatness of black
people. He had a deep and abiding faith in "the ultimate redemption and
elevation of Africa and her children." This was based on a profound love
for his race. His son wrote that "he was a race man in every possible way."[3]
Holly himself declared in season and out of season, "I am a Negro, I love
my race, I am not ashamed of my identity with them."[4] He was aware of
the proud history of the black race. He wrote that "the black faced, wooly
haired, thick lipped and flat nosed Egyptians of ancient times" were members of the same race "who [had] been the victims of the African slave
trade for the past four centuries."[5]

For Holly the race had not only a noble past but also a great destiny.
He based this notion on his understanding of the Old Testament. He
believed there were three historical epochs: the Mosaic dispensation carried
out by the Semitic race, the Gospel dispensation carried out chiefly by the
Japhetic [white] race; and the Millennial dispensation which had not yet
arrived. The Millennial dispensation would be one thousand years of justice
and peace resulting from human submission to divine rule. The Millenium
would follow an awful cataclysm in which corrupt political, economic, social
and ecclesiastical institutions under the control of Japhetic [white] societies
were to be overthrown. Holly believed that the black race had developed
a sense of righteousness, justice, forbearance, and love of peace out of
centuries of oppression and therefore would be the fit agents for the final
age. In one place, he put it as follows:

> The condition of servitude meted out to our race for four thousand
> years, since the days of Noah, has been our training for greatness
> in the Kingdom of God.[6]

This role of the black race as the servants of God he saw foreshadowed by
New Testament events. At the crucifixion, the Semitic race in the person
of the Sanhedrin and multitude crying "crucify him" had united with the
Japhetic race in the person of the White Romans, Pontius Pilate and the
army to crucify the Saviour, but the Hamitic or black race in the person
of the African Simon of Cyrene served the Saviour by assisting to carry
his cross. It was the black race which furnished the first pure Gentile
convert to Christianity, the Ethiopian eunuch baptized by Philip.[7]

As the living proof of the capacity of black men, Haiti was the key
to his vision of future black greatness. His major work written in 1857
and entitled *A Vindication of the Capacity of the Negro Race for Self
Government and Civilized Progress*[8] was a study in Haitian history. In
his day Haiti was the only nation outside Africa under black control. It

was also the only nation where enslaved blacks had successfully revolted, overthrown white domination, and established an independent nation. Moreover Haiti had done so without any assistance and in spite of the powerful opposition of France, England, and Spain whose armies had been defeated. For Holly, Haiti was therefore utterly unique among the nations of the earth:

> Never before in all the annals of humanity has a race of men, chattelized and almost dehumanized, sprung by their own efforts, and inherent energies from brutalized condition, into the *manly* status of independent, self-respecting freemen, at one gigantic bound; and thus took their place side by side with other mature nations.

Haiti was therefore "the strongest evidence and the most irrefragable proof of the equality of the Negro race, that can be found anywhere, whether in ancient or modern times."[9] Haiti was a sacramental sign of black potential greatness where "a strong, powerful, enlightened and progressive Negro nationality equal to the demands of the nineteenth century, and capable of demanding the respect of all the nations of the earth" could be developed.[10]

Holly's vision did not blind him to reality. He was not unaware of obstacles nor did he possess romantic notions about his black brothers and sisters. He recognized that Haiti was under developed in almost every way. He once referred to Haiti as the "Mary Magdalene of the nations" possessed by seven devils; the mulatto class; Roman Catholic clergy, all of whom were white; "extra-officious" diplomats from overseas; unprincipled businessmen from abroad; unjust impositions by the powers; African fetishism or vodun and the ignorance of the masses. He had little use for mulattoes who dominated economic and social life and prided themselves on their French language and culture. He dubbed them the "unpatriotic class of Haitians who would fain themselves the cream of society." Furthermore he alleged they "never had one grain of sympathy for the toiling masses who compose the majority of their countrymen." He almost despaired at the frequent revolution and consequent disorder in Haiti. In 1888 when he experienced his sixth rebellion since his arrival some seventeen years earlier, he called revolution "the chronic state of Haitian society."[11]

He believed that the experience of slavery and racism in its many forms had almost debilitated black people. He once spoke of his "shame for black Americans" and denounced "the servile character of the free colored people of the United States." He decried the fact that "many of the race themselves, are almost persuaded that they are a brood of inferior beings."[12]

This weakness could be overcome only by black people coming together and helping one another. His vision was always that of Black Solidarity, which was the means the race could realize its potential. In a letter to his friend Alexander Crummell, he stated "black men must hold up one another, for we have not much to expect from white men." Repeatedly he advocated some form of a union of black people in the new world. In 1851, he urged a "great league of colored people" of North America, South America and the West Indies. At the Cleveland emigration convention in 1856, he proposed the "North American and West Indies Trading Association." He outlined at a large convention held in Washington, D.C., of blacks in 1875 the steps for creating an independent West Indian Confederacy in which blacks would be "the dominant factor." Holly set forth in great detail twenty-six years later a "Negro confederacy plan" which he presented to President Theodore Roosevelt. Subsequently his plan was carried in all the Hearst newspapers. He was sympathetic with the objectives of the first Pan-African Congress which met at the call of Henry Sylvester Williams in London in 1900. Holly did not attend; however, he was named as regional officer for Haiti of the Pan-African Association formed to continue the influence of the Congress.[13]

His love and vision of the greatness of his own race included no denigration of whites. He wanted blacks to emulate the "vim and vigor" of American whites in education and business. Realizing that whites possessed skills in short supply in the black community, he sent his own sons and urged others to attend the best colleges and professional schools in the United States and then to "pass on their skills to their brethren in order to build up a politically and economically independent black nation." He consciously sought and worked with white allies. During his years in Canada he was considered by many as a tool of whites because of his support of the Refugee Home Society owned and largely controlled by whites. In Haiti, he looked to the Protestant Episcopal Church to provide episcopal supervision and subsidies to foster his "infant church." But always he wanted allies to "fulfill the behests of our race."[14]

Bishop Holly had a vision of the Church. By Church, he generally meant the Anglican Communion which he called "the Church of our love." Strictly speaking he did not consider Anglicanism to be the whole Church; however, it was his church about which he generally wrote. He believed strongly in the Episcopal Church, "the Reformed Church of Christ" which taught "the pure scriptural and Catholic truths." Its glory was its scriptural liturgical order in its clear, systematic presentation of "the whole mystery of Godliness." For him the Church was Catholic. His Catholicism was not so much that of his Anglo-Catholic Contemporaries with their renewed emphasis on the sacraments, the supernatural character of the Church, and the apostolic succession. Holly rather took these things as given. Perhaps his Roman Catholic upbringing predisposed him to this outlook. For him, the Church was Catholic in that it was meant for all mankind regardless of race or nationality. William White, he called "a Catholic-hearted Prelate" not because of what commonly went for High Churchmanship but because he "had the courage [in 1795] to ordain a man of the Negro race [Absalom Jones]." The Church was Catholic, not European or white, in its primitive and pristine state because it was an amalgam of the Greek, Asiatic, African, and Latin. He was fond of quoting Cyprian "an African Father of the Church." The Church was no more European [white] than mankind was European [white] although whites dominated and thereby corrupted both the Church and mankind. The Church, for Holly, was the instrument for actualizing the full manhood of all people through its spiritual and moral teaching and its means of grace. And that included black people. On one occasion he put it as follows:

> ... the African race must find in the Churches of the Anglican Communion the powerful lever, which under God, will elevate them to the full stature of their Christian manhood. That race is under a dark and heavy cloud of spiritual ignorance.

The Church remained the divine means of elevation despite the fact that its administrators were white and racist. In writing to his friend, George Freeman Bragg, Jr., in 1899 after the diocesan councils in Virginia had voted to exclude black representation, Holly explained why blacks should "not abandon the Churches of the Anglican Communion."

> There is still virtue in them by the Sovereign election of the Almighty, and with no thanks to those temporarily invested with their administration. It is not moral character, nor knowledge, nor personal control nor the dignity of those administrators that pre-serve the Divine grace in those Churches . . .but it is the Sovereign will and power of Almighty God that preserve this grace in the Church in spite of unworthy administrators.[15]

"The preaching of Christian doctrine never appeared to me to be more than one-half of the gospel message," stated Bishop Holly whose vision always was of Christianity ministering to the whole man. This was a necessary consequence of his deeply incarnational theology.

> The very fact that Our Lord took a human body of flesh, blood and bones is the palpable demonstration that He came to redeem the bodies as well as the souls of men.

Holly believed that "care for the infirmities of the body as well as for those of the soul" was "the Divine Plan of human redemption" and that the neglect of the healing ministry by the post-apostolic Church had very much weakened the witness to "the Divine Incarnation, as the central and fundamental fact of redemption."[16]

Medical work was thus a constant aspect of his ministry. This was especially needed in a country like Haiti with its frequent epidemics of smallpox, yellow fever, and typhoid. From his arrival in 1861, Holly "always kept medicines and treated . . . the sick poor."[17] Constantly he pleaded with the Board of Missions for a physician. In 1892, Holly's son Dr. Alonzo Potter Burgess Holly began to practice in Gunaives and treated the poor "as a Christian physician" in addition to his private patients. By the next year he had treated without pay 597 patients.[18] This was the beginning of Holly's medical mission. By 1898 a clinic and dispensary had been built and a team of several physicians, all sons of Haitian clergy, voluntarily served a circuit of treatment points.[19] Although Dr. Holly opened in 1901 a somewhat more permanent facility, St. James Clinic, Holly was never to have the well-staffed hospital he always desired. Inadequate funds also meant that his physicians devoted the bulk of their time to private practise or left his service completely.[20]

Education was also a part of the Gospel ministry for Bishop Holly. He established schools not only so his converts could read the Bible and Book of Common Prayer but also "to make them useful in the ordinary things of life." His schools combined both religious and secular instruction. He himself conducted a school both as pastor of St. Luke's Church, New Haven and also at Holy Trinity Church, Port-au-Prince. As early as 1880 he had seven small parochial schools in operation. The next year he began "a Normal School and Collegiate Institute" which he envisaged as the nucleus for a future "University of the Antilles."[21] He also initiated a mechanical and agricultural school located on 57 acres of land outside the capital city.

Integral to his vision of the Church was the notion that in a black nation the Church should be led by black men. Holly was the first Episcopal priest in Haiti. He saw to it that every other one was also black. He tutored candidates privately and then sent them to the Philadelphia Divinity School. In 1876 he opened a theological college staffed by three Haitian clergy. The concordat between the Protestant Episcopal House of Bishops and the Eglise Orthodoxe Apostolique Haitienne stipulated that the bishops would elect a bishop for Haiti from "one of the Clergymen of the . . . Church in Haiti."[22] Holly himself was so elected and consecrated on November 8, 1874, at Grace Church in New York City. Holly was fond of saying that only three Haitian institutions were under Haitian control: the government, the Masonic fraternity, and the Episcopal Church.

Holly also had a vision of a society free of injustice and oppression. He denounced imperialism which he considered as any organized exploitation and control of others as "[blasting] the happiness of nations, and [debasing] the multitudinous peoples of the earth." He regarded socialism; that is, the equitable distribution of the resources of the earth as "the fundamental social principle in the Bible." Holly believed that every family had the inalienable right to land and to the means of living in dignity. Although his writings have Marxian overtones he was a disciple of the

Utopian Socialist Francois Marie Fourier whom he considered a "Christ-hearted man." Holly believed that the present "long organized social injustice" and "the whole Babylonish fabric of Christendom ecclesiastical, political, and financial" would be overthrown "in one general crash." After this cataclysmic overthrow of society debased by the domination of the "Japhetic nations of Europe" would come the Millenium, the age of justice, socialism, and peace, the age of the Hamitic or black race.[23]

His Example

Bishop Holly left not only a vision but also an example. He labored his whole life to actualize his vision. Gandhi once wrote as follows:

> I am indeed, a practical dreamer. My dreams are not airy nothings. I want to convert my dreams into realities, as far as possible.[24]

The same could have been said by Holly. First he struggled to provide himself with the educational tools he needed as a prophet and organizer for his race. All the formal schooling he had was the few years at Holy Trinity School as a boy in Washington, D.C. Yet by assiduous private study he was able to pass the rigorous canonical examinations of the Episcopal Church, given to ordination candidates ordinarily college and seminary trained. Holly even mastered Latin, Greek, and Hebrew. When the bishop offered to dispense him from proficiency in those languages in consideration of his meager schooling, Holly replied: "I could not respect myself if I did not pass all the required examinations."[25] A perusal of his writings which include some seven books or pamphlets and about eighteen articles, reveals his familiarity with history, economics, Biblical theology, English and French literature. In Haiti he added to his native English fluency in creole and French.

Holly was a man of independent thought. During the crisis of the 1850's when most black spokesmen such as Frederick Douglass and John Mercer Langston advocated blacks remaining in the United States and fighting for their rights, Holly believed that blacks should emigrate because they had no future here:

> ... In the United States, the numerical weakness of the colored people; the public sentiment of the dominant race against them, stronger than law; and the social repellancy of whites manifest toward blacks ... place the black man under barriers of caste he will never be able to surmount.[26]

Holly's independence of mind was also shown by his religious preference. Whereas the bulk of his race supported the AME and other black denominations, Holly left his native Roman Catholicism and affiliated with the aristocratic Episcopal Church whose free black membership was a tiny minority with less than a half-dozen black clergymen.

One of Bishop Holly's outstanding traits was his perseverance. He appealed to the Board of Missions over a four year span for an appointment as the first Episcopal missionary to Haiti. On one occasion he awaited a reply in New York with no means of support other than occasionally working as a laborer on the wharfs. His application was denied three times. Finally he led a group of 110 made up largely of his own parishioners to Haiti with no support from the Church and nothing more than a letter dimissary from the Presiding Bishop.[27] His perseverance and loyalty to his vision is shown by the fact that of all those who advocated emigration such as Martin R. Delaney, Robert Campbell, and Henry Highland Garnet only he actually emigrated and established a colony for black Americans.[28] Holly never looked back. Aside from brief visits to the United States and to England for the 1878 Lambeth Conference, Holly remained in Haiti until his death on March 13, 1911, a period of nearly 50 years.

Holly persevered in spite of personal loss and tragedy. His two children, Anna and Ella, "all we had" died in less than two months after his taking up in 1856 his rectorship in New Haven. Holly's colonists landed in July 1, 1861. Within seven months the impure water, crowded conditions, intense heat, and disease had taken their toll. Holly buried his mother Jane, his wife Charlotte, his daughter Cora, and his infant son Joseph Geffrard. Only Holly's two sons aged three and five survived. These deaths he took to be a "baptism of fire." He married again in November, 1862, and eventually had eight more children.

He stuck to his task in spite of the desertions from his colony. Rumors in the Afro-American press had it that he had gone insane or left Haiti for greener pastures in California. Through those trying early years, Holly prayed, preached, baptized, celebrated Holy Communion, taught school, made boots, and led his little colony in tilling the soil.[29]

Bishop Holly was never financially secure but persevered in spite of personal poverty. His personal property in New Haven was valued at $100 and he owned no real estate. He worked to support himself and his large family throughout most of his episcopate, making shoes, teaching, tutoring, or serving as secretary and advisor to the United States minister. At times he allowed himself but one substantial meal a day and wore "quite shabby dress." At one time his home was more of a "hovel" than a house. For most of his episcopate he never owned a horse but had to rent one for his arduous visitations and travel around Port-au-Prince on his "apostolic shanks."

Holly never had the solid support and encouragement of the Episcopal Church but he persevered in spite of neglect, misunderstanding, and even opposition from the Board of Missions. Before his consecration, he had great difficulty in finding bishops willing to visit Haiti and to confirm, ordain, and inspect the work. Repeatedly he was forced to accept reductions in his salary and was not granted the travel allowance enjoyed by other missionary bishops. In a land nominally Roman Catholic and actually devoted to syncretism of African practises and Catholicism, Holly would compromise with neither. So his Church faced small growth in numbers. In 1874 it numbered 1,000 communicants. It had reached only 2,000 by 1911. Yet Holly continued his labors.[30]

His Family and Church

Andrew Billingsley has observed that the primary and most crucial institution in the black community is the family because the family instills in its young "the requisites for survival" which are "a sense of mastery, a quest for achievement, a set of interpersonal values and the desire to acquire technical skills in order to function in the world."[31] Second to the family, continues Billingsley, is the "Black Church." Holly's legacy is not only his vision and his example but also two concrete realities, his family and his church.

Ten of Bishop Holly's children survived him. He was determined to provide them with Christian values and to educate them so they could be useful in the uplifting of their race. He and his wife taught them English, geography, science, mathematics and music. He instructed his eldest sons in Latin and Greek. He taught all his boys the trade of shoe-maker which had been in the Holly family for four generations. The boys also served in turn without pay as sexton of the church. Mrs. Holly taught all the children how to cook.

Holly was engaged for twenty-five years in providing higher education for his nine sons. He prepared his son Theodore Faustine Holly for the priesthood. He served for nearly twenty-three years as curate to his father at Holy Trinity Cathedral. Occasionally he acted as overseer of the model farm school. John Alfred Lee Holly was also ordained after studies at Codrington College in Barbados and then General Theological Seminary in New York City. Alonzo Potter Burgess Holly studied at Harrison College in Barbados and then entered the Atherstone Grammar School in England where he was the only black student. There he won the gold medal for "best scholarship." He then attended Cambridge and obtained the M.D. from the New York Homoeopathic Medical College. After practising for awhile in Haiti, he migrated to the Bahamas and then to the United States, eventually operating a medical practice and drug store in Miami, Florida. Dr. Holly was a prolific writer.[32] Ambroisie Theodore Holly studied at L'Ecole Nationale de Pharmacie d'Haiti. In 1891 he became the first black graduate of the Massachusetts School of Pharmacy. He received his M.D. two years later from the University of Pennsylvania. He was awarded Haiti's highest decoration, "La Croix d'Honneur et de Merite," for his faithful and distinguished medical career. He was also the author of several religious books. Sabourin Holly studied dentistry in Philadelphia.[33] Louis

Holly attended the Boston Conservatory of Music and returned to a teaching career in Haiti. Arthur Cleveland Coxe Holly was awarded the M.D. in 1893 from the University of Boston. Later he qualified as a surgeon of eye and ear diseases at the New York College of Opthalmy.[34] He also practised in Haiti. Bishop Holly's daughter, Grace Theodore, was apparently the child most devoted to her father. Although she never studied outside Haiti, she wrote several articles on Haiti which were published in Afro-American newspapers and magazines.[35]

Holly founded and built the Episcopal Church in Haiti, the first autonomous Anglican Church in a non-English-speaking country.[36] That church continues to serve Haiti, making a witness not unworthy of its great apostle. In Haiti, there are 39,260 baptized persons of whom 15,738 are communicants ministered to by 43 clergy in 82 churches. The Church maintains 61 parochial day schools with 293 teachers and nearly 8,000 students. College St. Pierre in Port-au-Prince is widely regarded as the best secondary school in Haiti. The only facility in Haiti for handicapped children, St. Vincent's School, is operated by the (Episcopal) Sisters of St. Margaret. The Church also maintains a model farm project and is constructing a large condominium for families of moderate income.[37]

One of the striking facts of the history of black Americans is the prominence of the Black Church and its leader, the Black Preacher. DuBois expressed this preeminence as follows:

> The Preacher is the most unique personality developed by the Negro on American soil. A leader, a politician, an orator, a "boss," an intriger, an idealist—all these he is, and ever, too, the centre of a group of men, now twenty, now a thousand in number. The combination of a certain adroitness with deep-seated earnestness, of tact with consummate ability, gave him his preeminence and helps him to maintain it.[38]

Bishop Holly was all of that. In his magnificent eulogy at the funeral of Malcolm X, Ossie Davis sought the central meaning of the life of that remarkable black minister and exclaimed, "Malcolm was our . . . living black manhood!"[39] The same can be said for James Theodore Holly. He was our living, black manhood.

Notes

1. Proverbs 29, 18.
2. Quoted in David L. Lewis, *King: A Critical Biography* (Baltimore, 1970), 227–28.
3. Alonzo Potter Burgess Holly, *God and the Negro* (Nashville, 1937), 14.
4. Quoted in David Dean, "James Theodore Holly, 1829–1911, Black Nationalist and Bishop" (Unpublished Ph.D. dissertation, University of Texas, 1972), 164.

5. James Theodore Holly, "Thoughts of Hayti: The Important Position that This Nationality Holds in Relation to The Future Destiny of the Negro Race," *Anglo-African Magazine*, I, 6 (June, 1859), 186.

6. James Theodore Holly, "The Divine Plan of Human Redemption in Its Ethnological Development," *African Methodist Episcopal Church Review*, I (October, 1884), 83.

7. George Freeman Bragg, *The First Negro Priest on Southern Soil* (Baltimore, 1909), 70.

8. Reprinted in Howard W. Bell, ed., *Black Separatism and the Caribbean 1860* (Ann Arbor, 1970), 17–66.

9. "Thoughts on Hayti, Future Destiny," 185.

10. Quoted in Dean, 73.

11. Dean, 171, 169, 168.

12. Bell, 22.

13. Dean, 199, 18–19, 51, 201, 204, 202–203. For Crummell, see Otey Scruggs, *We the Children of Africa in This Land: Alexander Crummell* (Washington, 1972). For Williams, see Clarence G. Contee, *Henry Sylvester Williams and Origins of Organized Pan Africanism 1897–1902* (Washington, 1973).

14. Dean, 199, 22–24, Chapter IV, especially 91–104.

15. Bragg, 59, 67–68, 64, 65. For Jones, see Carol V. George, *Segregated Sabbaths: Richard Allen and the Rise of Independent Black Churches, 1760–1840* (New York, 1973).

16. Protestant Episcopal Church, Domestic and Foreign Missionary Society, *Proceedings and Annual Report 1893* (New York, 1893), 137.

17. *Ibid., 1894*, 144.

18. *Ibid., 1893*, 143–44.

19. William Louis Wifler, "The Establishment and Development of L'Eglise Orthodoxe Apostolique Hatienne (Unpublished S. T. M. Thesis, General Theological Seminary, 1955), 26.

20. Dean, 191; *Church Advocate* (December, 1909), 1.

21. Dean, 188, 55–56, 188–91.

22. Wifler, 28–29, 32–33.

23. James Theodore Holly, "Socialism from the Biblical Point of View," *AME Church Review*, IX, 3 (January, 1893), 250, 253, 254, 256.

24. Quoted in Lewis, 12.

25. Quoted in Dean, 48.

26. James Theodore Holly, "Thoughts on Hayti: 'Emigration as a Means of Removing the National Diabilities of the Haytian People,' " *Anglo-African Magazine*, I, ?? (August, 1859), 242.

27. Dean, 44, 76–80.

28. *Church Advocate* (September, 1921), 2. See also Hollis R. Lynch, "Pan-Negro Nationalism in the New World Before 1862," in Okon Uya, *Black Brotherhood: Afro-Americans and Africa* (Lexington, Massachusetts, 1971), 41–62.

29. Dean, 84, 90, 81–88.

30. *Ibid.*, 115–16, 99, 186, 92–114, 185–86, 217.

31. Andrew Billingsley, *Black Families and the Struggle for Survival* (New York, 1974), 19.

32. Frank Lincoln Mather, *Who's Who of the Colored Race, 1915* (Chicago, 1915), 141.

33. Letter from Mrs. Victor Emmanuel Joseph Holly to Hayden, January 21, 1975.

34. Domestic and Foreign Missionary Society, *Annual Report 1894*, 144.

35. Dean, 193–97 for all of above concerning Holly's family except where noted.

36. William R. Curtis, *The Lambeth Conferences, The Solution for Pan-Anglican Organization* (New York, 1942), 255–56.

37. 1971 Statistics conveyed with letter from Canon Jack C. Potter, Diocese of Indianapolis to Hayden, January 23, 1975. Conversation with Mgr. Luc Anatole Garnier, Bishop of Haiti, February 9, 1975.

38. William E. Burghardt DuBois, *The Souls of Black Folk* (Greenwich, Connecticut, 1961), 141.

39. Quoted in Earl E. Thorpe, *The Central Theme of Black History* (Durham, North Carolina, 1969), 9.

Harold M. Kingsley:
Preaching to the White Collar Class

Herbert M. Smith

The Church Portrait

1. Environment

This church is located on the southwest corner of Fifty-Seventh Street and Prairie Avenue. Prairie Avenue is one of the main arteries of travel and traffic running north and south through the south side of Chicago. One block south is Fifty-Eighth Street, a busy cross street which is completely commercial, while Prairie Avenue is a curious blend of residential, rooming house, and home-business establishments. Although this neighborhood is not blighted, it shows unmistakable signs of decay. The ugly barrier of the elevated system crosses Fifty-Seventh Street just a half block east of the church. Wherever there is a grass plot or a lawn, it has been left to struggle alone and unaided by man in its losing fight with city soot, trespassers, and litter. So, these spots planned originally as beauty-places in a crowded city neighborhood only add to the feeling of neglect and disorder.

The various signs in the windows of the home-business establishments suggest a neighborhood which, while not impoverished, still feels the need of turning to account any marketable skill its occupants may possess. Here are a few of the many seen within a block of the church:

"Rooms"
"Manicuring and Hairdressing"
"First Class Dressmaker"
"Radio Repairs by an Expert"
"Hats Styled to Your Own Personality"

2. The Building

The church suggests, in architecture, the Tudor country houses of the English countryside of the seventeenth century. Unfortunately, its warm

141

maroon-colored bricks in the lower half, and the heavy timbered construction in its upper half have both suffered from the grime and dirt of the city. The church is built close to the sidewalk on both sides of its corner lot. There is no shrubbery or grass. Instead, the earth has been packed hard by the careless passage of city crowds and by the children of the neighborhood who have played in the shadow of this church which seems to have lost much of its countryside beauty within a stone's throw of the city's sprawling elevated structure.

This building is another reminder of the fate of recent migrants to a great city. It, like the homes of most of its members, is second-hand. In 1928, before the depression had slowed the Negro's march from rural simplicity to urban complexity, it was purchased for its present occupants from its builders and original worshippers—a white Presbyterian congregation. This group did not re-locate in some other section, but simply scattered in all directions, a few of them now being found in nearly all of the white Presbyterian churches of the Chicago area.

A double flight of concrete steps facing north and south lead to the one entrance of the church. Entering, one finds oneself in a rather small oblong-shaped vestibule. Behind, at the right and left, two doors open to stairs leading to the gallery. Also on the right and left two doors lead into the main auditorium of the church. In the center of the vestibule as one enters is a table filled with packages of offering envelopes marked with the names of the members of the church. An officer was busy seeking to hand the right package of envelopes to members as they passed into the church.

The exterior of the church, as well as the small vestibule, are both plain, if not positively ugly. They certainly do not prepare one for the simple beauty of the auditorium into which I entered. It is practically a perfect square. The walls on the two sides and the rear are panelled in dark oak for about eight feet from the floor; the rest of the wall above the oak panelling is dark red brick. Four windows of amber stained glass break the wall space on each side. In the rear, a large gallery sweeps across the church. It will seat about 150 people. Three amber stained glass windows light the rear wall behind the gallery. The vaulted roof of dark oak reminds one again of the timbered and brick models of the Tudor period, but now with a rich vividness which the exterior of the building lacks. The cross beams of the roof are enriched by a geometric design painted in warm deep greens, blues, and reds. The pews, panelling of the choir, and the pulpit furniture are all a dark oak. The furniture of the pulpit is that of the conventional Protestant church. The pulpit or reading desk with the three usual chairs behind the desk are there. The choir is behind and slightly above the level of the pulpit. There are two side aisles running from the two vestibule entrances straight through the auditorium to two doors to the right and left of the pulpit facing the congregation. The church is lighted by eight massive circular iron chandeliers, each studded with about twenty frosted bulbs which give one the impression of a ring of pearls set in iron. To the left of the pulpit is a grand piano. A vase of white and pink carnations has been placed upon it. To the right of the pulpit also on the floor level is the communion table.

But the attention and interest of the worshipper is drawn at once upon entering this building to the large mural which adorns the front wall of the church. Above the pulpit and choir, and balanced on both sides by panels of organ pipes is the painting which dominates the room as well as gives its name to the church—a natural, reverent, and beautiful conception of Christ, the Good Shepherd. As a border for this mural thirteen plaques of a geometric design suggest the influence of Persian and Arabic art. The rich blend of rose, green, and blue in this conventional design makes a perfect foil for the masterful and yet compassionate figure of the Good Shepherd.

The remainder of the building is devoted to a Sunday School annex of two stories in the rear of the auditorium. Eight fair sized rooms, which by means of curtains and folding partitions, can be used as private classrooms, open on each floor into the large central space which is furnished in the usual Sunday School assembly room fashion. A large well-kept basement extends under the church auditorium and Sunday School rooms. The entrance to the basement and the rooms and offices in the rear is on Fifty-Seventh Street.

3. *The Congregation*

As one looks over this congregation, and the building comfortably crowded with about 700 people, one has the feeling that a person poorly dressed would be both conspicuous and uncomfortable in this fellowship. These people are not so much over-dressed as they are well-dressed. It is the first Sunday in January, and in this church fur coats among the women are commonplace.

In the front half of the church women outnumbered the men in the congregation three to one. In the rear half, and especially in the gallery, men came very close to accounting for from one-third to one-half of the congregation.

There seems to be an exceptionally large number of young people in the congregation. Children, on the other hand, were quite conspicuous by their absence from the preaching service.

With full appreciation of the inconclusiveness of appearances in urban gatherings, it may be said that this congregation had the appearance, if not the substance, of prosperity. It certainly was not shabby or down at the heels.

Forty-one automobiles were parked around the church during the morning service.

4. *The Service*

On this particular Sunday morning I reached Good Shepherd Church at 10:30 o'clock. The church was about one-quarter full. There was a constant stream of people entering the auditorium. For fifteen minutes we listened to an unusually fine program of organ music. At 10:45, the minister, Reverend Mr. Kingsley, entered the pulpit from a door to the right. He wore a black pulpit robe. His plump, pink face and twinkling eyes behind his nose glasses suggested a man at home in his world. As he stepped to the central reading desk, the choir of sixteen mixed voices in black vestments filed into the choir loft behind the pulpit.

Immediately the congregation rose and joined the choir in singing one verse of 'O Worship The King." The pastor uttered the call to worship.

The Lord's Prayer was repeated in a novel fashion. The minister announced a phrase of the prayer. The choir repeated this same phrase in a chant. The congregation, meanwhile, stood and listened to this antiphonal rendition of the Lord's Prayer by the pastor and choir. A hymn in which the congregation joined was now sung, "Dear Lord and Father of Mankind."

The 139th Psalm was next read responsively by the pastor and congregation. This psalm, "O Lord Thou Hast Searched Me and Known Me . . ."—was read very poorly by the congregation. There was a lack of unity in their reading.

Following this the choir chanted, "May the words of my mouth and the meditation of my heart be acceptable in thy sight, O Lord, my Strength and my Redeemer."

The congregation sang, "Come Thou Almighty King."

The pastor then read the Scripture lesson for the morning which he announced as "The psalm of this church." It is the Twenty-Third Psalm— "The Lord is My Shepherd." An annoying phase of this part of the service was the fact that the ushers sat late-comers during the reading of the Bible.

Following the brief organ voluntary the pastor prayed. He possesses a fine, clear speaking voice. His speech is direct and concrete. There is little suggestion of the flowery or oratorical. There is an absence also of the stereotyped phrases which have become associated with conventional Negro religion. Here are a few of the sentences of his prayer:

> "We thank Thee for this strong, sweet note of confidence and faith" (a reference to the Twenty-Third Psalm just read).
> "We pray that our nerves may be strong, and our grit may be unending."

The choir chanted a response following the pastor's prayer. The congregation rose and sang, "Just As I Am Thine Own To Be."

The announcements for the service were now made by the pastor. He referred to the offering envelopes for the new year. Special emphasis was placed upon the Building Fund Drive now in progress, by means of which $1,000 is paid each year on the church property. He appealed for the support of the church's lecture program. Three speakers were to be presented: Dr. W. E. B. DuBois, James Weldon Johnson, and Rabbi Louis Mann. A frank statement was made concerning the business details of these lectures and the purchase of tickets urged. A definite note of race consciousness was struck by the pastor as he announced a declamation contest to be held in the church next Sunday night by remarking, "Thus we are seeking to give our children here in Chicago an opportunity for self-expression which they do not often find in our northern public schools."

The friendly attitude of the pastor in personal relations was seen in the personal remarks he made as he announced the sick and burdened of the church community.

The church and gallery were comfortably full by 11:20.

The choir and congregation sang, "Blessed Assurance, Jesus Is Mine."

The pastor announced as the subject for his sermon, "One Aspect of the Spiritual Equipment with which to Face the New Year." It was a discussion of courage based on the Twenty-Third Psalm.

The sermon, which was in manuscript, had a decided literary emphasis. There were quotations from Sidney Smith, Gobden, Emerson, and Goethe. There was a strong, realistic note also as he spoke of the tremendous handicap to a poor people of the vicious luxury of gambling. The congregation listened closely as the preacher read his message. The sermon may be described as concrete, practical, forceful, vivid, and analytical. It was closed with a prayer by the pastor. A choir response followed the pastor's prayer. It was "Jesus My Saviour."

The choir sang, "Lord, I'm Coming Home." Three persons came forward to join the church. One was from the Bethel A.M.E. Church of Chicago. Two were from the Second Baptist Church of Detroit, Michigan.

The church clerk, a mature, well-poised woman, now read the names of seven persons who were to be welcomed into the membership of the church at this service. Two were present and were so welcomed.

The reception of the morning offering was now in order. A special appeal was made by the church treasurer concerning the church Building Fund. Nine male ushers came to the pulpit; they faced the preacher as he offered a brief prayer. A very beautiful organ offertory was played by the organist while the ushers collected the offering from the congregation.

Following the offering the pastor made a few general announcements. At the close of these the choir rendered a brilliant and spectacular anthem. This is very definitely a "trained" choir. But the .conscious emphasis on musical excellence rather than on religious worship was a discordant note. It seemed to be music for its own sake rather than as an aid to worship.

The congregation stood to receive the pastor's benediction, following which the congregation and choir joined in singing a four-fold amen.

The minister hurried from the pulpit to the vestibule where he greeted the departing congregation.

The Pastor Portrait

My conference with Mr. Kingsley took place in the pastor's office in Good Shepherd Church. This room was almost barren as far as personal effects were concerned. There was the usual flat top desk, a table, a couch, and three or four chairs. There were no pictures on the wall, no books or personal touches to give any insight into the personality of this man. This is a workshop rather than a study.

As Reverend Mr. Kingsley entered the office he was wearing a soft, tan topcoat, brown business suit, tan colored shirt with collar attached, and brown shoes. He looked like a prosperous, alert business man. One feels that he consciously avoids even in his habits of dress any suggestion of the traditional role of the clergyman. Here are his own words telling the story of his life:

> My father was a white aristocrat of Mobile, Alabama. My mother was colored. They were the parents of twelve children, ten girls and two boys. I am the fourth oldest of the children. My father died only a few years ago. The relationship between him, my mother and all of us children was of the most cordial type.
>
> Father was born in Virginia and reared in the Episcopalian Church. Like many another wealthy southerner, he was ruined financially by the Civil War.
>
> My mother was a member of the oldest Negro Baptist church in Mobile. She taught in the Sunday School there for years. But the dominant personality in our family was neither my mother nor my father, but my maternal grandmother. She ruled not only our home, but our entire community as well. I can remember her well—slender, black and proud. She was a pillar in the Negro Baptist Church of Mobile. I recall her saying with disgust to a shouting sister in church as I sat by her side in wide-eyed boyish wonder: "My God-a-mighty, why do you holler so, the Lord can hear a whisper."
>
> She had spent all of her life during and after slavery as a trusted house servant in the home of cultured and wealthy southerners. Her habits, attitudes, and interests all reflected their aristocratic background. Then, too, Mobile during and after the Civil War became a center for ambitious Negroes who fled from plantations all over Alabama at the approach of Northern armies which were thought of as the bringers of freedom. This southern pride and Yankee ambition found an instant response in her own spirit. For

example, although she was a Baptist, she advised that all of us children should go to the Episcopal church maintained in Mobile by northern missionaries for colored people. And in our family her advice was law and gospel.

At this time the program of this Negro Episcopal mission was religiously high church or Anglo-Catholic. But for us children the most attractive features were the tennis and croquet games, the story-telling hours, and the gentle and sincere interest of these cultured celibate men and women who found a home in the church, and discovered love in their ministry to black boys and girls.

As I look back across the years, I think the real religion of my grandmother was education. Her constant refrain to us was, "I don't want my grandchildren to be raised ignorant." With this driving passion in her heart we were sent to the Episcopal church on Sundays and to a Congregational private school for freedmen (Emerson School) during the week. This, mind you, by a grandmother who was herself a member of a Baptist church and without any formal training.

There was a definite religious environment in our family, but always under the clear-sighted, non-emotional guidance of grandmother; it was a religion that stressed the rational rather than the mystical. There was no parade of piety. Rather, she took her religion for granted, insisting that religion is as religion does. For example, the playing of cards and the giving of private dances in the homes of church people was not at all unusual in our group in Mobile. This, in spite of the fact that many religious leaders raised a great hue and cry against the "sin" of such practices by Christians.

Thinking of it all today I am afraid that in the striving ambition of the maternal mistress of our family there was a great deal of downright snobbishness. As a heritage of her house-servant days in slavery she rigidly divided all Negroes into two classes: Field Negroes and house Negroes—to her mind like the Jews and the Samaritans, they should have no dealings with one another.

I was my grandmother's favorite grandchild. She was the greatest influence in my entire life.

From Emerson School in Mobile, I went to Talladega College (a Congregational institution in Alabama for the education of Negroes maintained by the American Missionary Association). Two facts stand out in my mind as I think of my college life at Talladega. The growing influence upon me of the Y.M.C.A. program and outlook on life, and my rebellion against that which was considered "proper and correct." In a student strike in which I had had some part, I think now of the president, a white New Englander, who sought first to frighten the students by threats; this failing, he sought to move them by tears. My remark to the students then was typical of my attitude at that time—"Any baby will cry when he can't get what he wants."

From Talladega I went to Yale Divinity School. At first my objective was to prepare to teach, and to teach Greek at that. Then I became interested through the department of practical philanthropy in the field of social work. A significant experience for me at this time was the discovery that many of the student leaders at Yale were genuinely interested in religion. This was both a revelation to me and a corrective for my feeling gained while at Talladega that religion was a field for misfits and "yes-men."

Here I must say a word about my "call to the ministry." In a word, I was not called to the ministry, I didn't hear anything or see anybody; but I sensed the need of our churches for the best possible leadership. To that need I have tried all my life to respond.

I entered Yale a member of the Episcopal church who had spent all of his school life in Congregational institutions. While in New Haven, my desire to get in touch with the masses of the Negro group caused me to leave the Episcopal church and to enter the African Methodist Episcopal church. Personally, I am not anti-Episcopal, but I am anti-class, and the Episcopal church as I have found it is a class church. After an experience of less than a year in an A.M.E. pastorate at Bridgeport, Connecticut, I became disillusioned and left the A.M.E. church. I now entered the Congregational ministry. This, you will remember, is the church I had never joined, but under whose influence and domination I had received all of my education from the Emerson grade school in Mobile to Yale University in New Haven.

Here is a record of my work up to date:

1911   Bethel A.M.E. Church, Bridgeport, Connecticut. I spent one year there.

1912   Union Congregational Church, Newport, Rhode Island. I spent two years in this the oldest Negro Congregational Church in America.

1914   Director of Congregational field work among Negroes in Texas and Oklahoma. During the three years on this job my headquarters were located at Tillotson College in Austin, Texas.

These years in Texas I think of as being of especial value. They developed my self-confidence. They helped me to make simple, direct contacts with all kinds of people. They were invaluable in practical training in public speaking and social approach.

1917   Director Central District Congregational Field Work Among Negroes, serving at the same time as pastor in the following cities. My salary has been paid by the Congregational Board, and not by the local church.
    1917   Detroit, Michigan, 1½ years
    1918   Cleveland, Ohio, 4½ years

1918   Director of Northern Congregational Field Work Among Negroes with headquarters in Chicago. I have served at the same time these pastorates:
    1923   Detroit, Michigan, 2 years
    1925   Chicago, Illinois

When I came to Good Shepherd Church ten years ago I found sixty-six people who were a split from the other Negro Congregational Church in Chicago, Lincoln Memorial. In less than two years our membership had grown to four hundred. The migration from the South was still at flood tide. At the present time our membership is nearly a thousand.

It has required some nerve and courage to break away from the older orthodox religious customs current in most Negro churches. For example, we met with a great deal of opposition when we first did away with the prayer meeting service here. And yet it was dead, only the people didn't know it. A handful of old people coming to church repeating to God in their prayers the same old stereotyped phrases and calling it a prayer meeting.

The real problem of the Negro church is our great need for a social and economic ministry. Theological pietism is played out. We have overemphasized other-worldliness too long. An ideal that challenges the Negro church to rise up and realize it is that of the Denmark cooperatives. We should buy coal, stockings and bread on a cooperative basis in our churches. Here is an opportunity to demonstrate the validity of a social and economic ministry.

Conditions in our neighborhood around the church, in fact, throughout the entire Negro south side, are much worse than people outside this section realize. Prostitution, gambling, economic and political exploitation of Negroes by other racial groups go on without interference from any constituted civic authority. I have preached frequently about the peril of whores, policy gambling, economic starvation to our common life. It is hard to make some people see that these social evils are much more dangerous than the old individual "sins" of card-playing, dancing, and going to the theater.

My attitude toward white people may be characterized as friendly but realistic. I do not think of all white people as playing the role of Santa Claus. I refuse at the same time to make personal devils of them as a class.

Chicago Negroes have had wide and varied contacts with Communists. I don't think Communism is really significant, however. My greatest personal objection to the Communists is that they won't play the game. You can't trust them. They will do anything to win their point. They will burn down the barn to destroy the rats. We should ignore them, in my judgment. They thrive on publicity and opposition.

Reverend Mr. Kingsley, with his round face, bald head and athletic body, reminds one immediately of the well-fed preachers of middle-class America rather than of the prophet of a disadvantaged minority group. His business acumen and friendliness suggest the manager, not the mystic. In one of his sermons assailing the evils of gambling, he revealed middle-class standards of success and snobbery thus: "Playing the races causes you to know people you ought not to know." This may be good advice from Mrs. Grundy, but it seems a little too worldly-wise for a man whose religious commission makes the world his parish. His emphasis on the virtue and value of labor and character makes you feel that this practical, positive and aggressive churchman represents more nearly than he realizes the pragmatic ideals of Booker T. Washington brought up to date. He is not a religious genius; instead he strikes one as a social engineer. His sermons do not discuss the golden streets of the New Jerusalem. He is more concerned with the challenge of the slums and dives of Chicago. The fact that men of this type and temper are so few and far apart in the religious history of Black America makes them all the more valuable and significant when they do appear.

Patriarch McGuire and
The Episcopal Church

Gavin White

"What the distant future may accomplish in the way of obliterating racial lines in State, in Church, or in Society, is no very grave concern of ours. The fact cannot be denied that at present there must be total cleavage—complete separation—all along these lines, if we desire peace, success, and full development for all parties."[1] That was the programme of George Alexander McGuire, at that time Archdeacon of the Convocation of Arkansas and later to be Chaplain-General of Marcus Garvey's Universal Negro Improvement Association and founder of the African Orthodox Church. It was a programme derived from his experiences of racial tensions in the Episcopal Church, but it has had its most marked effect overseas where it has been the incidental cause of a new sense of missionary vocation in the Orthodox Church of Greece. It originated in an able and eloquent man who had the misfortune to find himself linked at critical periods of his life with some of the most unstable figures in Christian history.

George Alexander McGuire was born in the West Indian village of Sweets, Antigua, on March 26th 1866. His father was Anglican, his mother a member of the Moravian Church. Yet amongst the Moravians of that day it was often felt that the "Unity of the Brethren," as they termed themselves, was more a missionary movement than a denomination, and there was a tendency to adopt the liturgy and customs of the predominant or established local church, be it Lutheran or Anglican. A man could thus pass from Moravianism to Anglicanism, or even vice versa, without any sense of disloyalty. McGuire seems to have been baptized in the Anglican Church and then educated in the Moravian, and his parents, apparently well-to-do, saw him through the island school system until he entered the Mico College for teachers, which had a branch in Antigua. He studied there for a year and a half, graduating in 1886. He then entered the Theological Seminary of the Moravians at Nisky, St. Thomas, in what were then the Danish West Indies. The name "Nisky" was confusing since the main Mission College of the Moravians was at "Niesky" in Prussia,[2] but it is quite clear that McGuire attended the Caribbean and not the European seminary.

The seminary was modest enough. It opened in 1886 with Augustus Romig, son of a veteran missionary, as sole tutor, while a couple named Warner looked after the catering. There were three students, including McGuire. But within a few months Romig and the Warners all fell sick and left the island, turning the seminary over to a new missionary named Edward Foster. It cannot have been easy. Foster, though he sometimes had an assistant, was responsible for the Nisky congregation as well as the seminary, and the congregation was a constant disappointment. Like the widow's curse it seems to have declined steadily without ever having the grace to give out completely. It did have a Sunday school in which the seminarians taught; they also preached both at St. Thomas and in what was called "St. Jan."[3] Nisky must have been a very personal sort of seminary, typical of its day, with Foster imparting to his disciples whatever he knew. The weakness of such training is that it cannot be called education, since there is no opportunity to compare opposing viewpoints. Yet in the hands of an able teacher even seminaries such as Nisky can produce trained pastors, and if McGuire showed evidence of ability and intelligence in later days, some of the credit may have been due to Edward Foster.

McGuire apparently graduated from the seminary in 1888 and was posted to a congregation at Frederickstead in St. Croix where a large proportion of the people were immigrants from the British West Indies.[4] Contemporary Moravian records suggest that the work around Frederickstead progressed rapidly during McGuire's ministry, but there is no mention of his name.

Meanwhile, things were changing throughout the Caribbean. The sugar industry had been hard hit by a slump, unemployment was rising, and many young men were off to the United States. Perhaps McGuire had some specific reason for leaving St. Croix. We cannot say. What we do know is that he arrived in Wilmington, Delaware, sometime in 1894. And on January 2nd 1895 he was confirmed in the Episcopal Church.[5] It is not clear who arranged this; we are told that he was sponsored by the priest of St. Matthew's Church but he was American-born and must have made contact with McGuire through another immigrant. In any event, McGuire was soon enrolled as a candidate for ordination in the Episcopal Church and spent some time working under Dr. H. L. Phillips, the energetic and patriarchal Jamaican who was archdeacon for "coloured work" and in charge of the Church of the Crucifixion, Philadelphia. Whatever McGuire had not learned from Foster, we may assume he must have learned from Phillips. In 1896 he was made deacon by the co-adjutor bishop of Southern Ohio, ordained priest the followng year, and sent to St. Andrew's Church in Cincinnati.[6] In 1899 he moved to Richmond, Virginia, but after only two years returned north to serve from 1901 to 1905 as Rector of St. Thomas First African Protestant Episcopal Church in Philadelphia, the venerable parish founded by Absalom Jones, the first Negro Episcopal priest. It may have been at this time that he became interested in studying medicine, in the tradition of West Indian clergy who tried to make up for a shortage of qualified doctors. It has been said that McGuire graduated from Jefferson Medical College in Philadelphia,[7] and while it is quite certain he did not,[8] he may have begun some courses there. Be that as it may, in 1905 he left Philadelphia to be archdeacon in the convocation for "coloured work" under the Bishop of Arkansas, William Montgomery Brown.

Bishop Brown's name is seldom mentioned in Episcopalian circles to-day; he was the sort of bishop that Episcopalians would prefer to forget. Some have suggested that he was paranoiac, and perhaps he was. Suffice it to say that it was a calamity that one of the ablest Negro churchmen of his day should have been committed to Brown's care and guidance.

William Montgomery Brown had this in common with George Alexander McGuire: both were largely self-educated. Brown had been an orphan sent out to work for a local farmer, then turned over to the care of a wealthy Episcopalian lady whose daughter he subsequently married.[9] Since he had next to no schooling in childhood he was obliged to read privately before entering a seminary admittedly a little more ambitious than Nisky, and it may have been this which left him with a seriously unbalanced world-view. But with all the originality of the self-educated genius he wrote a book on why everyone should be Episcopalian, and thus became Bishop of Arkansas. He continued to write books and he built up missions all over Arkansas, but illness forced him to retire in 1912. He promptly recovered his health and lost his faith; some would say that he lost his mind. In one of his later books he called himself, "Episcopos in partibus Bolshevikium et Infidelium," remarking that, "I consider going to a church and praying to a God to be bad habits, and if I could live my life over, I would not allow myself to become addicted to them."[10] Instead he took up Marxism and Darwinism and had himself re-consecrated by an "episcopus vagans" or churchless bishop whose claims seemed entirely reasonable to Brown.[11] The Episcopal Church eventually tried him for heresy and he was deposed in 1925, an event which was recently remembered in the furor over Bishop Pike. Brown characteristically wrote a book about it and lived happily on until 1937.

But what concerns us most about Bishop Brown is the view which he held on race, and that view was way out. On the one hand he maintained that, "if the Southern negro is ever raised from the slough of degradation into which he is sinking deeper and deeper, the white people of the south must extend him a helping hand,"[12] but on the other hand, "among all the races of mankind there are no more widely differentiated peoples than the Anglo-American and the Afro-American."[13] And in 1907 he told the House of Bishops of the Episcopal Church that, "The Protestant Episcopal Church in the United States of America is a national racial branch of the Catholic Christian Church. It is, so to speak, an Anglo-American racial chapel in the great all-inclusive national Cathedral with its many Chapels. Negroes have as much right in this Cathedral as we have, and they are equally entitled to a racial chapel."[14] All this was based on the fact that the Episcopal Cathedral in New York, a monstrous structure the incompletion of which has somehow become a contribution to solving the urban problem, was equipped with a variety of chapels named for European racial saints. (In actual practice they are all open to anyone and always have been.) On the possibility of mixing races, Brown wrote, "I pass this nauseating theory by with the observation that it is the solution of the problem upon which the great majority of Negroes have set their hearts and that, if this Church wants to further them in the realization of their abominable desire, the creation of an Afro-American Episcopate of either the Missionary or Suffragan type, with any degree of representation in the General Convention, would be along the right line; otherwise it would be as fundamentally as it would be ruinously wrong."[15] Summing up, he insisted that "it is wrong for different races even to try to get along with one ecclesiastical Chapel,"[16] and, "A God-implanted race prejudice makes it impossible, absolutely so, that Afro-Americans and Anglo-Americans should ever occupy the same footing in a dual racial Church."[17]

All of this argument was presented in connection with the projected Negro Episcopate. There were two points of view, and neither was very satisfactory. Some wanted Negro clergy to be consecrated as Suffragan or Assistant Bishops, which would prevent formally dividing the Church on racial grounds but would also deprive the Negro bishops of any vote in the General Convention. Others wanted special Missionary Districts erected all over America to deal with all Negro work under Negro Missionary Bishops;[18] this would give those bishops some authority of their own and a vote in General Convention, but it would formally segregate the Church. Brown was willing to accept suffragan Negro bishops, provided they did not sit in the House of Bishops, but he really wanted a quite separate denomination of Negro Episcopalians, analogous to the African Methodist Episcopal Church. Anything rather than a "combination mess of Anglo-Afro pottage," for, "the Negro is degenerating morally,"[19] save for a tiny minority of men like McGuire who would make good bishops.

What effect can all this have had on McGuire? He originally held that white and Negro work must be separate, though equal, and he went to some lengths to satisfy white prejudices on this issue. Speaking to a mainly white gathering at the Arkansas Convention of 1907, he even went so far as to ask their support for Negro work because that would enhance white security; McGuire's argument was that non-Episcopalian Negro ministers were self-seeking and did not teach morality, whereas Episcopalians did. He drove this point home by saying that the "crime" which led to lynching in the U.S. was unknown in the British West Indies through the influence of the Church of England.[20] Yet McGuire seems to have been horrified to discover that his bishop believed that mixed blood led to early death, that Negroes were uneducated because they were lazy, and that the Negro population might soon disappear through emigration or a falling birth-rate.[21] He wrote a spirited protest, pointing out what the Negro American people were already achieving. "Bishop," he added, "can you duplicate this achievement among the nations of the ancient or modern world? You cannot, sir." Brown next adumbrated a theory that Negroes had no civil rights in America, and that their emancipation only permitted them to leave; ecclesiastical status should likewise permit them to pull out of the Episcopal Church and set up their own.[22] He also speculated on the cause of Negro degeneration which he attributed to mulattoes "born of Negro women by impure white men who are degenerates. The white women of the South are pure."[23] Ultimately, Brown would have had to argue that the thing which made Negroes inferior was their non-Negro heritage. He did this by oscillating between two theories both common in his day. One, seen above, was that the Negroes received the degenerate heritage of the whites, which was thus syphoned off from the whites of the next generation. The other theory was the more common one that whites and Negroes were distinct species, originally equal, but with contemporary Negroes debased by an infusion of white genetic characteristics which could not live in an alien host. It must be remembered that Brown had never gone to high school.

But McGuire *had* gone to something rather like a high school, and this was too much for him. Originally he had been willing to accept the idea of suffragan bishops, but he now swung his support behind separate missionary districts for Negro Churchmen, writing that, "Like the two rails of the track, we may parallel each other throughout the journey, supporting the same train, without meeting at any point.... An entire race ... appeals to the fair-minded, liberty loving Catholic Church of the Anglo-Saxon, as a court of last resort."[24] Nonetheless, "no legislation, nor lack of it, shall drive me from the Anglican Communion."[25] Eventually, of course, he did leave the Anglican Communion, and immediately he left the jurisdiction of Bishop Brown.

The story is told in the pages of the *Church Advocate*, a Baltimore monthly edited by McGuire's friend and admirer, the Rev. George F. Bragg, Jr. Bragg had always been in favour of missionary rather than suffragan bishops, and it must have been with some satisfaction that his

March 1908 issue printed a letter from McGuire advising of his conversion. As for McGuire's earlier views, "Baptized in the Church of England, reared in the West Indies, where there has existed no need for special or racial episcopal supervision, although the overwhelming majority of the laity and a large number of the clergy are of African descent, I failed to fully appreciate at first the necessity for this movement."[26] Two months later Bragg wrote that McGuire was leaving since, "'The Arkansas Plan' under which, of necessity, he must work, is radically at variance with what the late Archdeacon, and his brethren, believe to be fundamentally necessary for the growth and expansion of the Church among our people." Yet there was, wrote Bragg, "no rupture" with Bishop Brown.[27] And this was confirmed by Brown himself, who told his next convention that he still had a great liking for McGuire, though in Brown's version the archdeacon had been sent east to raise money and had there succumbed to the lure of a "call."[28]

McGuire had learned two things from his Arkansas experience. First, that Negro suffragan bishops or archdeacons could never have full authority if the white diocesan bishops wished that authority to be limited. Second, that at least one of those white Episcopalians who had seemed most sympathetic to Negro aspirations was actually moved by strange and erroneous doctrines of race. What must be done for the Negro Episcopalian must be done, it seemed, without reliance on whites.

By this time McGuire was known throughout Negro Episcopal circles as an outstanding preacher and an able organizer, though the attempts to build on the stony ground of Arkansas had been singularly unsuccessful in actual numbers, Brown's publicity notwithstanding.[29] McGuire had no difficulty in finding a new post and by July 1st 1909 he was at the head of a group of forty-seven Churchmen establishing a new congregation in Cambridge, Mass. They had the building of St. Bartholomew's, first put up for poor immigrants from the Canadian Maritimes, but later handed over to the equally poor immigrants from the West Indies who found themselves rather unwelcome at St. Peter's or Christ Church or other parishes. In the words of St. Bartholomew's present rector, "These Churchmen of colour, forever hating segregation, but denied fraternity with their fellow Churchmen were driven into segregation because, as their initiating petition said, they wanted 'to worship in freedom, peace, and harmony without any limitation as to numbers, rights, and privileges,' which conditions were denied them in neighboring congregations."[30] The congregation flourished, but difficulties were made about their becoming a full parish of the Diocese, while McGuire was suspected by the Boston clergy for his High Church ways. It became clear that the congregation would not be given the independence that McGuire and others sought, and in February of 1911 he resigned.

There was one bizarre note to his stay in the Boston area. It was there that he became Dr. McGuire, thus acquiring the title which has led a string of commentators to call him a prominent physician or intellectual.[31] But the title was next to worthless. It was given by the Boston College of Physicians and Surgeons, but from its opening in 1880 to its closing in 1927 that College had only known one brief period of three years in which its graduates were eligible for examination by the state medical society. In 1898 that society was noting that the officers of the College who had been responsible for the illegal sale of diplomas were still in control, and by 1918 the state attorney-general was trying to have the College's charter revoked since a dozen students swore that the advertized instruction was not given, while there was extortion of irregular sums of money before diplomas were granted.[32] McGuire was not a student during the period when his diploma might have admitted him to practise in Massachusetts, and it is doubtful if it would have allowed him to sit for examination anywhere; when the College closed it was unrecognized by any state licensing board or by the American Medical Association.[33] Why, we might ask, did McGuire waste his money and at least a little of his time on what he must have known to be a worthless degree? His brother was a physician, and regularly practicing in America; McGuire cannot have been ignorant of the true nature of his qualification. Perhaps it was some sense of insecurity, of working for recognition and finding it snatched from his grasp, that led him to seek some other road to solid ground, even while he must have realized how ephemeral that road was. It was in 1910 that Abraham Flaxner published the famous report that was to wipe out the accreditation of two-thirds of America's medical schools; in the same year McGuire graduated from a school that was so weak that it wasn't even accredited in the first place.

Meanwhile he had cut his ties with St. Bartholomew's in Cambridge. From 1911 to 1913 he was based in New York as Field Secretary of the American Church Institute for Negroes, on whose behalf he preached and spoke across the country. It was an invaluable experience in seeing the Episcopal Church as a whole, and there was no better place for discovering what the Episcopal Church thought was good for its Negro members. And then, in 1913, McGuire went home to Antigua. Whether he did so in disgust or frustration or because things were going badly in his home village or because his mother was ill, we know that he went, and for five years held the rectorship of St. Paul's, Falmouth, with St. Barnabas' Chapel in Liberta and All Saints in his native Sweets. In those years he was able to use his medical ability, in the absence of licensed practitioners, while his preaching was famed across the island. One gets the impression that he and his wife were as happy then as at any other time, and as happy there as at any other place. And yet, in 1918, he called upon the Bishop of Antigua and "handed in his resignation but gave no reasons."[34] And so he returned to America, leaving behind his home and his family estate, Magnola, which was suffering from yet another decline in the sugar trade.

He seems to have been primarily drawn by the name of Marcus Garvey, though it is uncertain how much he knew abut him at this stage. Nor can we be sure quite what McGuire did with himself in the first few years after his return to New York, though he was certainly associated with Garvey and became Chaplain-General of Garvey's Universal Negro Improvement Association long before he founded his own church. As for Garvey, his name has emerged from obscurity in recent years,[35] and only the briefest reference will be sufficient here. Born in Jamaica and a Mico College graduate, he had spent some time in England where he met African nationalists who influenced his thinking.[36] Garvey himself carried to America the West Indian demand for independence on equal terms, rather than the more usual Negro American demand for assimilation. Arriving for the second time in the United States in 1918, Garvey founded the U.N.I.A. He exalted blackness. He had a Black Star shipping line (as against Cunard White Star) and a Black Cross Nursing Corps and talked of the day when he would occupy a Black House in Washington. His programme, which was at one time supported by millions, envisaged the liberation of Africa and the return of at least some Negro Americans to build up a model state on that continent. That programme has had a great deal of influence on later African nationalists. The flag of modern Ghana carries Garvey's Black Star, and that country operates a Black Star line of freighters. Malawi uses Garvey's banner, almost unchanged, as its national flag, while the same colours dominate the Kenya flag. But Garvey's movement was shortlived. Though he declared himself Provisional President of Africa and appointed Dukes of the Nile and Uganda, his organization was financially shaky. Some of his associates proved untrustworthy, all of his steamships proved unseaworthy, and he himself was imprisoned for using the mails to defraud and in 1927 deported. The U.N.I.A. split into two parts, one of which Garvey tried to operate from Jamaica, but neither part prospered and Garvey's death at London in 1940 was virtually unnoticed.

Naturally, Garvey's movement met with opposition. Almost the entire range of Negro intellectuals, clergy, businessmen, and Dr. DuBois of the N.A.A.C.P. were against him. That the Negro churches were influential bodies could not be denied, and Garvey therefore set out to neutralize their opposition. First, he accused them of being organized to worship a white God, and he told his audiences to worship a Black God and a Black Christ. Garvey was himself a Roman Catholic, though hardly a very active one, and he may have underestimated the violent reaction against this idea amongst the Negro Baptist and Methodist ministers. Yet his idea was not all that radical. As he later explained, "Christ's ancestry included all races, so that He was Divinity incarnate in the broadest sense of the word."[37] Thus Garveyites in general, and McGuire's followers in particular, used black crucifixes and black pictures of the saints, though the African Orthodox Church to-day is not particular about the colours of its statues and uses whatever is available. Obviously this is a tricky question, and there has been a great deal of discussion about it in Africa. Christianity claims to be founded on historical fact, and specifically the birth of Christ in a particular time, place, and even race. There cannot be a multiplicity of Christs. Yet there is a sense in which Garvey's statement was very true, and if our common pictures of Christ represent Him as an Anglo-Saxon, it may be desirable to counteract this with pictures of Christ as a human being of the race most commonly known in any given society. The African Orthodox Church of Dr. McGuire was in no sense unique with its pictures of a Black Christ and a Black Madonna; perfectly ordinary Anglicans in Africa have such pictures in their official service books.[38]

But it was not enough to describe God as Black; Garvey had to establish a substitute church organization, allied in spirit if not in letter to the U.N.I.A. And here we come to the distinction between what McGuire wanted and what his followers seem to have wanted. McGuire appears to have aimed at a united single church which would encompass all Negro Americans, and ultimately all Africans and West Indians as well. Just as Garvey leant heavily on the image of a free Liberia and a free Ethiopia,[39] many Negro churches in America have used the word "Ethiopian" (or the less suitable "Abyssinian") to remind themselves of the ancient Christianity of that country.[40] The use of the word "Orthodox" in the church which McGuire duly founded seems to have been partly derived from this source and partly from the fact, more stressed to-day, that McGuire was to receive the episcopate from someone claiming that tradition. Such was the purpose of George Alexander McGuire. But it was not his intention to provide a mere pseudo-church, a buttress for Garvey's political movement. Despite many statements to the contrary, Garvey did not found the African Orthodox Church and he did not control it.[41] He was not a member of it. Those who were members were by no means all Garveyites; it is doubtful if more than a small fraction ever supported the U.N.I.A in other ways. The link was in the person of McGuire himself.

So much for McGuire, but the purpose of his followers was less ambitious. They were gaining their independence from the Protestant Episcopal Church. Hardly any of them were non-Episcopalians, if we except the Moravians who had, as noted above, a symbiotic relationship with Anglicanism. And before we study the history of those who joined McGuire, we must note that his movement was only a limited success. He did not touch the great mass of Negro American Christians, mainly Baptist or Methodist. He only reached the Negro Episcopalians, who knew him and were known by him. And of these last he only really touched the West Indian immigrants; of all the men who have ever been leaders in McGuire's church, only one was American-born.

It surprises many to know that there are such people as Negro Episcopalians. There are not very many, but they are thought to be anything up to 6% of all Episcopalians,[42] and that despite those Episcopalians who prefer that Negroes be Baptist, and even despite those more broad-minded Episcopalians who prefer that both Negroes and white Southerners be Baptists. Their history is not a particularly successful one, but it has its fascination. There had long been Anglican work amongst slaves in Colonial days, and this continued through the early nineteenth century with Episcopalianism strongly identified with the slaveholder planters, and a consequent tendency to work from the top down. After the Civil War, this work fell in ruins. It was estimated that in some states 90% of Southern Negro Episcopalians opted out and became either African Methodist Episcopal or Coloured Methodist Episcopal.[43] The reason was that the Protestant Episcopal Church was never split between North and South except during the actual conflict. Northern Presbyterians or Methodists, especially the latter, could support Southern Negro congregations which were independent in their own area, since Southern Presbyterians and Methodists formed separate denominations. But Negro Episcopalians in the South were under white Southern bishops who might or might not be personally acceptable, but were regarded as part and parcel of white rule. A noted Southern historian has cheerfully observed tnat, "The devotion of Episcopal churchmen to the catholic aspects of their religion had outweighed whatever concern there may have been for social and political issues which had disturbed and divided other churches."[44]

In a sense this paralleled the famous "Hayes agreement" in which the North agreed to let white Southerners run their own show in the political field. For better or worse, in the Episcopal Church there was no North nor South, but only one great fellowship, suitably graded, of course. To this fact Dr. W. E. B. DuBois has attributed the near-eclipse of Negro Episcopalianism.[45] And by this fact, Negro Episcopalians could not have what their Methodist neighbours had, Negro bishops responsible for Negro churches. When the first post-war General Convention met and the roll was called from Alabama, and someone answered, the quest for the Negro episcopate was doomed. Of course they struggled along, and hence the argument over suffragan or missionary bishops, already mentioned. In fact it was the suffragan scheme which won out in theory, but long before that the Sewanee Conference of 1883 had recommended total separation and, while that failed to win a majority in General Convention, separation on a parish and diocesan level became the norm. Nor were Negro Episcopalians trusted to provide their own clergy in many dioceses; it was while McGuire was in Arkansas that the Bishop of Georgia warned against Negro priests who led to "Socialism" and "Unionism," the Negro being a "but twice removed child of the jungle."[46]

Negro Episcopal congregations in the North were somewhat more independent, but even there one found limitations. When Absalom Jones led his people into the Episcopal Church he was not made a member of Convention since his ordination contravened certain rules about educational standards, and this peculiar argument was even used to prevent his laity having a voice in diocesan matters.[47] Even in England it was known that the Negro American was established in the Episcopal Church, but only at a level which fluctuated somewhere below that of the white.[48]

So it was that at the beginning of this century Negro Episcopalians were not very numerous when their numbers were suddenly swelled by a development totally unexpected and not particularly welcomed. Indeed, one can search the correspondence of certain bishops without finding evidence that it was even noticed.

That development was immigration from the West Indies, which ran strongest in the twenty years before 1930. For the period of 1920 to 1933, it is estimated that a quarter of Harlem's population was immigrant. In 1930 there were 54,754 so-called "foreign Negroes" in New York City, ten times the number found in Miami, which ranked next on the list.[49] Those immigrants flocked in from all the islands of the Caribbean, but especially from the British West Indies, where Anglicanism was long established. Thus the religious balance changed in places like Harlem, since most of the immigrants were either Anglican or Roman Catholic, rather than Baptist or Methodist.[50] For the first time there was a body of aggressive, articulate, and concentrated "Negro" Episcopalians in Eastern cities. But their presence does not seem to have attracted much attention. For the bulk of white-skinned Episcopalians, any dark-skinned person was a Negro and that was that.

But there were differences between West Indians and Negro Americans. The former were accustomed to class rather thas colour consciousness, and were particularly insulted by the American colour bar; Negro Americans had long been forced to accept it. The West Indians were poor or they would not have emigrated, but they were determined to succeed and they tended to do so. West Indian militants had always looked to independence with their own social structures run by themselves; Negro Americans looked more to acceptance in a common American way of life. And, as one West Indian immigrant has written, "West Indians in Harlem always seemed to have precious things that others around them wanted but usually didn't have—most important, a faraway 'home' to retreat to when America balked on its promise."[51] From a consideration of these factors, it can be understood that when McGuire began his new church the West Indians, or some of them, pulled out of the Episcopal Church while the native-born stayed put.

Of course there were specifically religious differences as well. While modern Negro Episcopalians have a liturgical tone which is neither High nor Low but a distinct blending of their own, in the 1920's it was much Lower than it is now. And the background of West Indian Anglicanism was ultra-High, save for the Jamaicans who were either Low or near the centre. As late as 1942 one of McGuire's bishops was preaching that separation from American Episcopalianism had been necessary in order to practise those Catholic customs which West Indian Anglicans had always known.[52] And of course there were differences associated with family life and such minor things as hymns; the African Orthodox Church to-day still uses a hymn-book produced for the Church of England, and in a conservative version at that.[53]

Finally, there were Negro Episcopal parishes where West Indian immigrants were as unwelcome as European immigrants would have been in certain white Episcopal parishes. In the year that McGuire formed his church there was one particularly notable row, "Wealthiest Negro Church in Throes of Dissatisfaction," as a Harlem paper described it. The issue was whether a Negro American rector should dismiss his Jamaican assistant, and one of a large number of charges, many rather nasty and mostly very personal, was that the aforesaid rector had first encouraged West Indians to join the congregation, and then "expressed himself in uncomplementary manner concerning the intelligence of this new element in the church body."[54] Whatever the truth of all this, there was antagonism. And that this has now been almost entirely overcome in American life is an indication of what might have been possible between white and Negro Americans whose differences are relatively minor. So far as our subject is concerned, however, the important point is that the West Indians felt they had little to lose by pulling out, and some did pull out. We should next ask why they did so at the particular time when McGuire broke with the Episcopal Church.

Obviously, they were unable to pull out until there was an alternative structure, and until McGuire laid the groundwork for it. Of course they could have left Episcopalianism for another denomination, and many did, but except for the Reformed Episcopal Church there was no place where they could remain even vaguely Episcopalian, and that church was both white-dominated and very Protestant.[55] But there were other factors which controlled their timing. The 1920's had introduced unprecedented violence against Negro Americans. The American dream had never seemed falser, and the West Indian immigrants with all their ambition lacked the patience of the native-born. Nor were events in the Episcopal Church itself very encouraging. In 1921 alone there were three incidents which showed the mind of the church.

The first was the response to the Tulsa riot with its deathroll of 81 persons; the Bishop of Oklahoma managed to accept rumours that a Negro had attacked a white girl, and that armed Negro appearances had provoked the violence.[56] The second incident was the attempted assassination of an Episcopalian deaconess in Galesburg, Illinois, allegedly by a Negro; the normally liberal *Living Church* described this as an act of "sheer atrocity" even before the facts were known, whatever they may have been.[57] But neither of these events had anything like the consequences of the "Miami outrage," in which Archdeacon P. S. Irwin, an Irishman responsible for work amongst Bahamian immigrants in the Missionary District of South Florida, was tarred and feathered by a gang of local patriots who told him that "all the Kings in England and Ireland can't save you."[58] The authorities then hustled Irwin out of the city with the excuse that his continued presence might cause violence against his Bahamian parishioners. The "Living Church" was especially scathing about the failure of the Miami police to find the culprits, arguing that, "If Liberian officials can protect missionaries and Miami officials cannot, which demonstrates that it has the higher civilization?"[59] And Bishop Mann of South Florida, who had previously promoted his Bahamian work on the dubious grounds that teaching honesty and temperance to Negroes was good for the welfare of the South,[60] told his Convention that it was the duty of every churchman to encourage Negroes to rise in the world, and as for religion, "they are entitled to as full membership in the Catholic Church as we are."[61] It was a courageous thing to say in Miami, but Mann was aware as was everyone else that he did not carry his people with him,[62] and it seems to have been felt that Irwin received what he deserved.

Quite apart from such incidents, there were newly aroused feelings over the Negro episcopate. The General Convention of 1916 had opted for suffragan rather than missionary bishops. By the 1919 Convention there were a number of suffragans, but only two of them were Negro Americans, one in Arkansas and the other in North Carolina; the former, at least, was never given any real authority by his diocesan bishop.[63] Opinion was against the Negro episcopate throughout the South; only a few years earlier a South Carolina priest had published a pamphlet comparing a hypothetical Negro bishop to "an educated parrot."[64] The suffragan bishoprics were generally a disappointment.

But if there were not to be separate missionary districts within the Episcopal Church as desired by Dr. Bragg, nor a separate Negro Episcopal denomination as desired by Bishop Brown, but an even more separate Negro church as desired by Dr. McGuire, how was it to derive its episcopate? McGuire turned to the East, but he was by no means the first Negro Episcopalian to think of this. His friend Dr. Bragg of Baltimore seems to have had a positive fascination for schemes of independent episcopacy deriving from Eastern Orthodoxy. As early as 1898 Bragg noted in his *Church Advocate* that the appearance of one René Vilatte in America, claiming consecration from the East, would prove an important factor for Afro-Americans.[65] And in 1908 Bragg noted that a certain Robert Josias Morgan had surfaced in Philadelphia after abandoning the Episcopal Church and having been ordained priest in "the Greek Church, by the Patriarch of Constantinople." And, Dr. Bragg went on, there was nothing to prevent the Greek Church "taking a hand in our American 'race problem' by bestowing a valid Episcopate among Afro-Americans."[66] The Morgan story is so utterly improbable that one tends to dismiss it as a hoax; it has much in common with that tale of a Greek bishop or pseudo-bishop who was used by John Wesley to ordain one of the· early Methodist lay preachers.[67] Morgan was a Jamaican, made deacon by Bishop Coleman of the Episcopal Church in 1895, the same year that Coleman confirmed McGuire. Dr. Bragg called him a former Methodist minister, which may have been true.[68] Contemporary directories of clergy list him as having been educated at "K.C.L."; if this is supposed to mean King's College, London, it is certain that he was not there.[69] In that period it was not uncommon for Negro clergy to remain deacons throughout their ministry, and it was as deacon that Morgan served in St. Matthew's, Wilmington, from 1896 to 1897, from 1897 at Charleston, W. Va., from 1902 to 1905 at Richmond, Va., in 1905 at Nashville, Tenn., and by 1906 at Philadelphia with his address care of the Church of the Crucifixion. In June of 1908 his bishop in the Episcopal Church, who for some reason was the Bishop of Asheville, suspended Morgan "from the exercise of his ministry for abandonment of the same," and on November 6, 1908, deposed him completely, the required six months having elapsed.[70] That his bishop bothered to suspend him in the same month that he claimed Greek ordination is not proof that he actually had Greek ordination, though it makes it seem more likely. If Morgan tried to organize a Negro American Greek Orthodox church in Philadelphia, its memory has vanished, and nothing whatsoever is known about Morgan in later years. Most Eastern Orthodox sources seem to agree that Morgan *could* have been ordained in Constantinople, and there is at least one secondary source which says that he was.[71] But whatever the truth about that, there can be no doubt that McGuire knew all about Morgan and it is very probable that he knew him personally. It is just possible that it was Morgan who first introduced McGuire to the Episcopal Church in Wilmington; it was almost certainly Morgan who introduced McGuire to the idea of Eastern episcopacy.

But first of all McGuire had to organize his following, and he did this with the formation of an "Independent Episcopal Church" in June of 1921. That body and title met the demands of most of McGuire's supporters, even if it did not meet his. According to Garvey's *Negro World*, McGuire was now the "Chaplain General of the Universal Negro Improvement Association and Titular Archbishop of Ethiopia," which was rather premature, and also, "Called of God, elected by Negro deputies from all over the world, and approved by the ministers of the Independent Episcopal Church of Ethiopia. . . ." The "deputies from all over the world" were probably officials of the U.N.I.A. who accepted McGuire as their Chaplain General. On the *Living Church* noticing these events,[72] Dr. Bragg hastened to inform them that, "I have before me the lists of negroes deposed from the ministry of the Church, and with very rare exceptions they were converts to the Church," McGuire being described as a former African Methodist Episcopal pastor, an error about which Dr. Bragg was at least consistent.[73]

But McGuire had still to receive the episcopate. He is said to have written seeking consecration, or at least recognition, from Cardinal Hayes of the Roman Catholic Church and from Bishop Manning of the Episcopal Church but, predictably, without success.[74] He then turned to the Orthodox Church and, since at that time the present overlapping jurisdictions did not formally exist, that meant the Russian Church, cut off from the mother-country but still undivided in New York. And since the Russian clergy of the day were unfamiliar with such problems, McGuire's request was turned over to a group of former Episcopalians who had found refuge in the Russian Cathedral where they constituted an "English Department." The foremost of these was a certain Ingram Irvine, D.D., who had been involved in litigation with his bishop while Dean of the Cathedral at Quincy, Illinois. The tale is not very edifying, but Irvine went on to be deposed by the Bishop of Central Pennsylvania after more litigation and probably some real injustice.[75] He must have been a difficult person, but there does not seem to have been anything else to hold against him. In any event, Irvine was next re-ordained by the Russian Orthodox, an event duly recorded by Adrian Fortescue as showing the true worth of Anglican orders,[76] and duly publicized by certain Greeks in London as showing the true worth of Russian respect for the British Empire.[77] Irvine then tried to bring about Episcopalian-Orthodox union on the grounds that "there is, so far as my individual self is concerned, dogmatic union between the Eastern and Anglican Churches."[78] Irvine was certainly over-optimistic in this belief, but he held that Anglicanism could become a Seventh Patriarchate of Orthodoxy,[79] and it was easy to transpose this idea to McGuire's body.

The other two ex-Episcopalians with whom McGuire was concerned were lesser men. James G. Mythen was a born rebel who had been connected with Bishop Grafton of Fond du Lac in a quasi-Benedictine community before being made an Episcopalian deacon in 1910 for work in a parish at Santa Fe. From there he went to New York for theological studies but by 1911 was off to Baltimore and the secretaryship of the "Men's Just Government League" for female suffrage, and subsequently the "Protestant Friends of Irish Freedom," until de Valera organized him out of the picture.[80] But Mythen made his biggest splash in 1914 when he told a meeting of Wobblies and assorted Anarchists to "Walk into the churches. Seize them. Turn them to Christian service."[81] And by 1921 Mythen, who seemingly ended his days as a Uniat, had joined the Russian Orthodox and become the Archimandrite Patrick. And with him went another convert, Father Anthony R. F. Hill; his identity has become hopelessly muddled through the similarity of his spoken name with that of Father Anthony Raphael, a Negro Roman Catholic priest who joined McGuire in the early 1930's and taught in his Seminary.[82]

We might ask how McGuire came to be in touch with these people. They are said to have read of him in the *Living Church* and then to have sought him out, as did an Archbishop Lloyd who represented a body called the American Catholic Church. But we must deal with the Russians first.

On September 2, 1921, McGuire and his associates began a synod in their "Independent Episcopal" Church of the Good Shepherd, New York. There were delegates from America, Canada, and Cuba; Dr. McGuire began by explaining how he had built up the movement from November 9, 1919, and how congregations were being formed in a variety of countries.[83] He then welcomed the Archimandrite Patrick and Father Anthony, expressing the hope that they would receive "consideration" from the Eastern Churches and eventual "union with the ancient and apostolic Abyssinian Church of glorious heritage, sacrifice, and continuity."[84] A report was then made of a "Preliminary Meeting" which had elected McGuire to be bishop and the Rev. J. N. Bridgeman to be assistant bishop; the synod ratified the former but postponed judgment on the latter. In the event, Bridgeman was neither consecrated nor active in the later A.O.C.; he was apparently a Moravian pastor from Barbados. At that meeting the name "African Orthodox" was unanimously accepted at McGuire's suggestion, but final action was postponed until the following day when Mr. Bridgeman spoke up for "African Episcopal" while others preferred "Holy Orthodox" with no racial title.[85] McGuire carried the day, though "Independent Episcopal" still survives as a secondary title for certain parishes, and "Holy African Orthodox" was used by Archbishop Nurse's organization until 1964.

Meanwhile, the Archimandrite Patrick and his Russians had dropped out of the competition and the new body was definitely looking to Lloyd for the episcopate. Almost certainly the failure of Mythen's attempt to join McGuire's church to Russian Orthodoxy was due to McGuire's and others' refusal to accept oversight by Russian bishops. It was not for this that they had left the Episcopal Church. On the other hand, McGuire was a married man and could not have been consecrated by the Russians even if they had been willing to give him a certain autonomy. On the doctrinal side there was no acknowledged obstacle; Irvine claimed that there were no doctrinal issues at stake while McGuire said his people could accept the Orthodox faith "unreservedly." Be that as it may, when it became evident that episcopacy from the Russians was impossible, Irvine is said to have written advising that the episcopal succession of Lloyd's group was as Orthodox as that of the Russians. But Mythen did not give up that easily. A few years later we find him typing up a letter from McGuire to Meletios Metaxakis, Patriarch of Constantinople, with whom McGuire actually had an interview when the patriarch was re-visiting New York. At that interview the patriarch asked about the African Orthodox Church and, says the church's history, "declared us to be ORTHODOX."[86] One may speculate on just how much Meletios meant by this; declaring people to be orthodox but not defining it further and not acting upon it may have led his successor into a false step in the Alexandria patriarchate when the Ugandans were under consideration.

Returning to the synod which was now seeking the episcopate else-where, there was some sort of delay since the Chancellor of the American Catholic Church told McGuire that he should not have given his references to Lloyd, and must retrieve them and send them to somebody else. There was apparently more delay while the A.O.C. made it clear that they had no desire to be merely a diocese in a white-run church, as desired by Archbishop Lloyd. Finally it was agreed that they should be independent, though McGuire was to sit on the Consistory of the other body, and on September 28, 1921, McGuire was consecrated by Joseph René Vilatte, assisted by Carl A. Nybladh, in Chicago.[87] And immediately there arises the question of what this consecration was worth.

About Nybladh little need be said, since he had himself been conse-crated by Vilatte. Originally an Episcopalian priest from the Galesburg already mentioned for its "atrocity," he was running a Swedish American Church in Chicago under the Vilatte organization.[88] Of Vilatte, more needs to be said, and much has been said. Indeed, by 1921 he had acquired a certain notoriety. Born in France, he had changed denominations on numerous occasions before being taken up by the Episcopal Diocese of Fond du Lac for work amongst Belgian settlers, being sent to Switzerland for Old Catholic ordination. It has been asserted that after a few years Vilatte accepted some form of Russian Orthodox oversight in this work,[89] but in 1889 he went to Ceylon and was consecrated bishop by one Arch-bishop Alvarez. This last was a priest who had headed a schism from Rome and then obtained the episcopate from the Patriarchal party in the Malabar Church by permission of the Patriarch of Antioch.[90] That that patriarch ever gave permission for Vilatte's consecration has never been proved.[91] In any event, the Syrian Orthodox Church washed their hands of Vilatte when he started consecrating bishops uncanonically, nor do they regard his consecrations as valid. Indeed, some would say that Vilatte's American Catholic Church existed primarily as a refuge for dissident clergy and a source of "valid" orders,[92] and such reality as it had derived from Lloyd rather than Vilatte. The latter was primarily a consecrator of bishops, there being over sixty "bishops" who claim the episcopate through Vilatte and who are virtually all without churches, quite apart from the number deriving through McGuire whose status is a little different. Vilatte finally returned to France and died as a Roman Catholic, which he had been from time to time before.[93]

Therefore, was not the consecration of McGuire in an indisputable line of succession? Much ink has been spilt to prove this, and it is rather difficult to point out to those who have spilt the ink that there is more to be proved than mere succession alone. For it takes more than a bishop to make a bishop. He must be made a bishop in the Church, and when the thing is managed outside of any real or evident Christian body and for the personal status of the candidate, has it any religious significance? The East would say not; there is no ministry outside the Church. The West would be more inclined to admit that if ordination meets the normal minimal requirements, the circumstances are irrelevant. But the recent flood of "episcopi vagantes" or wandering bishops has forced even the West to consider the circumstances. The Roman Catholic Church seldom admits the validity of orders received from such sources; they usually require the person in question to retire to lay life or, if they consider the person suitable, which is not often, to receive conditional ordination. Anglican churches do likewise, and the non-recognition of "episcopi vagantes" by a string of Lambeth Conferences has now become a valuable means of demonstrating to Presbyterians and others that Anglican views of apostolic succession are not entirely mechanistic. Thus there is no possibility of anyone descended through Vilatte being recognized by Orthodoxy, Roman Catholicism, or Anglicanism. Yet one may sympathize with the African Orthodox Church. After all, they are a church. Almost alone of the bodies having an episcopacy dependent on Vilatte and such "episcopi vagantes," the African Orthodox Church exists for the Glory of God and the salvation of souls, and not to lend dignity to a particular pseudo-bishop. It may be argued that they owe their separate existence to racial factors, but such a criterion would eliminate quite a few very respectable bodies, and it will be shown that the racial aspects of the A.O.C. have been exaggerated. Moreover, their line of episcopal succession passes through but one churchless bishop, Vilatte himself. And yet the principle of there being no episcopacy outside the Church is of such importance that no recognition may be expected now or in the foreseeable future.

The subsequent history of the African Orthodox Church is complex and need not be covered here; it had moved out of the Episcopal Church though it always remained within the Anglican ethos. Whatever the connection with Garvey might have been, it ceased when Garvey's movement faded, though McGuire was to be one of the leaders of the New York U.N.I.A. opposed to the other U.N.I.A. which Garvey himself sought to direct from the West Indies.[94] That the connection was not a vital one is shown by the continued life of the A.O.C. when Garvey and the U.N.I.A. were totally eclipsed. The African Orthodox Church was McGuire's work and not Garvey's; it was only fitting that McGuire should have been elected Patriarch in 1924 with the title of Alexander I.

His immediate problem was to prevent disintegration of his following. Normally this might stem from two sources, the tendency of his lieutenants to split off for themselves, and the difficulty of finding replacements as his clergy died. Only four Episcopalian priests joined McGuire, yet he had to man his parishes. Naturally he was offered the services of almost every man deposed from the Episcopal ministry—and naturally he was sometimes unwilling to accept such services. Instead he founded the Endich Theological Seminary, in the lower rooms of the Holy Cross Pro-Cathedral, a large house in Harlem. There he lectured, and there Father Anthony lectured, and however unsatisfactory it must have been, it at least demanded some attempt at theology and it weeded out the totally unsatisfactory. Of course the degrees meant little, since the Seminary was accredited by no one, but as an instrument of discipline it must have proved its worth, and it did supply the parishes after a fashion. As for the other danger, revolt of the lieutenants, this was minimal while McGuire lived, but proved nearly fatal after his death in 1934.

The Church soon spread to the West Indies, where it never had much success, and to Cuba where it had a little more, and from the start it had a parish in Nova Scotia. But its great strength was in the cities of the Eastern Seaboard, in New York, in Miami, and to a lesser extent in Philadelphia, Boston, and Chicago. Perhaps at its height it had twenty thousand adherents, perhaps more. That it did not grow larger was due to a number of factors. Bishop Brown and his fellow-thinkers had provided some of the stimulus, but they were becoming increasingly rare in the Episcopal Church, and the picture was improving in both New York and Miami. We have already seen how Bishop Mann was finally stirred to action by the Irwin affair, and once stirred, he was not to slumber again. As for New York, McGuire began his work just as an ailing bishop gave way to the iron rule of Bishop Manning. A survey of Bishop Manning's correspondence does not indicate that he gave much attention to Negro affairs, but he thought of himself as a friend to Negro Episcopalians, and, "The most notable thing about his policy was his insistence that fine sites be procured for the negro churches where the work would have dignity and independence."[95] Fine sites were not enough, but to see the importance of dignity and independence was to be lightyears ahead of some other bishops. And, on occasion, Manning could be firm. In 1932 it seemed that the vestry of All Souls had closed that church to

discourage Negro membership, since they claimed they had "an obligation
to perform to the white people who founded, supported, and built up
All Souls' Church," though they would admit Negro guests.[96] Manning
had a locksmith open the doors so that he and the rector might take
service for all comers. Whether better recognition of Negro Episcopalianism
was in any way due to the McGuire challenge is questionable. Dr. Bragg
of Baltimore, however annoyed at McGuire for going off on his own,
seemed to think so. When the African Orthodox Church was founded, Bragg
wrote that only the "Missionary Episcopate" could stop it,[97] and the following year one of his editorials deplored schism on the one hand but
called the A.O.C. a "necessary evil" on the other—necessary because it
alone could force the hand of the Episcopal Church, evil because it was
schismatic. Others would say that the existence of the African Orthodox
Church was scarcely noticed by Episcopalian leadership.[98]

Perhaps that was not entirely their fault. It was a time when many
new Orthodox churches were coming into being. Not only was there the
rash of pseudo-churches headed by part-time patriarchs who presided only
over their immediate families, but the single structure of Russian Orthodoxy
in America had crumbled. There were to be, and there still are, as many
Orthodox jurisdictions in America as could be found in the old world;
one might almost say twice as many jurisdictions since in due course
most American bodies would suffer division over their relationship to
home patriarchates closely related to Communist regimes. Though the
chaos contained the seeds of its own re-order, that was not immediately
apparent, and Orthodoxy seemed to have so many heads that one extra
jurisdiction could be easily overlooked. Yet the African Orthodox Church
had nothing "Orthodox" about it—only the title of Patriarch, only the
Creed without its "filioque" clause, only the origin of its episcopate joined
it to the East. For the rest, it was and is a very conservative expression
of West Indian High Church Anglicanism. Its "Divine Liturgy" is thoroughly Anglican, though it does follow American rather than English usage
on some major points, and the church is equipped for such things as
Sunday schools and ladies' teas and all that is culturally not of the East.
Yet by many it was thought to be an Eastern body, and to many more
it seemed a purely racial body. It does have a prayer in the Eucharist
for "thy Church throughout the world, and especially that portion thereof
which thou hast graciously planted among our race,"[99] which is about as
racial as its worship ever becomes. And it is constitutionally controlled
by Negro members, though open to all races.[100] It is, of course, a little
illogical to leave a church which is white-controlled and to then establish
one on equally Negro-controlled lines, and this is now admitted, at least
by some. But McGuire did not invent this idea; the first Negro Episcopal
parish in America restricted the vote to those of African descent.[101]

But if the church was not much noticed in high circles, it was at least surviving, and it was beginning to overcome its earlier financial difficulties. Disaster struck in 1934; McGuire died and his church broke up into at least four fragments. Some priests and laity, including the founder's widow, Lady Ada McGuire, and his daughter, returned to the Episcopal Church.[102] That a body should split into fragments on the death of its founder is all too common; that the fragments should swallow their pride is less often seen and shows that there still lives some vision in the African Orthodox Church. For the two major groups are re-united. To replace McGuire, the former Bishop W. E. J. Robertson had succeeded as the Patriarch James I. His leadership was not universally accepted, and a large proportion of the A.O.C. either broke off or stayed out under the leadership of Bishop R. G. Barrow, McGuire's closest associate and father of the present Prime Minister of Barbados. This group passed under the leadership of Bishop F. A. Toote, and then that of Archbishop Gladstone St. Clair Nurse, under whom it was re-united with the other body on February 22, 1964, the patriarch of the latter having meanwhile died and been replaced by Bishop R. G. Robinson. This last was the bishop who had the unique distinction of being native-born, and he adopted the patriarchal name of Peter IV, the other three Peters being those of Antioch. Unfortunately Peter IV had barely begun the work of renewal, for which he seemed admirably suited, when he died in turn. At present there is no patriarch; Archbishop Nurse is primate of the re-united body. That church now has approximately 4,000 adherents which figure may be more or less than it was ten years ago; there are about thirty clergymen, mainly, of course, working in secular occupations during the week.[103] Parishes are concentrated in New York, which has nine, with two more in Brooklyn. There are two around Boston, and one each in Chicago, Philadelphia, Miami, and Sydney, Nova Scotia. Those of McGuire's following who are not in the present-day A.O.C. are relatively few and can mainly be found in such small bodies as the North American Old Roman Catholic Church or St. Thomas' Liberal Catholic Church in New York.

Since their reunion, the A.O.C. have found themselves with more bishops than are actually required, so no consecrations are likely for some time to come. In New York City there are probably more than enough priests, though it is hoped that the Seminary will be re-opened. One does hear of a priest being received from England for work in the A.O.C., and this raises one of the two reasons for the international importance of this body.

First, it has a great deal to teach the Church of England. It is not entirely certain that there will not come to be a Province of the African Orthodox Church in England where so many West Indians are settled. Of course this depends on the response of the Church of England, and on the social patterns that are formed in that country during the next few years.

Secondly, there is the work within Africa itself. And about that work there is considerable misunderstanding. The lines of communication are long and somewhat roundabout, where they exist at all. It began with Daniel William Alexander, half Negro American and half South African, who was consecrated by McGuire in 1927 as Primate of the African Province of the A.O.C. and built up a small following around Kimberley, South Africa.[104] That work was and is primarily amongst ex-Anglicans. In 1960 two bishops from the American Province visited South Africa to join in consecrating a successor,[105] so the work will probably outlast Alexander himself, though it does not seem to have much capacity for real growth and is now scarcely in touch with the American body. But the consecration of McGuire, noted in Garvey's magazine, had attracted the attention of a young man who had taken the name of Reuben Spartas in his native Uganda, which, it must be emphasized, is in East Africa and not in South Africa and has no contact with the latter.[106] In 1931–1932 Archbishop Alexander visited Uganda at Spartas' request and expense and ordained Spartas and his companion Obadiah Basajjakitalo. On travelling homewards through Kenya he chanced to meet a representative of one of the independent schooling associations in Kikuyu territory.[107] These groups had left mission churches, mainly Presbyterian, over the issue of female circumcision, though it is generally held that behind this argument was a stronger motive of ordinary nationalism. That may also have been the prime motive in Uganda, though a secondary motive was certainly churchmanship—in both countries one still finds a few African Orthodox who insist that they are the equivalent of High Anglicans in an area handed over to Low Church societies.

But the influence of Alexander in East Africa could never be very great. In 1935 he entered Kenya at the request of his new friends and stayed for a year and a half, ordaining clergy for the Kikuyu associations. When he returned to his South African base, thousands of miles away, his influence in East Africa ended completely. It had already dawned upon Spartas in Uganda that Alexander was not Orthodox in the sense that he and his friends wished to be Orthodox, and they soon turned to a Greek priest who put them in touch with the Greek Patriarch of Alexandria. Union with Greek Orthodoxy was ultimately achieved in 1946, but from 1934 Spartas was in correspondence with that same Meletios IV whom McGuire had met in New York, and who had now become Patriarch of Alexandria. Meletios was welcoming but cautious; he probably did not wish to undermine his close relations with Anglicans by welcoming converts from Anglicanism too enthusiastically, and the Orthodox in Uganda were all from the Anglican fold. Yet his successor but one, Christophoros II, either read into Meletios' letters more than was intended or was misinformed on the origins of the A.O.C. At any rate he accepted the African Orthodox Church as it existed through East Africa, and also accepted its clergy as if they had been canonically ordained clergy of the Orthodox East who had fallen into what he called "an Eastern heresy." The subsequent history of what may be referred to as either the Archdiocese of Irinoupolis (Dar-es-Salaam, Hellenized), or the African Greek Orthodox Church, is told elsewhere.[108] Suffice it to say that it has about eight to ten thousand adherents, and has been under the supervision of a Greek metropolitan until 1968; that metropolitan has just been elected to the Patriarchate of Alexandria which will create a problem of succession. Though a Ugandan might be consecrated, the centre of gravity has now switched to Kenya where a Ugandan might not be welcomed, nor is there a Kenyan monk readily available at this point. Probably the next metropolitan will be Greek, though an African bishop will be introduced eventually.

As for the African Orthodox Church, without the qualifying word "Greek," it no longer has any adherents in Kenya or Uganda. The contrary is believed both in America and by a few well-informed persons in Britain, but the most exhaustive enquiries on the spot have failed to find anyone regarding himself as subject to Archbishop Alexander. The name of Alexander is barely remembered, and that of McGuire is utterly unknown.[109] The man in East Africa who should have known most about Alexander, and was ordained by him, told this present writer that Alexander was a "Uniat" consecrated in South America, and this is believed by others than him. The Orthodox of Kenya are busy collecting the remnants of their pre-Mau Mau following, and busy bringing their Church into line with Orthodox practises in liturgy and devotion. They are not very interested in speculations about an incident in their earlier history. Nonetheless, the American factor was decisive in bringing the A.G.O.C. into existence, and also decisive in shocking world Orthodoxy into a reconsideration of its missionary vocation. Political and social pressures had long forced most jurisdictions of Eastern Orthodoxy to abjure evangelism, and since they sometimes found Roman or Protestant missionaries trying to evangelize the Orthodox, they had tended to regard all missionary activity as suspect. The discovery that they had a mission in East Africa, however gingerly they accepted it, roused the Orthodox to a new vision, especially in Greece. Unhappily that vision was somewhat muddled by the perennial problem of Hellenism, and unhappily the actual facts of the East African experience tended to become distorted by the time that they had been broadcast through Greece. The work in East Africa has not been primarily missionary, in that the members of the A.G.O.C. were mainly Anglican or Presbyterian in origin. Yet the most significant achievement of the A.O.C. in either continent was their awakening of

Greek Orthodoxy to the non-Greek world, however unintentional this may have been.

Finally, what is to be learned from all this by the Episcopal Church in America? There are, we are told, 85 predominantly Negro parochial congregations and 178 mission congregations in the Episcopal Church; between them they have over 75,000 communicants with about a tenth of that number of Negro communicants to be found in predominantly white congregations.[110] Another survey states that there are 320 Negro Episcopalian congregations,[111] and there are 283 Negro Episcopal clergy.[112] Altogether, they make up a sizable group of people, and it has been demonstrated that they do not lag behind other Episcopalians in self-support at the parish level.[113] They are not a captive church; indeed, they include a high proportion of the wealthier and more highly educated Negro population. Yet somehow this group is not influential in the higher levels of church government, and that may be at least partly due to certain preconceptions of white Episcopalians.

The most obvious problem is the practical segregation which keeps all but a small number of Negro clergy circulating in Negro missions, or stationary in Negro parishes. But this is not due to crude racism; Episcopalians are sophisticated people and when they become racist, do so in a sophisticated way. The average white Episcopalian is opposed to segregation as a matter of principle. Thus he feels he should be opposed to Negro Episcopal churches which were born out of segregation. The mere existence of such is a cause of shame. That people should be obliged to worship in such bodies is a travesty of justice, and all Negro Episcopalians should be called out of them and welcomed to take their rightful place in the real Episcopal Church, which is, of course, white, but welcomes all men. Naturally that would make Negro clergy redundant, but something can be done about that. After all, the Negro clergy have also experienced the injustice of segregation, and have only been given inferior Negro congregations. The thing to do is to welcome the Negro laity to white congregations where they will be ministered to by white clergy, who will be much better. But the Negro clergy must also be cared for, so they can be introduced into white congregations, which will be better for the clergy. Then everyone will be happy. And there will be no Negro Episcopal churches.

It is hard to answer that sort of thinking. Integration is coming. There are Negro clergy who should be working in predominantly white parishes. There should be places for them. And there are Negro laity who should and will seek for themselves places in predominantly white congregations. But Negro Episcopal churches are an asset which should not be thrown away. It is easy to despise them for being so middle-class, and there are some Episcopalians who think that any Negro who prefers the Book of Common Prayer to the storefront church is a traitor to his people.[114] It is easy to regard integration as a one-way street, in the words of Father Hughes of Cambridge, "Negroes absorbed into white congregations, as if institutions run by Negroes have no intrinsic validity. Only in the most isolated instances do you ever hear of the reverse process: white people being transferred to so-called Negro churches; and this only among white people of strong Christian conviction and compunction of conscience regarding this disgrace to the Church of segregated congregations."[115] The non-American reader of these words cannot but wonder that so much conviction is required to join a congregation about which the most frequent complaint regards its excessive respectability. And in point of fact there are odd families of white Episcopalians, as well as individuals, who have united with Negro Episcopal parishes without any particular conviction or compunction of conscience. Either they like the music or the preaching or the churchmanship or the place is nearby. They have not had to grit their teeth to enter in.

Again, it has been argued that the Negro Church will be the last Negro institution to disappear in America, and that it will be necessary as long as there is a racial problem. Why should it ever disappear? If it has a life of its own, it will survive integration, though the faces of its members may be of more varied hues. And for Episcopalians, the Negro Episcopal Church is, in its small way, a success story. There has been a real accomplishment in surviving, and more than surviving, even though others have given up and gone out. And this survival allows all Episcopalians who face the race problem to begin *as* Episcopalians, working out in their own household, where it hurts most, what they believe must be done in their society as a whole.

So much for George Alexander McGuire. He came to Anglicanism partly by birth and partly by choice. He was ordained with the minimum of training and, when he had proven his ability, handed over to the care of a near-paranoic. He went to the Russians, who handed him over to the care of a man not much better, and finally he received the episcopate from a man whose name is a by-word for irresponsibility. That the African Orthodox Church survives at all is mainly due to McGuire. That he succeeded in leaving his mark on church history was largely by accident. In his primary object, the foundation of a church for all peoples of African descent, he failed. Indeed, he ended up placing Africans under a Greek bishop instead of under an African one. And in trying to create a church for Negro Episcopalians McGuire failed also, since changing circumstances cut the ground from under his feet. Yet his personal reputation has survived all contact with those whose reputations have not. His church has survived, a church which he founded on the ideas which came to him from Brown and Bragg and Irvine and Morgan. And it must be admitted that where McGuire failed, he did so with a certain patriarchal flair. May he rest in peace.

Notes

1. Quoted in W. M. Brown, *The Crucial Race Question—or Where and how shall the Color Line be drawn?* (1907), p. 174.

2. *Periodical Accounts, relating to the Missions of the Church of the United Brethren established among the Heathen* (1893), p. 161.

3. *Periodical Accounts,* 1885, p. 325; 1886, p. 523; 1887, p. 117; 1893, p. 24.

4. J. Pinnington, "A Note on Anglicanism in the Danish West Indies," *Historical Magazine of the Protestant Episcopal Church,* Vol. XXXVII, No. 1 (March, 1968), p. 67.

5. *The Church Advocate* (Baltimore, March, 1908).

6. A. C. Terry-Thompson, *The History of the African Orthodox Church* (1956), p. 49.

7. *Idem.*

8. Communication from the Alumni Association of Jefferson Medical College.

9. W. M. Brown, *My Heresy*, pp. 3–19.

10. W. M. Brown, *Communism and Christianism* (1920), p. 144.

11. H. R. T. Brandreth, *Episcopi Vagantes and the Anglican Church* (Second Edition, 1961), p. 39. Brown's reconsecration may not have been as pointless as it seemed. Though he himself did not place this interpretation upon it, it was apparently thought by others that it would bring him into relationship with the "Living Church" schism in Russia, where his books were circulated by the Soviet authorities who considered him a great gift to their anti-church propaganda.

12. W. M. Brown, *Five Years of Missionary Work in Arkansas* (1906), Chap. III.

13. W. M. Brown, *Great Problems, Local and General, and How to Solve Them* (1909), p. 24.

14. W. M. Brown, *The Catholic Church and the Color Line* (1910), pp. 11–12.

15. *Ibid.,* p. 12.

16. *Ibid.,* p. 13.

17. *Ibid.,* p. 17.

18. The idea of Missionary Districts for Negro Americans was copied from a similar scheme for American Indians put forward in 1854 by Bishop G. W. Doane of New Jersey. The ultimate source of this scheme was theological; it was hoped that missionary bishops would prove that bishops were successors to the apostles, who were the first missionaries.

19. W. M. Brown, *The Catholic Church and the Color Line,* p. 23, and *Crucial Race Question,* p. 43.

20. *Journal of the Convention of the Missionary District of Arkansas, 1907.* In fairness to McGuire, the inverted commas around the word "crime" are his.

21. W. M. Brown, *Crucial Race Question,* pp. 28, 50, 118.

22. *Ibid.,* p. 77.

23. *Ibid.,* p. 106.

24. Quoted by Brown, *Crucial Race Question,* p. 274.

25. *Ibid.*, p. 281.
26. *The Church Advocate*, March 1908.
27. *Ibid.*, June 1908.
28. *Journal of the Convention of the Missionary District of Arkansas, 1908.*
29. *Ibid.*
30. K. de P. Hughes, *The History of St. Bartholomew's Protestant Episcopal Church* (Cambridge, Massachusetts, 1958), no page.
31. Amongst others, Terry-Thompson, *op. cit.*, p. 49, and G. Myrdal, *An American Dilemma* (1944), p. 746.
32. W. L. Burrage, *A History of the Massachusetts Medical Society* (1923), pp. 184–88, 267.
33. Physicians' Record Section, American Medical Association.
34. Communication from the Very Rev. G. S. Baker, Dean of Antigua.
35. The best accounts of Garvey are in E. D. Cronon, *Black Moses*, or for the non-American reader, G. Padmore, *Pan Africanism or Communism?* There is also A. J. Garvey, *The Philosophy and Opinions of Marcus Garvey.*
36. Richard B. Moore, in J. H. Clarke's *Harlem, a Community in Transition*, p. 84, ascribes the phrase "Africa for the Africans" to a "Sudanese Egyptian Nationalist," one Duse Mohamed, who did influence Garvey. The claim of R. H. Brisbane, "New Light on the Garvey Movement," *Journal of Negro History*, Vol. XXXVI (January, 1951), pp. 56–57, that Garvey knew both John Chilembwe and (Simon) Kimbangu while in London during 1912, has no foundation. Neither of these independent churchmen was, regrettably, in London at the time.
37. E. D. Cronon, *Black Moses*, p. 178.
38. *Missa Takatifu*, the Missal of the Dioceses of Zanzibar and Tanga, Masasi, S-W. Tanganyika, and Dar-es-Salaam, is but one instance.
39. There is a story that Garvey sent an agent named Homer to Ethiopia, but Homer found the Ethiopians unsympathetic. Since he could never get fare-money to return, Homer, when last heard of, was still in Ethiopia.
40. For a fuller discussion of Ethiopianism from a different viewpoint, see G. Shepperson, in C. G. Baeta's *Christianity in Tropical Africa* (1968), and the same author's "Negro American Influences on the Emergence of African Nationalism," *Journal of African History*, Vol. I, No. 2 (1960).
41. This view probably stemmed from a report in the *Living Church* (June 11, 1921), based on reports in the *Negro World*.
42. American Institute of Public Opinion, *Gallup Opinion Index: Special Report on Religion* (1967), p. 23. On the other hand, there is a figure of 3.7% in J. Nicholson, *What is Happening to the Negro in the Protestant Episcopal Church?* (1968), and this agrees with the paper, *The Placement and Deployment of Negro Clergy in the Episcopal Church*, Special Report, ESCRU (1967), p. 14.
43. For the early period, see S. B. Lines, *Slaves and Churchmen: The Work of the Episcopal Church among Southern Negroes, 1800–1860* (1960), unpublished thesis, Columbia University.
44. W. B. Posey, "The Protestant Episcopal Church: An American Adaptation," *Journal of Southern History* (February, 1959), p. 29.

45. W. E. B. DuBois, *The Negro Church* (1903), p. 139. According to him, the Episcopalians had "probably done less for black people than any other aggregation of Christians."

46. Quoted in the *Church Standard* (Philadelphia, 1906), p. 12.

47. G. F. Bragg, *Richard Allen and Absalom Jones* (1916), p. 5.

48. S. Wilberforce, *A History of the Protestant Episcopal Church in America* (1844), has a chapter on this. Wilberforce's brother tried to interest J. H. Newman in the Negro American and segregated Episcopalianism, but apparently without success.

49. G. Osofsky, *Harlem: The Making of a Ghetto*, p. 131.

50. *Ibid.*, p. 134.

51. G. Moore, in *Life* (June 30, 1967), p. 78.

52. Bishop Richard Grant Robinson, in a sermon quoted in the *Orthodox Messenger* (Miami, October, 1942).

53. B. Aron, *The Garvey Movement* (unpublished M.A. thesis, Columbia University), p. 31. Actually the Revised Version of *Hymns Ancient and Modern* is used at Holy Cross, and the Standard Version used elsewhere.

54. *New York Age* (June 25, 1921).

55. Nonetheless, the Reformed Episcopal Church in a previous generation had welcomed large numbers of Negro Episcopalians after St. Mark's, Charleston, was refused regular admission to the Convention of the P.E.C. Though they were led out by a white priest, racial factors were by no means incidental. Negro membership still accounts for a large proportion of Reformed Episcopalians.

56. *Living Church* (June 25, 1921).

57. *Living Church* (October 15, 1921).

58. *Living Church* (November 19, 1921).

59. *Living Church* (September 10, 1921).

60. *Journal of the Convention of the Missionary District of South Florida, 1916*, p. 42. See also *Church Advocate* (September, 1921).

61. *Journal of the Convention of the Missionary District of South Florida, 1922*, pp. 44–45.

62. *Ibid.*, 1924.

63. D. M. Reimers, *White Protestantism and the Negro* (1965), p. 124.

64. J. H. Woodward, *The Negro Bishop Movement in the Episcopal Diocese of South Carolina* (1915), pp. 30–34.

65. *Church Advocate* (March, 1898).

66. *Church Advocate* (July, 1908).

67. Professor George Tsoumas concludes that the "bishop" in that case was not Greek Orthodox; see *Greek Orthodox Theological Review*, Vol. II, No. 2 (Christmas, 1956), pp. 62–73. But he may well have been a bishop in the Byzantine Rite of the Roman Church.

68. *Living Church* (June 25, 1921).

69. Communication from the Registrar's Office, King's College, London.

70. G. F. Bragg, *History of the Afro-American Group of the Episcopal Church* (1922), p. 273. The suspension of Morgan is recorded in the Convention

Journal of the Bishop of Asheville, but his deposition in that of the Bishop of Pennsylvania.

71. Article by the late Metropolitan Anthony Bashir in *The Word* (Brooklyn, December, 1965) to the effect that Robert Morgan was "reordained" at Constantinople in 1907. But the mention of Morgan is incidental, and there could have been no re-ordination since he had never been an Episcopal priest, so the Metropolitan may well have been misled on this.

72. *Living Church* (June 11, 1921).

73. *Living Church* (June 25, 1921). See also *Church Advocate* (March, 1908).

74. Terry-Thompson, *op. cit.*, p. 51.

75. B. Ravenswood, *A Grave Question Submitted for Consideration to Thomas March Clark, etc.* (1900).

76. A. Fortescue, *Orthodox Eastern Church* (1907), p. 262n.

77. *The Union of the Churches* (London, January 15, 1906).

78. I. N. W. Irvine, *A Letter on the Anglican Church's Claims* (1906), p. 13.

79. *Ibid.*, p. 10.

80. I am indebted for much of this information to the Rev'd. P. W. S. Schneirla.

81. *New York Times* (April 19, 1914).

82. I am indebted for this information to the Rev'd. Julian Smith.

83. Terry-Thompson, *op. cit.*, p. 53.

84. *Idem.*

85. *Ibid.*, pp. 54–55.

86. *Ibid.*, pp. 35–36, 43.

87. *Ibid.*, p. 52.

88. Brandreth, *op. cit.*, p. 63. Two priests of the Episcopal Church serving at Galesburg in that era were named Carl Nybladh.

89. *Ibid.*, p. 48.

90. That is to say, the West Syrian or Jacobite Patriarch of Antioch.

91. Brandreth, *op. cit.*, p. 51.

92. There is still a congregation of the American Catholic Church, St. Mary's, on Lenox Avenue in New York City.

93. Brandreth, *op. cit.*, p. 54. In using this book one should depend on the Second Edition and not the First where McGuire is concerned. There is also a good deal about Vilatte in Peter Anson's *Bishops at Large*. What is said here about orders received from churchless bishops applies, of course, to the Anglican Orthodox Church, a Southern white splinter group, as much as to McGuire and his followers.

94. Cronon, *op. cit.*, p. 160.

95. W. D. F. Hughes, *Prudently with Power* (1964), p. 128.

96. *New York Times* (October 24, 1932).

97. *Church Advocate* (November, 1921).

98. *Church Advocate* (March, 1922).

99. *The Divine Liturgy and other Rites and Ceremonies of the Church, according to the use of the African Orthodox Church, together with Selections from the Psalms* (Reprint of 1945), p. 48.

100. Terry-Thompson, *op. cit.*, p. 129, Constitution, Art. I, Sec. 3 & 4.

101. G. F. Bragg, *Richard Allen and Absalom Jones* (1916), p. 4.

102. The title was conferred upon her by Marcus Garvey.

103. For the re-union, see *The Trumpet*, Vol. I, No. 4 (February-March, 1964), p. 7. I am indebted for certain other items of information in this section to Msgr. Clement H. Gordon.

104. Brandreth, *op. cit.*, pp. 56–57. In the Corfield Report, *The Origins and Growth of Mau Mau: An Historical Study* (Colony & Protectorate of Kenya, Sessional Paper No. 5 of 1959/60 [1960]), much wickedness is attributed to Alexander. It is said, for example, on p. 173, that Alexander falsely claimed birth in Mauritius in order to obtain a French passport, which he used until it was taken away by authority. The author of this historical study evidently did not know that Mauritius had ceased to be French in 1814.

105. P. Anson, *Bishops at Large*, p. 264 ff.

106. F. B. Welbourn, *East African Rebels* (1961), p. 79. This is the definitive work on the subject.

107. C. G. Rosberg and J. Nottingham, *The Myth of "Mau Mau": Nationalism in Kenya* (1966), p. 129.

108. Notably in Welbourn's book, but for a later interpretation, see G. White, "Eastern African Orthodoxy," in *Sobornost*, Series 5, No. 5 (Summer, 1967), pp. 357–64; and D. E. Wentink, "The Orthodox Church in East Africa," in *The Ecumenical Review*, Vol. XX, No. 1 (January, 1968), pp. 33–43.

109. Perhaps not quite utterly unknown, since the Corfield Report, mentioned above, p. 173, tells us that the A.O.C. was "founded in 1921 by one G. A. Maguire" [*sic*].

110. Nicholson, *op. cit.*, pp. 10, 14.

111. The *Special Report* of ESCRU, quoted above. There is nothing in that report to show how this figure was reached.

112. Nicholson, *op. cit.*, p. 10.

113. *Ibid.*, p. 15 *et al.*

114. It is hard to tell to what extent this is really a way of saying that Negro Americans cannot appreciate the Book of Common Prayer which is not intended for them.

115. K. de P. Hughes, *op. cit.*, no page.

Reverdy C. Ransom:
The Making of an A.M.E. Bishop

David Wills

Reverdy Cassius Ransom (1861–1959) was one of the most important black churchmen of the first half of this century. Within the A.M.E. Church, he can justly be classed with Richard Allen, Daniel Alexander Payne, and Henry McNeal Turner as among the church's greatest bishops. Outside the church, he was for decades an eloquent and influential spokesman for racial justice. Yet Ransom has received very little scholarly attention. Not only is there no full-length study of his career, but apart from a few pages in S. P. Fullinwider's *The Mind and Mood of Black America* there is not a single published interpretation of his work. Such a lapse in scholarly attention clearly needs correction.[1]

Ideally, that correction should take the form of a book-length account of Ransom's long and productive life. A southwestern Ohio boyhood lasting from the eve of the Civil War through the end of Reconstruction; five troubled college years at Wilberforce and Oberlin; twenty-six years as the increasingly prominent pastor of A.M.E. congregations in Pennsylvania, Ohio, Illinois, Massachusetts and New York, and as an influential member of such racial protest groups as the Afro-American Council and the Niagara Movement; twelve years as editor of the *A.M.E. Review*; twenty-four years as the leading bishop of a denomination struggling to overcome severe internal divisions and to adjust to a reduced role in black American life; and seven years as a retired observer of the desegregation struggle of the 1950's—Ransom's life is clearly rich enough to sustain such a lengthy account.

The present essay, however, attempts no such ambitious task. It is, rather, quite limited both in the period it emphasizes and the topics it most fully treats. More is said here about Ransom's youth, education, and early years in the pastorate than about his later career as editor and bishop. Greater attention is given to his place within the A.M.E.

tradition than to his role in black protest movements. The controlling purpose of the essay is to trace through the personal experiences, ecclesiastical developments and public affairs of those earlier years—the emergence of the distinctive style of churchmanship which Ransom brought with him to the bishopric in 1924. The rest of the story, hopefully, will be told elsewhere.[2]

"Harriet Ransom's son," as Reverdy termed himself in the title of his autobiography, was born on January 4, 1861, in the village of Flushing, Ohio.[3] His mother, a woman of "light bronze complexion, with clearly cut features, high cheek bones and a straight, well-formed nose," was the daughter of an Indian father and an ex-slave mother. She was also, by her son's account, the dominant influence of his childhood and youth. She selected from the black and white worlds around her those ideas and values which seemed most commendable and impressed them upon young Reverdy with all the forcefulness that a strong and independent woman could muster. Her place in the title of his life story was earned, not merely honorary.

At birth, Reverdy was a frail child, whose appearance gave no hint of the long life that was to follow. He also had red hair and no admitted father, two facts possibly related to one another. His first two names were bestowed upon him, curiously enough, by Congressman John A. Bingham, who paid five dollars in gold for the privilege of naming his new constituent after two politicians, Reverdy Johnson of Maryland and Cassius M. Clay of Kentucky.[4] He also at some point gained a surname from George Warner Ransom, the "silent, taciturn man" who eventually married Reverdy's mother and became, by his "son's" account, "a father to me for more than fifty years." By temperament and affection, however, young Reverdy remained "Harriet Ransom's son."[5]

For the first four years of his life—the Civil War years—mother and son lived with Harriet's mother, Lucinda, in whose two-room log house Reverdy had been born. Lucinda was a brown-skinned woman from Virginia, who always impressed her grandson with her "exceptionally bright mind." Like a considerable number of other blacks in southeastern Ohio, she had been settled in the area (along with some relatives) by her former master.[6] She owned, in addition to the house, a plot of land that Reverdy, at least, regarded as "sizable." She was also literate, having learned to read in Virginia.

For some reason, perhaps having to do with her relationship with George Ransom, Harriet in 1865 left her mother's home and took Reverdy with her to Washington, Ohio, a slightly larger town a few miles to the west, in Guernsey County. There she boarded her son with George's parents, Louis and Betsy Ransom, who owned a farm on the outskirts of town. She herself worked in Washington as a domestic servant. At night,

Reverdy would join her, sleeping on a pallet in the cold, unheated attic of one of the homes in which his mother worked. Reverdy cared neither for the sleeping nor the eating arrangements. The attic was uncomfortable and the Ransoms, with a large family of their own to care for, seemed to him short on both food and affection for their boarder. He especially did not get along with George's sister, who persisted in calling him "that little red haired devil."

Both the Ransoms and his mother's employers, however, made a mark on his life as lasting as these memories of childhood deprivation. The Ransoms were regular attenders of the local African Methodist Episcopal Church, and they trained the children, Reverdy included, to emulate their piety. (They also were confirmed whiskey drinkers who shared their toddies with the children, a practice which also may have influenced Reverdy's later habits.) His mother's employers, mostly affluent, pro-slavery northern Democrats, were influential in a more indirect but no less important way. According to Reverdy, their "speech, manners and ideals" in rearing their own children were observed and emulated by his mother, who became, in the eyes of Reverdy's playmates, bent on turning her son into a "'white folks' nigger.'" Most especially, convinced that "ignorance" lay at the heart of black America's problems, she became determined that her son go to college.

The prospects for this were not encouraging. Reverdy began his education in Washington at a black school which met in the local A.M.E. Church. Apparently it offered little beyond instruction in literacy. When Ransom and his parents moved eight miles west to Cambridge in 1869, he was able to attend the town's somewhat more advanced black public school (which also met in the local A.M.E. Church). But by the time he was thirteen, he had exhausted the education available from this "noisy undisciplined ungraded" school and its white teachers. Harriet Ransom then took her son to the principal of the Cambridge Public School and requested that he be admitted to the white school, but they were met with a firm refusal. (She also took him at some point to the white Presbyterian Church's Sunday School. There, the teacher to whom he was assigned burst into tears, which probably ended that experiment as well.) Undaunted, Reverdy's mother pieced together a more advanced education for him by taking in the washing of several white families in exchange for their instructing her son in various subjects. Meanwhile, Reverdy himself did janitorial work in a shoe store in order to receive algebra lessons from its owner. Later on, after working in a brickyard, a barber shop, a saloon and a bank, he secured a position as house-boy in the bank cashier's home. This post, he later recalled, both expanded the horizon of his readings and gave him the opportunity to "absorb . . . and assimilate . . . the best in these people and their friends who came and went."

The friends who came and went in these white homes were, indeed, sometimes national celebrities to whom a black boy in small town Ohio would not ordinarily be exposed. Ransom recalled, for example, that Henry Wadsworth Longfellow, visiting in a home his mother was working in, had come around and paid a call at the Ransoms' home, too. Yet most of the impressive out-of-town visitors who attracted young Reverdy's interest were not white poets or politicians who might happen to take a momentary interest in a bright, red-haired black boy. They were, rather, black community leaders, particularly A.M.E. churchmen, who passed through Cambridge frequently and were no doubt well acquainted with some of the local African Methodists. The church's leading bishop, Daniel Alexander Payne, had his headquarters across the state at Wilberforce University, but travelling widely in the pursuit of his episcopal duties, he must have passed through Cambridge often, for the town lay on the old National Road at an important railroad junction.[7] Ransom also recalled, among others, the visits of Benjamin Arnett, an Ohio A.M.E. pastor and politically active Republican, and Henry McNeal Turner, the church's fiery Georgia leader, whose duties as Manager of the A.M.E. Book Concern took him after 1876 on nationwide travels. Each of these men proved important to Ransom's future.[8]

One immediate mark of their influence was Ransom's decision to make Wilberforce University the goal of his educational efforts. The A.M.E. school was in many ways a synthesis of the white and black influences that Harriet Ransom had tried to cultivate in her son's life. In curricular content, in the moral standards it sought to inculcate, and in the evangelical Protestantism it confessed, Wilberforce was very much in tune with the ethos that reigned in "the best white homes" in Cambridge. But it was also a black institution firmly committed to equal rights for black Americans. That must have mattered to Harriet Ransom, for Reverdy remembered that, of all his relatives, it was she who most bristled and spoke back when taunted with racial insults. Wilberforce, then, must have seemed a fitting culmination for her son's education.

At the last minute, however, Harriet Ransom's goal for her son almost went unachieved. Everything seemed in order for Reverdy to enroll in Wilberforce in the fall of 1881. He had completed his preparation by taking a summer normal school course and then teaching two short terms in a county school. The necessary funds had somehow been put away. Then, late in the winter before Reverdy's planned departure, he decided he was ready for marriage. The object of his affections was Leanna Watkins, a "comely" teenager whose "correctness of life and conduct" seemed to Reverdy to set her apart from the "community of free morals" in which they both lived. They were married in mid-February and immediately thereafter Leanna became pregnant. She herself had long since quit school to enter domestic service and it was readily apparent that if Reverdy undertook to support his wife and prospective child, his education must come to an end as well. Harriet Ransom, therefore, relieved her son of this responsibility. To secure additional funds, she mortgaged the house the family had acquired and, when in November Leanna gave birth to Harold George Ransom, she took her grandson into her home and reared him herself. Reverdy went to Wilberforce, after all.[9]

Wilberforce University was, in 1881, the "intellectual center of the A.M.E. Church."[10] It was also the lengthened shadow of one man, Daniel Alexander Payne. By then seventy, the church's senior bishop had been associated with the school since 1856, when it was first launched by the Cincinnati Conference of the Methodist Episcopal Church, North. In 1863, having arranged for the school's purchase by the A.M.E. Church, he had become the first black president of the first black-controlled college in America. He retired from this post in 1876, but remained a resident of "Tawawa Springs" and a major influence in the life of the school.

Payne was, moreover, the single most important figure in the A.M.E. Church as a whole.[11] Elected to the bishopric in 1852, he had soon become and long remained the dominant influence among the handful of bishops who ran the church. An intense, rigidly self-disciplined, bookish man, Payne had tried for years—especially through the church's educational program—to reshape African Methodism in his own ascetic image. Theologically, he was a strict biblicist who admired the Princeton scholastic Charles Hodge above all other American theologians. He also was convinced that the Bible, properly read, taught one to respect authority and restrain contention in the conduct of church business, to worship "in a rational manner," and to adhere strictly to an ascetic code of personal conduct. He therefore fought vigorously throughout his career against those in the church who seemed to him to lack proper respect for church law and episcopal authority, who engaged in such "heathenish" worship practices as the "ring-shout" or insisted on singing the spirituals ("corn-field ditties"), and who violated or refused to enforce the church's strict moral disciplinary rules. Not surprisingly, some of these people fought back, and the result was a half-century struggle between Payne and his adversaries that at times sharply polarized the church.

In the ante-bellum period, when the restrictive laws of the southern states generally excluded the A.M.E. Church from slave territory, the line of cleavage seemed roughly to follow the major class division of northern black communities. Payne spoke from the point of view of a relatively affluent black elite strongly imbued with the middle-class ethos of white America, while his opponents were more likely to view things from the vantage point of more impoverished blacks with closer ties to Afro-American folk culture. As a result of the church's rapid expansion in the south during the Reconstruction period, however, the controversy increasingly came to have a geographical cast. Payne now represented a beleaguered northern leadership elite struggling to maintain its control of an overwhelmingly southern church, while his most visible opponents were younger southern churchmen. Naturally, there were many exceptions to and variations on this pattern. Payne's northern opposition did not disappear, he had imitators as well as enemies in the south, and the play of personal idiosyncracies made for curious alliances on any given issue. But there was in the church a general sense that a division was there and that it ran roughly along sectional lines.

There was also a sense that the south was on the offensive and gradually gaining in power. At the General Conference of 1880, the south had elected two bishops—Richard H. Cain and Henry McNeal Turner— over the opposition of Bishop Payne. In the early 1880's, moreover, the southern Annual Conferences launched a series of educational ventures that created unprecedented competition for Wilberforce. The South Carolina Conference led the way in 1880 by reorganizing Payne Institute as Allen University and locating it at Columbia. The next year, the North Georgia Conference took initial steps to organize Morris Brown College (it opened in Atlanta in 1885), while Paul Quinn College was established at Waco, Texas. Edward Waters College was launched in Jacksonville, Florida, in 1883. There was also already an A.M.E. school, Western University, in Quindaro, Kansas, which had evolved from the earlier efforts of a white Presbyterian minister, and several more A.M.E. schools were to follow in the latter half of the decade. In a way, of course, these schools demonstrated the hold of Payne's educational concerns on the southern wing of the church. He was, however, not pleased. He feared that the rapid creation of new schools would divide the church's already meager resources and undermine the quest for excellence at Wilberforce itself. He therefore issued increasingly strident warnings against the effort to build up more than one college at a time.[12]

Whatever Payne's worries about this southern threat to the church in general and Wilberforce in particular, the college itself seemed perfectly to exemplify—within the limits imposed by its small budget—the kind of African Methodism the old bishop was so determined to create.[13] The emerging theological liberalism of the time had not made a dent in the school's orthodoxy. Though it regularly culminated in an annual revival in which students might even "fall down in the classroom and plead with the Lord to pardon their sins," the extensive worship life of the college (two required services daily, six days a week) did not include "bush meetings," "ring shouts," or "the frenzy" in their most intense forms. Individual conduct was strictly regulated from the rising bell at 6:00 a.m. until lights out at 9:30 p.m. and the lessons of hard work and self-discipline were inculcated at every turn. There were stern prohibitions against "immoral books and papers, fire-arms, card-playing, games of chance" and unsupervised encounters between members of the opposite sex. Administrative and faculty authority to enforce these rules and generally govern the institution went unchallenged by the disrespect for authority and general boisterousness that Payne thought his southern brethren had brought to the General Conference of 1880. It was, in sum, Daniel Alexander Payne's world.

It also became, in the fall of 1881, Reverdy Ransom's world—though, finally, a world he was more "in" than "of." Especially during what seems to have been a difficult first year, Ransom struggled over the direction of his life and Wilberforce's place in it. The religious life of the school he found thoroughly congenial. "Though reared in an atmosphere of prayer by a devout Christian mother" and long familiar with the life of the A.M.E. Church, Ransom had neither been "converted" nor joined the church. Regarded by some of his friends and relatives at home as a stone-hearted reprobate, Ransom knew his problem lay not in a lack of Christian conviction but in an unwillingness "to go to the mourner's bench and kneel on the bare floor with a great crowd of singing, shouting, perspiring men and women surrounding me." At Wilberforce, he found a religious atmosphere in which submission to this sort of "spectacle" was not a required rite of passage. Able at last to pursue his own path, Ransom struggled on his own for grace until one night, alone in his room, he experienced "one of those rapturing moments . . . when earth and heaven meet and blend in the happy consciousness that God has entered into our life making Himself known." In his own estimation, achieving this "knowledge of the conscious, inward presence of God was worth more to me than all other things gained during my first year at Wilberforce."[14]

Other aspects of campus life, however, he found much less satisfactory. In *School Days at Wilberforce*, published some half-dozen years after his graduation, Ransom described the carefully regulated, once a month socials, where men and women were allowed two carefully chaperoned hours of polite conversation, as "among the most pleasant . . . experience . . . of our college days." Writing a half-century later, however, he admitted they had been "dull and tame" affairs which he had generally avoided. Indeed preoccupied with sorting out his feelings about Leanna and their baby, Ransom must have felt remote indeed from Wilberforce's regime of highly circumspect courtships. He also, however, felt increasingly remote from his uneducated bride at home, so much so that he finally secured a divorce. The whole business, which Ransom regarded as the most painful experience of his life, clearly made his first year at Wilberforce an unhappy one.[15]

He was also discontented with the education which Wilberforce offered. Influenced, perhaps, by his mother's persistent efforts to place him in white schools or to secure white tutors for him, Ransom had come to the black college doubting that "a Faculty composed of colored men was as good as one composed of white men." Though he eventually came to greatly admire Wilberforce's small and overworked faculty and to insist that black schools could teach a lesson in self-respect that "mixed schools" could not, he was still troubled by what he later called the "cramped and narrow quality of academic life." Aware no doubt that a number of prominent blacks—including Wilberforce's own well-regarded young classicist, William Sanders Scarborough—had been educated at Oberlin College, Ransom decided that he too should avail himself of that school's "broader and more liberal educational advantages." He also hoped that he would find it easier there to make ends meet financially— another real problem for him at Wilberforce.[16]

Ransom's arrival at Oberlin in the fall of 1882 was, however, an untimely one. A free tuition scholarship and a variety of odd jobs solved his financial problems and, if one can judge by his lack of complaint, the quality of education seems to have met his expectations. He also enjoyed the friendship of his black classmates—though he had neither the money nor leisure fully to share their social life. But liberal Oberlin was in the process of adapting to the racially more conservative ethos of the early 1880's and Ransom soon found himself in the thick of a fight over segregated eating facilities. Ladies Hall, the college's main dormitory, had long had an integrated dining room. In the fall of 1882, however, pressure from white students led to the establishment there of a separate table for black women. Counter-pressure from black students and from many alumni and administrators led finally to the restoration of integrated dining, but not before Ransom had become a casualty of the battle. By his account, his organizing and addressing a protest meeting provoked the faculty to terminate his scholarship. This made his position at the college untenable. Resentful in any case of "the outward friendliness which subtly, but firmly, closed so many doors to the freedom of the larger life about us to colored students," Ransom left Oberlin and returned to Wilberforce.[17]

By now, knowing more clearly the limited character of his options and having a no doubt heightened appreciation of Wilberforce's commitment to black equality, Ransom was ready to make his peace with the A.M.E. school. He was enormously helped in this reconciliation by a change in his vocational plans. As a result of the religious deepening that had occurred during his first year at Wilberforce, and in response to what he regarded as a call "so vividly clear and impressive as to leave no doubt," Ransom had decided to enter the A.M.E. ministry. The decision had not been easy, for Ransom, since his youthful fascination with the doings of the Cambridge Court of Common Pleas, had intended to pursue a legal career.[18] The choice for the ministry once made, however, the advantages of Wilberforce were obvious. There he could combine his collegiate and theological education and graduate in four years. There he could also move within the circle of men important in shaping the institution he proposed to serve.

But there were still problems. As always, Ransom was short of money. Even after Harriet Ransom sold the family cow to pay his initial expenses and Reverdy secured a steady Saturday job in a Xenia barbershop, life at Wilberforce meant "often going hungry and always poorly clad." He had also somewhere acquired a taste for liberal theology, a set of ideas equated with rank heresy at Wilberforce. Keeping his forbidden views hidden from the watchful eye of the college's strictly orthodox theological instructor, T. H. Jackson, proved a difficult and painful task, and led to much brooding about whether he was truly suited for the ministry. There was also the continuing problem of Wilberforce's stilted social life—though he managed to get around this difficulty in his senior year by courting Emma S. Connor, a girl who belonged to his student charge at nearby Selma, Ohio.[19]

By June 1886, Ransom had completed his studies and was ready to graduate—an accomplishment that most of the students who enrolled in Wilberforce in those days never achieved.[20] He did not depart inconspicuously. His address at the college literary society's commencement meeting was, by one account at least, "the finest students' oration ever delivered at Wilberforce. . . ." On commencement day itself, moreover, Ransom was involved in a scene that the same observer thought quite unprecedented:

> When Mr. R. C. Ransom had concluded his oration and amid the deafening applause that followed (wrote John G. Brown in the *Christian Recorder*), his mother, who sat in the audience, forced her way to the stage and fell upon the neck of her son. Overcome with emotion, realizing the fulfillment of her prayers, she could not contain herself. Well she might rejoice with love that is a tender mother's when her mind wandered back a few years ago when this, her only child, was a wayward lad. Now she beheld him graduating with honors. Her prayers had been answered and he who was the wayward lad stood before her prepared to go forth preaching the gospel that she had made her staff through life. Those who witnessed the scene are not likely soon to forget it.

Ransom often told his mother "that she and I had graduated together."[21]

Ransom's career in the pastorate fell into three phases. From 1886 to 1890, assigned to small, difficult parishes in western Pennsylvania, he served the typical apprenticeship of a beginning A.M.E. preacher. From 1890 to 1896, he rose to regional prominence as the pastor of two important Ohio churches, North Street Church in Springfield (1890–1893) and St. John's Church, Cleveland (1893–1896). From 1896, when he was assigned, at the age of thirty-five, to Bethel Church in Chicago, until 1912, when he was elected editor of the *A.M.E. Review*, Ransom achieved a church-wide reputation as the pastor of a series of important churches in Chicago, Boston and New York. He was, then, from a relatively early age, a "successful" pastor and well-known A.M.E. churchman.

Such success was important to Ransom for he was clearly an ambitious man. When, as a theological student he became sufficiently troubled by his doctrinal doubts to question his calling, he experienced the conflict as one between honestly abandoning the ministry to "dwell in poverty obscure" or hypocritically preaching his way to "the honors the Church can give." A few years later, as a novice pastor, he became angry when he was assigned once too often to a tiny, impoverished congregation. He had willingly served for two years a circuit near Altoona, Pennsylvania, where his major charge had only thirteen members. But when Bishop Payne assigned him in 1888 to the even smaller and poorer Manchester Mission in Allegheny City (now part of Pittsburgh), Ransom at first refused to go. (Sixty years later, he was still complaining about "the theory and practice among us that a young man in the ministry, regardless of his ability and training, should be sent out to small churches and made to suffer hardship and deprivation for a few years before being given a living charge.") He was also a willing, if not always eager, candidate for hïgher church office, who did not rest content until he had won his way to the bishopric.[22]

Ambition alone, however, could scarcely have secured Ransom's rapid rise to churchly prominence. Neither could his personal charm, general administrative abilities, or exceptional oratorical skills—though all of these no doubt helped. What he needed as well were "connections," particularly among the bishops, who could so easily make or break a young pastor's career.

Here Wilberforce served Ransom well, for it placed him within the immediate circle of men highly influential in the church. Indeed, Ransom shortly found himself under the benevolent protection of Bishop Payne himself. In spite of his adamant assignment of Ransom to the obscure Manchester Mission in 1888, the old bishop clearly liked the young Wilberforcian. In 1890, telling Ransom that he was sending him to a church with "carpets on the floor, cushioned pews, stained glass windows and a marble pulpit," Payne transferred him from the Pittsburgh to the Ohio Conference and assigned him to North Street Church in Springfield. This was a congregation of several hundred members which included "a majority of the most intelligent and most prosperous colored people in Springfield." In 1893, after carefully checking beforehand to make sure that the thin young pastor considered himself hardy enough to face the city's winters, Payne moved Ransom to the equally prestigious St. John's Church in Cleveland. Shortly thereafter, Payne died at the advanced age of eighty-two. He had, however, already brought Ransom to a position of considerable regional prominence within the church.[23]

The old bishop's favoring of Ransom is not hard to understand, for Ransom clearly had begun his career as a loyal member of the Payne wing of the A.M.E. Church. Through his education at Wilberforce, he had not only become personally acquainted with Payne, but was identified as well with the institution that, above all else, embodied Payne's vision of the church. This was an important identification, for Wilberforce and its place in the church were in those years matters of considerable church-wide controversy. On the very day that Ransom graduated, the denomination's weekly newspaper, *The Christian Recorder*, carried a long article attacking the existing financial arrangements by which Wilberforce received support from the whole church while the other A.M.E. schools were financed on a regional basis. Benjamin F. Lee, a former President of Wilberforce and now editor of *The Recorder*, tried to meet the attack by explaining that the denomination must concentrate its resources on its oldest school because "we can make Wilberforce a great college much sooner than we can any other." But such attacks persisted and Wilberforce was clearly on the defensive—as was evidenced by Lee's own concession that the shift in membership perhaps required that "we should concentrate just as strongly on establishing one great university in the South, perhaps in Atlanta. . . ." Still, he warned, "two respectable universities are all we should be able to build up. . . ."[24]

Ransom, as a Wilberforcian, would presumably have been more or less identified with the ideals and interest of his alma mater even had he not actively worked to underscore the association. The identification must therefore have been all the greater when, from an early point in his ministry, he energetically espoused Wilberforce's cause. In 1890, he published a vigorous plea for the concentration of the church's educational resources on Wilberforce, warning that equal support for the many "so-called colleges being set up in nearly every one of the episcopal districts" would lead to a pointless dissipation of A.M.E. efforts. (The piece caught the eye of Bishop Payne, who published a reply in which he gently chided Ransom for not sufficiently praising the school's present strengths but generally agreed with his "just and timely" assessment of the school's needs.) Ransom also made it clear in *School Days at Wilberforce*, published shortly thereafter, that he regarded the college and its community as the pinnacle of black America's highest educational and cultural achievement. Wilberforce, he declared, "has gathered around itself a community as intelligent, refined and Christian as can be found anywhere in our land." He also openly acknowledged that his book had been written precisely to quicken support for the school.[25]

Ransom identified himself, moreover, not only with the institution and its needs but also with the general ethos of "colored Christian civilization" that was associated with it—particularly as it applied to the ministry. His first article in the *Christian Recorder*, published in the fall of 1886, was an apology on behalf of the educated and morally disciplined minister. Acknowledging that sometimes a minister seemed "too cultured for his flock," he insisted that the gap be closed by an elevation of the congregation's tastes. He also sharply criticized those clergymen whose ministries seemed to have the opposite effect:

> Many preachers [he complained], by the manner in which they associate with their members, and in the community generally, are imparting to the people a false education on the subject of ministerial culture and decorum. When a man follows who has proper ideas concerning preaching and pastoral work, one who uses the pastoral visits as a means of spiritual instruction, one who prays from hour to hour, instead of feasting and joking from hour to hour, one who spends his otherwise unemployed time in study and with his family, instead of loafing around barber shops and the like—he is often styled "stuck up" or as being unsociable.

To get to the root of the problem, he called, in another *Christian Recorder* article, for conference examining committees to be stricter in applying the educational tests for admission into the A.M.E. ministry. "No amount of sympathy," he insisted, "should be sufficient to pass a man who has not made proficiency in his studies." These views also caught the attention of Daniel Alexander Payne, who was happy to count Ransom as a new recruit in his battle against "ignorance." At a meeting of the North Ohio Conference, for example, Payne put Ransom on an examining committee with explicit instructions to block a rumored effort to deny ordination to Oscar J. W. Scott, a young Ohio Wesleyan graduate. "I need more men like you and Reverend Scott," he told Ransom, "because we have so few educated men in the ranks of our ministry." It is evident, then, why Payne liked Ransom and so quickly advanced him to large and prestigious churches.[26]

What is not so clear is whether Ransom himself deliberately exaggerated his conformity to Payne's ideals in order to secure advancement. It has already been noted that Ransom's post-graduation enthusiasm for Wilberforce masked misgivings about the school which he only acknowledged much later. More striking is Ransom's April 1890 assault on C. S. Smith of the A.M.E. Sunday School Union for using a revised version of the Apostles Creed in the agency's literature. Although, according to his autobiography, he had himself abandoned as a college student the doctrine of the Trinity ("as it was usually taught"), he assailed Smith for changes that were more verbal than substantive. He hinted that Smith had eliminated the phrase "He descended into hell" because he did not believe it and lamented the fact that "in the publications of the Sunday School Union this important link in the golden chain of faith is broken." He warned that "those who have rejected the statement of doctrine contained in the Apostles Creed have ultimately drifted into mysticism and pantheism" and cited with approval A. A. Hodge's declaration that creedal revision amounted to a "'dreadful violation'" of Christian solidarity. He also took time to discuss the historic importance of the Nicene and Athanasian Creeds. If he had wanted to please Payne, he could scarcely have found a more effective way to do so than by this spirited defense of a learned orthodoxy.[27]

It is also possible, however, that Ransom had not by this time really made peace with himself about his own deviations from Payne's version of African Methodism. At Wilberforce, his struggle with his own heresy had been a private one, for he had found there "no sympathetic human counsellors" with whom to share his views.[28] Since the beliefs he developed were therefore lacking in public acknowledgment and support, they may have been quite unstable, and he may well at times have genuinely adhered to the orthodoxy he at other moments only pretended. Indeed, it is conceivable that by attacking Smith he was unconsciously trying to silence his own doubts—to appease the Payne within as much as to please the bishop without. The same might be said of his exaggerated enthusiasm for Wilberforce and his general effort energetically to align himself with the Payne wing of the church.

In the long run, however, neither calculation nor conscience could disguise the fact that Ransom simply was not cast from the same mould as his patriarchal sponsor. Differences of temperament, background, and generation, obscured by their common immersion in the Wilberforce ambience of the late 1880's and early 1890's, increasingly came to the fore after Payne's death. Gradually, Ransom developed his own perspective on the nature and task of African Methodism. His mature views were identical neither with Payne's nor with those of that disparate group of southern churchmen whom Payne counted as his opponents. They were rather a blending of the two, a synthesis shaped by his own experience and organized around his own special concerns. This is evident in a number of areas.

For one thing, Ransom did not share Payne's view that the church must strictly enforce an ascetic morality—not even in the early years of his ministry. When, for example, the young, unwed, church organist at Manchester Mission became pregnant during Ransom's pastorate there, he refused the demands of the congregation's officers that she be brought to trial and expelled from membership. "'Now that she is in this trouble and disgrace,'" he insisted, "'she needs us. We must not cast her out. . . .'" No doubt, Ransom's leniency for those who in one way or another departed from the church's teaching about sex and marriage, in part reflected a personal sympathy based on his own experience. But it also seems to have been based on a deliberate shift of emphasis from "law" to "gospel."

Speaking of a very different and much later case in which he also declined for the sake of mercy to carry out the requirements of the Book of Discipline, Ransom remarked: "I knew in my heart of hearts that a sinner like me could not refuse to give that which he hopes to receive when he comes at last to stand before the Judge of all the earth." Nevertheless, conventional Methodist morality as such was not directly challenged by Ransom. He was careful to see that the wayward organist eventually married the father of her child. He was also, by this time, a respectable family man himself, having married Emma Connor, in 1887. (During their two years in Allegheny City, their family grew as Reverdy C. Ransom, Jr., their only child, was born, and Harold George Ransom, Reverdy's older son, came to live with them.) Even in the area of "temperance," moreover, Ransom never presented his own non-compliance with the ethic of abstinence, which became increasingly notorious in his later years, as anything other than a sinful (but presumably forgivable) failing.[29]

Ransom was similarly more flexible and tolerant than Payne in his attitude toward black folk worship practices—without becoming a practitioner or partisan of the "ring shout." He was enough the Wilberforcian that one of his earliest parishioners was moved to refer to his sermons as "gospel lectures," but when a visiting Kentucky revivalist greatly stirred his Springfield congregation, Ransom tried the next week to imitate the musical cadences of the revivalist's delivery. (Another parishioner ended the experiment by telling him that such preaching, coming from him, sounded "ridiculous.") He had no sympathy, moreover, for the Cleveland parishioner who reported that "she had outgrown the old-fashioned and sometimes noisy manner of worship in St. John" and was going to become a Congregationalist. And when he later served, in New Bedford, Massachusetts, a congregation that seemed ignorant of and uninterested in "Negro spirituals and other forms of religious expression so characteristic of the Negro Church," he judged "their mode of worship . . . rather cold and formal." Still, worship in one of Ransom's more typical churches would have been readily distinguishable from the practices of the storefront or "bush meeting."[30]

Ransom was also more an ecclesiastical democrat (and politician) than Payne, though he remained, on the whole, more an enemy than a friend of "lawlessness." He shared enough of Payne's commitment to parliamentary decorum and the rule of law to respond with disgust when, as a first time delegate to the General Conference of 1896, he witnessed the general tumult, electoral corruption, and even physical violence that had become typical of these assemblies. Yet Ransom's reverence for episcopal authority never matched Payne's. In 1888, when Payne refused to change his assignment of Ransom to Manchester Mission, Ransom submitted. But in 1904, when Bishop C. T. Shaffer seemed bent on banishing him from Chicago to the hinterlands of Indiana, Ransom simply left the bishop's jurisdiction and went, without the proper transfer papers, to New England, where he knew he would be more favorably treated. He was also, throughout his career, generally sympathetic towards efforts to democratize church life and he had an undeniable taste for church politics.[31]

In sum, while Ransom did not altogether abandon Payne's strictly ordered vision of what African Methodism should be, he greatly softened its rather authoritarian and even repressive cast. Where Payne had sought to conquer and rule the passions that informed "heresy," "immorality," "heathenish worship," and "strife and contention," Ransom was willing to come to terms, to negotiate a settlement that allowed more play to individual imaginings, bodily indulgence, emotional enthusiasm, and the spirit of rebellion. This, after all, was Ransom's private settlement—as a stern asceticism had been Payne's. Ready, apparently, to acknowledge and accept in himself both "the wayward lad" and the Wilberforce trained preacher, Ransom could scarcely do otherwise. His private struggles thereby bore public fruit and, more and more his own man, he was increasingly able to lead.

Personal autonomy could not, however, be translated into ecclesiastical independence without considerable risk, and Ransom was therefore still dependent on episcopal sponsorship even after Payne's death and his own maturing. Fortunately, he found in Bishop Benjamin W. Arnett an ally who was personally less formidable than Payne but nonetheless effective in advancing and protecting his career. Elected to the bishopric in 1888 at the age of fifty, Arnett was known for his wooden leg, his active involvement in politics, his oratorical skills, and his compilation as Financial Secretary of a series of important denominational reports. A resident of Wilberforce, he had employed Ransom during his student years and was therefore by the early 1890's an old friend. From Payne's death in 1893 until his own demise in 1906, Arnett was an energetic and reliable defender of Ransom's interests.[32]

In 1896, after Ransom had served at St. John's A.M.E. in Cleveland for three years, Arnett arranged to transfer him to whichever of the church's two major Chicago congregations Ransom preferred. Choosing Bethel Church, "a well built structure with a seating capacity for about nine hundred people" and a congregation that was willing to pay him $1800 a year, Ransom moved that October to the "big, wicked, but splendid city" of Chicago. There, "play[ing] to a crowded house" that included some of Chicago's most prominent black families and linked through Arnett's political connections to several members of the city's white elite, Ransom achieved both considerable local prominence and a nationwide reputation among black leaders. He also developed a new style of ministry that was at once a clearer expression of his own deepest concerns and an important innovation in the urban work of the entire denomination.[33]

The change in the method of Ransom's ministry was rooted in his growing concern to bring together in the church "the Negro who is up and the Negro who is down, the Negro who is good and the Negro who is ignorant." Difficult enough in Bishop Payne's day, this task was severely complicated by the socio-cultural milieu of a modern industrial city such as Chicago. There, and across the urban north, one could discern the emergence both of an "up Negro" who was increasingly critical of the black church and progressively more susceptible to an altogether secular view of life, and of a "down Negro" who was by the desperate living conditions of urban poverty separated ever more sharply from the world of black respectability. Sympathetic to the currents of thought which were influencing the disaffected elite and bound by the memories of his own economic struggles to the life of the black poor, Ransom sought to overcome this growing fragmentation.[34]

The methods which he employed in this enterprise were partially an adaptation of the newer patterns of urban church work recently developed among white Protestants. Ida B. Wells-Barnett, the well-known anti-lynching crusader and one of Ransom's Chicago parishioners, reported enthusiastically to the *Christian Recorder* early in 1900 that Ransom had "enlarged and broadened the church horizon" in part by creating at Bethel a series of "auxiliary movements."

> The most prominent of these [she wrote] was "The Men's Sunday Club," an organization which has gathered young men off the streets and out of saloons . . . , together with the best representatives of our professional and business manhood every Sunday afternoon for intellectual culture. . . . [Another] child of Rev. Ransom's brain . . . is . . . "The Woman's Conference" which purposes to do the same thing for women. The industrial school for children, The Twentieth Century Club, a literary organization, and a kindergarten were all fostered by this pastor and his church. In like manner have the physical necessities of, not Bethel Church alone, but whoever in the church district needed it, been looked after. Rev. Ransom districted that part of the city . . . and created an order of deaconesses, twelve women, who cover that district seeking strangers, visiting the sick, and feeding, clothing and making warm the poor and needy.

Ransom himself, however, was apparently less satisfied than Mrs. Wells-Barnett with the impact of all these "auxiliaries," for he became persuaded that what was needed was an entirely new organization. Securing the assistance of Bishop Arnett, who used his influence as president of the Church's Financial Board to obtain denominational funds to support Ransom's new venture, Ransom left Bethel in 1900 to launch the Institutional Church and Settlement House.[35]

Located in what had at one time been known as "the Railroad Chapel" ("a magnificent stone and brick ... building ..., with an auditorium holding nearly two thousand persons, ... the finest pipe organ, save one, in Chicago ... [and] rooms up and down stairs for almost any imaginable purpose"), the "only colored Social Settlement in the world" was modelled after Jane Addams' Hull House and Graham Taylor's Chicago Commons. Its program included a day care center, a kindergarten, boys' and girls' clubs, a mothers' club, music classes, sewing classes, cooking classes, an employment bureau, a penny savings bank, and a public forum. On its staff, among others, were two later prominent University of Chicago students, Monroe Work, who ran the boys' club, and Richard R. Wright, Jr., who served for a year as the assistant pastor. The Institutional Church and Settlement House attracted favorable comment in the Chicago press and served as a model for similar A.M.E. efforts elsewhere. Already by Christmas 1902, the *Christian Recorder* was declaring it a successful experiment.[36]

Ransom did not, however, rely solely on these innovations in church organization and programming to achieve the results he was seeking. He also took a leading part in a number of wider efforts to promote the general welfare of Chicago's black community. Early in his ministry at Bethel, he disregarded the raised eyebrows of some of his parishioners and worked with black saloon keeper Robert T. Motts to defeat a city alderman who refused to arrange for the paving of Dearborn Street. In 1903, as pastor of the Institutional Church, he launched a major campaign against the South Side's numbers racketeers, during which the church was dynamited and his own life threatened. The following year, 1904, he became actively involved in efforts to mediate the violent stockyards strike, which pitted hundreds of imported black strikebreakers against the largely white ethnic union workforce in a confrontation that created racial tension all over the city. Not surprisingly, he soon became, according to Ida B. Wells-Barnett, "the best known colored preacher Chicago has ever had."[37]

He meanwhile became active in racial advancement efforts at the national level. In this—especially to the extent that it involved him in electoral politics—he followed the example and benefitted from the sponsorship of Benjamin Arnett. Bishop Payne had early decided to forego abolitionist lecturing and political involvement in order to concentrate his energies entirely on the church, but Arnett had chosen a different course. Active in racial advancement organizations and Republican politics from the beginning of his ministry, he had served a term in the Ohio legislature (1885–87) and introduced one of the bills that ended school desegregation in the state. He had also carefully cultivated William McKinley, Ohio's governor from 1892 to 1896, and Mark Hanna, his political manager. After McKinley's election to the White House, he became perhaps his most influential Afro-American adviser. All this clearly was to Ransom's advantage when he sought to widen the scope of his own activities.[38]

Ransom had also developed his political ties of his own. Among the members of his Cleveland congregation was George A. Myers, owner of the elite Hollenden House barbershop and wielder of significant influence in Ohio Republican circles. Also on good terms with Mark Hanna, whom he both barbered and supported politically, Myers along with Arnett arranged for Ransom himself to become at least casually acquainted with the Cleveland kingmaker. Myers helped Ransom secure $500 from Hanna to help pay off the mortage at St. John's Church, while Ransom himself was subsequently able to talk Hanna into contributing $800 toward the rebuilding of Bishop Arnett's fire-damaged Wilberforce home. When Ransom moved to Chicago, moreover, he was linked through Bethel Church member Ida Wells-Barnett to Ferdinand Barnett, who ran the Afro-American Bureau for the Republican National Committee in both the 1896 and 1900 campaigns. He was, then, well placed to pursue a career of mounting political influence.[39]

The nature of Ransom's interest in politics differed, however, from that of Arnett, Myers or Barnett. These men were all enormously interested in patronage. On the basis of his good service in 1896, Barnett angled for a presidential appointment and then secured in Illinois a position as assistant state's attorney, a post he held for a decade. Myers, though declining Hanna's offer of a position for himself, tried very hard, albeit unsuccessfully, to secure appropriate places in the McKinley administration for his friends and political allies. Similarly, but more successfully, Arnett worked to secure appointments both for two of his sons and for a variety of other political and ecclesiastical allies. Ransom, however, was at this time uninterested either in personal office holding or political empire-building. When Hanna offered him a position as army chaplain (a prestigious post for a black cleric) he turned it down, and there is no record of his having tried systematically to influence the appointments of others. His concern seems to have been more exclusively focussed on securing the election of candidates sympathetic to the interests of black America.[40]

Ransom also seems to have differed from these men in being too independent and outspoken to have easily played the role of a power-seeking party regular. He especially differed from Arnett, whose continuing political influence depended heavily on his partisan reliability and discreet silences. When, for example, McKinley was sharply criticized by many black leaders for his failure to condemn the Wilmington, North Carolina, race riot in November 1898, Arnett not only failed to join the criticism but was later discovered to have recommended to McKinley the policy of silence. Ransom during this same period publicly warned that the failure to check such mob outrages would eventually drive blacks to defend themselves with dynamite. He also privately called upon the president to "give more attentive ear to the great mass of people who are Republicans from principle and who seek no office, rather than its professional champions in church and state."⁴¹

Given these limitations in his taste for partisan politics, it is not surprising that Ransom found racial protest organizations an important vehicle for his own efforts to secure racial justice. When the Afro-American Council was revived in 1898, he quickly became an active member. Perhaps through the influence of Ida Wells-Barnett, a veteran of the old Afro-American League who was elected secretary of the new Council at its first meeting, the group's second meeting was convened at Ransom's church in Chicago. More prominent as host than he otherwise might have been, Ransom emerged from the session as the eighth of the Council's nine vice-presidents.⁴²

He also emerged from the meeting, however, as the center of a storm of controversy over the Council's relation to Booker T. Washington. Washington, in bad repute with some of the Council's members over his failure forcefully to condemn the brutal Sam Hose lynching of a few months earlier, had decided prudently to avoid the annual meeting even though he would be in Chicago during its sessions. His absence itself proved a further irritant, especially after he summoned the Council's president, A.M.E. Zion Bishop Alexander Walter, to meet with him privately in his hotel room. When Mrs. Washington requested toward the end of the meeting that her name also be removed from the program, that proved the last straw—at least to Ransom. Having already blocked in committee a resolution to endorse Washington, he now publicly rebuked the Tuskeegean for his absence and moved that he be removed from the Council's list of members. Accounts of the proceedings vary, but according to one newspaper, Ransom made his attack in these stinging words:

> I know of no man who has received more advertising from his connection with the Negro race than has Booker T. Washington. He has posed as the leader of the colored people and the Moses who was to lead his people out of the wilderness. Yet he has hung around the outskirts of this council casting aspersions and contempt on its proceedings. He has refused to come inside. He sat in his room at the Palmer House and sent for our president to wait upon him. No such man ought to claim to be our leader. We want the country to know he is nothing to us. We hold him in contempt. He is trying to hold us in line. From his room in the Palmer House, he says "Sh! Sh!," but he's afraid to come in. I move that Mr. Washington's name be stricken from the roll.

With cries of "traitor," "trimmer," and "coward" arising from the floor, the motion went down to tumultuous defeat. More conservative members of the Council soon rallied their troops and rushed through the closing session a ringing endorsement of Washington. Early press reports, however, carried the mistaken news that the Council had repudiated Washington and even when, amidst a shower of editorial condemnation of Ransom, the truth emerged, "the Wizard" was not pleased.[43]

Under considerable pressure from all sides (DuBois, for example, who was there, referred to his remarks as "ill-timed and foolish"), Ransom backed down. In a letter to the Chicago *Inter-Ocean*, published less than a week after the meeting, he admitted that his attack on Washington might have been "unwise." He also sought to excuse himself by explaining that he had meant Washington no harm but simply felt that if Washington had wished to influence the Council's deliberations he should have directly participated in its meetings. After all, he concluded weakly, "we needed the help of our best and wisest minds." A few days later, in replying privately to an "earnest letter" from Washington himself, Ransom blamed the whole affair on the misrepresentation of Washington's "overzealous ... friends and admirers." He assured him that "I regard your career as one of the most fruitful and remarkable of any man of our race, and your work as the most fundamental and helpful of any that is being done for the great mass of our people who, if they rise at all, must do so through habits of industry, frugality, character and thrift." To clinch the matter, he wrote Washington again two weeks later requesting a copy of the latest Tuskeegee Conference program for use in preparing a forthcoming *A.M.E. Review* article on "what the wisest and best among us are doing in the direction of mapping out a program for the race." Washington apparently obliged, and when the article appeared the following April it listed the Tuskeegee program ahead of those devised by the National Association of Colored Women, the Afro-American Council, and the Hampton Conference, and came no closer to a criticism of Washington than the observation that his program made "no reference ... to political action, which has been thought for so long by many to be the lever by which the race would be lifted to the enjoyment of its rights." He did not even attempt, moreover, to fight the ensuing Bookerite take-over of the Afro-American Council. Convinced that the Chicago delegations' expenses for the 1900 Indianapolis meeting were paid in full, through Bishop Arnett, by Mark Hanna and the Republican National Committee, Ransom concluded that the Council was "useless as a weapon [for] political and social justice" and withdrew.[44]

Ransom's retreat before Washington and resignation from the Council were, however, less indicative of the long range direction of his ministry than was his initial attempt to participate in the group and press it toward militancy. The Sunday after the "Boston riot" of July 30, 1903, in which William Monroe Trotter and several other black Bostonians directly challenged Washington at a crowded public meeting, Ransom declared from his pulpit that for all his virtues,

> Mr. Washington . . . does not believe as his people believe, and
> in promulgating his propaganda of surrender of rights he does
> not represent his people. The revolt at Boston was the first that
> has reached the public. There would be others if Mr. Washington
> did not control the strong papers conducted by colored men. . . .
> I . . . insist that a colored man should have the right to vote, to
> own his own home, to transact his business, have a fair trial if he
> commits a crime, just as a white man does, and that he should
> be deprived of none of these. These are the things the colored
> people stand for and they will not countenance any surrender.

When the militant challenge to Washington took organizational form two
years later in the Niagara Movement, Ransom soon became an active
participant—an involvement facilitated by his move to Boston in the
summer of 1905. That winter, William Monroe Trotter invited him to deliver
the main address at the New England Suffrage League's celebration of the
Garrison centennial, and Ransom responded with an oration that an
enthusiastic W. E. B. DuBois wrote from Atlanta to praise as a "splendid
. . . speech . . . [,] worthy of our best traditions." Afforded a similar opportunity at the August 1906 Harper's Ferry meeting of the Niagara Movement, Ransom created one of the most memorable moments in the
organization's brief history.

> Mr. Ransom [delivered] the most eloquent address the writer has
> ever listened to [wrote J. Max Barber in *The Voice of the Negro*].
> He spoke on "The Spirit of John Brown," and before he was
> through speaking everybody in the house must have felt that John
> Brown's spirit was with us. Men and women who had attended
> the New England anti-slavery meetings fifty years ago said that
> they had witnessed nothing like the enthusiasm in that meeting
> since the dark days of slavery. Women wept, men shouted and
> waved hats and handkerchiefs and everybody was moved.

Other such oratorical triumphs followed, and Ransom broadened his organizational participation to include the Constitution League and, later,
the N.A.A.C.P., as well as a number of more ephemeral organizations. In
the division of the times between Bookerites and anti-Bookerites, there
was no mistaking where Ransom finally stood.[45]

Not surprisingly, this increasingly forthright militancy, combined with
his continued churchly success, gradually earned for Ransom a number
of ecclesiastical adversaries. After 1900 his career within the church
became increasingly vulnerable to the machinations of these opponents.
At that year's General Conference, Bishop Arnett—who remained Ransom's
protector in spite of their political disagreements—was reassigned to another episcopal district, and Ransom's area came under the jurisdiction
of Bishop Abram Grant. Grant was not only the closest A.M.E. ally of
Booker T. Washington, but also an apparent good friend of Archibald J.

Carey, Ransom's chief Chicago rival. A well-educated Georgian then serving as pastor of Quinn Chapel, Carey, along with A. L. Murray, the new pastor of Bethel Church, persuaded Bishop Grant to forbid Ransom to preach at the Institutional Church on Sunday mornings. This ban lasted only until Henry McNeal Turner, as senior bishop of the church, overruled Grant and ordered Ransom to preach, but Carey's opposition continued to plague Ransom throughout his Chicago pastorate. Finally, in 1904, when C. T. Shaffer replaced Grant as presiding bishop over the Chicago area, rumors began to reach Ransom that he would soon be sent from the city to serve as a Presiding Elder (regional superintendent) in Indiana. Unable to negotiate a more satisfactory transfer with Bishop Shaffer, Ransom resigned his position at the Institutional Church and, in effect, walked out of the Illinois Conference.[46]

Arnett, then presiding over the New England area, took Ransom in and temporarily assigned him to a church in New Bedford, Massachusetts. He had, indeed, been at work for some time trying to rescue Ransom from his Chicago troubles. In 1901, he had tried to secure Ransom an appointment to Metropolitan A.M.E. Church in Washington, D.C., one of the denomination's most prestigious congregations. Though not within his own jurisdiction, the church was within the domain of another Wilberforcian friend of Ransom's, Bishop Benjamin T. Lee, and Arnett apparently tried to arrange the transfer through the Bishops Council. Local opponents, however, including John Wesley Cromwell, the historian and A.M.E. layman, protested that they "did not want Ransom with all his eloquence" and, Arnett's personal pleadings notwithstanding, "the game was blocked." In 1905, however, Arnett was able to offer Ransom a good appointment within his own jurisdiction as pastor of the Charles Street A.M.E. Church in Boston. Grumbling at the initial salary (which was only two-thirds of what he'd made when starting at Bethel twelve years before) but no doubt pleased to be assigned to the center of northern black radicalism, Ransom surely thanked Arnett for the transfer. It was, however, the Bishop's last favor to Ransom, for in October 1906, Arnett died.[47]

After Arnett's death, Ransom was on his own in the A.M.E. Church. No more would his career be looked after by a powerful episcopal sponsor. The negative effects of this were already evident in the spring of 1907. Henry McNeal Turner—who, as senior bishop, temporarily assumed some of Arnett's responsibilities—wrote to Ransom "private, private, private" about the possibility of transferring him to New York. Though, as his earlier helpfulness in Chicago suggests, Turner had generally been cordial to Ransom, he now presumably knew that Ransom did not wish to leave Boston and nevertheless proposed to move him for reasons of his own. Ransom, at least, regarded Turner's warm correspondence on the matter ("I wish I could make you President of Morris Brown College....") as a rather disingenuous attempt to humor him into leaving town peacefully. Acquiescing, Ransom went quietly, though "with reluctance and with [a] heavy heart..." to serve Bethel A.M.E. Church in New York City.[48]

If Turner's reappointment of Ransom indicated his vulnerability, however, the manner in which it was done suggested that the forty-six year old Boston preacher had become a formidable power within the church in his own right. Ransom himself recalled years later that his transfer "created quite a sensation, not only in my own church, but in church circles throughout the city of Boston." It was, presumably, a respect for Ransom's ability to mobilize such support on behalf of his continued appointment to the Charles Street Church that prompted Turner so carefully to secure Ransom's consent beforehand. Sending Ransom to New York's large and prestigious Bethel Church also showed more respect for Ransom's talent—and influence—than Bishop Shaffer's earlier plan to pack him off to Indiana. In New York, Ransom was able both to pursue his concern for an effective urban ministry and to participate actively in black politics and protest organizations. He was also able to mantain a position of high visibility in the life of the denomination as a whole.[49]

His effectiveness in this regard was evidenced by his election in 1912 to the editorship of the *A.M.E. Review*. This victory, which permanently established Ransom as an independent power within the church, came after at least two unsuccessful attempts at churchwide office. In 1900, when *Recorder* editor H. T. Johnson was rumored to be due for elevation to the bishopric, Ransom was mentioned as a possible successor. But Johnson's campaign for higher office failed and he did not vacate the editorship. Nine years later, when the position finally did open, it was filled not by Ransom, but by his former junior colleague at the Institutional Church, R. R. Wright, Jr. In the middle of the following quadrennium, however, H. T. Kealing, editor since 1896 of the *A.M.E. Review*, resigned his post, turning the magazine over temporarily to C. V. Roman, and at the General Conference of 1912, Ransom defeated Roman for the editorship. He was re-elected in 1916 and 1920.[50]

In that it freed him from direct dependence on the bishops and made him instead responsible only to the General Conference for the retention of his post, Ransom's election to the editorship marked a major departure from his ministerial past. Yet, in the substance of his daily work, it represented a far less sharp break from his years in the pastorate than did his subsequent election to the bishopric. Largely this was due to Ransom's own initiative. Convinced that the editorship of the *Review* was not really a full-time job, Ransom started on his own the "Church of Simon of Cyrene," a mission church intended to serve the " 'bad Negroes' ...the Negroes of the slums." Since Benjamin W. Arnett, who had succeeded Ransom as pastor of Bethel Church, successfully insisted that Ransom not take any of Bethel's members with him, the new congregation was never very large. But it afforded Ransom an outlet for his pastoral energies and served as a reminder to the church at large of the type of ministry he wished African Methodists to undertake. Meanwhile, his editorial work allowed him to continue in print the political commentary and protest against racism that had previously found its way into his sermons and orations.[51]

Whatever the satisfactions of life as a part-time pastor and editor, Ransom was willing to abandon them for the bishopric. Politically, the editorship allowed Ransom to develop personal ties with western and southern church leaders, whom he had not much known as a midwestern and northeastern pastor. By 1920, he had sufficiently overcome southern resistance ("'sectionalism,'" he termed it) to make a strong showing at the St. Louis General Conference, losing, he claimed, only because the clerk deliberately stopped reading his name. Four years later, working closely with fellow candidates John A. Gregg, the president of Wilberforce University, and A. L. Gaines, the southern-born leader of the Baltimore Conference, Ransom—at the age of sixty-three—succeeded. "God has answered my prayer," said the aged Harriet Ransom: "He let his glory shine about [you]."[52]

As bishop, however, Ransom had more to do than rest on his laurels. The church which had elected him bishop was confronted both by an increasingly inhospitable milieu without and deepening divisions within.[53] Urban, industrial America had never been as susceptible to the dominance of evangelical Protestantism as its small-town, agricultural predecessor, and as the Great Migration increasingly carried blacks from the latter realm to the former, black churchmen more and more experienced the same frustrations that had earlier beset their white brethren. Able to retain their hold on the middling groups within the urban black community, but unable to embrace the ghetto masses or shape the thinking of the cultural elite, the mainline black churches found it increasingly difficult to speak for black America as a whole. Of no church was this more true than the African Methodist. As late as 1903, W. E. B. DuBois could justly describe the A.M.E. Church as "probably...the greatest voluntary organization of Negroes in the world,"[54] but by 1924 such claims were scarcely more plausible than the parallel claims that Wilberforce was "the Black Athens" and the *A.M.E. Review* the race's leading journal. Ransom, having watched this transition occur during the years of his own ministry, understood the problem well. His own early innovations in the church's urban ministry had been intended precisely to overcome African Methodism's growing separation from both "the Negro who is up" and "the Negro who is down," and he had been confronted firsthand, as editor of the *Review,* with the problem of reversing the declining prestige of that journal.

Ransom also knew, from his own experience, the depth of regional, class and personal divisions within the church. His own career, after all, had at various times run afoul of southern opposition to his northernness, the resistance of middling respectables from all regions to his attempts to minister across class lines, and the personal spite of envious colleagues. He also knew the abuse of episcopal power and disregard of church law that such divisions often prompted. Even he, however, was apparently surprised by the growing tendency of the church to fragment into ecclesiastical baronies dominated by some entrenched bishop or lay reader who resisted all outside interference in his private realm. More than once in Ransom's bishopric, the integrity as well as the influence of the church was in doubt.[55]

In meeting these challenges, Ransom drew on both his own mature sense of the church's nature and purpose and on the insights and concerns of his predecessors. Symbolic of his renewed ties with the latter was his moving back to Wilberforce, where he lived beside Bishop Payne's college in Benjamin Arnett's old house.[56] Chairman of the Wilberforce Board of Trustees from 1932 to 1948, he became more deeply involved with Payne's school—and his—than he had been for decades, playing a crucial and controversial role in the final, angry separation of Wilberforce and what became Central State University. (The latter was the outgrowth of the "Combined Normal and Industrial Department" which State Senator Arnett had persuaded his fellow legislators to establish at Wilberforce in the 1880's.)[57] He also became deeply involved in Ohio politics, playing for the state's Democrats something of the role that Arnett had once played for its Republicans and enjoying as a reward an appointment to the state's Board of Parole and an invitation to offer the opening prayer at the 1940 Democratic National Convention.[58]

As important as he was as a living link to the past, Ransom's chief service to the church during these troubled years was offering it a way into the future. "I see little hope for the survival of the A.M.E. Church," Ransom warned the General Conference of 1936, "... if we do not so apply the Gospel of Christ as to make it a vital force in the life of society."[59] This, of course, was what Ransom had tried to do in his own ministry, and his work as bishop was therefore largely a matter of trying to get the church to follow his example. In this he experienced failure as often as success, and the church from whose service he retired in 1952 was no doubt not the militant and activistic community he would have wished it to be. Still, it was far better prepared for the struggles of the 1960's than it would have been without him. Watching from retirement the emergence of the southern civil rights movement in the late 1950's, he must have taken satisfaction in that.[60]

Notes

1. S. P Fullinwider, *The Mind and Mood of Black America: 20th Century Thought* (Homewood, Illinois: Dorsey Press, 1969), pp. 41–47. There are also important general comments on Ransom in August Meier, *Negro Thought in America, 1880–1915: Racial Ideologies in the Age of Booker T. Washington* (Ann Arbor: University of Michigan Press, 1963), pp. 180, 182, 185, 220–21, 229–33. Richard R. Wright, Jr., *The Bishops of the African Methodist Episcopal Church* ([Nashville]: A.M.E. Sunday School Union, 1963), pp. 287–92, contains the best biographical synopsis.

2. Two doctoral dissertations on Ransom are currently in progress: Donald A. Drewett, "Ransom and Race: A Social, Political, and Ecclesiastical Study, 1861–1959" (Drew University), and Frank E. Moorer, "Reverdy C. Ransom and the Transformation of the A.M.E. Church, 1860–1950" (Johns Hopkins). I have also discussed Ransom's economic ethics in an unpublished essay, "The Meaning of Racial Justice and the Limits of American Liberalism," pp. 32–38.

3. Except where otherwise indicated, the factual information and direct quotations contained in the following account of Ransom's childhood and youth are drawn from his autobiography, *The Pilgrimage of Harriet Ransom's Son* (Nashville: Sunday School Union, n.d.), pp. 15–27. His birthdate is supplied by Wright, *Bishops of the A.M.E. Church*, p. 287.

4. Bingham (1815–1900), who served in every Congress save one between 1854 and 1873, was a resident of nearby Cadiz, Ohio. He later played an important role in the impeachment proceedings against Andrew Johnson. Reverdy Johnson (1796–1876), a well-known constitutional lawyer active in politics as a Whig and then as a War Democrat, served twice in the United States Senate. A gradual emancipationist, he argued the pro-slavery side in the Dred Scott case, was prominent in the abortive Washington peace conference of 1861, and later was one of President Johnson's main senatorial defenders. Cassius Marcellus Clay (1810–1903), an anti-slavery Kentucky Whig and Republican, was prominently mentioned for the vice-presidency in 1860. Thomas D. McCormick, "John Armor Bingham"; E. Merton Coulter, "Cassius Marcellus Clay," and Mary W. Williams, "Reverdy Johnson," in *DAB*, ed. Allen Johnson and Dumas Malone (New York: Scribner's, 1928+), II, 277–78; IV, 169–70; X, 112–41.

5. Wright, *Bishops of the A.M.E. Church*, p. 287, identifies George Ransom as Reverdy's father. I have concluded otherwise strictly from a reading of Ransom's autobiography. The phrasing of Reverdy's initial allusion to him, and the declaration that he knew "nothing" of his "paternal forbearers," seem to me to indicate that George Ransom was actually his step-father. I have not, however, been able to confirm this interpretation by any other documentary evidence, so it must be accepted with considerable caution.

6. On the general pattern of antebellum black settlement in Ohio, see David A. Gerber, *Black Ohio and the Color Line* (Urbana: University of Illinois Press, 1976), pp. 14–24.

7. Henry Howe, *Historical Collections of Ohio*, I, 728–30.

8. Ransom, *Pilgrimage,* p. 23, also mentions the visits to Cambridge of Richard T. Greener, Francis E. W. Harper, and John G. Mitchell—all prominent blacks and members of the A.M.E. Church.

9. The records of the Probate Division, Court of Common Pleas, Guernsey County, Cambridge, Ohio, show that the marriage occurred on February 17, 1881, and that Harold George Ransom was born on November 4, 1881. Reverdy and Leanna were divorced on February 3, 1886. Ransom later described this marriage as a "youthful folly."

10. Wright, *Bishops,* p. 81.

11. The standard accounts of Payne's life and influence are his own autobiography, *Recollections of Seventy Years* (Nashville: A.M.E. Sunday School Union, 1888; reprint ed., New York: Arno Press and *New York Times,* 1969), and Josephus R. Coan, *Daniel Alexander Payne: Christian Educator* (Philadelphia: A.M.E. Book Concern, 1935). These have been supplemented recently by two doctoral dissertations: Charles Denmore Killian, "Bishop Daniel A. Payne: Black Spokesman for Reform" (Ph.D. dissertation, Indiana University, 1971), and Arthur Paul Stokes, "Daniel Alexander Payne: Churchman and Educator" (Ph.D. dissertation, Ohio State University, 1973). My own interpretation of Payne is more fully developed and documented in "Aspects of Social Thought in the African Methodist Episcopal Church, 1884–1910 (Ph.D. dissertation, Harvard University, 1975), ch. 1 and *passim;* "The Meaning of Racial Justice and the Limits of American Liberalism" (unpublished essay), pp. 19–26; and "Daniel Alexander Payne in Charleston, 1811–1835" (unpublished essay).

12. Charles Spencer Smith, *A History of the African Methodist Episcopal Church . . . from 1856 to 1922* (Philadelphia: Book Concern of the A.M.E. Church, 1922; reprint ed., New York: Johnson Reprint Corporation, 1968), pp. 351–69; Daniel A. Payne, "Some Thoughts About the Past, Present and Future of the African M. E. Church," *A.M.E. Church Review,* I (July, 1884), 5–8; Reverdy C. Ransom, ed., *Response of Bishop Payne to Rev. R. C. Ransom, B.D.* (n.p., 1890).

13. The standard history of Wilberforce University is Frederick A. McGinnis, *A History and an Interpretation of Wilberforce University* (Wilberforce, Ohio: n.p., 1941). The ethos of the school's early years is best conveyed by Hallie Q. Brown, *Pen Pictures of Pioneers of Wilberforce* (Xenia, Ohio: Aldine Publishing, 1937), and, especially, Reverdy C. Ransom, *School Days at Wilberforce* (Springfield, Ohio: New Era, 1890). My own account relies heavily on the last volume, especially pp. 20–24, 35–40, and 63–66.

14. Ransom, *Pilgrimage,* pp. 31–33.

15. Ransom, *School Days,* p. 65; Ransom, *Pilgrimage,* pp. 27, 39

16. Ransom, *School Days,* pp. 19–20; Ransom, *Pilgrimage,* p. 33; Francis P. Weisenburger, "William Sanders Scarborough: Early Life and Years at Wilberforce," *Ohio History,* 71 (October, 1962), 203–26, 287–89.

17. W. E. Bigglestone, "Oberlin College and the Negro Student, 1865–1940," *Journal of Negro History,* 55 (July 1971), 199–201, describes both the general changes of the 1880's and the Ladies Hall dining room dispute but makes no reference to Ransom. Ransom himself omitted from *School*

Days all mention of his stay at Oberlin, describing it only in *Pilgrimage*, pp. 33–34.

18. Ransom, *Pilgrimage*, pp. 23, 37, 49.

19. Ransom, *Pilgrimage*, pp. 37–40, 42. Wright, *Bishops of the A.M.E. Church*, p. 289, suggests that Emma Conner was also a "school mate" of Ransom's at Wilberforce.

20. Reverdy C. Ransom, "The Class of 1886," typescript, Reverdy C. Ransom Papers, Wilberforce University Archives, Wilberforce, Ohio, states that his graduating class consisted of eight men and one woman. He documented and criticized the tendency of many Wilberforcians not to complete their degrees in "Why This Haste?" *Christian Recorder*, 28 (August 28, 1890), 1.

21. John G. Brown, "Wilberforce University: Twenty-Third Commencement Exercises—A Brilliant Closing," *Christian Recorder*, 24 (July 8, 1886), 1; Ransom, *Pilgrimage*, pp. 41–42.

22. Ransom, *Pilgrimage*, pp. 38–39, 43–47, 50, 261–64.

23. Ransom, *Pilgrimage*, pp. 55, 57, 65; Gerber, *Black Ohio*, pp. 144–46. Payne died on November 29, 1893.

24. A. J. Kershaw, "The A.M.E. Church—Its Educational Department: No. 6," *Christian Recorder*, 24 (June 17, 1886), 1; Benjamin F. Lee, "Our Schools—Their Location," *Christian Recorder*, 24 (June 24, 1886), 2.

25. R. C. Ransom, ed., *Response of Bishop Payne to Rev. R. C. Ransom, B.D.*, pp. 1, 2 (unnumbered); Ransom, *School Days*, p. 8 and preface (unnumbered). In introducing Payne's reply, Ransom indicates that the article which occasioned it had appeared in the *Christian Recorder* during September, 1890, but I have been unable to locate it there. Presumably it appeared in another periodical or at a considerably earlier or later date.

26. Reverdy C. Ransom, "Too Cultured for His Flock," *Christian Recorder*, 24 (November 18, 1886), 2; Reverdy C. Ransom, "Annual Conference," *Christian Recorder*, 26 (September 27, 1888), 4; Ransom, *Pilgrimage*, pp. 65–66.

27. Reverdy C. Ransom, "Dr. C. S. Smith's Version of the Apostles Creed," *Christian Recorder*, 28 (April 24, 1890), 1; Ransom, *Pilgrimage*, p. 38.

28. Ransom, *Pilgrimage*, p. 38.

29. Ransom, *Pilgrimage*, pp. 45, 47–50, 290–91, 304. Ransom's marriage to Emma Connor, who proved to be an exceptionally effective minister's wife, lasted until her death in 1941. Two years thereafter, Ransom married Georgia Myrtle Teal, the Dean of Women at Wilberforce University. Wright, *Bishops*, pp. 291–92.

30. Ransom, *Pilgrimage*, pp. 53, 58, 72, 143.

31. Ransom, *Pilgrimage*, pp. 75–76, 135, 267–70; George A. Singleton, *The Romance of African Methodism* (New York: Exposition Press, 1952), pp. 162–69.

32. The standard biographical account of Arnett is Wright, *Bishops*, pp. 78–82. There is also a biography, Lucretia H. Newman Coleman, *Poor Ben: A Story of Real Life* (Nashville: A.M.E. Sunday School Union, 1890), which does not, however, cover Arnett's years in the bishopric. Most helpful is Gerber, *Black Ohio*, especially pp. 350–69 *passim*. Singleton,

Romance of African Methodism, p. 129, reports on Ransom's having worked for Arnett at Wilberforce.

33. Ransom, *Pilgrimage,* pp. 81–82; Reverdy C. Ransom to George A. Myers, October 17, 1896, Box 2, George A. Myers Paper, Ohio Historical Society, Columbus, Ohio; Allan H. Spear, *Black Chicago: The Making of a Negro Ghetto, 1890–1920* (Chicago: University of Chicago Press, 1967), pp. 63, 91–93.

34. Ransom, *Pilgrimage,* pp. 82–83, 230; Spear, *Black Chicago,* pp. 91–97.

35. Alfreda M. Duster, ed., *Crusade for Justice: The Autobiography of Ida B. Wells* (Chicago: University of Chicago Press, 1970), p. 297; Ida B. Wells-Barnett, "Rev. R. C. Ransom, B. D.," *Christian Recorder,* 47 (January 25, 1900), 1; Ransom, *Pilgrimage,* p. 103.

36. Thomas W. Henderson, "Manager's Weekly Letter: A Visit to Chicago," *Christian Recorder,* 47 (March 15, 1900), 3; Reverdy C. Ransom, "The Institutional Church and Social Settlement," *Christian Recorder,* 48 (November 29, 1900), 1; Reverdy C. Ransom, "The Institutional Church," *Christian Recorder,* 48 (March 7, 1901), 1; Ransom, *Pilgrimage,* pp. 103–10; Spear, *Black Chicago,* pp. 95–96; Richard B. Wright, Jr., *87 Years Behind the Black Curtain: An Autobiography* (Philadelphia: Rare Book, 1965), pp. 94–96; "St. Paul Social Settlement," *Christian Recorder,* 50 (December 25, 1902), 2.

37. Ransom, *Pilgrimage,* pp. 83–84, 113–14, 117–35; Spear, *Black Chicago,* 36–39, 63; Wells-Barnett, "Rev. R. C. Ransom, B. D.," p. 1.

38. Payne, *Recollections,* pp. 66–68; Gerber, *Black Ohio,* pp. 350–64; Meier, *Negro Thought,* p. 57.

39. Felix James, "The Civic and Political Activities of George A. Myers," *Journal of Negro History,* 58 (April, 1973), 166–78; Gerber, *Black Ohio,* pp. 345–70; Ransom, *Pilgrimage,* pp. 68–71; Reverdy C. Ransom to George A. Myers, October 17, 1896, October 28, 1896, December 15, 1896, January 9, 1897, January 13, 1897, January 26, 1897, February 18, 1897, March 3, 1897, Boxes 2–3, George A. Myers Papers, Ohio Historical Society, Columbus, Ohio. Ransom's correspondence with Myers suggests that he was something of a mediator between Myers and Arnett, who though allies, were also rivals for influence with Hanna and McKinley.

40. Ransom to Myers, February 18, 1897, March 3, 1897; Spear, *Black Chicago,* pp. 60–61; Gerber, *Black Ohio,* pp. 345–70; Ransom, *Pilgrimage,* pp. 66–67. Ransom recalled that Hanna's offer came during his last year in Cleveland, but since McKinley was not elected to the presidency until after Ransom had moved to Chicago, the offer may, in fact, have come later.

41. Gerber, *Black Ohio,* pp. 353, 361–62; Willard B. Gatewood, Jr., *Black Americans and the White Man's Burden, 1893–1903* (Urbana: University of Illinois Press, 1975), pp. 253–54; Reverdy C. Ransom, "Chicago Paragraphs," *Christian Recorder,* 47 (July 6, 1899), 1; Reverdy C. Ransom to John P. Green, June 27, 1899, William McKinley Papers, Manuscript Division, Library of Congress, Washington, D.C.

42. *Autobiography of Ida B. Wells,* pp. 254–56, 262; Chicago *Inter-Ocean,* August 20, 1899, clipping, Container 1031, pp. 102–103, Booker T.

Washington Papers, Manuscripts Division, Library of Congress, Washington, D.C.

43. Louis Harlan, *Booker T. Washington: The Making of a Black Leader, 1856–1901* (New York: Oxford University Press, 1972), pp. 263–66; Theophile T. Allain to Booker T. Washington, August 20, 1899, Container 161, and *Minneapolis Times*, August 22, 1899, clipping, Container 1031, p. 128, Booker T. Washington Papers, Manuscript Division, Library of Congress, Washington, D.C. Allain's letter and some of the other correspondence pertaining to this episode have been published in Louis R. Harlan and Raymond W. Smock, eds., *The Booker T. Washington Papers*, Vol. 5, 1899–1900 (Urbana: University of Illinois Press, 1976), pp. 175–206. Ransom's only mention of this episode in his autobiography (*Pilgrimage*, p. 83) is an account mistakenly associated with the Council's 1900 Indianapolis meeting. He recalled Washington's coming late one night to summon Bishop Walters, who was Ransom's house guest, for a sidewalk lecture on the need to restrain the Council.

44. *Chicago Inter-Ocean*, August 20, 1899; Reverdy C. Ransom, letter to the editor, *Chicago Inter-Ocean*, August 25, 1899, p. 6, as cited in Harlan and Brock, *BTW Papers*, Vol. 5, p. 187; Reverdy C. Ransom to Booker T. Washington, August 31, 1899, and September 12, 1899, Container 160, Booker T. Washington Papers, Manuscript Division, Library of Congress; Reverdy C. Ransom, "A Programme for the Negro," *A.M.E. Review*, 16 (April, 1900), 423–30; Ransom, *Pilgrimage*, pp. 84–85. Sadie Harlan, to whom, along with Louis M. Harlan, I am indebted for assistance in locating A.M.E. materials in the Booker T. Washington Papers, reports that the letter from Washington to which Ransom alludes in his own letter of August 31, 1899, is not contained in this collection.

45. Stephen R. Fox, *The Guardian of Boston: William Monroe Trotter* (New York: Atheneum, 1970), pp. 49–54, 97–100; Reverdy C. Ransom, sermon of August 2, 1903, the Institutional Church and Settlement House, Chicago, as quoted in *Literary Digest*, XXVII (1903), 188; Ransom, *Pilgrimage*, pp. 148–71, 196–97, 219, 221; "William Lloyd Garrison: The Centennial Oration Delivered . . . in Faneuil Hall, Boston, Mass., December 11, 1905," and "The Spirit of John Brown: Before Second Annual Meeting of the Niagara Movement, Harpers Ferry, West Va., August 17, 1906," in Reverdy C. Ransom, *The Spirit of Freedom and Justice* (Nashville: A.M.E. Sunday School Union, 1926), pp. 5–14, 16–25; W. E. B. DuBois to Reverdy C. Ransom, January 20, 1906, Reverdy C. Ransom Papers, Payne Seminary Archives, Wilberforce, Ohio; J. Max Barber, *Voice of the Negro*, 3 (October, 1906), 403; Meier, *Negro Thought*, p. 182; Nancy J. Weiss, *The National Urban League, 1910–1940* (New York: Oxford University Press, 1974), p. 26.

46. Ransom, *Pilgrimage*, pp. 88, 95–96, 111, 115, 135; Wright, *Bishops*, pp. 191–94 (on Grant), 127–29 (on Carey) and 301–303 (on Shaffer); Harlan, *Booker T. Washington*, pp. 206, 225; correspondence between Grant and Washington, particularly in Containers 3, 41, 45, 50, 51, Booker T. Washington Papers, Manuscripts Division, Library of Congress, Washington, D.C.; *Autobiography of Ida B. Wells*, pp. 191–92, 294, 297–98, 361, 393. On Carey, who eventually became a highly influential figure in Chicago politics, see also Spear, *Black Chicago*, pp. 64–65, 84–85, 95–96, 113, 118, 124, 187, and Harold F. Gosnell, *Negro Poli-*

ticians: The Rise of Negro Politics in Chicago (Chicago: University of Chicago Press, 1935), pp. 39, 49–51, 55–56, 58, 73, 98–99, 199–251, 275, 320.

47. Ransom, *Pilgrimage*, pp. 143, 148–52; John W. Cromwell to F. H. M. Murray, April 3, 1915, Freeman Henry Morris Murray Papers, The Moorland-Spingarn Research Center, Howard University, Washington, D.C. I am indebted to Randall K. Burkett for calling my attention to this letter.

48. Ransom, *Pilgrimage*, pp. 199–201.

49. Ransom, *Pilgrimage*, pp. 201–25.

50. (H. T. Johnson), "Editorial; Catch 'Ear and Hold 'Ear," *Christian Recorder*, 47 (September 2, 1899), 2; Ida B. Wells-Barnett, "Rev. R. C. Ransom, B. D.," *Christian Recorder*, 47 (January 25, 1900), 1; Wright, *Bishops*, p. 372; Ransom, *Pilgrimage*, pp. 226–27.

51. Ransom, *Pilgrimage*, pp. 227–57.

52. Ransom, *Pilgrimage*, pp. 261–64; Wright, *Bishops*, pp. 171–72 (on Gaines) and 199–202 (on Gregg).

53. The following interpretation of the situation confronting the A.M.E. Church at the time of Ransom's election to the bishopric is more fully developed and documented in Wills, "Aspects of Social Thought in the A.M.E. Church," pp. 235–42. See also pp. 42–87.

54. W. E. B. DuBois, ed., *The Negro Church . . .* (Atlanta: Atlanta University Press, 1903), p. 123.

55. The major instances of such strife during these years are recounted in Ransom, *Pilgrimage*, pp. 264–74, 303–19; and Singleton, *Romance of African Methodism*, pp. 86–88, 162–82. Singleton's account is generally sympathetic to Ransom. For a more critical assessment of Ransom's role in one of these episodes, the "trial" of Bishop Joshua H. Jones by the General Conference of 1932, see Wright, *87 Years*, pp. 219–22.

56. Ransom, *Pilgrimage*, pp. 70, 323. The house, known as "Tawawa Chimney Corner," is still occupied by Ransom's widow.

57. Ransom, *Pilgrimage*, pp. 277–86; Wright, *87 Years*, pp. 222–23; McGinnis, *Wilberforce University*, pp. 103–19; Gerber, *Black Ohio*, p. 331.

58. Singleton, *Romance of African Methodism*, p. 156; Wright, *Bishops*, pp. 290–91; Ransom, *Pilgrimage*, pp. 286–90, 294–96.

59. Reverdy C. Ransom, "The Church That Will Survive," cited in full by Singleton, *Romance of African Methodism*, pp. 146–56. The quotation is from p. 152.

60. The contention of S. P. Fullinwider, *Mind and Mood*, p. 45, that Ransom's gospel became "increasingly . . . race centered until it was a racial Christianity he was preaching," is, in my judgment, exaggerated and misleading. Because this essay carefully examines only Ransom's earlier years and emphasizes his career within the church rather than the course of his thought, it has not been possible fully to discuss or defend this conclusion. I have, however, offered elsewhere (Wills, "The Meaning of Racial Justice and the Limits of American Liberalism," pp. 32–38) an alternative reading of Ransom's approach to the problem of race in America. My contention there is that one finds in Ransom a rather unsystematic blending of the liberal individualism exemplified by Daniel Alexander Payne, the black nationalism expressed by Henry McNeal

Turner, and the democratic socialism which Ransom seems to have become interested in on his own in the mid-1890's. Since the second strand may have been more prominent in the latter half of Ransom's life than in the first, Fullinwider's interpretation is perhaps not altogether without foundation—though even here the loaded terms in which his thesis is expressed seem to me to distort the reality of Ransom's thought. In any case, what is most distinctive and noteworthy about Ransom's social thought is not this motif but rather his early engagement with socialism and life-long concern with the problems which arise at the intersection of race and class. Viewed from this angle, Ransom's thought is anything but the "intellectual prison" 'Fullinwider claims it to be.

William J. Seymour: Father of Modern-Day Pentecostalism

James S. Tinney

Pentecostalism, that radical expression of Christianity which emphasizes ecstatic speech in an unknown tongue as a proof of the presence of the Holy Ghost, has attracted the attention of the world. It has become, some say, the fastest-growing religion both in the United States and the world, causing it to become to some the most respected, and to others the most feared, religious development.

At the turn of the century there was not a single American Pentecostal church denomination anywhere, although Pentecostalism was represented in several "prophetic movements" on the continent of Africa. Today, however, there are more than 6 million Pentecostals, both Black and white, in the U.S. Worldwide there are approximately 30 million Pentecostals, most of these belonging to Third World countries. What is not so well known is the fact that this new world religion, which now embraces every nationality, began in a small Black church in Los Angeles, under the leadership of a Black American minister, William J. Seymour. Even the white Pentecostals trace their beginnings as *distinctively Pentecostal organizations* back to the church and that minister.[1] Unheralded and often recognized, or at least unpromoted, by those who are contemptible of his race, William J. Seymour is nevertheless the "father of modern-day Pentecostalism."

It is, of course, true that the Pentecostal experience of tongue-speaking was itself not an entirely new phenomenon. It was first mentioned directly in Scripture in Acts 2:4, having been manifested a few days after the ascension of Jesus Christ. Some scholars have even asserted that there are evidences of the manifestation, or a similar form of ecstatic speech, in both Jewish and other world religions prior to the Christian day of Pentecost.[2] Students of African religion have long been familiar with the speech-event.³ Throughout Christian history, tongue-speaking never completely died out as an observable event. Although it became infrequent, its practice was preserved in the more mystical branches and sects of Protestantism, Catholicism, and Orthodoxy; or at least the phenomenon reappeared throughout the ages in times of spiritual revival.⁴ Even in the U.S., speaking in *unknown*⁵ tongues was sometimes witnessed in connection with shouting, jerking, shaking, dancing, jumping, falling prostrate, and other motor phenomena during unsupervised Black worship, the New England Great Awakening, and the Holiness campmeetings of the Nineteenth Century. Again, however, these were isolated occurrences.

Tongue-speaking as experienced and promoted by William J. Seymour and his modern heirs was the beginning of an unprecedented religious development. In the following ways this was true: (1) For the first time, this manifestation was regarded as unique and superior to all other physical motor phenomena. (2) For the first time it was offered and sought for its own value, and given theological importance as a special sign and gift of God. (3) Seymour taught that tongues was the first evidence, the inevitable accompaniment, of possession by the Holy Ghost. (4) For the first time generally, a whole doctrinal framework called the Baptism or Filling of the Holy Ghost was attached inseparably to tongues. Previously this framework had been descriptive of either conversion or entire sanctification in Protestantism. (5) All other tongues-speaking occurrences were short-ended, limited to sporadic manifestations. For the first time, tongues were preached and practiced as a continuous and normal experience lasting until the present day. (6) Other events of the phenomenon were local in scope and isolated in circumference of influence. This Los Angeles event immediately became publicized and was given worldwide attention, drawing observers from every part of the U.S. and several foreign countries.⁶ (7) Other ministers, under whose ministries tongue-speaking had occurred, were identified often as eccentrics, quacks, or moral indigents, thereby discrediting the phenomenon itself. (Such was the case with Charles F. Parham, a white man some newcomers had tried to project as the founder of Pentecostalism.) Seymour had an impeccable reputation which gave credence to the phenomenon. (8) This was the first time every race was represented among those who received the experience in a single meeting. (9) This was possibly the first time the tongue-speaking was recognized by foreigners or immigrants as including words and messages in actual, discernible foreign languages. (10) Not only is there historical succession between this revival and every other Pentecostal organization, but key leaders and founders of every major U.S. Pentecostal denomination which developed attended the Seymour meeting and received the experience at his hands. (11) Historiographers of every major U.S. Pentecostal group have acknowledged the Los Angeles revival as the birthplace of the entire movement known as

Pentecostalism. (12) Without exception, all recognize Seymour as the acknowledged leader and pastor of the Los Angeles revival.[7]

Despite the fact that William J. Seymour occupies the distinctive position as founder/leader/father of modern Pentecostalism, little information has been made available to the public about his life. Whereas other religious movements have preserved and promoted records of their origins, Pentecostals generally know very little about the Los Angeles birthplace of their faith, and even less about the man who directed it. It appears that this "silent treatment" about Pentecostal origins by the leaders of the movement today is more than the result of neglect. It amounts to a veritable conspiracy on their part to keep the facts below surface, or at least subordinate to later historical developments within each denomination. Probably this has been done because (1) Pentecostalists prefer to think of the movement as a wholly divine, supernatural occurrence which happened spontaneously without human intervention; and (2) most of the available historical materials have been published by white Pentecostals to whom recognition of the movement's Black origins would be of obvious embarrassment, given the present status of race relations in this country.

This article does not presume to offer all possible information about Seymour. The author has neither the available time nor money required to gather the research documents which could contribute to a comprehensive study of this great Black church father. What it will attempt to do is consolidate what information has become available to this researcher into a unified article—the first of its kind in any periodical—about the man and his mission. Completion of this historical task will necessarily await opportunity. In the meantime, may the following information bring due recognition, at least partially, to one who has long deserved it.

William J. Seymour, the man whom God would use to usher in the Twentieth Century gospel of Pentecostalism, was of humble origins. The exact date of his birth is unknown, but it is supposed that he was born in the 1850's, possibly about 1855. This would make him at least 51 years old at the time of the Los Angeles inauguration of the movement. Historians are sure that Seymour was born in Louisiana, and some have described him as "poverty stricken." It may be assumed that he was born in a rural setting, and that both he and his parents were slaves. Emancipation came to the family, perhaps, while Seymour was a lad, perhaps 10 or 12 years old.

White historians have typically pictured Seymour as "a very untidy person," "dirty and collarless," with no pleasing physical dimensions.[8] A photograph reprinted by the Institute for the Study of the Negro Church, however, puts the lie to such negative descriptions.[9] Instead, this photograph taken in his adult life, at the time of the famed revival, depicts him as a well-groomed man with a pleasing countenance. He was neither the stereotyped example of poverty in dress, nor the harsh taskmaster some have imagined him to be. Short and stocky, he probably weighed

200 pounds or more, although he was well proportioned. He had a high forehead, a wide nose, and wore his hair naturale with a part near the center of his forehead. A full complement of sideburns and joining beard give him the distinguished look of a scholar and gentleman. He was fully suited, and a bow-type tie was barely distinguishable beneath his modest beard. It was hardly noticeable, but he was blind in his left eye, and wore a glass eye there.

Very early in his life, Seymour moved to Texas, whether with or without his parents. And his avid interest in the Bible caused him to early affiliate with the churches and seek to become a minister. There is some discrepancy about his church attachment however. Generally he is noted as a Baptist, although at least one of his contemporary acquaintances says he was a member of the African Methodist Episcopal Church (AME). It is possible that he was first a Baptist, and then later a member of the AME Church. In either case, he was a church member who was not genuinely converted, by his own admission, in those years.

Then he came into contact with a small group of Black Christians known as the "Evening Light Saints." This body was one of hundreds which participated in what was then known as the Holiness Movement, an offshoot of the Methodists who sought to preserve original emphases of John Wesley. The Evening Light Saints taught the necessity of a born-again experience or conversion, evidenced by a holy life. They also taught that there was a second experience necessary for final salvation, known as holiness or entire sanctification, which freed the Christian from all sinfulness of the heart and inner man. When Seymour heard the testimonies of these saints, he could not resist. He went to the altar and "prayed through" to salvation. Then he went back a second time and prayed until he testified to being wholly sanctified, he tells us. From that point on (although no precise dates are available for these experiences), he became a preacher for the Evening Light Saints. The name of his new religious affiliation was taken from Zechariah 14:8, where it says, "It shall come to pass that at evening time it shall be light." The symbolism was clear to Seymour: his life had become a light in a time of fast-approaching doomsday, a holy example in a time of great evil. From this time forward, he was installed as the pastor of a small Holiness church in Houston, Texas.

In the fall months of 1905, another dramatic development took place in Seymour's life. He met another Black saint by the name of Lucy Farrar (or Farrow) who told him of seemingly strange wonders, including the possibility of a third religious experience which would give him added spiritual power and enable him to speak in languages he had never learned. Ms. Farrar had attended a short-lived, small Bible school in Topeka, Kansas, where tongue-speaking had, in fact, happened four years prior.[10] She told Seymour how she had spoken in tongues. But Seymour's greatest difficulty was her insistence that sanctification and the fullness of the Holy Ghost were separate experiences. He had believed until this time that he had been filled and baptized with the Holy Ghost when he was sanctified wholly. Eventually he accepted the idea Ms. Farrar presented, although he did not at that time speak in tongues himself or profess the new experience.

The Evening Light Saints did not approve of Seymour's new doctrinal interest, since they did not accept tongue-speaking. So Seymour left his pastorate. Partially because of Ms. Farrar's insistence, and partially because of his own interest, he began attending a small Bible school led by a minister named Charles Parham, a white man, and a few others from Topeka, Kansas. Like the school which had earlier existed for a short while in Topeka, this was really a communal-type living arrangement in one house, where students and their instructor spent days and nights together praying and studying the Bible in informal fashion. Because of this, there is some question as to whether or not Seymour, Ms. Farrar, and the other Black saints were only daytime students, or whether they also lived in the house fulltime. At any rate, Seymour gradually developed his new interest in tongue-speaking, and formulated his own Pentecostal theology.

There are some who would like to imply that Seymour simply adopted the views of Parham and the other students on this and similar subjects. But the facts are otherwise. Instead, Seymour disagreed violently with Parham and some of the others on several issues.[11] Parham, for instance, did not believe in entire sanctification as a second, definite work of grace; Seymour did. Parham also had very liberal thoughts about permitting Christians to divorce and remarry. Seymour did not believe in remarriage of divorced persons for any cause. He was also in disagreement with Parham about other sexual liberties which the white minister/teacher permitted. (There are some who trace the entire "free love" movement within Pentecostalism—which flourished in the early 1900's in the Midwest—to Parham.) Further, Parham disliked much physical demonstration in worship services, and he ridiculed Seymour for encouraging "holly roller-isms." But the thing that broke Seymour's heart most, and caused him to rebel against these whites, was their prejudice and discrimination. We do not know the specific incidents Seymour suffered from his experiences at the "integrated'" Bible school, but they were sufficient for Seymour to feel the need to condemn the racism he encountered. "If some of our white brethren have prejudices and discriminations, we can't do it," he wrote.[12] Eventually Seymour was to become so disenchanted with the possibilities for whites to overcome their racial prejudices that he demanded that all officers in the church should be "people of color," although whites could be members. Parham retaliated by accusing Seymour of being "possessed with a spirit of leadership." But if Parham couldn't get ready for Black leadership, God could. The Lord, in fact, exonerated Seymour by sending Parham back to Kansas and obscurity, while leading Seymour to Los Angeles for the real founding of what would be the Pentecostal movement.

The chain of events which brought Seymour to Los Angeles developed rapidly. Early in 1906, Seymour was making plans to begin a new church in Houston's Black community, where he could preach and further develop his new "Pentecostal" doctrine. Unexpectedly, he received a letter from Ms. Neely Terry, another Black former student at the Bible school who had since returned to her home in California, but had not forgotten her dear friend and fellow-student Seymour, asking him to come pastor a Black congregation in Los Angeles which was affiliated with the predominantly-white Church of the Nazarene. Believing the letter to indicate the will of God for him, Seymour packed his belongings and arrived early in April of 1906. He later wrote:

> It was the divine call that brought me from Houston, Texas to Los Angeles. The Lord put it on the heart of one of the saints in Los Angeles to write to me that she felt the Lord would have me come there, and I felt it was the leading of the Lord. The Lord provided the means and I came to take charge of a mission on Sante Fe Street.[13]

Arriving at the small Nazarene church or mission, Seymour preached his first sermon on Acts 2:4. He told the congregants that they were mistaken in thinking they had received the Holy Ghost, since they had not spoken in tongues. "You are only sanctified," he said. Most of the members listened eagerly to this new gospel Seymour had brought with him. But when he returned for the afternoon service, he found that the doors of the church had been padlocked against him.

After a debate with a delegation of Nazarene ministers, and others associated with the local Holiness Association, Seymour was barred from further activities at the church. However, he accepted an invitation from one of the sympathetic Nazarene members to stay and conduct prayer meetings in his home. There was really little else he could have done, since he knew no other persons in town and didn't have the money to get back to Houston. He stayed with a Brother and Sister Lee at 312 Bonnie Brae Street. His popularity was quickly evident, and scores of persons began attending these prayer services and tarrying for the Pentecostal experience of speaking in tongues which Seymour promulgated. Realizing that he needed support in his ministry, especially the assistance of a knowledgeable woman who could assist the female seekers, Seymour collected donations from the prayer group to purchase a train ticket for his friend, Sister Farrar, and another saint in Houston to come to Los Angeles. Soon they arrived.

Finally, on April 9, 1906, the experience Seymour had been proclaiming arrived. Seymour and Sister Farrar were eating dinner in the Lee Home, when,

> Sister Farrar rose from her seat, walked over to Brother Lee, and said, "The Lord tells me to lay hands on you for the Holy Ghost." And when she laid her hands on him, he fell out of his chair as though dead, and began to speak in other tongues. Then they went over to the prayer meeting at Sister Asbury's house. When Brother Lee walked into the house, six people were already on their knees praying. As he walked through the door, he lifted his hands and began to speak in tongues. The power fell on the others, and all six began to speak in tongues.[14]

The same eyewitness records that they "shouted three days and nights. The people came from everywhere. By the next morning there was no way of getting near the house. As the people came in they would fall under God's power. And the whole city was stirred." Not only did the whole house become filled, but the newly Spirit-baptized saints moved the piano and other accessories to the front porch of the Asbury house, and began preaching to the hundreds that had gathered, filled the yard and spilling out into the street. At one point, as Seymour preached from a makeshift pulpit on the front porch, the weight caused the beams to give way and the floor to cave in. Fortunately no one was hurt; and sometime during that same evening, on April 12, 1906, Seymour himself experienced a mighty feeling of God's power and found himself speaking in tongues too. The long-awaited gift had finally come to the man whose preaching had caused others to obtain the blessing even before he did.

Aware that the house would no longer accommodate the gathering crowds, and harrassed by the police who deplored the "public disturbance," Seymour set out to find a larger shelter. He discovered an old, abandoned Methodist church in the business section of Los Angeles. The building, long out of use, had recently been converted into a part-tenement and part-livery stable. It was a two-story structure with five windows on each side, both above and below, and a double door on the front side set between two front windows. There were few glass panes left in any window opening, and the place was a general mess, but the saints believed its location—far from a residential area—would not attract further police attention. Little did they realize that the old Azusa Street Mission, at 312 Azusa Street, would soon become the most talked-about spot in the city, and the launching point for a world-wide movement.

The first floor was a large barn-like room which was unplastered. The upstairs was used by Seymour for lodging; and it also contained a room for prayer sessions where seekers could travail and cry out to God 24-hours a day, without stopping. On the outside, the mission was surrounded by only lumberyards, stables, and a tombstone shop. But the forlorn location did not discourage the attendance. By the literal hundreds, they came. Whites began coming also in response to the newspaper accounts. The *Los Angeles Times* spoke of the scene as "wild," "a new sect of fanatics," and described Seymour as "an old colored exhorter" whose glass eye was believed to hypnotize believers. The *Times* also ridiculed a prophecy one of the saints had given after claiming a vision of "awful destruction" in which people were "flocking in a mighty stream to perdition." But the following week the historic San Francisco earthquake occurred, adding to the validity of the prophecy, and no doubt frightening thousands more to seek out the revival at Azusa Street.

The power of God could be felt around the outside of the building, it was claimed. Scores of people were seen dropping in prostration in the streets, "slain by the power of God" before they could even get to the mission. Most would rise speaking in tongues, converted without any assistance from the saints. By summer time, the crowds had reached staggering numbers, often into the literal thousands, and the scene had become an international gathering. Although Blacks still predominated, there were whites, Mexicans, Jews, Chinese, Germans, and Russians noted in attendance.[15] One description said, "Every day trains unloaded numbers of visitors who came from all over the continent. News accounts of the meeting spread over the nation in both the secular and religious press." One critic stressed that "there was much kissing between the sexes and races."

Everyone within hearing distance was affected by the continuous roar of shouting, weeping, dancing, falling into trances, and speaking and singing in tongues. An observer at one of the services wrote these words:

> No instruments of music are used. None are needed. No choir— the angels have been heard by some in the spirit. No collections are taken. No bills have been posted to advertise the meetings. No church organization is back of it. All who are in touch with God realize as soon as they enter the meetings that the Holy Ghost is the leader.[16]

With the Spirit as the leader, Seymour was the head man-in-charge, the pastor, and sponsor. It was his humble ministry which seemed to attract all, and which caused even the critics to esteem him personally, regardless of how much criticism they offered about the general tenor of the services and the usual manifestations. Although Seymour was stationed at the front of the church, he had erected no platform for the pulpit. He remained on the same level as the congregants. Both he and they sat on backless benches—a custom dating from slavery times when Blacks often removed the back rails of chapel seats 'in order to have "room to pray." The seats were simply hewn planks nailed onto barrels. In front of Seymour's seat were two boxes or crates end-on-end, one on top of the other. Most of the time, while the Spirit moved, the "father of the movement" kept his head stuck inside the top box and prayed. No record exists of anyone else preaching at the mission, other than Seymour.

> At times he would be seen walking through the crowds with five and ten-dollar bills sticking out of his hip pockets which people had crammed there unnoticed by him. At other times he would preach by hurling defiance at anyone who did not accept his views, or by encouraging seekers at the woodplank altars to "let the tongues come forth." To others, he would exclaim: "Be emphatic! Ask for salvation, sanctification, the baptism with the Holy Ghost, or divine healing."[17]

When he concluded preaching a message, he would invite seekers to the altar or simply begin intercession himself. The whole congregation would follow suit, with hundreds dropping to their knees. Another written account described it in this manner:

> As soon as it is announced that the altar is open for seekers ... the people arise and flock to the altar. There is no urging. What kind of preaching is it that brings them? Why, the simple declaring of the Word of God. There is such power in the preaching of the Word in the Spirit, that people are shaken on their benches. Coming to the altar, many fall prostrate under the power of God, and often come out speaking in tongues.[18]

No one could record all the miracles that happened. Blind persons sometimes instantly received their sight for the first time. All manners of diseases were cured instantly. (Although Seymour himself remained blinded in one eye.) Immigrants speaking in German, Yiddish, and Spanish were interpreted by uneducated Black saints, who translated these languages into English by supernatural ability.

Missionaries were called from the Caribbean, India, and Africa to come home to witness the new phenomenon. Many came, and then returned to these countries with the new gospel. Within a year, Pentecostalism had already spread to several states and foreign nations. Aiding in this propagation was a periodical Seymour began to publish almost singlehandedly, called "The Apostolic Faith." Begun in September 1906, the circulation had increased to 20,000 within three months. In it, Seymour announced his intention to restore "the faith once delivered unto the saints" by means of "old time religion, camp meetings, revivals, missions, street and prison work."

> During the course of the three years, persons from every continent visited the revival. Many of them were "baptized in the Holy Spirit" and returned home to propagate the new doctrine in their own localities. For this reason, Azusa Mission is generally considered the center from which Pentecostal influence spread ... to the nations of the world.[19]

When the daily meetings and the revival were finally concluded in 1909, the whites soon withdrew to form their own church in another section of the city. The Azusa Street Mission (which some months earlier had been officially named the Apostolic Faith Gospel Mission by Seymour) continued with Seymour as its pastor for many years afterwards. And even though the Los Angeles church had been the Pentecostal launching-point for the founders or key leaders of several new Pentecostal denominations begun while Seymour still lived, the "father of the faith" refused to affiliate the mission with any one of them. He was fearful of "prejudicing the work of God," and did not want to show favoritism to any of the groups, hinder their expansion, or thwart other individual leaders by his affiliation.

Soon after the revival closed, he took Jennie Moon, one of the first six to receive the tongues of the Holy Ghost in Los Angeles, as his wife. In 1915, he wrote a "Doctrine and Discipline of the Azusa Street Apostolic Faith Mission of Los Angeles, California, with Scripture Readings by W. J. Seymour, Its Founder and General Overseer." The manual, which was more than 100 printed pages in length, served as the guidebook for a loose network of Black churches which bore the stamp of his approval. It was, except for the distinctive Pentecostal tenets and the racial requirements for officers, practically a word-for-word duplicate of the Discipline of the Methodist Episcopal Church at that time.

He also traveled extensively as an evangelist in his later years, helping to confirm the newly attached Pentecostal believers in faith, all across the nation. Little is known of the facts surrounding his death, sometime around 1920. In 1928, the Azusa Street Mission was torn down, after a white Pentecostal denomination refused to buy it for a historic memorial. "We are not interested," they said, "in relics."

Notes

1. While some predate Azusa as formerly non-Pentecostal, Holiness groups, these invariably experienced defections and/or official reorganizations at the times they embraced this additional experience, doctrinal change, and new designation. Thus even the Church of God—Cleveland, and the Pentecostal Holiness Church, with beginnings in the 19th Century, owe their distinctly Pentecostal designations to Azusa. The COG's first general overseer, A. J. Tomlinson, received his tongues experience during a meeting conducted in his own church in 1908 by a white minister, G. B. Cashwell, who had just returned from Azusa. Cashwell is also the link to three other bodies which reorganized and became the Pentecostal Holiness Church. Florence Crawford left Azusa to found the Apostolic Faith Movement. William H. Durham returned to Chicago after Azusa, and there communicated the Pentecostal message and experience to the founder of the Pentecostal Assemblies of Canada, and to E. N. Bell,

who would later become the first general chairman of the Assemblies of God in 1914. Kelsey states: "Not only the Assemblies . . . but the Foursquare church and a dozen others spring from this original prayer meeting in 1906. In all there are 26 church bodies which trace their experience with tongues and their Pentecostal doctrine to Azusa." Cf. Morton T. Kelsey, *Tongue Speaking* (New York: Doubleday, 1961), pp. 64–65; John T. Nichol, *The Pentecostals* (Plainfield: Logos, 1966), pp. 34–37; Klaude Kendrick, *The Promise Fulfilled* (Springfield: Gospel Publishing House, 1971), pp. 68–70; and Charles W. Conn, *Like A Mighty Army* (Cleveland: Pathway, 1955), pp. 84–85.

2. One of the clearest expositions on non-Christian instances of tongues is found in Donald S. Metz, *Speaking in Tongues: An Analysis* (Kansas City: Nazarene Publishing House, 1964), pp. 18–26. Also see Kelsey, p. 139; John P. Kildahl, *The Psychology of Speaking in Tongues* (New York: Harper, 1972), p. 11; and H. J. Stolee, *Speaking in Tongues* (Minneapolis: Augsburg, 1963), pp. 11–20.

3. Strange speech connected with spirit possession is identified with African traditional religious practices by Melville Herskovits, *The Myth of the Negro Past* (Boston: Beacon, 1941), pp. 211, 216–17; John S. Mbiti, *African Religions and Philosophy* (New York: Praeger, 1969), p. 82; Leonard E. Barrett, *Soul Force* (New York: Doubleday, 1974), p. 85; and Stolee, pp. 15, 68.

4. F. L. Cross' article on "Glossolalia" in *The Oxford Dictionary of the Christian Church* (London: Oxford, 1958), states, "Similar phenomena are constantly met with in religious revivals." One of the most extensive tracings of this exercise throughout church history is found in Wade H. Horton, *The Glossolalia Phenomenon* (Cleveland: Pathway, 1966), pp. 69–139.

5. For our purposes, the terms "other" and "unknown" tongues are herein used interchangeably, since in either case the words or language is unknown to the speaker (although perhaps not to the listener), because it is both unlearned, in the sense of not being a studied foreign language, and unintelligible to him, unless the "gift of interpretation" is also subsequently bestowed. The use of the terms in this sense (since it does not disallow divine reception of a genuine language in this speech-event) is acceptable both to those Pentecostals who distinguish between the terms, and those who do not.

6. Several authors have compiled lists of states and countries represented at the Azusa meeting. Cf. Vinson Synan, *The Holiness-Pentecostal Movement* (Grand Rapids: Eerdmans, 1971), p. 114. Nichol says while "it is hard to explain its magnetism," the Azusa mission "became a veritable Pentecostal mecca to which pilgrims from all over the world came" (p. 34). Kendrick says, "During the course of the three years persons from every continent visited the revival. For this reason Azusa Mission is generally considered the center from which Pentecostal influence spread not only to many places in the United States, but also to a number of other nations" (p. 68).

7. Because of Seymour's role, the United Pentecostal Association at Howard University, an ecumenical campus ministry embracing Pentecostals of many denominations, was renamed during the fall of 1975 during its

tenth anniversary celebrations. Led by Chaplain Steve Short, the student group chose to become known as the William J. Seymour Pentecostal Fellowship of Howard University—probably the first organization of any type in the U.S. to bear the name of the "father of the modern-day Pentecostalism."

8. Cf. Synan, p. 105.

9. The original photograph has not been located. Franklin C. Showell is director of the Institute, located at 5806 Royal Oak Avenue, Baltimore, Maryland 21207.

10. "How Pentecost Came to Los Angeles," *The Pentecostal Evangel* (April 8, 1956), p. 4.

11. Eventually the disagreements between Parham and Seymour on doctrinal issues led Seymour to bar him from attending or preaching at Azusa. This break between the two ministers was never healed. Cf. Synan, p. 112.

12. William J. Seymour, *Doctrine and Discipline of the Azusa Street Apostolic Faith Mission of Los Angeles* (published by the author, 1915), p. 2.

13. Robert C. Dalton, *Tongues Like As Of Fire* (Springfield: Gospel Publishing House, 1945), p. 38.

14. "How Pentecost Came to Los Angeles: An Eyewitness Account of the Momentous Events of the Year 1906," *Pentecostal Evangel* (April 8, 1956), p. 5.

15. See Dalton, p. 41; Nichol, p. 36.

16. Dalton, p. 40.

17. Synan, pp. 108–109.

18. Dalton, p. 41.

19. Kendrick, p. 68.

Bibliography

Barrett, Leonard E. *Soul Force: African Heritage in Afro-American Religion.* New York: Doubleday, 1974.

Bartleman, Frank. *What Really Happened at Azusa Street.* Published by the author, 1925.

Conn, Charles W. *Like A Mighty Army Moves the Church of God.* Cleveland: Pathway, 1955.

Dalton, Robert Chandler. *Tongues Like As Of Fire: A Critical Study of the Modern Tongues Movements.* Springfield: Gospel Publishing House, 1945.

Dyer, Luther B. *Tongues.* Jefferson City: LeRoi, 1971.

Herskovits, Melville J. *The Myth of the Negro Past.* Boston: Beacon, 1941.

Horton, Wade H., ed. *The Glossolalia Phenomenon.* Cleveland: Pathway, 1966.

"How Pentecost Came to Los Angeles," *Pentecostal Evangel* (April 8, 1956).

Kelsey, Morton T. *Tongue Speaking: An Experiment in Spiritual Experience.* New York: Doubleday, 1961.

Kendrick, Klaude. *The Promise Fulfilled: A History of the Modern Pentecostal Movement.* Springfield: Gospel Publishing House, 1961.

Kildahl, John P. *The Psychology of Speaking in Tongues.* New York: Harper, 1972.

Mbiti, John S. *African Religions and Philosophy*. New York: Praeger, 1969.

Menzies, William W. *Anointed to Serve: The Story of the Assemblies of God*. Springfield: Gospel Publishing House, 1971.

Metz, Donald S. *Speaking in Tongues*. Kansas City: Beacon Hill, 1964.

Nichol, John Thomas. *The Pentecostals*. Plainfield: Logos, 1966.

Seymour, William J. *The Doctrine and Discipline of the Azusa Street Apostolic Faith Mission of Los Angeles, California*. Published by the author, 1915.

Sherrill, John L. *They Speak With Other Tongues*. New York: McGraw Hill, 1964.

Stagg, Frank, et al. *Glossolalia: Tongue Speaking in Biblical, Historical and Psychological Perspective*. Nashville: Abingdon, 1967.

Stolee, H. J. *Speaking in Tongues*. Minneapolis: Augsburg, 1963.

Synan, Vinson. *The Holiness Pentecostal Movement*. Grand Rapids: Eerdmans, 1971.

Tinney, James S. "Black Origins of the Pentecostal Movement," *Christianity Today* (October 8, 1971).

Tomlinson, A. J. *Diary*. New York: Church of God World Headquarters, 1949.

Williams, Ernest S. "Memories of Azusa Street Mission," *Pentecostal Evangel* (April 24, 1966).

Bishop Turner's African Dream

Edwin S. Redkey

Among the various Negro responses to their American ordeal, the least known and understood is "black nationalism." It has embraced many forms but always there has been a call for extreme segregation of the races and the establishment of all-Negro governments.[1] Although a minority movement, it has existed in one form or another among American Negroes since before the Civil War. In the years between Reconstruction and World War I the chief prophet of black nationalism was Bishop Henry McNeal Turner (1834–1915), who urged his people to go to Africa.

Turner, a blunt, forceful man who pushed his way into the upper ranks of Negro leadership, lacked formal education or wide acceptance by Negro intellectuals. W. E. B. DuBois remembered him as the "last of his clan: mighty men, physically and mentally, men who started at the bottom and hammered their way to the top by sheer brute strength."[2] But Turner was soon forgotten because journalists and historians who could have kept his memory alive had been offended by his scathing attacks on American society and upon Negroes who disagreed with his solution to the race problem. Despite his influence in the African Methodist Episcopal (AME) Church, the strongest Negro organization in the United States during Turner's lifetime, few mourned the end of his uncomfortable prodding toward Negro achievement and his perpetual scheming to move American Negroes to Africa. If Turner is remembered at all, it is for his African dream.

During the quarter century after the Civil War, Negroes entertained a number of ideas about their status in the United States. The Fourteenth Amendment granted them political rights, but politics had proved unsatisfactory with the collapse of Reconstruction. In the face of increasing political oppression after 1870, many Negroes, nevertheless, continued to believe that government action could solve the race problem. Others began to stress economic achievement as the way to win respect of whites.

This idea, combined with white segregationist pressure, virtually necessitated Negro self-help and racial solidarity as a means to securing the good life. Most articulate Negroes also had a vague trust in education and hard work as a way to attain racial equality; they thought it best not to arouse white anger by protest or agitation against white proscription. Some black spokesmen could not walk this path of least resistance and, instead, protested. Turner was one of those who protested loudly.[3]

During those years of increasing Negro frustration, Turner read of explorers and colonizers who pushed Africa to a new zenith in the attention of the world, while the fortunes of Negro Americans reached their nadir. At the same time, migration was popular as millions of Europeans crossed the Atlantic in search of the "American dream" of life, liberty, and the pursuit of happiness; but the newly emancipated Negroes, who had for a time during Reconstruction seen, touched, and handled that dream, saw it begin to slip out of their hands as race prejudice increased both in the South and North. Bishop Turner transplanted the waning dream to newly opened Africa and bade his people to pursue it there.

His early life offers some clues to Turner's later hostile reaction to the United States.[4] The frustration of being a so-called "free Negro" in the antebellum South made him yearn for independence from white men. Despite laws against education for Negroes, he succeeded in learning to read, write, and preach. At the age of sixteen, he became a traveling preacher in the southern Methodist Church, but later, when he visited New Orleans and learned of the all-black AME Church, he transferred to it immediately. He tasted glory when President Lincoln made him chaplain to a Negro regiment but was frustrated again when white prejudice forced him out of the army during the early days of Reconstruction.

Turner's true love, however, was not the church but politics. As an adolescent, he learned about politics while sweeping floors in a South Carolina law office. His flair for public speaking made him not only a successful evangelist but also an effective mobilizer of Negro votes for the Republican party in postwar Georgia. He served in the Georgia constitutional convention and later in the state legislature. But with other Negro legislators, Turner was promptly thrown out of the assembly. Shortly thereafter, he was forced out of another position; he had been the first Negro postmaster in the state. These Reconstruction experiences confirmed his earlier suspicions that color prejudice made it impossible for Negroes to achieve equality or power in the United States.

Forsaking politics for church organization, he devoted his energies to building the North-based AME Church among the former slaves of Georgia. Success lifted him to ecclesiastical power in the denomination. He sensed, however, that church power was no real substitute for vanishing Negro political influence. Pessimistic about life in the United States, he was certain that the American dream was not for the black man. By the end of the 1860's, alienation had become the major theme of Turner's life.

To his despair over the Negro's future in America Turner coupled an infatuation for Africa. It is possible that he first became interested in the work of the American Colonization Society (ACS) while preaching in pre-Civil War Baltimore, where ACS activity was strong. According to Turner, in 1860 he preached a sermon entitled "The Redemption of Africa and the Means to be Employed," which advocated conversion of the heathen by American Negro colonists.[5] This concern for missions was an integral part of his African dream, and he badgered church officials to increase their missionary work wherever Negroes lived, especially in Africa. He later recalled that sermons by a Liberian missionary, Alexander Crummell, permanently converted him to the proposition that Africa was the true home of the American Negro and indicated a way of escaping the frustrations of segregation. As circuit preacher and Georgia superintendent he urged his people to sail for Liberia because "There is no more doubt in my mind that we are ultimately to return to Africa than there is of the existence of God."[6]

Turner's relationship to the ACS during Reconstruction was ambiguous; he both endorsed and operated outside that facet of the white-man's philanthropy. Because the colonization idea had a bad reputation among Negroes who believed that the ACS wished to deport them from their American homes, Turner advised Secretary William Coppinger of the ACS to change the name of the Society to remove the stigma. Even in the face of criticism, Turner preached colonization with such vigor that in 1876 the ACS named him a lifetime honorary vice president. Although he accepted the post and occasionally made public appearances for the ACS, he devoted more attention to non-ACS emigration projects such as the South Carolina "Liberian Exodus" in 1877–1878. When a group of Charleston AME ministers formed the "Liberian Exodus Joint Stock Company," Turner pronounced his benediction as the company's ship, *Azor*, took one group of emigrants to Africa in 1878.[7]

Two years later, with the support of church members in the South where his colonization scheme was well known, Turner was elected bishop. By 1883 other Negro clergymen and secular leaders, voicing their opinions in the AME *Christian Recorder*, openly began to attack the Bishop's ideas; and in his rejoinders Turner formulated the main points of his African dream.

A vision of Negro social equality with white men was the basic theme of Turner's dream. He believed "that the great Jehovah, in his allwise providence, had made a distinction in color, but not in political or social status of the human race."[8] When it became clear at the end of Reconstruction that whites of the North as well as the South were loath to see the Negro as their social equal, Bishop Turner was disconsolate. In the

South acts of violence, lynchings, and convict labor systems grew more oppressive. The equality of the races which Turner and others sought became less likely as political and social barriers were raised. According to Turner, the sequel to the increasing segregation would be "war, efforts of extermination, anarchy, horror and a wail to heaven. This is a gloomy picture," he acknowledged, "but there is only one thing that will prevent its realization and that is marriage between whites and blacks; social contact that will divide blood; blood that will unify and centralize the feelings, sympathy, interest, and abrogate the prejudice, race caste, color barriers and hair textures, is the only hope of our future in this country." Because miscegenation was a private matter and offered no solution for the race as a whole, he did not advocate it seriously. But this statement illustrated the kind of social equality he thought necessary if the two races were to live together, and he observed that "whoever the white race does not consort with, it will crush out."[9] This vision of equality, born in Turner's youth as a free, colored man, would not die when prejudice doomed racial equality in America. Consequently, he turned his back on the nation which had sired the vision and looked to Africa where his color would not govern his social status.

Most articulate Negroes considered emigration a price too great to pay for social equality. Frederick Douglass, the aging, abolitionist hero, reminded *Recorder* readers that Negroes had been in America for 250 years and owed no allegiance whatever to Africa. In his view the United States provided as good a place as any for achieving equality. Furthermore, in 1883, northern publicity of southern persecution of Negroes had subsided to so great an extent that one correspondent could predict that "the bloodshed of which Bishop Turner complains will never be seen by him or any of us again." Another reminded the bishop that a man's color is no evidence of his nationality and accused him of treason.[10]

But Turner viewed his American citizenship as all the more reason for objecting to his subordinate status. "We were born here," he wrote, "raised here, fought, bled, and died here, and have a thousand times more right here than hundreds of thousands of those who help to snub, proscribe and persecute us, and that is one of the reasons I almost despise the land of my birth." Turner would have claimed the United States if he could, but to stay meant to give up his ideal of equality and achievement, and he would rather surrender his birthright than give up his dream.[11]

Turner suggested that those optimistic northern Negroes who challenged him in the pages of the *Recorder* did not understand the situation in the South, where, he estimated, 200,000 Negroes had suffered "murder and outrage" between 1867 and 1883. "Many of us think that the acclimating headaches of Africa, though sometimes fatal, are not to be compared to such an orgy of blood and death," retorted the Bishop. Nevertheless, he held the North equally responsible with the South for the state of race relations because both sections had ignored the pleas of Negro victims. If the South had been guilty of slavery, the North had been guilty of slave trading and chasing fugitive slaves. Prejudice against the black man was as strong in the North as in the South, according to Turner; and he believed that, although the Negro might escape the violence, he could not really change his status by moving from the South unless he left the country.[12]

Turner reported that many southern Negroes were eager to leave for Africa rather than sit and listen to theoretical solutions to the race problem. He claimed that "there never was a time when the colored people were more concerned about Africa in every respect than at present. If the Northern Negro is satisfied with matters and things, we of the South are far from [so] being." Benjamin T. Tanner, editor of the *Recorder*, articulated an opinion skeptical of Turner's followers. Because Tanner knew "the thoughts of those Negroes who read and write," he claimed that "what one thoughtful man among us writes outweighs in value the whole Niagara of eloquence common to our people [who] talk in the vein that we know our hearers desire us to talk," and that Turner heard only what he wanted to hear.[13] Whatever the truth of Tanner's analysis of Negro dialogue, there was considerable interest in Africa among the southern colored people; and letters of inquiry about Liberia poured into the ACS headquarters.

If emigration were cowardice, as Tanner charged, Turner would answer, "What of it?" At a time when large populations were leaving ancestral homes and known dangers for unknown risks in new lands, emigration was not a dishonorable concept; and the Bishop exclaimed, "Yes, I would make Africa a place of refuge, because I see no other shelter from the stormy blast, from the red tide of persecution, from the horrors of American prejudice." Claiming that self-interest, self-preservation, and "self in all its aspects" stimulated every migration since the Tower of Babel, he saw no more shame in Negro emigration to Liberia than in the Pilgrim move to Plymouth Bay. But Tanner pointed out that men from all over the world were seeking out the United States as the main chance for achieving their dreams and that even African students stayed on here after their studies ended. "The idea of a people leaving a country like America to go anywhere to better their condition . . . is like running from the sun for both light and heat." Turner rejoined that America was different for the black man who had once been a slave in the "land of opportunity." To Turner a revolution was necessary, and it must take the form of emigration to Africa.[14]

Turner conceived of Africa as much more than a refuge for persecuted Negro Americans; it was the "fatherland" symbol for the entire colored race. More specifically, he saw it as a political symbol because he was essentially a political man. "I do not believe any race will ever be respected, or ought to be respected," he wrote, "who do not show themselves capable of founding and manning a government of their own creation." He advocated a complete state of "a half-million civilized Christian people upon the continent of Africa" where black men could have their own "high officials, dignitaries, artisans, mechanics, corporations, railroads, telegraphs, commerce, colleges, &c., &c."; and he dreamed "of the glory that would accrue to the whole race from such a seat of power and influence." Fiercely independent, refusing to fawn or plead for mercy and favor from the white race, he would not permit his people to lower themselves to begging. If they were to remove the racial stigma of the symbolic past, Turner argued, black men must earn their rights in their own symbolic nation.[15]

Responsible Negro nationhood would serve both as a symbol to the entire race and a model for the advancement of the individual Negro. Turner challenged his critics in the *Recorder* to prove that any race had ever "amounted to anything" if it had been "shut out from all honorable positions, from being kings and queens, lords, dukes, presidents, governors, mayors, generals...." Answering his own question he proclaimed, "Till we have black men in the seat of power, respected, honored, feared, hated and reverenced, our young men will never rise for the reason they will never look up." Recalling the biblical story of the nation of Israel, smitten by fiery serpents in the wilderness (Numbers 21:4–9), he cried, "Oh for some Moses to lift a brazen serpent, some goal for our ambition, some object to induce us to look up.... Let the bravehearted men who are advanced enough to peril land and sea in search of better conditions ... raise a banner standard." Tanner reminded the Bishop that Negroes already had nations and governments in Haiti and Liberia and that many colored men were doing well enough in the United States. But Turner, writing from the South, where he had seen men "sit down and cry because they were compelled to hire out their daughters as chambermaids, after spending all they had to give them an education," obliquely discounted Tanner's illustrations as incapable of producing the desired results. What was needed, Turner insisted, was "an outlet, a theater of manhood and activity established somewhere for our young men and women," a state "that the world will respect and [whose] glory and influence will tell upon the destinies of the race from pole to pole; our children's children can rest securely under [its] aegis, whether in Africa, Europe, Asia, America or upon the high seas."[16]

Turner's symbolic African nation embodied most elements of the classic American dream. He was echoing the old chorus heard among American colonials and immigrants: hope for a fresh start where men had self-government and freedom from persecution and aristocracy; where land was available and where economic opportunity beckoned; where every man was judged on his merits and could even become President;

where there was freedom from old proscriptions; where there was the challenge of a land to be developed by the democratic process and civilized by Christianity.

Turner also had a well-defined theological view of Negro history which divined a great destiny for his black people. He explained that God had allowed white men to bring black men to America because the African needed the civilization and the Christianity of the United States, a nation consecrated as a sanctuary from persecution and peonage. Not that God endorsed slavery as such, Turner asserted, but He permitted it as a test of the white-man's obedience, because the two races were to embrace one another to work out the problem of civilizing and redeeming Africa. Turner acknowledged that the white man had exploited the Negro; this had been a historical necessity of natural growth, but the white man defaulted his obligation to God and the black man by forbidding his servants to improve themselves. "We gave the white man our labor, yes!" the Bishop proclaimed. "In return he should have educated us, taught us to read and write, at least, and seen that Africa was well-supplied with missionaries." To Turner, a redeemed continent, a "city upon a hill," was still God's goal for Africa; and it would be accomplished by former slaves. "Any person who opposes the return of a sufficient number of [Africa's] descendants to begin the grand work, which in the near future will be consummated," he insisted, "is fighting the God of the universe, face to face."[17]

Turner saw the mission of the emigrant Negro as not only to convert the African but also to help him to withstand the white invaders. The European scramble for Africa was well underway by 1883, and Turner feared that the same Europeans who once stole Africans from Africa would now steal Africa from the Africans. He chided Tanner for being content just to meditate and "wait till the whites go over and civilize Africa, and homestead all the land and take us along to black their boots and groom their horses. Wait till the French or English find some great mines of gold, diamonds or some other precious metal or treasures, so we can raise a howl over it and charge the whites with endeavoring to take away our fathers' inheritance, and lift a wail for the sympathy of the world." Turner urged Negroes to seize the initiative to make Africa the black man's preserve.[18]

Contrary to misinterpretations by his critics, the Bishop did not recommend a wholesale migration of all Negroes to Africa. The anti-emigrationists confused Turner's stand with that of the antebellum colonizationists who wanted to remove all free Negroes. After emancipation, even the ACS had necessarily changed its approach; and Turner never advocated the idea of shipping millions of black paupers into Africa. "Such a course would be madness in the extreme and folly unpardonable," he wrote. "Five or ten thousand a year would be enough." Half a million civilized Christian Negroes would be enough to build a nation of which Turner could be proud. But those half-million repatriates would have to be well-chosen for "all the riffraff white-men worshippers, aimless, objectless, selfish, little-souled and would-be-white Negroes of this country" would be useless in Africa, since they had no confidence in themselves or other black men. Only the proud and resourceful could contribute to his symbolic state; brave, ambitious, educated young men and women would be necessary to raise a nation worthy of respect. Furthermore, capital and technical ability would be needed to carve a strong republic from the wilds and to lead the natives of the dark continent to their destiny. "All this jargon about 'Bishop Turner trying to get all us colored people out of the United States' is not only nonsense, but absolutely false," Turner insisted, "for two-thirds of the American Negroes would be of no help to anyone anywhere."[19]

Unfortunately for his plans, those Negroes who came closest to his specifications were the ones least likely to forsake the gains they had made in the United States. Moreover, as wealthy George T. Downing, who spoke for many urban northern Negroes, reminded Turner, the most cultured, experienced, energetic, and moral Negroes were "the very persons we are most in need of at home.... We are not sufficiently represented in the needed character to upbuild Africa; we have not sufficient of it for home needs; this is our great misfortune; certainly we have not a scholar or business man to spare."[20]

One promising young Negro accepted Turner's challenge. T. McCants Stewart had been born free in Charleston, South Carolina, and received his education at the University of South Carolina and Princeton Seminary before being assigned to the large and affluent Bethel AME Church in New York City. In February 1883, in the midst of the debate between Turner and his critics, Stewart dramatically resigned his pulpit and announced that he would soon sail to teach in Liberia College. His Liberian letters were optimistic, but in 1885 Stewart was back in New York, complaining that the school was too weak to deserve the name of college. Turner chided him, suggesting that he go back and strengthen it himself; but Stewart remained in the United States to seek his fortune in Brooklyn politics. Twenty years later, when white politicians thwarted his progress, he returned to Liberia; but his ambivalence demonstrated with what reluctance cultured, ambitious young Negroes turned their backs upon the American dream. They were ever hopeful of success in the United States; and even when they wavered, they doubted that going to Africa would actually bring the dream to reality.[21]

American Negroes asked many questions about the suitability of the dark continent, questions raised by ignorance, by deliberate misinformation, and by the grim accounts of some disillusioned emigres and travelers. Chief among these threats to Turner's scheme was the complaint about the climate and the fever. Some of the *Azor* emigrants had returned to South Carolina with accounts of how ten percent of their group had died on arrival off the African coast, and the letters from those who remained in Liberia told of death and disease in the fever swamps. Furthermore, during the "Liberia Exodus" of 1878, some South Carolina white men who feared the loss of their labor supply had magnified the tales of horror about death and slavery in Africa. Negroes who were disposed to stay in the United States did little to brighten that image of Africa.[22]

Turner answered the "nonsensical jargon that the climate of Africa is against us, we can't live there, [and] the tropics are no place for moral and intellectual development." God had created Africa, and to deny that it was good "charges God with folly" because "man is a cosmopolitan [and] his home is everywhere upon the face of the globe." Although he admitted that there would be problems adjusting to the new climate and deaths from the "mysterious African fever," he insisted that the white men then working in Africa were disproving the old myths about African health. Even the fever, he argued, was better than dying at the hands of lynch mobs in America; why should Negroes balk at the risks of undertaking a divine errand into the wilderness? Turner assured self-sacrificing pioneers that in losing their lives for the dream, they would indeed find them.[23]

For the practical questions of money and transportation, he had two ready answers. First, he believed that the United States government should appropriate money to assist Negroes who volunteered to settle in Africa. According to Turner's calculation, the nation owed American Negroes about forty billion dollars, "estimating one hundred dollars a year for two million of us for two hundred years" for services rendered during slavery. Because other nations were turning their attention to Africa, he believed the United States should perform its role and send its Negroes to evangelize, civilize, and commercialize the "new" continent. But if government funds were not forthcoming, he had a second plan which called on American businessmen, both white and Negro, to establish regular trade and transportation links with Liberia. Because "there [was] a general unrest and a wholesale dissatisfaction" among his people, Turner promised that "if a line of steamers were started from New Orleans, Mobile, Savannah or Charleston, they would be crowded to density every trip they made to Africa." He ignored the fact that the ACS-chartered ship *Monrovia* made its annual trip to Liberia with only four families of immigrants. Nevertheless, the ACS noted that "so numerous have the applications become that the . . . Society will hereafter give the preference . . . to those who will pay a part of the cost of their passage and settlement in Liberia."[24]

Negro ideas about the race problem were in flux at the time of the debate regarding colonization. Most articulate Negroes, nevertheless, opposed emigration. Like Tanner, Douglass, and Downing, Turner's other opponents lacked clearly defined ideologies. They fluctuated between protest and accommodation, integration and Negro solidarity; but they concurred that going to Africa would not help. John W. Cromwell, editor of the *People's Advocate*, insisted that Negroes were doing all right in the United States; they needed only to work harder.[25] Charles W. Porter, physician and AME pastor, suggested that Negroes had better learn to be self-reliant in the United States before heading for Africa.[26] "What in the name of sense," asked the Reverend James H. Turner, "will a legion of insignificant, dejected mendicants do toward the reforming of that benighted land?"[27] Most Negroes who wrote asserted simply that they were Americans and intended to stay in their homeland. J. C. Embry, later an AME bishop, asserted that the climate of Africa would drain off all the energy of the American Negro. "The truth of the present and all future time," he added, "is the Negro cannot escape from the presence and influence of the white race in any habitable part of the globe. . . . To human view, the stern, irreversible decree of heaven has sealed these two peoples in a common destiny."[28]

Although most Negroes who wrote about the issue opposed emigration in any form, several spoke out in support of it. Among them was AME Bishop R. H. Cain, a congressman from South Carolina during Reconstruction, who predicted that, like Israel in the wilderness for forty years, Negro Americans might have to wait until the old generation had died out before the new would follow Turner to the promised land.[29]

More cautiously, T. Thomas Fortune, young editor of the New York *Globe*, reserved judgment. "Emigration may yet play a very important part in the solution of the question of our position in this country," he acknowledged. "We will say this much, that Dr. Tanner may speak, in his view, the prevailing opinion of northern colored men, while Bishop Turner may speak that of the south." But "whatever may be the wishes of the thoughtful men of the race, the masses of our people in the south are growing fearfully restless."[30] Whatever the impact on others, the debate had led Turner to formulate the ideas which had been ripening for years, and there would be little change in those ideas throughout the rest of his long and active life. Only the intensity of his vision of Africa would change as the status of the Negro in America fluctuated.

That status was drastically reduced in 1883 when the Supreme Court nullified the Civil Rights Act of 1875 in a decision which declared that the federal government could not prevent racial discrimination by private parties. To Bishop Turner, hypersensitive to the question of social equality, the civil rights rulings symbolized all that was wrong with the American attitude toward the Negro. He believed civil rights to be "as far above politics as heaven is above earth. Instead of being a political issue," he wrote, "it involves existence, respect, happiness and all that life is worth." As Turner viewed the decision, it sent the Negro back from the federal government, which granted and guaranteed his freedom, to the states which had opposed that freedom in the first place; and it was now up to the "white people of the respective states to decide whether we shall be treated as people or dogs." And, as if to clear the way for emigration to Africa, he declared that the Court decision "absolves the Negro's allegiance to the general government [and] makes the American flag to him a rag of contempt instead of a symbol of liberty." Moreover, the Constitution itself was a "dirty rag, a cheat, a libel and ought to be spit upon by every negro in the land."[31] The only alternatives he could see were Africa or extermination. Thus, the Bishop reiterated his disillusionment with the United States and urged more strongly than before that his people leave the land of broken promises for Africa. But disillusionment, strong and bitter as it was, did not move Turner himself out of the country any more than it removed the Negro masses.

During the next decade, although he was engrossed in ecclesiastical business, it was impossible for him to ignore the racial problem. He never renounced the appeals of Africa but he used his growing church and civic influence to make the best of the bad situation in America. Convinced that the Republican party had been defeated in 1884 because it had abandoned the Negro, Turner exerted his leadership to pull colored men into the Prohibition party. He even endorsed a number of Democratic leaders, especially after Senator John T. Morgan, an Alabama segregationist, introduced a Senate resolution calling for federal assistance for Negro emigration. Even though by 1895 Turner wielded enough political power to have his candidate named minister to Liberia, he never found enough success in political maneuvering to warrant relinquishing his African dream.[32]

If he grew more irenic toward white politicians, he was less accommodating to the Negro people, and his blunt evaluation of "scullion" Negroes who opposed colonization schemes alienated many people. He accused three fourths of the Negro Americans of "doing nothing day and night but cry: Glory, honor, dominion and greatness to White." To achieve either the American dream or its dark reflection, the African dream, Turner demanded a basic change of heart in the colored man, for "a man must believe he is somebody before he is acknowledged to be somebody.... Neither Republican nor Democratic party can do for the colored race what [it] can do for [itself]. Respect Black!" To stress the point, he proclaimed that "God is a Negro: Even the heathen in Africa believed that they were 'created in God's image.' But American Africans believe they resemble the devil, and hence the contempt they have for themselves and each other!" All the more reason, he urged, for a "Negro nationality where black men can be taught to respect themselves."[33] His personal manner and his emigration ideas offended so many middle-class Negroes that he received little cooperation when he worked for unity among several colored Methodist denominations.

In 1891 the AME Council of Bishops authorized Turner to visit Africa. He had long wanted to travel to the "fatherland," but his church was financially weak; it could not afford to send him, and its small missionary effort had been confined to a few workers in Haiti and British Guiana. There were a few AME churches functioning in Liberia and neighboring Sierra Leone. Without substantial support from the home organization, the African churches struggled along, ministering to the immigrants, converting a few natives, and attracting dissident members of white-dominated mission churches. Although officially Turner was to organize the AME churches to achieve better supervision and support, the Bishop viewed his trip as a pilgrimage to compare the real Africa with his dream Africa. Despite continuing unfavorable reports from other travelers, Turner confidently expected to "see or hear nothing that would change [his] convictions."[34]

His first contacts with Africans on board ship brought ecstatic reports. In his letters to the *Recorder* Turner reported that he had received a tumultuous welcome in Sierra Leone, which was matched by his own emotional embrace of Africa. When the people of Freetown heard of his arrival they streamed to the waterfront to meet him. He wept as he set foot on African soil; he was enraptured with the continent's geography and people. Instead of miasmic swamps, he described a clean, healthy city on hills rising from the harbor and black men standing erect and proud. He spoke to the governor of the colony, visited prosperous homes and businesses owned by blacks, and worshipped with natives "right from the bush, with a mere cloth over them," but who were "full of the Holy Ghost." All that he saw he pronounced good.[35]

Turner moved on to Liberia and recorded similar impressions with one major addition. Liberia was a free republic, not a colony, and it boasted a black president and government—the ultimate in political and social achievement. "One thing the black man has here," wrote the Bishop, "and that is manhood, freedom and the fullest liberty; he feels like a lord and walks the same way." Turner traveled about the country visiting the immigrant settlements, mission stations, and native villages, reporting the great promise of the coffee plantations, coal and iron deposits, and the general potential for rapid economic growth. If other travelers spoke adversely of the weather and fever, Turner scarcely mentioned the problems, since he visited Liberia during the dry, healthy season. In any case, he noted, the highlands were always healthy; if white missionaries could safely live there, so could Negroes.[36]

African people impressed Turner as much as African land; he praised the well-educated Muslim teachers who were present in all of West

Africa. Their learning and wisdom awed him at first, and he had to rationalize that their strong, African-based religion, a keen competitor for the faith of the natives, was actually preparing the way for Christianity by forbidding the terrible liquor traffic by which white traders debauched the people. He differentiated between the various tribes of natives who lived in Liberia, noting that the Negroes from the Congo region, released from slave ships and planted in Liberia by the American navy, were the least of the Africans. Furthermore, an ancient citizen of the place told Turner that in the slave days they never "used to sell 'big blood' Africans to white men except we catch him in war." This statement convinced the Bishop that most American Negroes, especially those who disagreed with him on emigration, were descended from the weaker Congo people who had always been slaves, even in Africa. (Turner himself claimed descent from royalty.) Most of the people in Liberia were worthy inheritors of the bishop's dream, and his glowing accounts beckoned Negro Americans to repatriate themselves and take advantage of the opportunities in trade, mining and agriculture, and most of all in equality and respect.[37]

Africa was all Turner dreamed it could be, and more: "I get mad and sick," he wrote, "when I look at the possibilities God has placed within our reach, and to think that we are such block-heads we cannot see and use them." The native Africans, doubtless following Turner's lead, could not understand why "the black man in America is at home across the sea." By the time he left for the United States, he was more convinced than ever that the status of the Negro in America was closely tied to the condition of Africa. "I see the wisdom of my position now as I never dreamed before," he wrote. "If the black man ever rises to wealth, . . . he will never do it by trying to be white or snubbing his native country," Africa.[38]

As in earlier years, few Negroes followed Turner's advice, in part because of the style of his leadership. When speaking to colored men he was callous and contentious, particularly as he grew old and survived to become senior bishop in the church. Starting in 1893 he edited his own newspaper and could use unrestrained language to attack the anti-emigrationists, the rich, the ignorant, and the would-be-white Negroes who lacked race pride. "We have been denounced and ridiculed a thousand times," he sneered, "by a number of these mushroom pimps who know how to scribble a little on paper for the public press." It was "these northern coons" who made the color problem worse by presuming to advise the southern Negro on the race issue, and it was "scullion" Negroes in the South, lacking the ambition or "animal instinct to either fight or run," who drew his scorn. He could categorize the opposition into either "this young fungus class" or "those old fossils who were in the slave pen when [I] was an officer in the army, trying to move heaven and earth to rescue their freedom."[39]

In 1893, alarmed at the increasing tempo of lynching and race violence, Turner summoned a representative gathering of "the friends of African repatriation or Negro nationalism elsewhere," but not the "stay-at-home portion" of the race.[40] Many Negro leaders agreed to attend, but they opposed mass emigration, although a few acknowledged that some colored men might find homes elsewhere.[41] In the face of strong opposition Turner shifted the emphasis of the meeting from emigration to general protest and, in an eloquent opening address, pleaded for action to alleviate the condition of southern Negroes. Conceding that he might be "overgloomy, too despondent . . . on the plane of despair," he put the choice to the convention: "It devolves upon us to project a remedy for our condition, if such a remedy is obtainable, or demand of this nation . . . five hundred million dollars to commence leaving it."[42] The more than six hundred delegates, with little hesitation, chose to seek the remedy at home rather than in exile. They sent memorials to Congress, to the state governors, and to the American people; and they formed an Equal Rights Council with Turner as chancellor. The pleas went unheeded; the Council never functioned, and the Negro press generally labelled the "Turner Convention" a failure for their editors were on guard against emigration ideas. Turner retorted in sour-grapes fashion, "What under heaven would [I] want with a national convention . . . to endorse African emigration when at least two million of colored people here in the South are ready to start for Africa at any moment."[43]

There is considerable evidence that a large number of southern colored people were willing, if not eager, to escape from the violence of America to the dreamland of Africa. A few Negroes wrote letters and articles supporting Turner's position, but a more relevant indication is found in the large number of applicants for transportation to Africa and in the persistent appearance of assorted companies and societies designed to provide such transportation. In fact, letters of inquiry and application overwhelmed the emigration companies, the ACS, and Turner himself, who, since 1893, had served as Liberian consul in the southern states. Turner hailed each new emigration scheme, endorsed a number of them, and reported their progress. Most such schemes failed, and some were surely fraudulent; but enough were genuine to keep a trickle of emigrants moving to Africa.[44] Financial problems were the primary barrier to actual emigration. Petitions asking for money to emigrate flowed continually to Congress and the state legislatures during the 1890's and increased in number as the depression in the South became severe in 1896. These petitions were usually tabled without action.[45]

By and large, Booker T. Washington rather than Turner set the norm for southern race relations after 1895. In a long editorial accompanying the full text of Washington's "Atlanta Compromise" address, Turner admired the professor's speech yet took exception to the statement that "the wisest among my race understand that the agitation of questions of social equality is the extremest folly." He was unwilling to surrender his claim to Negro rights, and while the professor stressed economic struggle, the Bishop maintained that political equality was a necessary precondition to racial peace. He concluded his editorial by prophecying that "With all due respect to Prof. Washington personally, for we do respect him personally, he will have to live a long time to undo the harm he has done our race."[46]

When Turner returned to Liberia and Sierra Leone again in 1893 and 1895 to supervise church conferences, he saw an ominous shadow. The European (and white American) encroachment was evident not only in the colonial governments and commercial enterprises but also in the missions where their race prejudice often debased the Africans. Turner wrote from West Africa in 1893 that it was common to meet white people in every direction. "Indeed, I do not like to see such an array of white faces," he complained. "It means the capture of the only spot upon the face of the globe that the black man can ever hope to be in power and demonstrate the ability of self-government."[47] As a result Turner stepped up his colonization campaign to save Africa for the Africans. Even more portentous, the same idea took root wherever the Bishop traveled in Africa.

Visiting South Africa in 1898, Turner consolidated a new branch of the church composed of native Christians who had rebelled against the race prejudice in the Wesleyan Missions; they had formed their own "Ethiopian Church" in 1892 and later had united with the AME Church.[48] In a region troubled by growing tension between Briton and Boer, he traveled for five weeks in the Cape Province and the Boer republics, organizing churches, ordaining new ministers, meeting government officials, and, above all, being seen and heard by the Africans. Turner reported that the white men in South Africa received him courteously, but "the Africans and colored people went wild by the thousands."[49] There are varying accounts of what he actually said to the people; nevertheless, all who have written of the tour agree that, either directly or indirectly, he stirred up a nationalist spirit within the hearts of the Africans which spread rapidly throughout southern Africa. One historian claims that Turner actually advocated a conspiracy to overthrow the white government so as to regain Africa for the Africans.[50] The official South African investigation into the native churches did not accuse him of such agitation; yet the government panel reported that "this close connection between the Ethiopians and the Negroes of the Southern States is viewed with grave misgivings by many South Africans, who fear that, by stimulating the spirit of racial jealousy and exclusiveness, it may have a sinister influence on the future of South Africa."[51] It is likely that he shared with the Africans his dream of black equality because, as one scholar states,

"Turner was a man full of the concept of the 'manifest destiny' of coloured Americans to redeem their unhappy brethren in Africa."[52]

When he returned from South Africa, Turner threw himself into the unsuccessful fight to prevent Georgia from adopting a disfranchising law. He attracted nationwide attention when he reportedly proclaimed from a Macon platform that "to the Negro in this country, the American flag is a dirty and contemptible rag," and that "hell is an improvement over the United States when the Negro is involved."[53] When President Roosevelt complained about the statement to his Negro adviser, Booker T. Washington, the professor soothed the President while Turner claimed that he had been misquoted. It was clear, however, that the contempt with which he held American race discrimination steadily deepened in Turner as he grew older.[54] Until his death in 1915 he never ceased to berate the United States and advocate his African dream.

Turner's emigration campaign failed for a number of reasons. Negroes were too captivated by the American dream to be tempted in an African nightmare. No matter how brightly he painted the map of Africa, most Negroes still considered it an ominous, unhealthy, dark continent. Furthermore, the opinion that Negroes lived better in the North or West of the United States provided a safety-valve nearer home.

The results of Turner's exhortations were not entirely negative. He did persuade some American Negroes to seek better lives in Africa. Negro intellectuals, while declining to emigrate, compensated by claiming an identity of interests with Africans, an identity which led to missionary activity and united protests against the excesses of colonialism. Turner, with others, aroused among Africans a sympathetic outcry against the excesses of American race prejudice. This reciprocal concern, a pan-Negro nationalism, has continued to play an important role in both American and African Negro thought.

Bishop Turner's career and teachings exemplify an important force in American Negro thought. He urged neither integration nor accommodation with white society. A black nationalist, he was totally disenchanted with the United States. Virtually rejected or ignored by Negro historians, Turner's African dream was the link between the pre-Civil War colonization movement and the later Chief Sam and Marcus Garvey back-to-Africa movements. Although unpopular with most articulate Negroes and ignored by most whites, Turner and his followers manifested a nationalism that has always been an option for free Negro Americans.

Notes

1. For studies of Negro nationalism see Edmund David Cronon, *Black Moses: The Story of Marcus Garvey and the Universal Negro Improvement Association* (Madison, 1957); C. Eric Lincoln, *The Black Muslims*

in America (Boston, 1961); E. U. Essien-Udom, *Black Nationalism: A Search for an Identity in America* (Chicago, 1962); Howard Brotz, *The Black Jews of Harlem* (New York, 1964); Robert A. Bone, *The Negro Novel in America* (New Haven, 1958); August Meier and Elliot Rudwick, *From Plantation to Ghetto* (New York, 1966); William E. Bittle and Gilbert Geis, *The Longest Way Home* (Detroit, 1964); Howard H. Bell, "A Survey of the Negro Convention Movement, 1830–1861" (doctoral dissertation, Northwestern University, 1953); Howard H. Bell, "Negro Nationalism: A Factor in Emigration Projects, 1858–1861," *Journal of Negro History*, XLVII (January, 1962); E. U. Essien-Udom, "The Black Nationalist Movements in Harlem," in John Henrick Clarke, ed., *Harlem: A Community in Transition* (New York, 1964); Harold W. Cruse, "Revolutionary Nationalism and the Afro-American," *Studies on the Left*, II (No. 3, 1962); Eugene D. Genovese, "The Legacy of Slavery and the Roots of Black Nationalism," *Studies on the Left*, VI (November–December, 1966); A. James Gregor, "Black Nationalism: A Preliminary Analysis of Negro Radicalism," *Science and Society*, XXVII (Fall, 1963).

2. *Crisis*, 10 (July, 1915), 132. A number of historians credit Henry M. Turner with having been the first Negro chaplain in the army, an able Reconstruction legislator, or a dominant personality in later years; but none until August Meier (*Negro Thought in America, 1880–1915: Racial Ideologies in the Age of Booker T. Washington*. Ann Arbor, 1963, pp. 59–68) wrote of him as a Negro nationalist. Benjamin Quarles, *The Negro in the Making of America* (New York, 1964), does not mention Turner. John Hope Franklin, *From Slavery to Freedom: A History of American Negroes* (New York, 2nd ed., 1956), 287, 306, 314, briefly mentions his Civil War and Reconstruction activities. Rayford Logan, *The Betrayal of the Negro* (New York, 1965), 289, mentions Turner once in an insignificant passage. Richard Bardolph, *The Negro Vanguard* (New York, 1961), 96–111, writes only of Turner's early life. E. Franklin Frazier, *The Negro in the United States* (New York, 2nd ed., 1957), 502, mentions Turner only as a pamphleteer. Among the older historians, Carter G. Woodson, *The Negro in Our History* (Washington, 5th ed., 1928), 434, devotes only a few lines to Turner. W. E. Burghardt DuBois, in his autobiographical *Dusk of Dawn: An Essay Toward an Autobiography of a Race Concept* (New York, 1940), 195, briefly mentions Turner and his ideas but dismisses them as impractical.

3. Meier, *Negro Thought*, 3–82.

4. For biographies of Turner see Dumas Malone, ed., *Dictionary of American Biography* (20 vols., New York, 1928–1936), XIX, 65–66; Mungo M. Ponton, *The Life and Times of Henry M. Turner* (Atlanta, 1917); J. Minton Batten, "Henry M. Turner, Negro Bishop Extraordinary," *Church History*, VII (September, 1938), 231–46; E. Merton Coulter, "Henry M. Turner: Georgia Negro Preacher-Politician During the Reconstruction Era," *Georgia Historical Quarterly*, XLVIII (December, 1964), 371–410.

5. *Christian Recorder*, June 21, 1883. See also Bell, "A Survey of the Negro Convention Movement, 1830–1861"; and P. J. Staudenraus, *The African Colonization Movement, 1816–1865* (New York, 1961).

6. Turner to editor, *African Repository*, November 28, 1874, published in *African Repository*, 51 (April, 1875), 139; Turner to editor, *Washington*

Post, January 25, 1895; Turner to William Coppinger, July 18, 1866, American Colonization Society Papers, Domestic Letters Received, vol. 184 (Manuscript Division, Library of Congress).

7. Turner to editor, *African Repository*, 52 (July, 1876), 84; *ibid.*, 51 (July, 1878), 77; see also George Brown Tindall, *South Carolina Negroes: 1877–1900* (Columbia, South Carolina, 1952), 153–68.

8. *Atlanta Constitution*, September 4, 1868.

9. Turner to editor, *Christian Recorder*, February 22, 1883; editorial, *ibid.*, June 4, 1885.

10. Frederick Douglass to editor, *ibid.*, February 1, 1883; J. C. Embry to editor, *ibid.*, February 1, 1883; John P. Sampson to editor, *ibid.*, January 18, 1883.

11. Turner to editor, *ibid.*, February 22, 1883.

12. *Ibid.*, and January 4, 1883.

13. *Ibid.*, February 22, 1883.

14. *Ibid.*

15. *Ibid.*, February 22, June 21, 1883; see also *Atlanta Constitution*, September 4, 1868.

16. *Christian Recorder*, January 25, June 21, 1883.

17. *Ibid.*, February 22, 1883; also see Turner's speech in *Augusta* (Ga.) *Colored American*, January 13, 1866.

18. *Christian Recorder*, February 22, 1883.

19. *Ibid.*, January 25, February 22, 1883.

20. *New York Globe*, January 27, 1883.

21. *Christian Recorder*, February 22, December 6, 1883; November 19, 1885. See also T. McCants Stewart, *Liberia, the Afro-American Republic* (New York, 1886), *passim*; and *Liberia Bulletin*, 31 (November, 1907), 30–32.

22. J. C. Embry in *Christian Recorder*, February 1, 1883; Tindall, *South Carolina Negroes*, 156. See also Philip D. Curtin, *The Image of Africa: British Ideas and Actions, 1780–1850* (Madison, 1964). American Negroes generally shared the view that West Africa was the black man's as well as the white man's graveyard.

23. *Christian Recorder*, February 22, 1883.

24. *Ibid.*, February 22, July 26, 1883.

25. J. W. Cromwell to editor, *ibid.*, February 22, 1883.

26. C. W. Porter to editor, *ibid.*, March 8, 1883.

27. J. H. Turner to editor, *ibid.*, February 22, 1883.

28. J. C. Embry to editor, *ibid.*, February 1, 1883.

29. *Ibid.*, July 12, 1883.

30. *New York Globe*, January 13, 1883.

31. *Memphis Appeal*, November 6, 1883, quoted in *Christian Recorder*, December 13, 1883; *St. Louis Globe* [n.d.], quoted in *Christian Recorder*, November 8, 1883. See also Henry M. Turner, *The Barbarous Decision of the Supreme Court Declaring the Civil Rights Act Unconstitutional* . . . (Atlanta, 1883, 1893).

32. Turner in a symposium of Negro letters on Cleveland's election in *AME Church Review*, 1 (January, 1885), 246. See also Clarence A. Bacote,

"The Negro in Georgia Politics, 1880–1908" (doctoral dissertation, University of Chicago, 1955), for documentation of Turner's political activity in this period.

33. Turner in *AME Church Review*, 1 (January, 1885), 246; *Voice of Missions*, November, 1895.

34. Lewellyn L. Berry, *A Century of Missions of the African Methodist Episcopal Church, 1849–1940* (New York, 1942), 71–72; Turner in the *Illinois State* (n.p., n.d.), quoted in *Christian Recorder*, July 23, 1891; *Atlanta Constitution*, September 15, 1891.

35. Turner's letters appeared irregularly in *Christian Recorder*, October, 1891 through January, 1892, and were collected in *AME Church Review*, 8 (April, 1892), 446–98.

36. *Ibid.*, December 5, 9, 1891.

37. *Ibid.*, November 29, December 4, 5, 7, 9, 1891. Turner claimed that his grandfather had been freed under a British colonial law forbidding the enslavement of royalty. Ponton, *Life and Times*, 33. It is more likely that Turner's free status at birth derived from a white grandmother, *New York Globe*, April 21, 1883.

38. Turner letters, *AME Church Review*, December 4, 1891.

39. *Voice of Missions*, August, 1893; March, October, 1895.

40. *Ibid.*, August, 1893.

41. *Ibid.*, October, 1893; *Indianapolis Freeman*, November 25, 1893.

42. *Voice of Missions*, December, 1893. Turner published the full text of his own speech but did not report the remarks of the many other speakers nor the minutes of the convention. The amount requested from Congress varied from $100 million to $500 million, depending upon the occasion.

43. *Voice of Missions*, January, 1894. See also *Cincinnati Commercial Gazette* and *Cincinnati Enquirer*, November 28, 29, 30, December 1, 2, 1893; *Denver Statesman*, December 2, 9, 1893.

44. *Voice of Missions*, March 1894, May 1895, May 1896. The most productive of these groups was the International Migration Society, Birmingham, Alabama, which sent about 600 Negroes to Liberia in 1895 and 1896.

45. *Ibid.*, May, September 1894, January 1895, February 1900; *New York Tribune*, April 16, 1896.

46. *Voice of Missions*, October, 1895. Later Turner generally supported Washington, but at times differed with both Washington and his "radical" critics.

47. *Voice of Missions*, June, 1893; *Christian Recorder*, November 21, 1891.

48. Josephus R. Coan, "The Expansion of Missions of the African Methodist Episcopal Church in South Africa, 1896–1908" (doctoral dissertation, Hartford Seminary Foundation, 1961). Coan deals with the ecclesiastical side of Turner's visit. Other works mention Turner in connection with the birth of African nationalism: George Shepperson and Thomas Price, *Independent African: John Chilembwe and the Origins, Setting and Significance of the Nyasaland Native Rising of 1915* (Edinburgh, 1958), 73, 93–109; Daniel Thwaite, *The Seething African Pot: A Study of Black Nationalism, 1882–1935* (London, 1936), 35–39; Bengt G. M. Sundkler, *Banta Prophets in South Africa* (London, 1961), 41, 65; South African Native Races Committee, ed., *The South African Natives: Their Progress and Present Condition* (New York, 1909), 192–205.

49. *Voice of Missions*, June 1898.

50. Thwaite, *Seething African Pot*, 35–38. The charge is suspect, for Thwaite does not give documentation and his general attitude toward African nationalism is quite negative.

51. South African Native Races Committee, *South African Natives*, 194–99. Turner's letters were first published in *Christian Recorder* and *Voice of Missions* and then collected in *AME Church Review*, 15 (1899), 809–13.

52. Shepperson and Price, *Independent African*, 73. See also George Shepperson, "Notes on Negro American Influence on the Emergence of African Nationalism," *Journal of African History*, I (1960), 299–312; Shepperson, "Ethiopianism and African Nationalism," *Phylon*, XIV (March 1953), 9–18.

53. For example see the *Portland* (Ore.) *New Age*, March 17, 1906. See Bacote, "Negro in Georgia Politics," for Turner's fight against disfranchisement.

54. Booker T. Washington to Turner, March 9, 1906; Turner to Washington, February 21, March 10, 1906, Booker T. Washington Papers (Manuscript Division, Library of Congress); Turner to editor, *Atlanta Constitution*, February 24, 1906.

The Social Mission of
Bishop Alexander Walters

George M. Miller

Panel: Is the Black Church Preserving Its History?*

The Social Mission of Bishop Alexander Walters (August 1, 1858–February 2, 1917) provides an insight into the struggle of Afro-Americans in one of the most turbulent periods of American history. The end of Reconstruction, the establishment of Jim Crow, and the various responses of blacks to an oppressive society occurred during his life. His ministry in one of the independent black Methodist churches presents an insight into one of the richest periods of American church history. His long identification with black protest organizations, as seen through his participation in the Afro-American League, and his initiative in founding the National Afro-American Council are worthy of scholarly investigation. Also, the relationship between Walters and Booker T. Washington needs to be studied, especially in light of the national political affiliations of the two Black leaders and their distinctive responses to disfranchisement. The concern of Alexander Walters for the freedom of subject peoples in Africa, South America and the West Indies can be studied by analyzing his role in the First Pan-African Conference which met in London in 1900. Walters' active political involvement can be seen in his tenure as president of the National Colored Democratic League, his extensive activities on behalf of Woodrow Wilson in the election of 1912, and his advocacy of black independence in politics. The concern by Afro-Americans to determine their destiny during the era of disfranchisement and recurring lynchings aroused the conscience of this dynamic clergyman. On several occasions Bishop Walters declined federal appointments so that he might continue to speak from a base in the black man's church.

---

*Sixtieth Annual Meeting of the Association for the Study of Afro-American Life and History, Atlanta, Georgia, October 18, 1975.

Alexander Walters was born two years before the Civil War (August 1, 1858), in Bardstown, Kentucky. He was an eyewitness to the early expressions of the newly freed slaves. The free black church (African Methodist Episcopal Zion Church) provided him an opportunity to attend school in his hometown. For several years he waited tables in Louisville and worked on steam boats on the Mississippi and Ohio Rivers. While in Louisville he continued his education by studying privately with white tutors for several years prior to 1875. In 1876 he joined a crew of waiters and was sent to work at the Bates House in Indianapolis, Indiana. On Agust 28, 1877, he married Katie Knox and to this union five children were born.

Entering the ministry of the African Methodist Episcopal Zion Church he was licensed to preach by the Quarterly Conference of the Blackford Street A.M.E. Zion Church of Indianapolis in May, 1877. In September, 1878, he was admitted to the Kentucky Conference, Croydon, Kentucky. He was ordained a deacon on July 8, 1879 in St. Louis and an elder on September 12, 1882 in Louisville. After serving several churches in Kentucky he was appointed pastor of Stockton Street A.M.E. Zion Church, second oldest black Protestant church on the West Coast (now First A.M.E. Zion Church), San Francisco, California in 1883. While pastoring in San Francisco he spoke out against the 1883 decision of the Supreme Court in the Civil Rights Cases, and urged President Arthur to protect the citizenship and political rights of black Americans. On his return from the East in 1884, he visited the Republican National Convention in Chicago and was unimpressed with its action on civil rights. After three years in San Francisco, Walters was moved east to Thompkins Chapel A.M.E. Zion Church, Chattanooga, Tennessee. Illness forced Walters to move from Chattanooga, after one year to Knoxville, and there as at previous appointments, new members were added to the church, social consciousness and "race pride" were emphasized. He served Loguen Temple Church, Knoxville for two years and was moved to Mother "Zion" A.M.E. Zion Church (founded 1796, mother church of the denomination), New York City, after the Quadrennial General Conference in May, 1888. During his tenure at Mother Zion, the interior was renovated, over 700 members added and finances reached new heights. Pastor Walters not only ministered to the spiritual needs of his parishioners, but to their social needs as well. He actively participated in the civic activities of the communities in which he served. In San Francisco he became the first black member of the Men's Bible Club sponsored by the Young Women's Christian Association. While at Mother Zion he was appointed agent of the Denominational Book Concern by the Board of Bishops of the A.M.E. Zion Church. In 1889 he was appointed as a delegate from his denomination to the World Sunday School Convention meeting in London. Afterwards he traveled in Europe, Egypt, and Palestine. In April, 1891, in recognition of his meritorious record as a successful pastor and his advocacy of race uplift, Livingstone College, Salisbury, North Carolina, conferred on him the honorary degree of Doctor of Divinity (D.D.).

At Pittsburgh, Pennsylvania, May, 1892, he was elected the twenty-fourth bishop of the A.M.E. Zion Church by the members of the Nineteenth Quadrennial Session of the General Conference of the A.M.E. Zion Church. In the short period of fifteen years at the young age of 33, Alexander Walters had risen to the highest office in Zion Methodism.

Closely akin to Walter's interest in his church and the ecumenical movement was his zeal for the welfare of his race. In 1890 he joined T. Thomas Fortune and others in issuing a call for a meeting to organize for race protection. As a result, the Afro-American League came into existence in Chicago in January, 1890. The League appears to have lapsed after a second meeting in Knoxville, Tennessee in 1891. But the problems and conditions which called the League into existence continued and so did Bishop Walters' social activism. After a number of outrages that had been perpetrated against blacks in the South, he called for revival of the League.

Bishop Walters secured over one hundred names to a petition addressed to T. Thomas Fortune, president of the Afro-American League. Mr. Fortune agreed to call another meeting of the group. The petition was signed by many of the leading blacks of the day. The group meeting in Rochester, New York, on September 15, 1889, decided not to revive the old League but to form a new organization, thus the National Afro-American Council was born. The high regard in which Bishop Walters was held by members of the new organization was evident when upon the refusal of Mr. Fortune to run (for the presidency), Bishop Walters was elected to the presidency of the Council. He served seven terms as president of the Council, from 1898 to 1907. The Council functioned as a national forum for the discussion of political, economic, and social problems affecting the race. Walters traveled throughout the country raising the visibility of the organization and keeping the historic "protest" tradition of the race alive. Unfortunately because of insufficient funds, lack of commitment, and racism the Council did not reach its full potential. Later Bishop Walters joined the Niagara Movement in 1905 and was one of the co-founders, member of the board of directors, and vice-president of the N.A.A.C.P.

In July, 1900, Bishop Walters was elected unanimously to the presidency of the First Pan-African Conference meeting in London, England. For several years the bishop was active in the American branch of the organization. He was a participant in the International Conference on the Negro, held at Tuskegee Institute, November, 1912. Later the bishop visited Liberia and the Gold Coast (now Ghana), in 1910.

Convinced that the Republican Party did not merit the support of the race, Walters in 1908 shifted to the Democratic Party and later was elected president of the National Colored Democratic League. The bishop was particularly active in supporting Woodrow Wilson for the presidency in 1912. A cordial relationship existed between the governor and the bishop which created the basis of the latter's endorsement of Wilson for the presidency. The basis of the Walters' endorsement of Wilson was formed from a letter he received in regard to his position on black-white relationships, the role of the federal government in protecting its citizens and securing justice for all blacks. Wilson in his now famous letter to Bishop Walters promised "to assure my colored fellow citizens of my earnest wish to see justice done in every matter, and not just mere grudging justice, but justice executed with liberality and cordial feelings" (Walters, *My Life and Work*, p. 195). With this supposedly genuine commitment from Mr. Wilson, the bishop spoke through the country in support of Wilson and helped persuade Dr. W. E. B. DuBois to endorse him. After the election the new president offered the bishop several traditional black federal appointments such as minister to Liberia but he refused because of his commitment to his church.

Later, when numerous blacks were dismissed in the federal government, lynchings continued unchecked, and the general deterioration of race relations went unabated, the bishop broke with President Wilson. It has been said that without the campaign activities of Bishop Walters in the election of 1912, Wilson could have been defeated because of the lack of black support in several pivotal northern states.

Bishop Walters was a founding member of the Federal Council of Churches in America, member of its Executive Council Committee, and served on several of its commissions; a vice-president of the World Alliance for Promoting International Friendship through the churches; a trustee of Livingstone College and Howard University; for many years a member of the Board of Trustees of the United World Society of Christian Endeavor; a delegate to the Ecumenical Conferences of World Methodism at Washington, D.C., London, England and Toronto, Canada; and a bishop of the African Methodist Episcopal Zion Church (1892–1917).

Alexander Walters' life was full of action, hard work and struggle to avoid any division in an already polarized society. His life as already pointed out previously was filled with travel, confrontation and sacrifice. For over a quarter of a century he had a heart condition but did not let it or the stubbornness of racial injustice stay him from speaking out against injustices.

Ultimately he paid the supreme price for his convictions without the benefit of comfort and power. It has been said that if a foreigner wanted to meet the three most influential blacks in the United States during the first two decades of this century, he was referred to Dr.

Booker T. Washington of Tuskegee, Alabama; Dr. W. E. B. DuBois of New York City and Bishop Alexander Walters of New York City.

Bishop Walters died on February 2, 1917. Undoubtedly the bishop was one of a new breed of socially conscious black churchmen. A further indication of his concern to "generations yet unborn" was the appearance of his autobiography *My Life and Work* the year of his death.

The following short comments underline the social mission of Bishop Alexander Walters as stated before the Fifth World's International Convention of the Christian Endeavor Society, Chicago, 1915:

> I admit that race prejudice is deep seated, stubborn, and one of the hardest things in all the world.
> Second, the great truth presented to the world was the Christ— the life and light of the world.
> Tyrannies, race discrimination, the burning of Negroes at stake, oppression of women, ignorance, poverty and crime coexist with the Christian religion in different lands. Still I am sure that the vital forces of which I have spoken, that mighty power which has uprooted gigantic evils, will overcome these evils.
> Fifth, the fifth great truth is the brotherhood of man is the acme of the teachings of Christ.
> America is the leader in present day civilization. . . . She is given a wonderful opportunity to do service for God and humanity in taking the lead in solving the race problem on Christian principles.

The social mission of Bishop Alexander Walters was affirmed for posterity by Reverdy Ransom in the April, 1917 issue of the *A.M.E. Church Review*:

> The passing of Bishop Alexander Walters marks the flight of one of the most alert and forceful personalities in Negro Methodism.
> The A.M.E. Zion Church had the honor to claim him as her son. She was quick to recognize his worth, electing him to the bishopric at the age of thirty-five. Like all extraordinary men, Bishop Walters was too broad visioned, and the scope of his activities was too large to be limited by the narrow boundaries of denominational lines. He was a man of the Church but not a churchman, in the sense of confining his activities within the range of the affairs of the Episcopacy. In the United Society of Christian Endeavor, he was a trustee; he was an influential member of the Executive Committee of the Federal Council of Churches of Christ in America; and in the field of national politics he was potentially active. Though lacking his astuteness, he was much like the late Bishop Arnett, in keeping his Church and race in touch with the larger national and international movements. . . . A Negro bishop should (take) an active, unswerving, outspoken position in advocacy of the interests of his people, whether they be industrial, moral, social, or political.
> The Negro race did not appoint the late Dr. Booker T. Washington

as its leader and representative. By force of circumstances he assumed it. On the all, the great questions he assumed to speak for the race. The bishops of the three great branches of Methodism, are the duly chosen and acknowledged leaders and advisers of a vast constituency. Their individual or united voice has great carrying power. Bishop Walters realized this and made the most of it. The bench of bishops of our Negro churches should never be without at least one such personality.

Alexander Walters spent most of his life in a conscious effort to improve the world for all Americans, but especially for the members of his race. His ministry was not confined to the "body of believers" in the church but included concern for the temporal existence of his congregants and others. The "this worldly ministry" of Walters can be best expressed in a letter to Booker T. Washington in 1900 where he stated "we are contending for his (Negroes) civil and political rights." When bishops, clergy and lay persons of his denomination eschewed his entrance into "politics and protest" he continued to preach "that we may all be one" in political as well as spiritual equality. Walters believed that the church's mission was to lead and not follow society.

> Stony the road we trod, Bitter the chastening rod,
> Felt in the days when hope unborn had died;
> Yet with a steady beat, Have not our weary feet
> Come to the place for which our fathers sighed?
> We have come, treading our path tho the blood of
> the slaughtered, out from the gloomy past,
> Till now we stand at last where the white gleam
> of our bright star is cast.

Reverend George Washington Woodbey:
Early Twentieth Century California Black Socialist

Philip S. Foner

In the *Ohio Socialist Bulletin* of February, 1909, Reverend Richard Euell, a black minister of Milford, Ohio, published "A Plan to Reach the Negro." The Negro, he wrote, "belongs to the working class and must be taught class consciousness." Blacks could be more rapidly recruited into the party if Socialists would go to them in their churches and point out "the way to freedom and plenty." Most of them had no experience with any organization other than the church and could think of committing themselves to action only in religious terms. The Bible, even motion pictures about the "Passion Play," could be used effectively to imbue religion with radicalism and convince the black working class of the evils of the capitalist system and the virtues of Socialism.[1]

The first black Socialist to conduct the type of work Reverend Euell recommended was Reverend George Woodbey (sometimes spelled Woodby), and he had already been performing this function for the Socialist cause for several years before a "Plan to Reach the Negro" was published.

George Washington Woodbey, the leading Negro Socialist in the first decade of the 20th century, was born a slave in Johnson County, Tennessee, on October 5, 1854, the son of Charles and Rachel (Wagner) Woodbey. Of his early life nothing is known other than that he learned to read after freedom came, was self-educated, except for two terms in a common school, and that his life was one of "hard work and hard study carried on together." A fellow Socialist who knew him wrote: "He has worked in mines, factories, on the streets, and at everything which would supply food, clothing and shelter."

Woodbey was ordained a Baptist minister at Emporia, Kansas in 1874. He was active in the Republican Party of Missouri and Kansas and was a leader in the Prohibition Party, and when he moved to Nebraska he became a prominent force in the prohibition movement in that state.

In 1896 Woodbey ran for lieutenant governor and Congress on the Prohibition ticket in Nebraska.

That same year, he made his first acquaintance with the principles of Socialism when he read Edward Bellamy's *Looking Backwards*, and his interest was further aroused by copies of the *Appeal to Reason* which came into his hands. Although he subscribed to the *Appeal*, he did not join the Socialists. Instead, he joined the Populist Party, and in 1900, he supported William Jennings Bryan, the Democratic and Populist candidate for President. But he also heard Eugene V. Debs speaking during the presidential campaign and was so impressed that when the Democratic Party asked Woodbey to speak for Bryan, he agreed but delivered speeches which were geared more to the ideas advanced by Debs than those by the Democratic candidate. After several such speeches, the Democrats stopped scheduling dates for Woodbey's speeches, and the black minister came to the conclusion that his place was in the Socialist camp. He resigned his pulpit and announced to his friends that henceforth his life "would be consecrated to the Socialist movement." A Nebraska Socialist recalls:

> We remember him in the stirring days of the inception of the Socialist movement in Omaha. Night after night he spoke on the streets and in the parts of that city. Omaha had never had the crowds that attended Woodbey's meetings.[2]

Woodbey visited his mother in San Diego during the spring of 1902, and immediately made an impression on the comrades in Southern California. A dispatch to the *Los Angeles Socialist* on May 31, 1902 expresses this clearly:

> Socialism is on the boom here in this county and city. We have had Rev. G. W. Woodbey, the Colored Socialist orator of Nebraska with us for nearly a month during which time he has delivered 23 addresses and will speak again tonight, and then he will do some work in the country districts where he has been invited to speak. . . .
>
> Comrade Woodbey is great and is a favorite with all classes. He came here unannounced ostensibly to see his mother who resides here but as he says that he is "so anxious to be free," that he feels impressed to work for the cause constantly. He has had very respectable audiences both on the streets and in the halls. He likes to speak on the street and it is the general verdict that he has done more good for the cause than any of our most eloquent speakers who have preceded him. He is full of resources and never repeats his speeches, but gives them something new every time. He requested me to state in my notes to the "Socialist" that he desires to visit Los Angeles later on if you folks can find a place for him. He makes no charges but depends entirely on passing the hat for his support. . . .[3]

Los Angeles did find a place for Woodbey, and he delivered a series of soap-box speeches and lectures in the leading hall. When after one of his speeches, Woodbey was denied admittance to the Southern Hotel and Northern Restaurant because of his color, the Los Angeles Socialist Party organized a successful boycott of the establishments and distributed leaflets reading:

> We demand as trade unionists and socialists, that every wage-worker in Los Angeles bear well in mind these two places that depend on public patronage—the Northern Restaurant and the Southern Hotel—keep away from them. They draw the color line.[4]

Woodbey accepted an offer to become minister of the Mount Zion Baptist Church in San Diego and made his home in California for the next two decades. He was elected a member of the state executive board of the Socialist Party, and soon became widely known in the state as "The Great Negro Socialist Orator." In a Los Angeles debate with Archibald Huntley, Ph.D., where Woodbey took the affirmative of the topic, "Resolved that Socialism is the True Interpretation of Economic Conditions and that it is the Solution of the Labor Problem," he was listed as a "well-known Socialist Lecturer."[5]

An announcement that Woodbey would deliver a reply to Booker T. Washington's "Capitalist Argument for the Negro" packed Los Angeles' leading hall on May 1, 1903. He paid tribute to Washington "as a gentleman" and educator, but added: "He has all the ability necessary to make a good servant of capitalism by educating other servants for capitalism." Woodbey charged that whether consciously or not, Tuskeegee Institute fulfilled the role of providing black workers to be pitted against white workers so as to bring about a general lowering of wage scales. What Washington failed to understand was that there was basically no unity between capitalists, white or black, and workers, white or black. "There is no race division industrially, but an ever-growing antagonism between the exploiting capitalists black or white, and the exploited workers, black or white." In this "industrial struggle," the working class was bound to "ultimately triumph."

> And then the men of all races will share in the results of production according to their services in the process of production. This is Socialism and the only solution to the race problem.[6]

A frequent target of the police of San Diego, Los Angeles, San Francisco, and other California communities, Woodbey was in and out of jail several times between 1902 and 1908, and was hospitalized more than once as a result of police brutality. But he gave as well as received. When he was attacked and driven off a street corner in San Diego in

July, 1905 by Police Officer George H. Cooley, Woodbey led a group of protesters to the police station to lodge a complaint. There Cooley again attacked the black Socialist, "using at the same time oaths and language too mean and vile to print." Woodbey was literally thrown bodily out of the station house. He immediately brought charges against the police officer for assault and battery and informed his California comrades:

> In the days of chattel slavery the masters had a patrol force to keep the negroes in their place and protect the interests of the masters. Today the capitalists use the police for the same purpose.

But slaves had rebelled despite the patrols, and he was following that tradition by telling the police that they could not get away with their brutality against enemies of the capitalist system.

Although Woodbey's case against the police was prosecuted by the County Attorney, assisted by Job Harriman, California's leading Socialist attorney, and although all witnesses testified that the Negro Socialist's conduct had been "perfectly gentlemanly," and that he had a perfectly lawful right to be at the station house, the jury, composed of conservative property owners, took only fifteen minutes to find the defendant not guilty. Woodbey was furious and published the names of the jury men, calling upon all decent citizens to have nothing to do with them. He followed this up by returning immediately to the soap box in San Diego and held one of the biggest street corner meetings in the city up to this time. As he wrote:

> The case has made more Socialists that I could possibly have made in many speeches. Had I not gone to the court with the matter the public would forever have contended that I was doubtless doing or saying something that I had not right to do or say. And when I complained I would have been told that if I had gone to the courts I would have got justice. Now, as it is, nothing of the kind can be said, and the responsibility is placed where it rightly belongs.

Many non-Socialists in San Diego, Woodbey noted, were learning the truth of the Socialist contention that "the police force are the watch dogs of capitalism."[7]

In more than one California city Woodbey was arrested and hauled off to jail for trying to sell copies of his Socialist booklets.[8] The writings made Woodbey's name known throughout the entire Party in the United States and even internationally.

Describing Woodbey as "the greatest living negro in America," a white Socialist noted that "his style is simple and his logic invincible. He knows the race question, and one of his most popular lectures relates to the settlement of this vexed question under Socialism." Woodbey's ability to explain Socialism in simple terms led to the demand that he "embody some of the things he has said to the thousands who have listened to his talks, in a written form. . . ." The response was the pamphlet *What To Do and How To Do It or Socialism vs. Capitalism.* A copy of a small edition, privately printed, fell into the hands of A. W. Ricker, a Socialist organizer in the West and South. While at the home of Socialist publisher Julius A. Wayland, in Girard, Kansas, he read it aloud to the Wayland family. "At the conclusion," Ricker wrote, "we decided that the book ought to be in the hands of the millions of American wage slaves, and we forthwith wrote to Rev. Mr. Woodbey for the right to bring it out."[9]

It was published as No. 40 of the widely distributed *Wayland's Monthly* in August, 1903. Ricker gave a send-off in the *Appeal to Reason* writing:

> The book in many respects is the equal of "Merrie England," and in the matter of its clear teaching of the class struggle, it is superior. It has been read by every negro in Girard, (Kansas), and has made Socialists of those who were susceptible of understanding after every other effort had failed to shake their unreasoning adherence to the Republican party. A good supply should be ordered by every local in the land, there is no book in the language that will excel it in propaganda value, and we expect to see it pass through one edition after another, as soon as it is read by the comrades.[10]

Since Robert Blatchford's *Merrie England,* published in England in 1894 and in the United States in 1900, was considered one of the best of the Socialist educational publications, the tribute to Reverend Woodbey's pamphlet was well understood by readers of the *Appeal to Reason.*

Woodbey's forty-four-page booklet carried the touching dedication:

> This little book is dedicated to that class of citizens who desire to know what the Socialists want to do and how they propose to do it. By one who was once a chattel slave freed by the proclamation of Lincoln and wishes to be free from the slavery of capitalism.[11]

In his preface Reverend Woodbey acknowledged that there was "nothing original" in his little book, his aim being simply to make the subjects treated "as plain as possible to the reader." It was not directed to those who were already convinced of the superiority of Socialism over Capitalism, but to "meet the demands of that large and increasing class of persons who have not yet accepted Socialism, but would do so if they could see any possible way of putting it into practice." Within this framework, Reverend Woodbey's booklet is an effective piece of Socialist propaganda, and so highly thought of in Socialist circles, that by 1908 it had been translated into three languages and gained for its author an international reputation.[12]

Basically, the booklet consisted of a dialogue between the author and his mother whom he has rejoined after nearly seventeen years of separation. She expresses her astonishment at having learned that her son had become a Socialist. "Have you given up the Bible and the ministry and gone into politics?" she asks. Her son attempts to convince his mother that it is precisely because of his devotion to the principles enunciated in the Bible that he became a Socialist, and that as the years passed, he became more and more convinced of the correctness of his decision. When his mother points out that among his comrades were a few who believed neither in God nor in the Bible, her son readily agrees, but reminds her that he found "a still larger number of unbelievers in the Republican party before I left it some twenty years ago," and that other parties had their "equal portion" of nonbelievers. More important, while he believed in the Biblical account of God, the origin of the earth and man, and members of his Party did not, he and they were able to agree that "man is here, and the earth is here, and that it is the present home of the race, at least." They did not, to be sure, see eye-to-eye about the "hereafter." Since Socialism was "a scheme for bettering things here first," he could be a "good Socialist" without surrendering his belief in God or the Bible. There was room in the Socialist Party for those who were interested only in what it could do for mankind in the present world and for those who, like himself, were "Socialists because they think that mankind is entitled to the best of everything in both this world and the next." Finally, his mother accepts the idea that under Socialism persons would be free to have "their own religion or none, just as they please, as long as they do not interfere with others."[13]

Having laid at rest his mother's anxiety and made her willing to listen to the fundamental principles of a movement which obviously had not destroyed her son's religious convictions, Reverend Woodbey proceeds to explain to her the evils of capitalist society and the way by which Socialism, gaining power through the ballot box, would set out to eliminate these evils. After he takes his mother through such subjects as rent, interest, and profits, all gained from labor's production, and value which is created only by labor but the fruits of which are appropriated entirely by the capitalists, she expresses bewilderment at the meaning of such words. Her son then illustrates what they mean in simple language and in terms of daily experience. Here, for example, is how he explained surplus value:

> Why didn't the slave have wealth at the close of the war? He worked hard.
> "Because his master got it," mother replied.
> "The wage worker's master got what he produced, too."
> "But wasn't he paid for his work?" asked mother.
> Yes, about seventeen cents on every dollar's worth of wealth he created. . . .

Under Socialism, he continues, the capitalist would have to turn over to the State a "large amount of capital created by labor" which he had taken from the worker while the latter, having been deprived of all he produced under capitalism, would have nothing to turn over. The very rich would have no reason to complain "since he and his children, who have done nothing but live off the labor of those who have nothing to turn over, are to be given an equal share of interest with those who have produced it all. So you see we Socialists are not such bad fellows as you thought. We propose to do good unto those who spitefully use us, and to those who curse us, by giving them an equal show with ourselves, provided that they will here-after do their share of the useful work."[14]

But his mother expresses concern that the capitalists will not yield peacefully to having the "land, factories, and means of production" turned over to the cooperative commonwealth by a Socialist Congress elected by the people, and that they would start a war to retain their holdings. Her son concedes that this would quite likely occur just as the slaveholders had refused to abide by Lincoln's electoral victory and precipitated a civil war. But the capitalists would never succeed in the war they would seek to stimulate, for the majority of the people had clearly become convinced that Socialism was the only solution to their problems, or else the Socialists could not have won their electoral victories. Hence, the capitalists would have no one to do the fighting for them:

> The slaveholder did not dare to arm the negro, on his side, without proclaiming emancipation, and to do that was to lose his cause; so with the capitalist, if he dares to offer all to the poor man who must fight his battles, he has lost his cause; and with this condition confronting the capitalist, there is no danger in taking over the entire industrial plant as soon as the Socialists can be elected and pass the necessary laws. And the Socialist party will go into power just as soon as the majority finds that the only way to secure to itself its entire product is to vote that ticket.[15]

Mother has only one question left about the transition from capitalism to Socialism: "Have the people a right to do this?" Her son reminds her of the Declaration of Independence which clearly affirmed the right of the people, when any form of government became destructive of the rights of life, liberty and the pursuit of happiness, "to alter and abolish it and institute a new government" which would be most likely to affect "their safety and happiness." On this the Socialists stand, the son declares firmly. Moreover, it was none other than Abraham Lincoln who, in his speech of January 12, 1840, in the House of Representatives, had said "just what the Socialist now say." He had then declared: "Any people anywhere being inclined and having the power have the right to rise up and shake off the existing government and form a new one that suits them better. . . ."16

His mother now fully satisfied, the son proceeds to describe how different departments of government—agriculture, transportation, distribution, intelligence, education, and health—will operate under Socialism providing for the needs of the people rather than under capitalism, for the profits of the capitalist. Occasionally, the mother interrupts the narrative with questions that bring answers that satisfy her. Thus, when she asks whether the workers who would own and operate the factories under Socialism, "would know how to do the work," the answer reassures her:

> Why, the workers are the only ones who do know how to run a factory. The stockholders who own the concern know nothing about doing the work. If the girl who weaves in the factory should be told that Socialism is now established, and that henceforth she is to have shorter hours of labor, a beautiful sanitary place to work in, and an equal share of all the wealth of the nation, to be taken in any kind of thing she wants, do you think she would forget how to work? And if on the other hand, all she produces is to go to the girl who does nothing but own the stocks, then she can work right along. Seems to me, you might see the absurdity of that, mother. "I believe I do see, now," she said, after a moment's hesitation. Then apply that illustration about the girls, to all the workers, and you will get my meaning.17

As might be expected, mother asks, "Like all other women, I want to know where we are to come in." Her son assures her that it was to the interest of "the women, more than the men, if possible, to be Socialists because they suffer more from capitalism than anyone else." For one thing, the Socialist platform demands "the absolute equality of the sexes before the law, and the repeal of the law that in any way discriminates against women." Then again, under Socialism, each woman would, like each man, have her own independent income, and would become "an equal shareholder in the industries of the nation." Under such liberating conditions, a woman would have no need "to sell herself through a so-called marriage to someone she did not love, in order to get a living," and, for the first time in history, could marry only for love. Under capitalism, the working man was a slave, "and his wife is the slave of a slave." Socialism would liberate both, but since it would give women political equality and economic freedom, it would actually do more for women than ever for men.18

By now mother has been converted, and the booklet ends with the comment: "Well, you have convinced me that I am about as much of a slave now as I was in the south, and I am ready to accept any way out of this drudgery, mother remarked as the conversation turned on other subjects."19

Here and there *What To Do and How To Do It* reflected Edward Bellamy's influence on Reverend Woodbey, and sections of the 1903 pamphlet are shortened versions of the 1887 *Looking Backward*.[20] In the main, however, the pamphlet revealed that the black minister had broken with Bellamy's utopianism. While Bellamy emphasized "equitable" distribution of wealth under Nationalism, Woodbey was convinced that the solution lay closer to Marx's maxim, "From each according to his abilities, to each according to his needs." Bellamy rejected the label "socialism" as dangerous and un-American.[21] But Woodbey welcomed it and believed its principles were in keeping with the best in the American tradition. Like many in the Socialist party, Woodbey believed that with the capture of sufficient political offices through the ballot box, socialism could be rapidly achieved. But he was one of the very few in the Party in 1903 who took into account the danger that the capitalists would not sit by and calmly watch their control of society eliminated by legislative enactments, and instead would, like the slave owners in 1860, resort to violence to prevent the people's will from being carried into effect. To be sure, unlike Jack London, who in his great 1908 novel *The Iron Heel*, predicted that the oligarchy of American capitalists would seize power from the Socialists and destroy the democratic process by violence, Woodbey was confident that the capitalists would fail.[22] Nevertheless, by even raising this issue in his pamphlet, Woodbey was in advance of nearly all Christian Socialists.

Early in *What To Do and How To Do It*, Reverend Woodbey assured his mother that he would at a future date tell her "more about what the Bible teaches on this subject" of Socialism.[23] He fulfilled his promise a year later with *The Bible and Socialism: A Conversation Between Two Preachers*, published in San Diego, California by the author. The 96-page booklet was dedicated to

> ... the Preachers and Members of the Churches, and all others who are interested in knowing what the Bible teaches on the question at issue between the Socialists and the Capitalists, by one who began preaching twenty-nine years ago, and still continues.[24]

As the sub-title indicates, *The Bible and Socialism* consists of a dialogue between Woodbey and another clergyman. The latter is a local pastor to whom Woodbey's mother has given a copy of the 1903 pamphlet and invited to her home to hear her son convince him that he was wrong in contending that "there is no Socialism in the Bible." When the skeptical pastor questions Woodbey about the Socialist claim that Karl Marx discovered the principles of Scientific Socialism and points out that this was centuries after the Bible was written, Woodbey notes, first, that no new idea is ever entirely new and is in some way based on what went before, and, second, that

> Marx, the greatest philosopher of modern times, belonged to the same wonderful Hebrew race that gave to the world Moses, the Lawgiver, the kings and prophets, and Christ the Son of the Highest, with his apostles, who, together, gave us the Bible that, we claim, teaches Socialism. Doubtless Marx, like other young Hebrews, was made acquainted with the economic teachings of Moses, and all the rest of the Old Testament sages and prophets, whatever we find him believing in after life.
>
> If we are able to show that the Bible opposes both rent, interest, and profits, and the exploiting of the poor, then it stands just where the Socialists do.[25]

After agreeing that Marx was not a Christian but noting that this was of no significance since Socialism had nothing to do with a man's religion or lack of it, Reverend Woodbey devotes the rest of his pamphlet to detailed references, quotations, and citations to convince the pastor that since the Bible—both the Old and New Testaments—did actually oppose "rent, interest, and profits, and the exploiting of the poor," it was a Socialist document with close affinity to such classics as *The Communist Manifesto, Capital* and other writings of Marx. As a Jew, Woodbey emphasizes, Marx was able to do "the greatly needed work of reasoning out from the standpoint of the philosopher, what his ancestors, the writers of the Old and New Testaments, had already done from a moral and religious standpoint."[26] This is not to say, he continues, that there is no difference between a Socialism based merely on a "moral and religious standpoint" and Scientific Socialism just as there was a fundamental difference between the Socialism advanced by Utopian reformers prior to Marx and that set forth by the father of Scientific Socialism. For Scientific Socialism was based on the class struggle which had dominated all history and dominated existing relationships in capitalist society. When the pastor asks Woodbey if the class struggle also exists in the church, there is the following discussion in which his mother joins:

> Master and slave, before the war, all belonged to the same church. They met on Sunday and prayed together, and one church member sold the other the next day. So now, in many cases, master and wage slave belong to the same church, meet on Sunday and pray together, and the one turns the other off from even the pittance he allowed him to take out of his earnings as wages or sets him out of house and home for non-payment of rent, or under mortgage, the next day. All that, notwithstanding the Bible says love brother and the stranger as oneself.
>
> It took the abolitionist, in and out of the church, to show the inconsistency of slavery and force a division, as the Socialists are now doing.

"Yes," said mother, "I belonged to one of that kind of churches, myself, before the war."[27]

Just as his mother was converted at the end of the 1903 pamphlet, so, too, the pastor by the close of *The Bible and Socialism*. He confesses he had learned little of economics while in college, and since he joined the ministry, he had been too busy to give more than a casual thought to the Bible's "economic teachings" and whether or not the churches adhered to them. But as a result of the "interesting evening conversations," he was a changed man.

> ... being convinced that Socialism is but the carrying out of the economic teachings of the Bible, I shall endeavor to study it and lay it before my people to the best of my ability.[28]

There may have been little new for white religiously-inclined Socialists in Woodbey's pamphlet since the Christian Socialists had already published a considerable body of literature demonstrating to their satisfaction that the Bible and Socialism were compatible. But to black church-goers much of what was in the pamphlet was new and certainly must have made an impressive impact. Moreover, while many Christian Socialists preached an emotional propaganda replete with Christian ethics, they tended to ignore the class struggle or to relate their biblical references to the contemporary scene. Not so Woodbey; he was a firm believer in the class struggle, had read Marx, and was not in the least reluctant to couple discussions of the Old and New Testaments with specific evils in twentieth-century American society.

Woodbey's third and last Socialist pamphlet was *The Distribution of Wealth*, published in 1910 at San Diego by the author. The sixty-eight-page booklet consists of a series of letters to J. Jones, a California rancher-friend of the author, in which Woodbey describes how the distribution of wealth created by productive labor would operate "after Socialism has overthrown the capitalist method of production." Pointing out in his preface that there was little in Socialist literature on how the future co-operative commonwealth would function, Woodbey, without the slightest hesitation, declared he would attempt to fill the gap. Affirming his right to do so, he noted:

> If the socialist movement is based upon truth, it cannot be destroyed by the utmost freedom of discussion, nor is the movement or the party necessarily in danger, because your views or mine are not at once adopted even should they be corrected. All I ask of the reader is a fair, honest consideration of what I have written.[29]

What he wrote is an interesting elaboration of how the different institutions under capitalism would operate in the new Socialist society.

Some of this had already been set forth in his 1903 *What To Do and How To Do It*, but here he develops it further. In 1903, it will be recalled, Woodbey had conceded that the capitalists would resort to armed resistance to prevent the Socialist society from coming into being. Now, however, he appears to believe that while capitalists would resist the transition to Socialism with "tremendous opposition," it would not necessarily lead to war. Once socialism had proven its superiority over capitalism even the capitalists and their children would acquiesce and decide to live under it. (A clear throw-back to *Looking Backward*.) He writes:

> Let us go back, for instance, to the slaveholder, by the way of illustration. He declared that he would go to war before he would permit himself and family to labor like the negro slave and live in poverty, rags and ignorance. He had been taught to believe that that was the necessary outgrowth of labor. And I submit that the condition of labor under chattel slavery was a poor school in which to teach the child of the master a desire to labor. So the capitalist of today and his children look upon the workers as he has them in the sweatshops, mines and factories of the country, putting in long hours for a bare existence, under the most unsanitary conditions, living in the worst of places, and eating of the worst of food; and, like his brother, the slaveholder, he is determined that he and his shall not be reduced to such straits. It has not yet dawned upon him that when the people who work own the industries in place of him, all of these disagreeable conditions will at once disappear. . . . It is my opinion that, notwithstanding the false education of the children of the wealthy, even they in the first generation will have so much of their distaste for labor taken away that we will have little or no trouble with them when the majority have changed conditions.[30]

Woodbey's rancher friend keeps asking whether people would work under socialism once the fear of poverty and unemployment were removed. Woodbey's answer is interesting:

> . . . when chattel slavery prevailed, as we said, men thought that labor must continue to be always what it was then, and that because the slave sought to escape he wouldn't work for wages. So now the capitalist, and those who believe in capitalism, think that labor must continue always to be just what it is now; and as some people won't work under the new and better conditions.
>
> It is a wonder to me that men are so willing to work as they are under the present conditions. The fact is, the mind of the child is such that it accepts what it is taught now, and will do the same then.
>
> The boy who was born a slave thought that it was natural for him to be one, and the young master took it for granted that he was intended to be master. But the boy that is born free, never thinks that any one ought to own him; nor does the youngster born

at the same time with him think that he ought to own him. But instead, they both go to school often in the same class. They at once accept the conditions under which they were born. No, my friend, there is no danger of the children not at once accepting the new conditions under Socialism, and we have proved there will be so little loss through idlers, even in the first generation of old folks, that it will not be found worth bothering about. And as the old and infirm should of necessity be looked after with the best of everything from the very beginning, it will be found when the time comes that the thing to do will be to let every one work and be sure that we have abundance of everything for all, and then let everybody help themselves, wherever they may be, to what we have on hand, as we do with what the public now owns. Indeed, they can be better trusted then than now, with all fear of the future banished forever.[31]

It is perhaps significant that this is the only one of Woodbey's pamphlets which ends without the second party convinced of the truth of the author's arguments and converted to Socialism. Probably Woodbey himself realized that he had tackled a difficult subject that his presentation was too tentative to be effective in total conversion. At any rate, he ended his last letter:

Hoping that I have been able to make it clear to you that under Socialism it will be possible to equitably distribute the products of industry and that you and your family will at once join the movement, I will close this somewhat lengthy correspondence by saying that I would be pleased to hear from you soon.

Yours for the cause of the Revolution,
G. W. Woodbey[32]

Reverend Woodbey was a delegate to the Socialist Party conventions of 1904 and 1908; indeed, he was the sole representative of the Negro people at these gatherings. At the 1904 convention Woodbey took the floor twice. On the first occasion, he expressed his opinion on the seating of A. T. Gridely of Indiana who was being challenged because he had accepted a position in the state government after passing a civil service examination. The question at issue was whether A. T. Gridely had violated the Socialist principle of not accepting a position under a capitalist government. Woodbey spoke in favor of seating A. T. Gridely, arguing that in Germany the Socialists boasted of the number of comrades in the army, and noting that certainly such Socialists were doing work for a capitalist government. "We all know," he continued, "that we work for capitalists when we work at all, and we would be pretty poor if we did not work for capitalists at all."[33] On the second occasion, he spoke up in favor of the Party National Secretary receiving a salary of $1,500 a year which he called "not a dollar too much."[34] But the failure of the convention to deal with the Negro question in the Party platform or of the delegates to discuss it once during the entire convention, aroused no comment from the only black delegate.

At the 1908 convention, Woodbey took the floor four times. On one occasion, in a discussion of franchises held by private corporations, he advanced what for the Socialist Party was the bold position that the Socialists declare themselves "in favor as fast as they can get in possession in any locality, of taking everything without a cent, and forcing the issue as to whether there is to be compensation or not. (Applause). I take the ground that you have already paid for these franchises—already paid more than they are worth, and we are simply proposing to take possession of what we have already paid for."[35] On another occasion, Woodbey recommended that the National Committee elect its own executive committee from its own members, and on still another, he opposed a time limit being imposed before a Party member could be nominated for office on the Socialist ticket to ensure that he would not betray the movement. Woodbey argued that the danger of such persons "selling out" was just as great if they were members for years instead of months. "In my judgment, a man who understands its [the Party's] principles is not more liable to do it after he has been in the party six months than five years."[36]

The other occasion in which Woodbey spoke at the 1908 convention marked the only time during the two national gatherings that he commented on an issue related to the race question. That was when he took a firm stand, during the discussion of the immigration resolution, against Oriental exclusion and, indeed, exclusion of any immigrants. His speech, coming as it did from a California delegate, was a remarkable statement and certainly not calculated to win friends among Socialists in his state. But it was in keeping with the tradition of black Americans since the era of Reconstruction: in 1869, the Colored National Labor Union went on record against exclusion of Chinese immigration. Woodbey conceded that it was generally believed that all who lived on the Pacific coast were as "a unit" in opposing Oriental immigration. But he did not, though a delegate from California, share this view:

> I am in favor of throwing the entire world open to the inhabitants of the world. (Applause). There are no foreigners, and cannot be unless some person comes down from Mars, or Jupiter, or some place.
> I stand on the declaration of Thomas Paine when he said "The world is my country." (Applause). It would be a curious state of affairs for immigrants or descendants of immigrants from Europe themselves to get control of affairs in this country, and then say to the Oriental immigrants that they should not come here. So far as making this a mere matter of race, I disagree decidedly with the committee, that we need any kind of a committee to decide this matter from a scientific standpoint. We know what

we think upon the question of race now as well as we would know two years from now or any other time.[37]

Woodbey scoffed at the idea that the entrance of Oriental immigrants would reduce the existing standard of living, arguing that regardless of immigration or no immigration, it was the "natural tendency of capitalism" to reduce the standard of living of the working class, and that if they could not get Oriental labor to do work more cheaply in the United States, they would export their production to the Oriental countries where goods could be produced more cheaply than in this country.[38] Woodbey's prediction that American capitalists would export production to cheap labor countries of the Orient, was, as American workers today fully realize, to bear fruit.

Continuing, Woodbey spoke eloquently of the contradiction between immigration restriction and the principles of international Socialism. As he saw it, Socialism was based "upon the Brotherhood of Man," and any stand in opposition to immigration would be "opposed to the very spirit of the Brotherhood of Man." Reminding the delegates that Socialists were organized in China and Japan as well as in other countries, he asked:

> Are the Socialists of this country to say to the Socialists of Germany, or the Socialists of Sweden, Norway, Japan, China, or any other country, that they are not to go anywhere on the face of the earth? It seems to me absurd to take that position. Therefore, I hope and move that any sort of restriction of immigration will be stricken out of the committee's resolution. (Applause.)[39]

It is unfortunate that while he had the floor, Woodbey did not attack delegates like Ernest Untermann and Victor Berger for the anti-Negro character of their arguments in favor of Oriental exclusion. Nevertheless, Woodbey's speech on the immigration resolution, ranks high in Socialist literature even though it has been ignored by all students of the subject.[40]

Only once at either the 1904 or 1908 conventions did the delegates take notice of the fact that Woodbey was a black representative. That was when his name was placed in nomination as Debs' running-mate in the presidential election of 1908. Delegate Ellis Jones of Ohio presented his name to the convention in a brief but moving speech. "Comrades . . . the nomination that I want to make for our Vice-President . . . is a man who is well known in the movement for many years. The Socialist Party is a party that does not recognize race prejudice and in order that we may attest this to the world, I offer the name of Comrade Woodbey of California."[41] But Woodbey received only one vote—that of Jones.[42] The nomination went to Ben Hanford who had been Debs' running mate in 1904. Possibly had Debs, who did not attend the convention, wired the delegates that Woodbey's nomination would be a major contribution of American Socialism in the struggle against racism, the vote would have been different. But Debs did not believe that the Party should do anything special on the Negro question, and this view was shared by all at the convention except the one delegate who nominated and voted for Woodbey. Since the fact that Woodbey was even placed in nomination has escaped the attention of every historian of the Socialist Party,[43] it is clear that the significance of the one vote he received has been generally overlooked.

Following the 1908 convention, Woodbey began a tour of Northern cities with fairly large black populations and delivered a series of soap-box speeches in favor of the Socialist ticket.[44] In addition, the National office of the Socialist Party circulated his four-page leaflet, *Why the Negro Should Vote the Socialist Ticket.* The author was described as a member of the State Executive Committee, Socialist Party of California, and formerly Pastor of African Church, in Omaha, Nebraska. Typical of Woodbey's propaganda technique, the leaflet consisted mainly of a speech, supposedly delivered by a Reverend Mr. Johnson, Pastor of the African Baptist Church, who had called his congregation together to explain why he had decided "to vote the Socialist ticket at the coming election."

The Socialist movement, he pointed out, sought to bring together all working people into a party of their own, so that through such a party "they may look after the interest of all who work regardless of race or color." Since Negroes were nearly all wage workers, it was clear that only such a party could really represent them. "All other parties have abandoned the negro, and if he wants an equal chance with everyone else, he can get it in no other way than by voting the Socialist ticket." No other party, including the Republicans, stood for eliminating poverty, and just as once, the elimination of slavery was crucial for the Negro, so today was the elimination of poverty. Socialism would create a society without poverty, a society in which the land, mines, factories, shops, railroads, etc., would be owned collectively, and the Negro "being a part of the public, will have an equal ownership in all that the public owns, and this will entitle him to an equal part in all the good things produced by the nation." In this future society, moreover, he would not have to abandon his belief in religion. On the contrary, by providing all with sufficient food to eat and decent places in which to live, Socialism would be fulfilling the fundamental ideas set down in the Bible.

Finally, Woodbey called for unity of white and black workers, urging them to "lay aside their prejudices and get together for their common good. We poor whites and blacks have fought each other long enough, and while we have fought, the capitalists have been taking everything from both of us." The Socialist movement was the embodiment of this unifying principle, for it was

> part of a great world movement which includes all races and both sexes and has for its motto: "Workers of the world unite. You have nothing to lose but your chains; you have a world to win."[45]

Woodbey's first published appeal directly to his people on behalf of the Socialist Party is an excellent illustration of the black minister's great ability to take a complex subject and simplify it so that even a political illiterate could understand it.

Woodbey expanded on several points in his leaflet in articles early in 1909 in the Chicago *Daily Socialist.* In "The New Emancipation," he emphasized the common interests of black and white workers under capitalism, condemned black strikebreaking and the doctrine that Negroes should seek to solve their problems by the accumulation of wealth. Even if a few Negroes could become wealthy, the fact still remained that "their brothers are getting poorer every day." What then was the answer?

> Give the negro along with others the full product of his labor by wrenching the industries out of the hands of the capitalist and putting them into the hands of the workers and what is known as the race problem will be settled forever. Socialism is only another one of those great world movements which is coming to bless mankind. The Socialist party is simply the instrument for bringing it about, and the negro and all other races regardless of former conditions, are invited into its folds.[46]

In another article, "Socialist Agitation," Woodbey called for the use of all forms of educational-techniques to reach the black masses, "the press, the pulpit, the rostrum and private conversation." Socialist agitators must understand that they would face imprisonment and other forms of maltreatment, but this was to be expected when one sought to overthrow an evil system. "For attempting to overthrow the slave system, Lincoln and Lovejoy were shot, John Brown was hung, while Garrison, Phillips and Fred Douglass were mobbed." Naturally, Socialist agitators "are equally hated and despised," and they faced constant distortion of what they stood for.

> Because the Socialists recognize the existence of a class struggle they are some times accused of stirring up class hatred. But, instead, they simply recognize the fact that capitalism, by its unequal distribution of wealth, has forced on us a class struggle, which the Socialists are organizing to put down and bring on the long talked of period of universal brotherhood.[47]

When Woodbey advised Socialist agitators to expect to be persecuted, he spoke from personal experience. At the time he was a delegate to the 1908 Socialist convention, he was out on bail, having been arrested in San Francisco early in the year with thirty other Socialist speakers for defying a ban against street-corner meetings. This was in the midst of the economic crisis following the Panic of 1907, and the Socialists were holding meetings to demand relief for the unemployed.

Even before the Wobblies made free-speech fights famous, Socialists had engaged in such battles and had used specific aspects of the strategy followed by the I.W.W. in their spectacular free-speech fights.[48] In the case of the 1908 San Francisco free-speech fight, the Socialists deliberately violated a city ordinance forbidding street meetings without police permits for all organizations except religious groups. When a speaker was arrested for speaking without a permit, his place was speedily filled on the soap box. Speaker after speaker, men and women, black and white, mounted the soapbox, were arrested, and dragged off to jail. Woodbey was one of the first to be dragged off and jailed. Along with his comrades he was released on bail.[49]

"The police can't stop us," Woodbey told a reporter during the 1908 convention. "They can and do arrest us when we speak, but they can't stem the tide that has been started no more than they can the ocean. The more they ill treat us, the more Socialists there are." Despite police opposition, the Socialists were determined to obtain relief for "the hordes of honest working men [in San Francisco] who are starving because they can't get the work they so earnestly desire."[50]

With the aid of liberals and labor groups, the Socialists were able to force the City Council of San Francisco to repeal the objectionable ordinance, and charges against Woodbey were dropped.[51] He continued to participate in free-speech fights, and in 1912 was a key figure in what was probably the most famous free-speech fight in American history—the free-speech fight in San Diego, California. San Diego was, of course, Woodbey's home town, and the place where he was the pastor of the Mt. Zion Church for several years until he was removed because, as one who knew him, wrote, he "loosened up his flock with the Bible, then finished his sermon with an oration on Socialism."[52]

On January 8, 1912, the San Diego City Council passed an ordinance creating a "restricted" district, forty-nine blocks in the center of town, in which street-corner meetings might not be held. Unlike ordinances in other cities banning street-speaking, that in San Diego made no exception for religious utterances. All street-speaking was banned in the so-called "congested district." The reason given was that the meetings blocked traffic, but it was clear that the real purpose was to suppress the I.W.W.'s effort "to educate the floating and out-of-work population to a true understanding of the interests of labor as a whole," as well as their determination to organize the workers in San Diego who were neglected by the A. F. of L. Among these neglected workers were the mill and lumber and laundry workers and streetcar conductors and motormen. This determination had infuriated John D. Spreckels, the millionaire sugar capitalist and owner of the streetcar franchise, and he and other employers had applied pressure on the Council to pass the ordinance. Certainly, San Diego had plenty of room for her traffic, and no one believed that this little town in Southern

California would suffer a transportation crisis if street corner meetings continued.[53]

Two days before the ordinance was supposed to go into effect, the I.W.W and the Socialists held a meeting in the center of the restricted district at which Woodbey was a leading speaker. The police broke up the meeting but did not intimidate the fighters for free speech. On January 8, 1912, the *San Diego Union* carried the following on its front page:

SOCIALISTS PROPOSE FIGHT TO FINISH FOR FREE SPEECH

Following a near-riot Saturday night during a clash between the police department, on the one hand, and Socialists, Industrial Workers of the World on the other, the Socialists and I.W.W. members held a running street meeting last night at Fifth and H streets, but the meeting was orderly, and there was not any semblance of trouble.

During the meeting members of the organizations policed the sidewalks and kept them clear, so that the city police would have no objection to make. Among the speakers were Mrs. Laura Emerson, Messrs. Hubbard and Gordon for the Industrial Workers of the World, and George Washington Woodbey, Kaspar Bauer and Attorney E. F. Kirk for the Socialists.

The part played by the police in the affair of Saturday evening was denounced, but none of the speakers grew radical. It was announced that the fight for free speech will be waged with vigor, but in a dignified manner.

The police, aided by vigilantes, responded with more than vigor and in anything but a dignified manner. The brutality against the free-speech fighters in San Diego was so horrendous that after an investigation ordered by Governor Hiram Johnson, Colonel Harris Weinstock reported: "Your commissioner has visited Russia and while there, has heard many horrible tales of high-handed proceedings and outrageous treatment of innocent people at the hands of despotic and tyrannic Russian authorities. Your commissioner is frank to confess that when he became satisfied of the truth of the stories, as related by these unfortunate men (victims of police and vigilante brutality in San Diego), it was hard for him to believe that he was not still sojourning in Russia, conducting his investigation there, instead of in this alleged 'land of the free and home of the brave.' "[54]

Woodbey was several times the victim of brutal police assaults as he insisted on exercising his right-of-free speech, and he filed charges of "Malicious and unofficial" conduct against the chief of police, captain of the detectives, and several policemen whom he accused of brutality.[55] As a leading figure in the Free Speech League, the organization which coordinated the free-speech fight, Woodbey was frequently threatened by vigilantes, and on one occasion, he barely escaped death. *The Citizen,* official organ of the Labor Unions of Southern California, reported in mid-April, 1912:

> Rev. Woodbey, a negro preacher, has been threatened for his activity. A few nights ago he was taken to his home by a committee from the Free Speech League. As the party left the car at a corner near Woodbey's home an automobile was noticed in front of the house. Upon examination it was found to contain two armed men. Across the street another vigilante was stationed, and in the alley two more armed men were found. The strength of the committee with Woodbey probably saved his life, as members of the League challenged the vigilantes to do their dirty work. The preacher's house was patrolled by armed men from the League all night.[56]

The free-speech fight in "Barbarous San Diego" was still in full swing in late April, 1912 when Woodbey left to attend the Socialist Party national convention in Chicago as a delegate from California. By the time he returned home, the struggle was still continuing and he did what he could to help the cause, faced with defeat as a result of the power of the police, vigilantes, and the state government. Wobblies continued to be clubbed and arrested, and there was little that could be done to prevent the wholesale violation of their civil rights. "They have the courts, the mails and funds," Laura Payne Emerson lamented.[57] It was not until 1914 that the right of the I.W.W. to hold street meetings was established. Although the ordinance still remained on the statute books, the police no longer interfered when Wobblies spoke at street corners in the forbidden district. On the invitation of the I.W.W., Reverend Woodbey was one of the regular speakers at such meetings.[58]

Woodbey's associations with the I.W.W. may not have pleased some California Socialists and his role in the free-speech fights probably disturbed members of his congregation. But he was candidate for state treasurer on the Socialist ticket in 1914 and was still listed as Pastor of Mt. Zion Church in San Diego and member of the state executive board of the Socialist Party in *The Christian Socialist* of February, 1915 which published two articles by the militant black Socialist minister. These, the last known writings of Reverend Woodbey on Socialism, were "What the Socialists Want" and "Why the Socialists Must Reach the Churches with Their Message." The first was in the form of a dialogue, a familiar Woodbey technique, between the minister (here called Parker) and George Stephenson, a black mail carrier. Stephenson asks to be told "in short, and the simplest way possible, just what it is you Socialists are trying to get any way," and Woodbey proceeds to enlighten him, pointing out the features of the Socialist society which he had presented in greater detail in his previous pamphlets. When the mail carrier leaves convinced that there was no way to answer the arguments in favor of Socialism, his teacher shouts after him: "Hold on a minute, we would solve the race problem of this and all other countries, by establishing the brotherhood of man which Christ taught."

In the second piece, Woodbey insisted that the Socialists would never succeed unless they won over "the millions of working people who belong to the various churches of the country," and proceeded to indicate how he did his part in this endeavor. His chief weapon was to play up the point that "the economic teaching of the Bible and of Socialism is the same, and that for that reason he (the church member) must accept Socialism in order to stand consistently by the teaching of his own religion." After having shown the church member that the Bible, "in every line of it," was "with the poor and against their oppressors," it was necessary to convince him that the solution for the ills of society was not charity which was at best "only a temporary relief," but the collective ownership and operation of the industries. The last point had to be reached slowly and step by step, but if the Socialist agitator keeps using the Bible as his authority, he will carry the church member along to that conclusion. The danger was that too many Socialists antagonized church members by linking anti-religion with Socialism. Hence, he advised against using agitators "who do not understand the Christian people, to carry this message, for the reason that they are sure to say something that will spoil the whole thing."

We know nothing of Reverend Woodbey after 1915. But we leave him at this point in his career as confirmed a Socialist as ever. "I would not vote for my own wife on a platform which did not have the Socialist message in it," he told an audience in December, 1914.[59]

Just how many blacks Woodbey converted by the method he outlined in his last Socialist writing is impossible to determine. But Hubert H. Harrison, a militant black Socialist in New York, said of Woodbey's work as a national Party organizer: "He has been very effective."[60] At least one prominent black Socialist attributed his conversion to Socialism to Reverend Woodbey. In the Chicago *Daily Socialist* of September 29, 1908, Reverend George W. Slater, Jr., Pastor, Zion Tabernacle in the Windy City, wrote:

> For years I have felt that there was something wrong with our government. A few weeks ago I heard Comrade Woodbey, a colored national organizer of the Socialist party, speaking on the streets in Chicago. He showed me plainly the trouble and the remedy. From that time on I have been an ardent supporter of the Socialist cause.

Notes

1. *Ohio Socialist Bulletin,* February 1909.
2. *Chicago Daily Socialist,* May 11, 1908; John Mather, *Who's Who of the Colored Race* (Chicago, 1921); A. W. Ricker in *Appeal to Reason,* October 31, 1903.
3. Reverend George W. Woodbey, *What To Do and How To Do It or Socialism vs. Capitalism, Wayland's Monthly,* No. 40 (August 1903), p. 4; A. W. Ricker in *Appeal to Reason,* October 31, 1903. Correspondence with the Omaha Public Library, the University of Nebraska Library, the Nebraska State Historical Society, and the United Methodist Historical Society at Nebraska Wesleyan University has failed to turn up any information on Reverend Woodbey in their files and his role as a Populist and Socialist in Nebraska.
4. *Los Angeles Socialist,* July 12, 1902.
5. *Ibid.,* December 17, 1904; *Common Sense* (Los Angeles, October 27, 1906).
6. *Los Angeles Socialist,* May 2, 1903.
7. *Common Sense* (Los Angeles, August 1905).
8. *Ibid.,* October 8, 1904; March 7, April 11, 1908.
9. A. W. Ricker, *Appeal to Reason,* October 31, 1903.
10. *Ibid.* Robert Blatchford's *Merrie England,* published in London in 1894, was a book of 26 chapters and 210 pages in which the superiority of Socialism over Capitalism is brilliantly set forth in clear, plain language.
11. Woodbey, *op. cit.,* p. 3.
12. *Chicago Daily Socialist,* May 11, 1908.
13. Woodbey, *op. cit.,* pp. 5–7.
14. *Ibid.,* pp. 15–19.
15. *Ibid.,* p. 20.
16. *Ibid.,* pp. 20–21.
17. *Ibid.,* p. 24.
18. *Ibid.,* pp. 37–38.
19. *Ibid.,* p. 44.
20. Compare, for example, Woodbey's discussion of an international credit system under Socialism (pp. 36–37) with Bellamy's discussion of the same system in Chapter 8 of *Looking Backward.*
21. In a letter to William Dean Howells a few months after the publication of *Looking Backward,* Bellamy wrote that "the word socialist is one I could never well stomach. In the first place it is a foreign word in itself, and equal foreign in all its suggestions. . . . Whatever German and French reformers may choose to call themselves, socialist is not a good name for a party to succeed with in America. No such party can or ought to succeed which is not wholly and enthusiastically American and patriotic in spirit and suggestions." (Quoted in Arthur E. Morgan, *Edward Bellamy,* [New York, 1941], p. 374).
22. For a discussion of *The Iron Heel,* see Philip S. Foner, *Jack London: American Rebel* (New York, 1964), pp. 87–97.

23. Woodbey, *op. cit.*, p. 7.
24. G. W. Woodbey, *The Bible and Socialism: A Conversation Between Two Preachers* (San Diego, 1904), Preface.
25. *Ibid.*, p. 7.
26. *Ibid.*, pp. 69, 83, 90.
27. *Ibid.*, p. 69.
28. *Ibid.*, p. 96.
29. G. W. Woodbey, *The Distribution of Wealth* (San Diego, California, 1910), p. 7.
30. *Ibid.*, pp. 41, 44–45.
31. *Ibid.*, pp. 54–55.
32. *Ibid.*, p. 68. Woodbey's fellow-California Socialist closed his letters, "Yours for the Revolution, Jack London."
33. *Proceedings of the National Convention of the Socialist Party Held at Chicago, Illinois, May 1 to 6, 1904* (Chicago, 1904), pp. 47–48.
34. *Ibid.*, p. 182.
35. *Proceedings, National Convention of the Socialist Party, Held at Chicago, Illinois, May 10 to 17, 1908*, pp. 208–209.
36. *Ibid.*, pp. 290–91.
37. *Ibid.*, p. 106
38. *Ibid.*, pp. 106–107.
39. *Ibid.*, pp. 107–108.
40. The most detailed discussion of the 1908 convention in relation to the immigration issue is Charles Leinenweber, "The American Socialist Party and 'New' Immigrants," *Science & Society*, vol. XLII (Winter 1968), pp. 6–12. It does not even mention Woodbey's speech in opposition to the resolution calling for a study of the necessity for immigration restriction.
41. *Proceedings, National Convention . . . 1908*, p. 163.
42. *Ibid.*, p. 164.
43. Neither Ira Kipnis nor Ray Ginger mention Woodbey's nomination in their discussion of the 1908 convention.
44. *New York Evening Call*, November 2, 1908.
45. Reverend G. W. Woodbey, "Why the Negro Should Vote the Socialist Ticket," four-page leaflet, undated, copy in Socialist Party Papers, Duke University Library.
46. G. W. Woodbey, "The New Emancipation," *Chicago Daily Socialist*, January 18, 1909.
47. G. W. Woodbey, "Socialist Agitation," *ibid.*, January 4, 1909.
48. Philip S. Foner, *History of the Labor Movement in the United States*, vol. IV (New York, 1965), p. 173.
49. *San Francisco Call, San Francisco Chronicle*, February 1–8, 1908.
50. *Chicago Daily Socialist*, May 11, 1908.
51. *San Francisco Call*, June 12, 1908.
52. In a letter to the author, Harland B. Adams of San Diego summarized a conversation he had with Dennis V. Allen, a black San Diegan who in

the years 1912 to 1916, as a postal clerk, delivered mail to the home of Reverend Woodbey. According to Mr. Allen, Reverend Woodbey lived at 12 Twenty-Ninth Street, San Diego. He described Woodbey as "a rather dark Negro, slender and about 5 feet 11 inches. Mrs. Woodbey was extremely stout, almost to the point that with her age and weight, it was difficult for her to get about. She was known by nearly everyone in the small Negro population of San Diego at that time, as Mother Mary or Mother Woodbey. She was a devout Baptist Christian and regularly attended the Baptist Church at 29th and Clay, which still exists." The Woodbeys, Mr. Allen continued, owned the property where he lived, as well as the house next door which he rented to a Negro who was a veteran of the Civil War.

According to Mr. Allen, he was in a group that drafted Reverend Woodbey as the pastor for the Mt. Zion Baptist Church, and was also part of the group which had him removed. Although extremely popular, and though he drew large crowds to his sermons, his dismissal "was a direct result of mixing too much Socialism with his Bible, and this the members of his church resented."

Dennis V. Allen organized the San Diego Race Relations Society in 1924, and held the post of president for thirty-six years.

53. Foner, *op. cit.*, vol. IV, pp. 194–95.

54. *Ibid.*, pp. 199–200.

55. *San Diego Union*, February 22, 1912. The charges were ignored by the authorities.

56. *The Citizen* reprinted in *St. Louis Labor*, April 27, 1912. In her study, "The I.W.W. Free Speech Movement San Diego, 1912" (*Journal of San Diego History*, Winter 1973, pp. 25–33), Rosalie Shanks does not once mention Reverend Woodbey.

57. *Industrial Worker*, October 17, 1912.

58. *The Wooden Shoe* (Los Angeles), January 22, 1914.

59. *California Social Democrat*, December 12, 1914.

60. *New York Call*, December 16, 1911.

Index

Compiled by Jacqueline Lee

About the Editors

Randall K. Burkett is Director of the Office of Special Studies, College of the Holy Cross, and editor of the *Newsletter* of the Afro-American Religious History Group, American Academy of Religion. He is the author of *Black Redemption: Churchmen Speak for the Garvey Movement* and *Garveyism as a Religious Movement: The Institutionalization of a Black Civil Religion.*

Richard Newman, formerly Chairman of the Department of Social Sciences, Boston University, is Senior Editor for reference publications at G. K. Hall & Co. He is the author of "The Origins of the African Orthodox Church," the introduction to the reprint edition of *The Negro Churchman.*